1985

The Young Einstein
The advent of relativity

Einstein in Zurich around 1900. © Lotte Jacobi.

THE YOUNG EINSTEIN
The advent of relativity

Lewis Pyenson

Adam Hilger Ltd, Bristol and Boston

British Library Cataloguing in Publication Data

Pyenson, Lewis
   The young Einstein: the advent of relativity.
   1. Einstein, Albert   2. Physics—Biography
   I. Title
   530'. 092'4   QC16.E5

ISBN 0–85274–779–9

Consultant Editor: **Professor A J Meadows**
University of Leicester

Published by Adam Hilger Ltd
Techno House, Redcliffe Way, Bristol BS1 6NX, England
PO Box 230, Accord, MA 02018, USA

Typeset in Great Britain by Input Typesetting Ltd, London and printed in Great Britain by Oxford University Press, Oxford.

For Nicholas and Catharine

Contents

Preface

The historian of science today enters the traditional realm of biography
with some hesitation. Historical treatments using cliometrics, semiotics,
structural anthropology, social psychology, demography, and prosopo-
graphy are widespread, and studies of these kinds are united in rejecting
explanations based on contingencies in one person's life. Discontent with
the biographical genre, however, is not a recent phenomenon. Whether
biographical narrative is a secure path to historical truth was questioned
by the mature Sigmund Freud. In 1936 he wrote to Arnold Zweig: 'He who
undertakes a biography commits himself to lies, dissimulation, hypocrisy,
embellishment, even the concealment of his own lack of comprehension:
for biographical truth is not to be had, and even if one did attain it, it
would be of no value.' By these words Freud meant to warn against an
overly simple approach when discussing individual motivation, one of the
oldest problems in historical writing; during his career Freud did not
avoid considering the immediate surroundings of Leonardo and Woodrow
Wilson, to mention two case studies of his. Several years before Freud's
pronouncement against biographical writings Einstein, too, expressed
doubts concerning this genre. In providing a short foreword for the
biography of himself written by his step-son-in-law, Rudolf Kayser,
Einstein noted how the book 'perhaps . . . overlooked . . . the irrational,
the inconsistent, the droll, even the insane, which nature, inexhaustibly
operative, implants in an individual'. Such forces could only be explained,
he believed, in the first person: 'These things are singled out only in the
crucible of one's own mind.'

The reservations of Freud and Einstein notwithstanding, an appeal to
biographical evidence lies at the base of a search for the environment that

encouraged, sustained, or inhibited the thought or actions of a historical figure. Although a chronicle of Einstein's youth and young manhood would need less justification than that of any other modern scientist, the present book does not have such a compilation as its goal. It focuses on the social circumstances of Einstein's formative years, as well as on the intellectual climate in Germany where, before 1919, Einstein's work on the theories of relativity received widest notice.

In the following pages, Einstein's early career is studied without much attention to the technical content of his publications. The reader will find no long discussions on the notions of simultaneity and covariance, on the true meaning of the Michelson–Morley experiments and eclipse photographs, or on the tensor calculus and the cosmological constant. These points are, and have been for many years, well-treated in the literature. I turn instead to consider the lesser known work of several of Einstein's contemporaries who were instrumental in elaborating his thought.

In view of the fact that little regarding Einstein's scientific papers is analysed in depth, it is natural to ask in what sense this book may provide information on Einstein's scientific *discourse*. My treatment assumes that a discourse extends beyond a text to encompass tacit understanding and shared beliefs. Distinguished critics, notably Timothy Reiss and (in some of his writings) Michel Foucault, have argued that a *text* carries in its language all that is necessary for properly understanding it. Though the text is surely important for writing history of science, many referents of a scientific text—many features of scientific life—remain *hors texte*, or in context. To understand a text it is often useful (if not perhaps always necessary) to reconstruct what at first glance may seem irrelevant discourses in areas such as pedagogy, banking, or eschatology. Over the past decade, indeed, the most interesting questions in the history of science have concerned the circumstances of scientific achievement and failure.

The book begins by examining three sides of Einstein's youth and young manhood to resolve apparent contradictions in his later career. Why did Einstein, who was an excellent mathematician, always view mathematics as something of a necessary evil in his pursuit of physical laws? How was it that the theoretician Einstein retained, throughout his life, a deep interest in experimental apparatus and mechanical objects? Why did Einstein always see himself as a stranger in all his many environments? I argue that Einstein's secondary-school and university teachers helped to mould his attitude towards the role of mathematics in physics; that the young theoretician always felt comfortable with instruments and mechanical objects because of his close contact with the family business in electro-technology; and that a number of features of Einstein's personal style may be understood from the perspective of the Jewish emancipation in southern Germany at the end of the nineteenth century.

Notwithstanding Einstein's strictures against formalism devoid of physical content, the theoretician's work on the theories of relativity has been, from its first appearance, of great interest to mathematicians. The middle four chapters examine how and why mathematicians in Germany transformed Einstein's original interpretation of special relativity to satisfy their own vision of the world. There I examine the views of pure mathematicians at Göttingen and elsewhere, men who used a four-dimensional space–time formulation of relativity to advance a theory of absolute, unphysical, ether-filled space—all that Einstein had laboured to dispel. I consider the motivations behind their manifest desire to uncover new mathematical harmonies in the physical world.

In assimilating and modifying relativity, pure mathematicians did not confront the possibility that the cherished beliefs of their discipline would have to be changed. It was otherwise among physicists and astronomers. In the last chapters I address the reception of relativity in Germany from two points of view. I consider how the distinguished editor of the most prestigious physics periodical at the time, Max Planck of the *Annalen der Physik*, evaluated incoming manuscripts dealing with Einstein's theories. I also investigate how physicists and astronomers interacted with Einstein's early scientific collaborators: the latter, unlike Einstein, fell victim to the retribution of their jealous and powerful colleagues.

For their having sped my archival research, I thank Klaus Haenel of the Niedersächsischen Staats- und Universitätsbibliothek, Göttingen; Alwin Jaeggli and Beat Glaus of the Eidgenössischen Technischen Hochschule, Zurich; Joan Warnow and Spencer Weart of the American Institute of Physics, New York; Hans Troxler-Keller of the Kantonsschule, Aarau; Paul Forman of the Smithsonian Institution, Washington; the late Helen Dukas of the Institute for Advanced Study, Princeton; Murphy Smith, late of the American Philosophical Society, Philadelphia; and John Stachel of the Einstein Project, Princeton. For sharing their memories of Einstein with me I thank Ramón Enrique Gaviola, Ruth Laub Wendt, the late Robert Alexander Houstoun, and the late Derek de Solla Price. Books have never constituted an important part of the culture of Montreal, especially in French-language institutions. Without the friendly collaboration of Maria Murphy and Wendy Knechtel of the Interlibrary Loan Service at Vanier Library, Concordia University, my work could not have proceeded. Several colleagues generously found time for critical reading of one or another chapter: Pierre Boulle, Paul Forman, John Heilbron, József Illy, Martin J Klein, Camille Limoges, Russell McCormmach, Horst Melcher, John David North, and Vladimir P Vizgin. To them I am especially grateful.

Portions of this book have appeared elsewhere in different form: chapter 1, *Isis* **71** (1980); chapter 2, *Historical Studies in the Physical Sciences* **12** (1982), reprinted here through the courtesy of the University of California Press; chapters 4, 5, and 6, *Archive for History of Exact Sciences* **17** (1977),

21 (1979) and **27** (1982), reprinted through the courtesy of Springer-Verlag; chapter 7, *Europa: A Journal of Interdisciplinary Studies* **2**, no 2 (1979); chapter 8, *Proceedings of the Ninth International Conference on General Relativity and Gravitation*, edited by Ernst Schmutzer (Berlin–DDR 1983); chapter 9, *Historical Studies in the Physical Sciences, Seventh Annual Volume*, edited by Russell McCormmach (Princeton 1976), reprinted by permission of Princeton University Press. Permission to cite from the published and unpublished writings of Albert Einstein is gratefully acknowledged from the Hebrew University, Jerusalem.

We live in an age that encourages economy of expression. The notes following each chapter accordingly employ, whenever possible, standard or readily understandable abbreviations for the titles of journals and sources. It is well, nevertheless, to signal several of these here:

Dict. Sci. Biog.: *Dictionary of Scientific Biography* ed Charles C Gillispie 16 vols (New York 1970–6);

Hist. Stud. Phys. Sci.: *Historical Studies in the Physical Sciences* annual vols 1–3 (1969–71) ed Russell McCormmach (University of Pennsylvania Press); annual vols 4–7 (1974–6) ed Russell McCormmach (Princeton University Press); annual vols 8–10 (1977–9) eds Russell McCormmach, Lewis Pyenson, and R Steven Turner (The Johns Hopkins University Press); from vol 11 (1980) issued semi-annually and edited by John L Heilbron (University of California Press).

Unless otherwise noted, all dissertations are doctoral (PhD or Dr phil) ones; references indicate year of printing (in Germany) or submission (in North America) instead of year of defence.

Credits and sources for the illustrations are given in the individual captions.

My research has been supported by the generosity of the Social Sciences and Humanities Research Council in Ottawa, the Deutschen Akademischen Austauschdienstes in Bonn, and the CAFIR fund of the University of Montreal.

> *Sie kann der Zufall gaukelnd nicht verwandeln.*
> *Hab' ich des Menschen Kern erst untersucht*
> *So weiss ich auch sein Wollen und sein Handeln.*

—Schiller, *Wallensteins Tod.*

Montreal West

1 Einstein's education: mathematics and the laws of nature

The misperceived legacy of the Luitpold Gymnasium

Einstein received formal, advanced schooling during the years 1888–1900. Over the past five generations there has never been more attention focused on the reform of science and mathematics teaching than in this thirteen-year period. The ferment spread throughout German-speaking Europe—from Königsberg on the Baltic to Berne in the foothills of the Alps, from German enclaves in Romania to the Hanseatic cities on the North Sea. Writers of the time spoke of it as the *Schulkrieg*, the war over the schools. It was a struggle between proponents of the classical values associated with education in Latin and Greek and supporters of instruction in modern languages and natural sciences. The question was asked over and again: which offered better preparation for life, abstract and impractical sensitivity to noble values or concrete training in practical arts? To characterise in a simple way the course of this complex struggle would be deceiving. It involved the professional and aesthetic goals of engineers, government officials, university professors, and secondary-school teachers. Kaiser Wilhelm II of Germany took a personal interest in the matter. Passions ran high as the new curricula and certifying procedures were debated, for the future of many professions hung in the balance.[1]

Two passages indicate the main lines of the great educational debate in late nineteenth-century central Europe. The first is from an 1886 address by the physicist Ernst Mach, a liberal-minded thinker whose writings produced a deep impression on the young Einstein. Mach was entirely opposed to the monopoly of classical philology on preparing pupils for university study. It was silly, he believed, to require familiarity with Greek and Latin of future doctors and scientists: 'In *modern* times the Greeks

1

and Romans are simply two objects, among others, for archaeological and historical research.' Exclusive instruction in mathematics and natural sciences, he continued, would in fact provide a better general education than would instruction limited to the philological specialities. Only mathematics and natural sciences, Mach argued, showed how to elucidate 'the economical organisation and organic association' of new concepts.[2] The second passage comes from a petition of 1888 circulated by the reactionary *Gymnasium* professor at Heidelberg, Gustav Uhlig. The petition attracted more than 4000 signatures, including 500 of the 1500 German university *Dozenten*. Uhlig's petition emphasised 'that the German nation has every reason to be grateful for that which the *Gymnasien* have attained and will attain'. It urged that the *Gymnasien* remain bastions of instruction in Greek and Latin. The signers would accept only minor changes in the educational system. They feared that the *Gymnasien*, 'a national blessing of the first order', would be weakened by 'the zeal of their opponents'.[3] Uhlig's and Mach's points of view defined the limits of debate for more than a decade.

The reform struggle centred on Germany, and within Germany on the kingdom of Prussia. Control of educational policy in the German Empire from 1870 to 1918 was retained by the individual German states, even though in practice the model set by Prussia, the largest and most populous state, was imitated widely. Throughout Germany the entire pattern of secondary education changed dramatically over the period 1890–1900. Before this period, graduates of the *Gymnasien* (the classical schools offering Greek and Latin) retained many official privileges not extended to graduates of the *Realgymnasien* (the semi-classical schools offering Latin but not Greek) and the *Oberrealschulen* (the non-classical schools offering neither Greek nor Latin). Although in the early years of the German Empire the Prussian *Realgymnasien* were awarded the right to send students to the universities to study modern languages and natural sciences and in 1882 the same privilege was extended to the *Oberrealschulen*, until 1900 most university programmes and many government positions remained closed to students trained in these *Realanstalten*. Only in 1901 did the Prussian educational authorities grant the *Realanstalten* virtual parity with the *Gymnasien*. The other German states soon followed the lead of Prussia.

Many more pupils attended *Gymnasium* in Prussia than in all the other states of Germany combined. In 1895 enrolment at Prussian *Gymnasien* exceeded 80 000, while in the state with the second largest school system, Bavaria, it reached only 18 000; in third place came Württemberg with 6400 pupils.[4] Einstein attended *Gymnasium* in Munich, capital of Bavaria. The smaller secondary-school system of nineteenth-century Bavaria differed from that of Prussia in several respects. The former was split for the most part between classical *Gymnasien* offering Latin and Greek and

Realschulen offering neither. In addition, Bavarian *Gymnasien* devoted more time to geography, history, and German than did their northern German counterparts.[5]

What can we say about Einstein's personal experience with Bavarian secondary-school education at his institution of instruction, the Luitpold Gymnasium in Munich?[6] By German standards it was a large *Gymnasium*. During the years of Einstein's attendance the school grew from 684 pupils in 1888 to 1330 pupils in the autumn of 1894.[7] Around the middle of the 1890s the school instructed seven per cent of all *Gymnasium* pupils in Bavaria. Most of the pupils were Catholic; only five per cent were Jewish, somewhat greater than the proportion of Jewish residents in the city of Munich.[8] In Einstein's time the Luitpold Gymnasium had a reputation as an enlightened school. The mathematician Abraham A Fraenkel, who entered the Luitpold twelve years after Einstein did, characterised the rector there, Dr Wolfgang Markhausen, as a kind and generous man who had established a liberal atmosphere at the school during the late 1880s and 1890s. Fraenkel contrasted Markhausen with his replacement in 1902, a slightly ridiculous martinet who invoked a curfew for his charges and forbade them to see many Munich plays, including some by Lessing and Schiller.[9]

At Markhausen's Luitpold Gymnasium Einstein enjoyed what passed for progressive instruction in the exact sciences. During his last year and a half he used as a text one of the later editions of Viennese school inspector Josef Krist's *Essentials of Natural Science*. Topics from the text included the distinction between chemistry and physics, the rigid and the fluid body, gases and gas laws, and heat.[10] In the 1864 preface to the first edition of his *Essentials* Krist was clear that experiments formed the basis for natural laws. Taking issue with the dominant view of the time in Prussia, where physics was taught as a branch of mathematics, Krist insisted that physics remained 'a science of experience' which had to be taught by appealing to intuition. By the fifth edition of 1872 Krist emphasised that he made less use of 'rigorous scientific systems' than of pedagogical and didactic principles. No dry prose could replace, in his view, the living word of a teacher. His book could only help the teacher instruct the pupil to distinguish 'through experiment the true from the untrue', and 'to draw the correct consequences from observations and thus formulate the correct laws in words'. Krist expressed the traditional hope that his pupils would obtain from physical instruction not only a strong dose of inductive logic but also the ability to express their thoughts precisely in words.[11] Though it differed from the usual *Gymnasium* fare, Krist's was an empiricist compilation. In the hands of an uninspiring teacher it could easily have become a burden for the pupils. We can only guess about how Krist's book was presented to Einstein by his mathematics and physics teachers Gottlieb Effert and Joseph Ducrue.[12]

We do know, nevertheless, that Einstein was privileged from 1888 to 1891 to have Adolf Sickenberger as a mathematics teacher. Sickenberger successfully completed *Gymnasium* at Aschaffenburg and in 1869 at the age of twenty-one became certified to teach mathematics and physics. He passed through various posts before arriving at the Luitpold Gymnasium. Sickenberger rose rapidly as the private tutor of crown prince Rupprecht, and in 1881 he became a member of the Bavarian chamber of deputies. A vocal partisan of school reform, he sat as director of the Realschulmännerverein, the German association that demanded reform of formal, sterile, and impractical instruction in the secondary schools. In 1891 Sickenberger was called to become the first rector of the Luitpold–Kreis Realschule in Munich.[13]

Throughout Einstein's five and a half years at the Luitpold Gymnasium, he was taught mathematics from one or another edition of the separately published parts of Sickenberger's *Textbook of Elementary Mathematics*. When it first appeared in 1888 the book constituted a major contribution to reform pedagogy. Sickenberger based his book on twenty years of experience that in his view necessarily took precedence over 'theoretical doubts and systematic scruples'. At the same time Sickenberger made much use of the recent pedagogical literature, especially that published in the pages of Immanuel Carl Volkmar Hoffmann's *Zeitschrift für mathematischen und naturwissenschaftlichen Unterricht*, the leading pedagogical mathematics journal of the day. Following in the tradition of the reform movement, he sought to present everything in the simplest, most intuitive way possible. He opposed introducing scientific rigour and higher approaches in an elementary text. He emphasised that he would follow neither the synthesis of Euclidean geometry nor the so-called analytical–genetic approach. He opted for a great deal of freedom in the form of presentation because he believed that a textbook was no more than a crutch for oral instruction. The spoken word, in Sickenberger's view, could infuse life into the dead forms of the printed text. Too often, he insisted in the preface to his text, mathematics was seen and valued 'as the pure science of reason'. In reality, he continued, mathematics was also 'an essential tool for daily work'. In view of the practical dimension of mathematics Sickenberger sought most of all to present basic propositions clearly rather than to arrive at formal conciseness. Numerous examples took the place of long, complicated, and boring generalities.[14] In addition to the usual rules of arithmetic Sickenberger introduced diophantine equations. To solve three linear, homogeneous, first-order equations with three unknowns he specified determinants and determinant algebra. Then he went on to quadratic equations and logarithms. In the second part of his book, Sickenberger treated plane geometry.

According to a biography of Einstein written by his step-son-in-law, Rudolf Kayser—one that the theoretical physicist described as 'duly

accurate'—when he was twelve years old Einstein fell into possession of
the 'small geometry book' used in the Luitpold Gymnasium before this
subject was formally presented to him.[15] Einstein corroborated Kayser's
passage in autobiographical notes of 1949, when he described how at the
age of twelve 'a little book dealing with Euclidean plane geometry' came
into his hands 'at the beginning of a school year'. The 'lucidity and
certainty' of plane geometry according to this 'holy geometry booklet'
made, Einstein wrote, 'an indescribable impression on me'. Einstein saw
here what he found in other texts that he enjoyed: it was 'not too
particular' in logical rigour but 'made up for this by permitting the main
thoughts to stand out clearly and synoptically'.[16] Upon working his way
through this text, Einstein was then presented with one of the many
editions of Theodor Spieker's geometry by Max Talmey, a medical student
at the University of Munich who dined with the Einsteins and who was
young Einstein's friend when Einstein was between the ages of ten and
fifteen. We can only infer from Einstein's retrospective judgment that the
first geometry book exerted an impact greater than that produced by
Spieker's treatment, by the popular science expositions of Aaron Bernstein
and Ludwig Büchner also given to him by Talmey, or by the texts of
Heinrich Borchert Lübsen from which Einstein had by the age of fourteen
taught himself differential and integral calculus.[17]

Which text constituted the 'holy geometry booklet'? In his will Einstein
gave 'all his books' to his long-time secretary Helen Dukas. Present in
this collection are three bearing the signature 'J Einstein': a logarithmic
and trigonometric handbook, a textbook on analysis, and an introduction
to infinitesimal calculus. The signature is that of Einstein's father's brother
Jakob, a business partner and member of Einstein's household in Ulm
and Munich. He presented the books to his nephew Albert. A fourth
book in Miss Dukas's collection, which does not bear Jakob Einstein's
name, is the second part of a textbook on geometry, a work of astronomer
Eduard Heis's which was rewritten after his death by the Cologne schoolteacher Thomas Joseph Eschweiler.[18] Without offering reasons for his
choice Banesh Hoffmann has recently identified Heis and Eschweiler's
text as the geometry book that made such an impression on Einstein.[19]
Yet, assuming that Kayser's unambiguous reporting is correct, it is far
more likely that the geometrical part of Sickenberger's text was what
Einstein referred to in his autobiographical notes. Sickenberger's exposition was published seven years after that of Heis and Eschweiler, and
unlike the latter it appeared with a Munich press. Because it was used in
the Luitpold Gymnasium, copies would have been readily available to
Uncle Jakob or to whoever first acquainted Einstein with Euclidean
geometry.

The Luitpold Gymnasium was, in the early 1890s, a good school of its
type, and Einstein could have received a fine education there. His grades

across the board were, in fact, excellent, in mathematics and German *as well as* in Latin and Greek.[20] Yet we know that the young man found it inflexible and stultifying. In an essay written shortly before his death Einstein elaborated on his passage through the 'authoritarian' Munich school. He contrasted instruction at the Luitpold Gymnasium with that which he would later receive in democratically inclined Switzerland. The Munich system, he noted, was based on 'drill, external authority, and ambition'. In the text of his essay there then follows an unusual sentence. 'True democracy', Einstein wrote, 'is no empty illusion.'[21] By these words he meant to emphasise the democratic quality of Swiss education and to indicate that it was something extremely precious. The sentence may be taken as a direct indictment of his Munich education in a second way, as well. In the course syllabus for Einstein's German class during his last year at Munich virtually an identical wording appears as the theme set for one of the pupil essays. There the sentence reads: 'The truth is no empty illusion.' Pupils were expected to comment on this thought by referring to a play written by the nineteenth-century poet, free thinker, and revolutionary Johann Ludwig Uhland: *Ernst, Duke of Swabia*.[22] Einstein's appeal to the *Gymnasium* essay—if, indeed, that is what he intended—is an unequivocal rejection of his years at the progressive Luitpold Gymnasium. We can only speculate on what irreparable damage might have been inflicted on the young genius had Einstein attended a more traditionally inclined secondary school.

Einstein's black picture of the Luitpold Gymnasium gives a misleading impression that the school offered reactionary and inhumane instruction. His retrospective vision was certainly coloured by intense feelings directed against a Germany that had allowed the rise of fascism. Recognition of this later antipathy must not obscure our knowledge that even as a youth Einstein was hostile to some of the dominant values of southern Germany. One suspects that at least a part of this hostility was directed against authority of any kind. In December 1894 Einstein left the Luitpold Gymnasium during the middle of his sixth year. He parted using a friendly physician's note citing the necessity of leave due to his 'nervous exhaustion', although Philipp Frank reports that before Einstein could use his fabricated medical excuse he was asked to go by one of his teachers because his disruptive presence disturbed the other pupils.[23] Einstein took with him a letter from his mathematics teacher attesting to his abilities, but he knew that without the final certificate called the *Abitur* he would be ineligible to become a higher-level secondary-school teacher; excluded would be higher positions in the military, postal, mining, and railway services and in all other government operations. Einstein placed himself outside the intellectual life of a society that valued culture and formal education highly. He wanted none of it.

Personal factors sped Einstein's decision to leave the Luitpold. For the preceding six months fifteen-year-old Einstein had been boarding at the home of an older woman. After some years of success the electrical manufacturing business of his father and his uncle Jakob had failed, and the extended family decided to relocate and set up shop in Milan. Einstein missed his family; letters that he received from Italy portrayed a happy life. Young Einstein liked to ramble in the countryside around Munich, but he had never been on a long trip.[24] He could not resist the temptation to flee south.

Italy, in the middle 1890s, was collecting its breath after having plunged into the Second Industrial Revolution. At the end of 1894 the kingdom had just come through a lustrum of financial austerity caused by rapid expansion, during the 1880s, in manufacturing, railways, and public ventures. Gross fiscal malfeasance on the part of the federal cabinet coupled with a state of apprehended insurrection forced the second Crispi administration to curb industrial expansion. Liquid capital was not readily available among Italian investors. An entrepreneur from northern Europe, bringing his own assets, could reasonably hope to set up a profitable venture. In looking south to Lombardy and the Piedmont, Hermann and Jakob Einstein focused on the most dynamic part of the industrialising nation. In the two provinces lay most of Italy's chemical and manufacturing plants. A rail grid connected the interior to domestic and foreign markets and to port facilities around Genoa and Venice. Electricity ran the northern economy. Hydroelectrical generating stations dotted the southern foothills of the Alps at the same time that smaller, coal-burning stations proliferated.[25]

Albert Einstein spent most of 1895 in Pavia, whence his family had moved from Milan in the hope of finding a better business climate. The Pavian site of the company Einstein and Garrone was typical of late nineteenth-century, northern Italian industrial architecture. The brothers Hermann and Jakob established separate households in the relatively small university town.[26] There, facing few responsibilities and no pressures in a serene, foreign country, Albert definitively rejected his homeland. Even before leaving Munich Einstein had thought about giving up German allegiance, but apparently he took this resolve soon after his arrival in Italy while on a hike to visit cousins in Genoa.[27] No longer a citizen of Germany, the young man avoided the opprobrium of spending three years in the German army as an ordinary soldier.[28] He was accordingly free to travel through Germany without risking arrest as a draft dodger.

The pleasure of Einstein's new Italian home was tempered by economic realities. As the family business continued to flounder, Einstein was persuaded by his parents to follow the solid career of electrical engineering, a known quantity in the Einstein household. To become an engineer required more education. Without the *Abitur* Einstein could not hope to matriculate at a German university, or even at a German institute of technology. The one path open to him in German-speaking Europe lay in nearby Switzerland.

'In 1895 at the age of sixteen I came to Zurich from Italy', Einstein wrote a lifetime later. His purpose in going to Zurich was to study at the famous Federal Institute of Technology, or Polytechnic. He knew that he could attend the Polytechnic if he passed an entrance examination. Beyond this clear goal, however, he had few thoughts. Let us listen to Einstein again: 'I was a conscientious but unassuming young man who had acquired his meagre store of pertinent knowledge of the essentials through self-study. Eager for deeper understanding but endowed with few prerequisites and burdened with a poor memory', formal study was hard for him. 'With a feeling of well-founded uncertainty', Einstein, apparently through the intercession of his mother, was allowed to sit for the entrance examination in the engineering section even though he was two years younger than the regulations specified.[29] He did very well in mathematics and physics but failed modern languages, zoology, and botany. Einstein remembered that his examiners were 'patient and understanding'. The rector of the Polytechnic, professor of engineering mechanics Albin Herzog, advised the young man to attend the technical division of the nearby cantonal secondary school in Aarau. In a year he could graduate and in this way satisfy the entrance requirements at Zurich.[30]

We can obtain some idea of the extent to which he would have impressed Herzog from an essay written by Einstein bearing the title, 'On the Investigation of the State of the Ether in the Magnetic Field'. Einstein sent the essay to his mother's brother, Cäsar Koch, a successful broker in Brussels of whom he was fond. Accompanying the undated manuscript was an undated letter, where Einstein explained that he was soon supposed to study at the Zurich Polytechnic. This course of action carried 'significant difficulties', for Einstein was then at least two years younger than he should have been to matriculate; Einstein added that he would write to Koch about the outcome. Because the entrance age at the Polytechnic was eighteen, from Einstein's remark it is certain that his letter and the accompanying manuscript were written after March 1895 and before the early autumn of the same year, the latest date when he could have taken the Polytechnic entrance examination.[31]

Although the essay was, in his words, more a 'programme' than a real contribution, it furnished his respected uncle with evidence of Einstein's having mastered much of Heinrich Hertz's electrodynamics. Einstein began by observing how an electric current set up a potential state in the ether, a state known as the magnetic field. He emphasised how Hertz—the only authority cited—had revealed the dynamic nature of electromagnetic phenomena. The programme that he wanted to follow, but at the moment could not see how to carry out, involved determining the potential state of the ether by measuring its elastic deformation, a phenomenon that could be related directly to changes in the velocity of ether waves. Most revealing in the essay is Einstein's methodological orientation. Near the end of his five-page text he remarked: 'Quantitative research on the absolute values of the density and elastic force of the ether can, so I believe, only begin if qualitative results exist which are connected with certain ideas.' Experiment formed the basis of physical knowledge, in his view, but the physicist had to be guided in the first instance by a clear, one might interpose an intuitive, apprehension of nature's laws.

The impact of the cantonal school at Aarau

With these views of physics in mind Einstein spent most of an academic year at the Aargau cantonal school in Aarau, capital of the fertile, northern canton that encompasses the area around the confluence where the Limmat and Reuss run together to form the river Aare. Aargau was a pastoral canton, supporting tobacco-growing, silk ribbon-weaving, and straw-plaiting occupations. At the end of the nineteenth century Aargau comprised 200 000 people, slightly less than seven per cent of the population of Switzerland. Nearly all residents spoke German, and somewhat more than half were Protestant. The 1885 constitution of Aargau reflected the increasingly democratic movement that had spread across late nineteenth-century Switzerland. The legislature that sat at Aarau contained one representative for every 1100 inhabitants, and all laws that it enacted had to be approved by an obligatory referendum. In 1900 around 7000 inhabitants lived in the capital and largest town in the canton. From Aarau Zurich was about half an hour distant by train.[32]

Einstein would have found Aarau congenial because of its historically progressive attitude towards Jewish residents. When in 1798 the French invaders proclaimed a Swiss republic, they preserved tradition by denying civil rights to Jews, who were treated as foreigners. Jews remained in Switzerland at the pleasure of municipal magistrates and their councils. The largest Jewish population in early nineteenth-century Switzerland established itself at Aarau, and in 1824 the far-sighted citizens of Aargau granted Jews the privilege of citizenship and guaranteed their schools and institutions. The Christian burghers did not see fit, however, to allow Jews free movement from one town to another. That right came a generation later in federal legislation following the ferment of 1848. Berne gave citizenship to all Swiss residents without regard to religion, although it, like other federal governments of the period, did not initially presume to dictate how its constituent members, the cantons, enfranchised voters for local elections. Aargau Jews became totally emancipated in 1863. Three years later Berne guaranteed freedom of belief to all Swiss citizens.[33]

Throughout Switzerland cantonal governments supported higher secondary schools as well as the eight Swiss universities, academies, or faculties. In the rich canton of Aargau, which had no university, the secondary school formed the apex of the educational pyramid. Founded by a public subscription of 6982 Swiss francs in 1802, the school originally offered instruction in the modern languages and natural knowledge. The city of Aarau placed it in a three-storey hospital building constructed during the 1780s and into the twentieth century still used for the school chemistry laboratory and a girls' school. In 1804 the private school split into two divisions. A technical division trained pupils for the world of commerce, and a philological division emphasised classical languages. Nine years later the school was sanctioned and partially funded by the canton of Aargau. At a time when senior teachers received around 1500 francs per year, the canton promised to provide annual support of 10 000 francs, and the city of Aarau donated 22 000 francs for a physical cabinet, library, mathematical instruments, and mineralogical collection.[34]

Over the next two decades the school acquired professors of mathematics, physics and chemistry, and natural history. After receiving private donations totalling 150 000 francs, in 1826 the technical division was elevated to form a three-class *Gewerbeschule*, or trade school. During the late 1820s and early 1830s pupils in the trade school were expected to spend a quarter of their time on physical sciences and a fifth on mathematics, which included the elements of differential and integral calculus. These requirements coincided with those at the most advanced *Realschulen* in German-speaking Europe at the time. Striking to a modern observer is the regulation of 1832 that pupils in the trade school spend one afternoon per week in the school chemistry laboratory.[35] This regulation is more remarkable when it is recalled that the first teaching laboratory in chemistry at a German university was that founded in 1832 by Johann Wolfgang Döbereiner at Leipzig.[36] Because of its consistently high standards and secure financial base, pupils and their parents expressed unwavering confidence in the school. From 1830 to 1900 attendance generally ran at over one hundred regular pupils.

With the establishment in 1855 of the federal Polytechnic in Zurich, the two highest classes of the trade school took on the character of a preparatory school. In 1860 the Polytechnic recognised the leaving certificate of the trade school at Aarau, along with that of schools at Frauenfeld, Berne, and Geneva, as an entry card that released its holder from the obligation to sit for an otherwise mandatory qualifying examination.[37] Because the school year at Aarau ended in April and in Zurich began in the autumn, the trade-school course of study was extended by a half-year to three-and-a-half years' duration. Among the first class entering the Polytechnic under the new arrangement was Friedrich Mühlberg, later Einstein's geology professor at Aarau. By the middle 1880s most Swiss higher secondary schools enjoyed the privilege of sending graduates directly to the Polytechnic, although the federal government seems to have held the Aarau institution in especially high regard.[38] When in 1885 it affirmed the *modus vivendi* of the Aarau–Polytechnic entente, the educational council of the federal Interior Department clarified how in principle it reserved the right to elect examiners for the leaving examination, or *Maturitätsprüfung*. In practice this reservation meant that several professors from the Polytechnic assisted in administering the examination at the trade school.[39]

Einstein found at Aarau, then, an unusual secondary school. It had three divisions. The oldest was a *Gymnasium*, offering instruction comparable to that achieved a decade later in the four highest years of progressive German *Reformgymnasien*. There Latin was mandatory and Greek optional. The second division was the trade school, where Einstein registered. It offered a curriculum like that in the highest years of a German *Oberrealschule*; because Greek and Latin were elective subjects, Einstein was freed from the grip of dead languages which had dominated his education at Munich. The third division was a two-year commercial school, just created that year for both girls and boys. As an annexe the cantonal school had a five-year *Progymnasium*, channelling pupils into the *Gymnasium* or, if they wished, into the trade or commercial school.

In his centenary retrospective of 1902 Einstein's physics teacher August Tuchschmid described Aarau in the 1890s as a *Reformschule* where there was free movement among *Gymnasium*, *Realgymnasium*, and *Oberrealschule* tracks. Tuchschmid was proud that at Aarau gymnasiasts could prepare for the Polytechnic and that technicians could take Latin in anticipation of medical or dental careers. In this multiplicity was unity, he offered. Healthy education lay neither in greater decentralisation and specialisation nor in stereotyped uniformity, 'but rather in an organisation by which individual talents—those generally determining the future direction of youth—are taken into account'.[40] This philosophy was precisely that outlined during the middle 1890s by the most radical German school reformers.

Einstein's fellow pupils were a homogeneous lot. In 1895/96 the cantonal school taught 163 regular pupils and 5 *Hospitanten*, pupils not in a diploma programme. The *Gymnasium* hosted 62 pupils, the trade school 65, and the commercial school 36. Of the 163 regular pupils only six were Jewish, two registered in the trade school. The six Jews constituted three per cent of the Jewish population of Aarau. Although many pupils came from Swiss cantons beyond Aargau, only five were foreigners, four of these in the trade school. At Aarau Einstein was seen by his fellow pupils as an unusual young man. He distinguished himself further by his stated career plans. In the autumn of 1896 eight of the nine pupils graduating from the *Gymnasium* sought to study law or medicine at a university; the ninth indicated chemistry as his choice, presumably at a university. Among Einstein's eight fellow graduates of the trade school most wanted to pursue a liberal profession at the Polytechnic; one went there to become a secondary-school teacher. Only Einstein was unconcerned with a profession. No longer did he want to become an engineer. Instead, he went to the Polytechnic as a student of 'mathematics and physics'.[41]

At Aarau Einstein lived close to one of the teachers in the cantonal school, and the experience furnished him with the measure of a teacher's independence. He boarded at the home of the professor of history Jost Winteler, at the professor's insistence.[42] Winteler was a distinguished philologist and an avid, amateur naturalist. Einstein became a member of the family, a brother to the young Winteler brood. He maintained ties with the family throughout his life. When in 1899 a Winteler daughter sought guidance about a marriage proposal, she wrote to Einstein. Following his urging, Einstein's younger sister Maja studied for three years at Aarau. She found a warm welcome at the Winteler household, for in 1910 she married Jost's son Paul. It seems that just at the time that Einstein's parents sent him out on a path leading to a profession, the young man discovered for himself a surrogate family.[43] Here I cannot dwell on Einstein's personal relationship with the Wintelers. Rather, I consider in some detail Einstein's science education at Aarau.

Einstein's passage was to some extent an unorthodox one. He arrived late in October 1895 for the third quarter of the term and sat in the third class of the trade school. There he was a year or more the junior of his classmates. The grades that he received for industry and mastery of his course material were at first uniformly poor. For the final quarter, ending in April 1896, he showed little improvement except in Italian, where he earned five from a possible six points. In arithmetic and algebra he received the lowest grade, one out of six. At his own initiative or at that of his teachers Einstein took private instruction in French, chemistry, and natural history. After Einstein registered for the final half-year at Aarau, his performance in the exact sciences improved dramatically. During the first quarter of the new year—May and June of 1896—he received a six in arithmetic and algebra, and in physics a six for industry and a five for mastery of the material.[44] Einstein remained at Aarau through early July, when he took part in the annual youth festival, and into early September.[45] On the fifth of the latter month the rector recorded Einstein's final course grades along with those of the other pupils in the fourth, two-quarter class at the trade school. The grades reveal that Einstein had made only some progress towards filling in the gaps revealed by his abortive Polytechnic entrance examination. Among his class he was the best in algebra (a grade of 6), geometry (6), physics (5/6), and in German (4/5); he was among the best in history (5) and natural history (5); he was middling in descriptive geometry (5) and chemistry (5); he was among the worst in freehand drawing (4) and technical drawing (4); he was absolutely the worst pupil in French (3/4) and geography (4).[46]

One of the principal attractions at Aarau during the summer of 1896 was a newly completed school building. When Einstein arrived late in 1895 he would have found himself in the midst of great excitement over its construction, for the physical plant—still in the eighteenth-century hospital—had remained unchanged for generations. The rooms were low, narrow, and dark, and the benches and desks carved with an intaglio of students' initials.[47] During the 1880s and the early 1890s school directors along with the Aargau Scientific Society urged the city and canton to provide more space, especially for instruction in natural sciences. The governments claimed poverty and refused. Finally, the Cultural Society of Aarau offered 100 000 francs for a new building provided that construction began at the latest during July 1894. The Society's gift was 250 000 francs short of the sum calculated by the city for erecting a new building—not counting purchase of the requisite land. Just at this time the city was able to acquire, with the help of a few local citizens, the estate of a politician for only 150 000 francs. The city reserved an existing structure for a trade museum and gave the eastern portion of land along with 50 000 francs for the cantonal school. The canton was then pressurised to come through with the remaining money.[48]

The new building opened in 1896. It was designed by Karl Moser, the architect who also drafted plans for the new quarters of the University of Zurich. The Aargau structure was a thoroughly modern, four-storey building capped with a small clock tower. By far its favoured laboratory was that housing the 'physical cabinet'. In place were a two-horsepower alternating-current motor with accessories, a lathe, a milling machine, a joiner's bench, a work bench, a grindstone, various tools, a gear transmission, a small dynamo with accessories for physical experiments, an accumulator battery with switchboard and Edelmann galvanometer, and a projector.[49] These provisions were nothing short of extraordinary for a combined *Gymnasium–Realanstalt* of the period. In very few other places across German-speaking Europe would a pupil have been in such close proximity to so fine a collection of physical apparatus.[50] It was, in the words of one former pupil, a physical institute that a small university could envy.[51] Einstein was among the first young men turned loose in this magnificent instrument collection.

The structure was inaugurated on a beautiful, sunny, spring day, 26 April 1896.[52] Einstein assembled with the rest of the pupils and teachers to witness and take part in the public events, one of which was awarding an honorary doctorate from the University of Zurich to the old Aarau philologist and historian Jakob Hunziker. If he were attentive, Einstein would have noted the reactionary Heidelberg *Gymnasium* professor Gustav Uhlig among the invited dignitaries; Uhlig, who opposed Mach over the issue of instruction in the classics, had earlier taught Latin and Greek at Aarau. At the opening ceremonies Einstein would have heard the address of the rector, his physics teacher August Tuchschmid. The school was to be a strong bulwark for higher principles in life, Tuchschmid emphasised. As the struggle for existence intensified in the world outside, so the school had to become increasingly stronger in pointing youth 'towards the love of the true, the courage to be right, to awaken and nurse the sense for the noble and good, and to struggle against egoism'. The cantonal school educated the individual to know the value of general learning, enabling him to lead a rewarding existence. At the same time, Tuchschmid continued, the school had always placed great value on useful learning.[53] This formula succeeded well. Einstein was not the only pupil of foreign origin at Aarau around the turn of the century who would later win a Nobel Prize. Also a graduate of the school was Paul Karrer, winner of the chemistry laurels in 1937.

Whereas throughout the nineteenth century most rectors at Aarau served for only a few years at a time, Tuchschmid held this position from 1889 throughout the First World War. His was the guiding spirit behind the remarkable expansion of the school. Upon arriving as physics teacher in 1882 he transformed his discipline from the most poorly served science to the most respected. Tuchschmid was, quite simply, one of Switzerland's most gifted native sons. He had come through the Thurgau cantonal school and, after a period of private study, passed the *Abitur* in 1873. From the beginning he wanted to become a secondary-school teacher of mathematics and sciences, and before he reached the age of twenty he was installed in such a school in the Bernese Jura, teaching in both German and French. After three years he moved to Zurich, to study at the Polytechnic and to teach at the Zurich Craft School as well. Upon receiving a diploma from the Polytechnic in 1880 he became assistant to the same physics professor who later taught Einstein, Heinrich F Weber. He remained an assistant for two years, until he landed a position teaching physics at Aarau. When he arrived in 1882 he was shocked at the small, dirty, and inadequate facilities reserved for physics. Fourteen years later he had one of the finest physical laboratories in Switzerland.[54]

In his inspired teaching Tuchschmid aimed for depth rather than breadth. He insisted before his classes that the concepts of the infinitesimal and the differential were keys to all advanced physics and mathematics. A former pupil of his recalled that Tuchschmid's introduction to electric current was a shining piece of experimental physics which equalled university lectures. In all his courses Tuchschmid strove for clarity, intelligibility, and precision. He omitted those parts of physics not based on rigorous scientific foundations or those areas giving play to theoretical speculations. He never engaged in chatter on physical subjects and spared no effort to convey fundamental laws and phenomena. As might be expected from his choice of physics apparatus in 1896, Tuchschmid's principal interest at

Aarau lay in the burgeoning field of electrotechnology. In 1888 the city of Aarau chose him as a member of its advisory commission on electrification. In part as a reward for this service, in 1918 the city made him an honorary citizen, the first teacher at the cantonal school to obtain such a distinction.[55]

Supporting Tuchschmid's pedagogical activity was the geologist Friedrich Mühlberg, also a teacher of Einstein's. At the school's centenary in 1902 Mühlberg observed how the harmony of nature was captured in the organisation of his school: just as the living organism depended on mutual interdependence among its organs, so in human affairs the highest aim was for the individual to serve his fellow man. If Tuchschmid was an educator–technologist, Mühlberg was an educator–scientist. By 1900 Mühlberg was widely recognised as a leader in the school movement. At the same time, scientific research dominated his restless activity. He wrote a definitive flora of Aargau, a treatise on glacial geology in the canton, and descriptions of the geology of the Jura mountains. By 1895 Mühlberg had well over 1300 pages in print, an output comparing quite favourably with that of university professors of the time. He attended around 450 sessions of the Aargau Natural History Society, delivering 90 addresses of which the majority communicated original research in geology. It was natural that he should have edited the Society's *Mitteilungen*. In 1888, at the age of forty-eight, he received an honorary doctorate from the University of Basle.[56]

When Einstein took Mühlberg's class in geology and physical geography, he was taught by one of Switzerland's greatest geologists, a kindly and distinguished man of fifty-five. The young man made an impression on his teacher. Mühlberg, who died in 1915, remembered Einstein as a clever pupil.[57] Einstein came to know Mühlberg in a personal way, too. It was the custom at Aarau to organise excursions every year for the pupils. In June 1896 twenty pupils in the highest classes at the trade school and the *Gymnasium* enjoyed a three-day walking tour led by Mühlberg. The group travelled to the eastern Swiss canton of Appenzell. There Mühlberg directed a climb of the 2700-metre peak Säntis. He and his fellow tourists crossed snow fields despite inhospitable weather.[58] Potential tragedy dogged the expedition. Einstein suffered a bad fall and was saved by the quick action of one of his fellow pupils.[59]

Einstein was fortunate in a third science teacher at Aarau. More traditionally minded than either Mühlberg or Tuchschmid was his mathematics teacher, Heinrich Ganter. A native of Baden, Ganter attended the *höhere Bürgerschule* in Freiburg im Breisgau and then continued at a private school in Frankfurt am Main. After working in industry for several years he served as a lieutenant in the Franco–Prussian War. He then entered his father's mill. The business failed, and he was forced to follow another calling. He chose teaching. By 1877 Ganter found himself an instructor at the *Realgymnasium* in Karlsruhe. His advancement limited by an incomplete education, thirty-year-old Ganter decided to return to school. He spent three years studying mathematics at the universities of Berlin and Zurich. While a student at Zurich he worked as an assistant for higher mathematics at the Polytechnic and at the local *Gymnasium*. He received a doctorate from Zurich in 1884. Two years later he arrived at Aarau.[60]

Ganter was a good mathematician, but also a leading mathematics teacher. He told a colleague at Aarau that he was not really talented enough for a career in higher mathematics, but he could teach, 'something that many speculative gentlemen cannot do'.[61] Ganter, together with his friend the Polytechnic professor Ferdinand Rudio, wrote a school textbook on analytical geometry.[62] It was a text that Tuchschmid used when teaching mathematics in the *Gymnasium* at Aarau. The book surely reflected Ganter's instruction in mathematics. A particular achievement of Ganter's lay in presenting rigorous concepts to pupils in the trade school, those who, in the opinion of Tuchschmid, 'generally see mathematics quite differently from gymnasiasts'.[63] A former pupil of Ganter's wrote that he 'never treated us demeaningly, but taught us as men'. From the 1890s Ganter's favourite author was Friedrich Nietzsche. A colleague saw Nietzsche's thoughts reflected in Ganter's deep commitment to mould in his pupils a beautiful and strong character. His former pupil the Polytechnic professor Ernst Meissner remembered Ganter as a teacher who, far from transmitting mere practical information to prepare a pupil for a career, educated the heart and character and truly civilised his charges. If all teachers were like Ganter, Meissner insisted, there would be no need for school reform.[64]

Later in life Einstein remembered his congenial year at Aarau. In 1952 he wrote to Guido Fischer of the Aarau Art Collection that the school remained for him 'the most satisfying image of this kind of cultural institution'.[65] What struck Einstein most forcefully, he went on, was the freedom of instruction and learning that he had experienced there. It was a freedom traditional at Aarau and, despite superficial resemblances, one not emerging from the process of school reform in northern Germany. The atmosphere created by Einstein's science and mathematics teachers would have appealed to a great many pupils, but in Einstein it struck a particularly resonant chord. Einstein would have found in Mühlberg a practising scientist who unpretentiously and arduously dedicated himself to understanding natural events. Ganter would have presented algebra and geometry as clear and vibrant domains of learning. From Tuchschmid Einstein would have received a feeling for the practical applications of physical laws and a prejudice to avoid encyclopaedic compilation in favour of seeking fundamental theories of nature. These values were among the ones that Einstein carried to his later career.

Einstein's final examinations at Aarau

How the Aarau experience affected Einstein is revealed in the record of his trade-school leaving examinations, which he wrote on 18, 19 and 20 September and defended orally on 30 September. In registering for the examinations he followed all the usual procedures, since he submitted a short *vita* to the canton's instructional commission.[66] By the time that he applied Einstein knew which of his teachers would formulate the examination questions. Among other examiners Ganter was responsible for algebra and geometry, Tuchschmid for physics, Mühlberg for natural history, and the old philologist Hunziker for French. Other written and oral examinations were set in German language and literature and in chemistry. History and descriptive geometry carried only oral interrogations.[67] Conforming to the federal policy in such matters, the Polytechnic sent two observers to Aarau, presumably to attend the oral defences; one of the two, in the autumn of 1896, was Einstein's sympathetic adviser Albin Herzog.[68] Einstein did not disappoint the Zurich engineer. He received straight sixes—the highest possible grades—in his mathematics and physics examinations, a record setting him clearly above the heads of his fellows.[69]

The three mathematical problems that Einstein answered in his examination papers were similar to those set during this period in Prussian *Realgymnasien*. They were easier than questions asked, for example, in Hamburg *Oberrealschulen*.[70] One of the geometrical problems was in trigonometry, where Einstein calculated the angles of a triangle after having been given its sides. He used logarithmic tables to obtain numerical results. His written answer was evidently a fair copy, for in marginal comments on the paper Ganter noted an error in transcription (*Abschreiben*).[71] A second problem in analytical geometry involved solving a second-order, inhomogeneous equation. This time Einstein was less sure how to proceed, and his answer is complete with false starts. At one point he began to solve a quadratic equation correctly, only to cross out his calculations. Something farther along must have caught his eye.[72]

The final geometrical problem inscribed a circle in a triangle and gave the line segments connecting the median to each of the apices of the triangle; their ratio was 1:2:3. Einstein had to find the radius of the circle in terms of the smallest line segment. This he did by remembering a general equality for the three angles of a triangle, α, β, γ:

$$\sin^2 (\alpha/2) + \sin^2 (\beta/2) + \sin^2 (\gamma/2) + 2 \sin (\alpha/2) \sin (\beta/2) \sin (\gamma/2) = 1.$$

With substitutions this identity reduced to a cubic equation. Einstein found the three roots by invoking the general formula for solving such an equation and by then evaluating the square-root discriminant in the formula with the help of a trigonometric substitution and logarithmic tables. Though it depended on instant recall of complicated mathematical formulae, Einstein's solution was the very opposite of one based on brute-force calculations. He was careful to arrive at numerical values only after having made general observations on, among other things, the rationality of the roots of the cubic equation and on the geometrical requirements that a solution would have to satisfy.[73]

A third examination where Einstein demonstrated outstanding talent was physics. In his four-page essay he discussed the theory and design of the tangent compass and the galvanometer. It was a question that could have been posed at this time on the *Maturitätsprüfungen* of few other schools in German-speaking Europe; few had facilities comparable with those in Tuchschmid's laboratory for providing pupils with first-hand experience in making electrical measurements. Einstein knew exactly how to proceed. He began by noting that any electrical current is based on the observable effects of lines of force. Magnetic force is indirectly proportional to the distance from the conductor and directly proportional to the standard current strength in the conductor. Then he described the construction of the tangent compass. In this instrument, a magnetised needle is freely suspended from its midpoint by a non-conducting thread mounted at the apex inside a vertical ring of conducting wire; when an electric current passes through the ring, the needle is deflected and orients itself at an angle to the axis of the coil, an angle depending on the strength of the current. In his paper Einstein gave the tangent of the angle as equal to the magnetic force of the current (a quantity directly proportional to the current) divided by the component of force in this direction coming from the earth's magnetism. He wrote $\tan \phi = Ik/H$, where k was a constant, I the current strength, and H the contribution from terrestrial magnetism. One could then compare, Einstein observed, two currents I and I', because since k and H remained constant, the observed ratio $\tan \phi / \tan \phi'$ was precisely I/I'. He continued by emphasising that a galvanometer worked like a tangent compass, except that a coil replaced the needle. Einstein concluded by describing the uses of both instruments.[74]

In his physics essay, unlike the manuscript that he had earlier sent to his uncle Cäsar Koch, Einstein almost pointedly made no use of the concept of an electromagnetic field. Such a concept did not then belong to the accepted body of physical theory in German-speaking Europe, and Einstein no doubt sought not to antagonise his examiner Tuchschmid by mentioning it. In writing his answer Einstein emphasised how general physical phenomena could be harnessed to design measuring instruments. He stressed the basic theory of the apparatus and concluded by describing practical applications. Einstein also included some technical details. He mentioned how light rays reflected from a mirror mounted on the suspending filament or magnet could provide an accurate display of displacement, and in passing he referred to the way that a small telescope could be used to observe the needle set into oscillation when current was introduced into the ring. To accompany his answer Einstein carefully and unnecessarily included a top and side view of the tangent compass, making use of his mechanical-drawing instruments to inscribe circles and draw straight lines; perhaps Einstein felt that, because of his poor performance during the year in mechanical drawing, it would be a good idea to demonstrate some facility in this area. Significantly, Einstein did not spend time discussing the mechanical parts of the apparatuses. Only implicitly did he introduce the notion of a restoring force for the needle in the tangent compass or the coil in a d'Arsonval-type galvanometer. He also avoided discussing the mathematical procedure for obtaining precise results by reducing multiple data readings with the help of the method of least squares. For him these were, and remained, far from fundamental questions.

In chemistry and natural history Einstein wrote good responses to simple questions. He set up a chemical equation for combining sulphuric acid with table salt, and he correctly calculated quantities of reagents and products using 'atomic weights'. Upon giving the desired solution Einstein set down a series of remarks on the origin and uses of the compounds that he considered.[75] In natural history Einstein wrote on the effect of previous glaciation on geological formations, the theme set by Mühlberg. In composing his answer Einstein would have been able to draw on first-hand experience gathered during Mühlberg's geological excursions.[76]

One is struck by the clear and unpretentious quality of Einstein's examination essays, strong points present as well in his later published writings. The essays begin with a statement of a generalisation of physical phenomena in terms of theoretical concepts, such as electromagnetic lines of force. Then the essays consider the problem at hand by omitting distracting albeit interesting detail in favour of the fundamentals. In view of his obvious literary talents it is not surprising that the seventeen-year-old Einstein was the best in his class in German. For his German essay Einstein wrote a summary of Goethe's play about the sixteenth-century Swabian military adventurer Götz von Berlichingen, a text in which Goethe recast the rough and unprincipled warrior into a moral and sympathetic thinker. In his summary, Einstein characterised the personalities and motivations of Goethe's characters much as a secondary-school essayist today would discuss the actors in Shakespeare's *Julius Caesar*. Einstein's direct and complete treatment earned him a grade of 5.[77]

If Einstein was at his best in German, he was incontestably the worst pupil in French. In April 1896, he passed into the fourth year at the trade school over the protest of his French instructor, a protest that continued into the summer.[78] His French essay for the *Maturitätsprüfung* was, in the view of the philologist Hunziker, only marginally acceptable. Amid misspellings and grammatical errors, nevertheless, Einstein elaborated a disarmingly cogent picture. The theme concerned his 'future plans'. It was, Einstein wrote at the beginning, natural for a 'serious young man' to be as precise as possible about his goals. If he were fortunate enough to succeed in his examinations, he would go to the Zurich Polytechnic. There he would spend four years 'studying mathematics and physics'. As a career, Einstein imagined becoming a teacher (*professeur*), specialising in the 'theoretical part' of the natural sciences. He was suited for this career, Einstein continued, because of his 'individual disposition towards abstract thoughts and mathematics', and his 'lack of imagination [*phantaisie*] and practical talents'. By the latter phrase Einstein probably meant to reject not only a career in the creative arts but also one in the world of human affairs and commerce, the very career that his father was then having such difficulty sustaining. Einstein concluded his short essay by noting that he looked forward very much to the 'independence' that characterised the learned profession.[79] With the models of Tuchschmid, Ganter, and Mühlberg before him, and living at the home of the congenial Jost Winteler, Einstein knew exactly what he wanted.

Uncongenial mathematics at Zurich

Several weeks after having acquitted himself with distinction in the most important of his leaving examinations at one of Switzerland's finest secondary schools, Einstein arrived at the Zurich Polytechnic. During the next four years he was a student there. Much has been written on Einstein at the Polytechnic, and for this reason I shall not provide details of Einstein's student years.[80] By 1896 the Polytechnic had achieved a reputation throughout German-speaking Europe as a leading centre of higher learning in mathematics and physics.[81] As the only federal educational institution in Switzerland, it benefited early in the 1890s when the country swelled with new revenues resulting from rising duties on imported goods. In 1896 it had an excellent physical laboratory, completed in 1890, and with it a first-rate teaching staff.

How did Einstein, with his formidable talents and with the special encouragement that he had received at Aarau, respond to the physicists and mathematicians at the Polytechnic? His love for the physical laboratory of Heinrich Friedrich Weber is well documented.[82] It was a passion that had been fanned, at the very least, under Tuchschmid's direction. Yet Einstein's achievements as a physicist lie not in experiment but in the realm of mathematised theory. For this reason I shall concentrate here not on the emotions that Einstein may have brought to experimental physics but rather on what he found in the mathematics lectures of Hermann Minkowski, his most distinguished teacher. Minkowski is remembered as the discoverer in 1907 of four-dimensional space–time, a formal representation for Einstein's special theory of relativity. He proposed this theory as the first step in formulating a more general approach to energy and matter which, before his death in 1909, he was unable to elaborate. He believed that pure mathematics might successfully resolve the problems confronting physics.

Minkowski's optimistic faith in the explanatory power of pure mathematics was quite different from the view on these matters of his pupil Albert Einstein. Einstein has recalled that after a short time at the Polytechnic he came to believe that mathematics presented many separate domains, any one of which might easily absorb the energies of a lifetime. In physics, though not in mathematics, Einstein felt that he could intuitively sense those problems that were most important.[83] In his early published work in physics Einstein followed his nose, so to speak, in dealing with physical problems. Maurice Solovine, Einstein's close friend during the period just after he graduated from the Polytechnic, remembered that 'Einstein, who handled the mathematical instrument with incomparable dexterity, often spoke against the abusive use of mathematics in physics. Physics, he would say, is essentially a concrete and intuitive science. Mathematics serves only as a means of expressing the laws that govern phenomena.'[84] The young researcher Einstein viewed mathematics with suspicion. 'I do not believe in mathematics', Einstein is reported to have affirmed before 1910.[85]

Although Einstein's antipathy to mathematics is reflected in the modest level of mathematical exposition characterising his early scientific papers, during his student years he expressed a strong interest in mathematics. Einstein's matriculation record reveals that he registered for nearly as many mathematics courses as did his classmates Marcel Grossmann and Louis Kollros, both of whom were preparing for careers as mathematicians.[86] Particularly striking in Einstein's school record is the presence of courses by the newly appointed professor of mathematics Hermann Minkowski. Einstein took nine courses from Minkowski, more than from anyone else. To a greater extent than any other source, the content of Minkowski's courses reveals the sort of mathematics that Einstein found uncongenial.

Einstein's decision to take three algebraic courses with Minkowski was unusual for a physical scientist of the period, even for one expressing strong interest in mathematics. Traditional mathematical preparation for physicists consisted of analysis, geometry, and mechanics, each defining a large domain in applied mathematics. Together with arithmetic, algebra constituted one of the most important fields of pure mathematics at the end of the nineteenth century. Algebra applied elementary arithmetical operations to abstract mathematical entities. Complex analysis, particularly the characterisation of solutions to polynomial equations, was the central focus of much algebraic research. In the section on algebra in the first volume of the encyclopaedia of mathematical sciences edited by

Wilhelm Franz Meyer, only three of the nine articles did not have applications to the solution of equations as their principal aim.[87] In 1896 Eugen Netto devoted the first volume of his widely used text on algebra entirely to the roots of algebraic equations.[88] Group theory and the theory of numbers were seen as two areas closely related to the main concerns of algebra. Although in 1895 the Strasbourg mathematician Heinrich Weber devoted the first volume of his vast survey of algebra to complex analysis, he emphasised that group theory was essential for the development of algebra, and number theory offered the best application for algebraic modes of thought.[89] To a young physics student who sought powerful mathematical syntheses that also held the promise of being solutions to practical problems, algebra might have seemed attractive. It would have been particularly appealing when taught by Minkowski, a professor who sought to relate the theory of numbers to geometry—a field in applied mathematics that required physical, spatial intuition.

Registering for courses carrying no examinations, as was the case at the Polytechnic, implies little about the familiarity that a student might acquire with the course material. If the instructor were unprepared or gave otherwise unexciting lectures, fewer than a third of his students might be expected to attend class. Such was the case with Minkowski, notorious among the students for his difficult and poorly delivered lectures.[90] Einstein later wrote that although he successfully received a diploma in 1900, he did not regularly attend most of his courses. As an aid in memorising the many unrelated facts required for his examinations, in March and April of 1900 Einstein pored over lecture notes meticulously compiled by his friend Grossmann.[91] One record of Einstein's examinations, a note written by Minkowski, indicates that in complex analysis Einstein received a grade of 5½ out of a possible 6, the same grade as that obtained by Grossmann and Jakob Ehrat but half a point lower than Kollros' perfect score.[92] (The registers at the Polytechnic are more obliging. There Einstein is recorded as receiving a 10 in complex analysis, a 10 in the physics laboratory, a 5 in astronomy, and an 18 for a special project. These grades added together in a complicated way to produce an average of 4.9, ranking below Kollros' 5.45, Grossmann's 5.24, and Ehrat's 5.14. Einstein's grades did not augur a brilliant career.[93])

According to the exposition in Grossmann's notebooks, the algebraic courses of Minkowski were one-semester introductions.[94] Just enough of the underlying theory was presented to arrive at some basic results. Then special topics were considered. No allusion to physics was made, and little emphasis was given to the general solution of polynomial equations by geometrically inspired techniques. Someone expecting a unified theoretical treatment that led to applications, probably what Einstein was waiting for, would have been disappointed.

Where one might have expected most attention to the introduction of geometrical intuition was in Minkowski's course on the geometry of numbers. The format of the course was much less analytical and abstract than was the book that he had published in 1896, which defined the field for his mathematician colleagues.[95] To judge from Grossmann's and Minkowski's notes[96], the course was an earlier version of the lectures that Minkowski later gave at Göttingen, lectures recorded by A Axer and published in 1907 as a text on diophantine approximations.[97] Presuming no familiarity with number theory, algebra, or geometry, Minkowski's Zurich lectures introduced one new topic each session and frequently illustrated general points with specific examples. Minkowski's introduction would have appealed to a pure mathematician, but a physicist like young Einstein might have been less impressed. Minkowski began by restating Leopold Kronecker's mathematical programme: 'Everything leads back to the whole numbers.' Rational and irrational numbers and all algebraic quantities, in his view, were created from the whole numbers. 'In the last instance all of mathematics is a science of the whole numbers, and there are only true laws where the whole numbers appear.' The study of the whole numbers belonged to the theory of numbers. One could say, in Minkowski's view, that pure number theory treated how whole numbers related to arbitrary magnitudes, specifically real numbers. Minkowski emphasised that he would treat applied number theory, especially how geometrical intuition could help find mathematical laws more easily.[98]

In the first section of his lectures Minkowski introduced the number lattice, a central concept around which his lectures would turn.[99] The number lattice in two dimensions was defined by an orthogonal coordinate system (later the orthogonal restriction was relaxed), interest focusing only on the planar coordinates composed of two integers. The power of Minkowski's number lattice was illustrated by a basic theorem relating the area of convex bodies in a lattice defined by nonorthogonal axes to the number of lattice points contained within the perimeter of the convex bodies. Minkowski's theoretical development of the many-dimensional number lattice proved fruitful in finding integer or rational solutions to diophantine equations. In the light of the critical role played by frames of reference in Einstein's special theory of relativity, it is noteworthy that in his lectures Minkowski appealed to coordinate transformations in deriving several of his results. At one point he introduced multiplication of two-dimensional transformation matrices; Grossman found the calculation so unfamiliar that in his notes he was at first not careful to maintain the order of multiplication.

In both Grossmann's and Minkowski's records of the course there is little advanced machinery for other areas of mathematics, and Minkowski's exposition was strikingly less elegant than treatments by other mathematicians who also wrote on number theory from a non-arithmetical point of view, for example those of Felix Klein.[100] Einstein's experience with

Minkowski's exposition of pure mathematics would have reinforced his opinion that it was of little use for the physicist. Although he gave a passing mention to group theory in his first paper on special relativity in 1905, this subject and the geometry of many-dimensional vector spaces did not become a regular part of Einstein's mathematical arsenal until around 1911, when he realised that they were indispensable for constructing general relativity.

If Einstein's disappointment with the limited utility of pure mathematics for understanding physical laws was an expected outcome, his rejection of Minkowski's applied mathematics requires further explanation. For a physics student around 1900, one of the most important subjects in applied mathematics was theoretical mechanics. Generally taught by mathematicians, mechanics established the physical foundations for more advanced work in thermodynamics and electromagnetism, as well as for that in the neighbouring fields of geophysics and astrophysics. Einstein registered for the two principal introductions to mechanics that were given in the teachers' section at the Polytechnic. One, taught by his former patron Albin Herzog, began with the concept of a continuous distribution of matter and investigated problems in elasticity, strength of materials, and hydrostatics.[101] Herzog assumed only that the students had a working knowledge of elementary differential and integral calculus; he introduced all the physics required, appealing frequently to empirical laws. Complementing Herzog's treatment, Minkowski gave a course on the mechanics of rigid-body motion. He carefully formulated the laws of transformations between coordinate systems and proceeded to rigid-body kinematics.[102]

For his lectures Minkowski drew heavily on the recently published first volume of Felix Klein and Arnold Sommerfeld's major statement on mechanics, the *Theory of Tops*.[103] Klein and Sommerfeld's text was a revisionist treatment based on intuitive, non-formalist mathematics. It drew strength from Edward John Routh's classic text on dynamics, the sixth English edition of which was then being translated into German with Klein's and Sommerfeld's help.[104] In their own text, Klein and Sommerfeld emphasised the importance of arriving at a geometrical, intuitive grasp of mechanics: 'We will only require that our knowledge of mechanics is not based on formalism, but rather the reverse, that the analytical formulation appears as the final consequence of a basic understanding of the mechanical relationships themselves.'[105]

While he accepted the pedagogical charm of Klein and Sommerfeld's text, Minkowski was unable or unwilling to infuse his course with an appeal to intuitive, physical examples and motivations. His lectures were dull, formal recitations. In his opening remarks Minkowski paraphrased the third sentence of Klein and Sommerfeld's first chapter on the kinematics of tops: 'One speaks of kinematics', Minkowski began, 'when one investigates only the geometrical possibilities of motion, where only the concepts of space and time are considered; one speaks of kinetics or dynamics when one treats the mechanical possibilities of motion, where the concepts mass and force are taken up and the effect of the laws in nature, the influence on masses by forces, is taken into consideration.'[106] What was meant by a rigid body? Minkowski offered no physical insight. All motion was referred to three mutually perpendicular spatial axes. A mass distribution over a three-dimensional region constituted a body. To describe the orientation of the body, Minkowski continued, it was necessary to affix three internal perpendicular axes to the body. When the body was subjected to motion, the first time derivatives of a unit vector on each of these axes became the velocity components of the net speed. Next Minkowski asked his listeners to consider a body of infinitely many mass points, with two points having specified axes. A body was said to be rigid when for any two points there was no net change in motion over time. Unlike Minkowski, at this point in their text Klein and Sommerfeld provided a long, intuitive, 'geometrical' treatment of kinematics, presenting no equations of any sort.

Minkowski was kinder to his old physics teacher Heinrich Hertz than were Klein and Sommerfeld. Previously, when he was *Privatdozent* at the University of Bonn, Minkowski had been an enthusiastic follower of Hertz's approach to physics.[107] At the time Hertz was working towards eliminating the concept of force from physics. In 1898, although he repeated Klein and Sommerfeld's strictures against Hertz's approach, Minkowski did not take them to heart. He merely cautioned that mechanics ultimately rested on experience: 'Of course we must make use of the equations for the motion of a body to arrive at true natural laws. Naturally we cannot advance here by mere speculation. Our formulae should convey motion as it is actually seen in nature, and for this we have to calculate with the precise facts of practical experience.'[108] Hertz's electrodynamics had made a profound impression on Einstein in 1895. One wonders how receptive Einstein would have been several years later to Minkowski's unconvincing criticisms of Hertz's excessive abstraction.

Minkowski's remarks on practical experience are the more surprising because they constitute one of the very few passages in his lectures where he appealed to empirical reality. He generally omitted providing an intuitive discussion of force, work, impulse, and momentum, all of which were emphasised by Klein and Sommerfeld. Neither did he make use of many physical concepts. One rare case occurred in a discussion of impulse and momentum, where he mentioned that integrating the impulse imparted by gas molecules to the walls of a container would give the gas pressure; there he inappropriately referred his listeners to Klein and Sommerfeld's text. Minkowski's notes represent only a preliminary version of his lectures on mechanics, but they indicate his general approach to physics. Natural laws, and mechanics in particular, had to be based in the last instance on observation. In practice, however, the development of mathematical theories of reality depended hardly at all on experimentally verifiable propositions. Minkowski's method of classical mechanics assumed space, time, coordinate systems, and the measurement process as operational concepts. Physical results were obtained by invoking new and independent mechanical idealisations and deducing mathematical relations among all these quantities.

Though Minkowski emphasised abstract development to a greater extent than did Klein and Sommerfeld, there is little reason to suppose that Einstein would have found the parent text more congenial. Not opposed in principle to mathematics, Einstein sought to understand fundamental problems of physics. In his early published work he investigated the meaning of the statistical mechanics of molecules, not the classical mechanics of points, bodies, and continua. Even more than statistical mechanics, electromagnetism was a subject in which the young Einstein expressed a strong interest. Though included in a mechanical picture of the world, it was not part of Minkowski's mechanics curriculum. Statistical mechanics and electrodynamics made use of many physical propositions that, by 1900, were not easily reduced to standard mechanical explanations. A course treating these problems might have appealed to Einstein. Minkowski's course on mathematical methods, based on assumptions concerning mechanical reality but not on investigations of the validity of these assumptions, served to reinforce Einstein's view that mathematics would be of little use to a physicist.

Einstein's classmate Louis Kollros has recalled that, in their last semester at the Polytechnic, Minkowski gave a lecture on capillarity. It consisted of Minkowski's earliest thoughts about a review of the subject which Felix Klein had asked him to write for the new encyclopaedia of mathematical sciences. After the lecture Einstein noted 'enthusiastically and melancholically', Kollros continued, ' "that is the first lecture on mathematical physics which we have heard at the Poly".'[109] Einstein may, indeed, have seen something in Minkowski's lecture, for several months later he finished his first scientific paper on the consequences of the phenomenon of capillarity.[110] To judge from Einstein's remarks, however, Minkowski's lecture on capillarity was a welcome relief from the usual way that he presented mechanics as a series of mathematical formalisms.

Conclusion

For the young Einstein mathematical formalism was only a tool in the service of that which he and others called 'physical reasoning'. Einstein believed that the fundamental physical laws were arrived at by close comparison with experimental phenomena. These are precisely the values that Einstein's secondary-school physics and mathematics teachers—Sickenberger, Tuchschmid, and Ganter—transmitted to him. The values were not emphasised in Minkowski's dry, formal procedures, and Einstein found his lectures uninspiring.

In view of Einstein's extreme independence of character one may ask whether the affinities between his thought and that of several of his early teachers indicate causal relationships or contingent ones. In presenting some circumstances of Einstein's youth I have described the textbooks and lectures that came to his hands as well as the styles and thought of some of the instructors who stood before him. How these men and materials struck Einstein is what appears most difficult for a historian to answer. I do not seek to claim exclusivity for these texts and teachers. Many other events happening outside school produced a strong impression on Einstein. Future scholars with access to new archival material may revise our understanding of the origins of Einstein's revolutionary ideas of 1905. They will have to take into account, nonetheless, that in his secondary schooling Einstein was taught a great deal of mathematics and physics at the hands of sympathetic teachers. By 1900 he knew about many branches of mathematical thought, and his rejection of advanced mathematics was based on familiarity rather than on ignorance.

The formative educational experiences of a scientific genius like Einstein may well lie not in advanced training but in events at the time of secondary schooling. His passage through Aarau was a significant one for Einstein, quite possibly far more influential than his years of education in Zurich. Einstein had left Munich as an inexperienced, precocious schoolboy of fifteen. He came to the Polytechnic in 1896 as an unusually mature and clear-minded young man with many of his basic sensibilities already fixed. He readily absorbed the scientific values of his teachers at the cantonal school, but he was considerably less impressed with a different—one might say an opposing—approach to natural knowledge in the lectures of Minkowski at Zurich.

The evidence presented here supports the view that Einstein's experience with secondary education infused him with a prejudice for approaching physical reality as a whole subject and for viewing mathematics as incapable in itself of providing a formulation for nature's laws. Other mathematicians and physicists educated in German-speaking Europe soon after Einstein—Max Born and Hermann Weyl, to mention just two—did adopt the belief elaborated by Minkowski and his mathematician colleagues that pure mathematics would be able to resolve long-standing problems in physical theory. The advocates of pure mathematics won many supporters among twentieth-century physicists. Though he came to have great respect for mathematics, Einstein could not accept mathematical manipulation as a substitute for physical reasoning. Einstein's suspicion of mathematics surely contributed to his rejection of quantum mechanics during the 1920s, when many physicists sought to articulate an indeterminist epistemology to justify the success of formal methods.[111] From this point of view Einstein was not the first of a new wave of twentieth-century physicists but rather the last great thinker in a nineteenth-century tradition that included Hendrik Antoon Lorentz, Heinrich Hertz, and Max Planck. None in this company shrank from mathematical calculations, but each invoked mathematics as nothing more than an aid to physical reasoning.

Einstein maintained his views on the appropriate place of mathematics in physical theory until the end of his life. A close physician friend of Einstein's in the 1920s clarified how Einstein remained suspicious of mathematical formalism. Einstein remarked on a problem that he had come up against: 'I'm afraid I'm wrong again. I can't put my theory into words. I can only formulate it mathematically, and that's suspicious.'[112] Leopold Infeld, the most perceptive writer among all the physicists who worked with Einstein, has relayed how in the 1930s Einstein believed that mathematical formalism was something to be mastered and then transcended before truth could be fathomed. Infeld reports Einstein's observation: 'God does not care about our mathematical difficulties. He integrates empirically.'[113]

Notes and references

1 The standard story is given in, among other sources, Friedrich Paulsen's *German Education: Past and Present* translated by T Lorenz (London 1908) pp 205 ff. A recent re-evaluation of events unrelated to mathematics and science instruction during the period 1880–95 is James C Albisetti's *Kaiser, Classicists, and Moderns: Secondary School Reform in Imperial Germany* (dissertation, Yale University 1976). Albisetti makes much use of August Messer's *Die Reformbewegung auf dem Gebiete des preussischen Gymnasialwesens von 1882 bis 1901* (Leipzig 1901). Polemical accounts are provided in Felix Klein's *Vorträge über den mathematischen Unterricht an den höheren Schulen, I: Von der Organisation des mathematischen Unterrichts*, recorded by Rudolf Schimmack (Leipzig 1907), and Schimmack's Göttingen *Habilitationsschrift, Die Entwicklung der mathematischen Unterrichts-Reform in Deutschland* (Leipzig 1911). Of great value is Herbert Göllnitz's *Beiträge zur Geschichte des physikalisch–chemischen Unterrichts an den höheren Schulen Deutschlands seit der Mitte des 19. Jahrhunderts* (Leipzig 1920) pp 68–163. A general picture based on statistics taken from published sources is painted in Fritz K Ringer's *Education and Society in Modern Europe* (Bloomington 1979) pp 32–112.

2 Ernst Mach, *Der relative Bildungswert der philologischen und der mathematisch–naturwissenschaftlichen Unterrichtsfächer der höheren Schulen* (Leipzig 1886) pp 11, 19.

3 Quotations from Paul Cauer's sympathetic review of Uhlig's *Heidelberger*

Erklärung, appearing in the *Berliner philologische Wochenschrift* **9** (1889) 541–5.

4 'Education in Central Europe', *Report of the Commissioner of Education for the Year 1896/97* **1** (Washington, DC 1898) 177, 299. Information was drawn from official German sources.

5 *75 Jahre Luitpold Gymnasium München* (Munich 1967) p 6.

6 The Luitpold Gymnasium that Einstein attended was completely destroyed during the Second World War. A replacement of sorts is found in the present Albert-Einstein Gymnasium. The present Luitpold Gymnasium was the former Luitpold-Kreis Realschule, founded in 1891 and elevated to *Gymnasium* status well into the twentieth century. *Ibid* p 11.

7 K Luitpold-Gymnasium in München, *Jahresbericht für das Studienjahr 1888/89* (Munich 1889) p 15; *Jahresbericht für 1894/95* (Munich 1895) p 23.

8 Abraham A Fraenkel estimated that around 1900 there were 8700 Jews in Munich. Fraenkel, *Lebenskreise: Aus den Erinnerungen eines jüdischen Mathematikers* (Stuttgart 1967) p 36.

9 *Ibid* pp 60–1.

10 *Jahresbericht 1894/95* (ref 7) p 12.

11 Quotations from the prefatory passages reprinted in Josef Krist's *Anfangsgründe der Naturlehre für die unteren Klassen der Mittelschulen* (Vienna 1877). Krist long wanted to provide first-hand experience with apparatus for his pupils. An extensive exposition of pedagogical apparatus is given by Josef Krist in 'Regnaults Apparate zur Untersuchung der Compressibilität, Ausdehnung, spezifischen Wärme, u.s.w. in der ihnen von S. Silbermann gegebenen Einrichtung' *Repertorium für physikalische Technik* **2** (1867) 65–105.

12 *Jahresbericht 1894/95* (ref 7) p 3.

13 *75 Jahre* (ref 5) pp 10–11.

14 Adolf Sickenberger, *Leitfaden der elementaren Mathematik* (Munich 1894). Citations from the preface to the first edition of 1888, reprinted in the 1894 edition. The first edition contained a part on algebra and a part on 'Planimetrie'. The second and third editions constituted a revision of the algebraic part of the first edition.

15 Anton Reiser [pseudonym of Rudolf Kayser], *Albert Einstein: A Biographical Portrait* (London 1931) pp 36–7.

16 A Einstein, 'Autobiographical Notes', in *Albert Einstein—Philosopher-Scientist* ed P A Schilpp (La Salle, Ill 1949) pp 9–11, 15.

17 Haig Gordon Garbedian, *Albert Einstein: Maker of Universes* (New York 1939) p 13. Max Talmey, *The Relativity Theory Simplified and the Formative Period of Its Inventor* (New York 1932) pp 161–4. Anton Reiser [Kayser], *Einstein* (ref 15) pp 37–9, mentions Spieker's book as different from a first, unnamed geometry book. Cf Ronald W Clark's *Einstein: The Life and Times* (London 1973) p 31. My identification of the geometry book is supported by discussion in Maja Winteler-Einstein's 'Albert Einstein: Beitrag für sein Lebensbild' (Florence 1924) pp 13–14. The text is a 39-page typescript available in the Einstein Archives, Princeton.

18 According to correspondence from Miss Dukas, the four books are, respectively: Georg Freiherr von Vega, *Logarithmisch–Trigonometrisches Handbuch*

ed C Bremiker (Berlin 1869); H B Lübsen, *Ausführliches Lehrbuch der Analysis zum Selbstunterricht mit Rücksicht auf die Zwecke des praktischen Lebens* (Leipzig 1868); H B Lübsen, *Einleitung in die Infinitesimal-Rechnung (Differential und Integral-Rechnung) zum Selbstunterricht* . . . (Leipzig 1869); Heis and Eschweiler, *Lehrbuch der Geometrie zum Gebrauch an höheren Lehranstalten* **2**: *Stereometrie* (Cologne 1881). Miss Dukas declined to let me examine the books, which until her recent death were located at the Institute for Advanced Study, Princeton.

19 Banesh Hoffmann, with the assistance of Helen Dukas, *Albert Einstein: Creator and Rebel* (New York 1972) pp 22–3.

20 In 1929 a former teacher of Einstein's looked through his records at the Luitpold Gymnasium. He found that Einstein consistently received very good grades in all subjects, including Latin and Greek. H Wieleitner, 'Albert Einstein am Münchner Luitpold-Gymnasium', *Münchener Neuste Nachrichten* 14 March 1929.

21 A Einstein, 'Autobiographische Skizze', in *Helle Zeit—Dunkle Zeit* ed Carl Seelig (Zurich 1956) pp 9–10.

22 *Jahresbericht 1894/95* (ref 7) p 11.

23 Philipp Frank, *Einstein: His Life and Times* transl George Rosen, ed Shuichi Kusaka (New York 1947) p 17.

24 A Reiser [Kayser], *Einstein* (ref 15) pp 37, 41–4.

25 Brunella Malvicino, Pier Enzo Peirano *et al*, 'La Bassa Valle di Susa industriale, 1870–1918: Lineamenti storici per l'analisi di un territorio', in *Patrimonio edilizio essistente: un passato e un futuro* (Turin 1980) pp 43–99. The story of Swiss manufacturers in northern Italy is recounted in Hans Rudolf Schmid's *Die Familie Abegg von Zurich und ihre Unternehmungen* (Zurich 1972). See also Pietro Regoliosi's 'Elettrotecnica', in the collection *Storia di Milano* **16**: *Principio di secolo (1901–1915)* (Milan 1962) pp 879–902.

26 Elena Sanesi, 'Einstein e Pavia', *Settanta* **3** no 29 (October 1972) 33–41.

27 H G Garbedian, *Einstein* (ref 17) p 19. On 26 January 1896, Einstein's father, on his behalf, petitioned the state of Württemburg to discontinue Einstein's citizenship. Zentrales Staatsarchiv Merseburg, Rep. 76, Vc, Sekt. 2, Tit. 23, Litt. F, Nr. 2, p. 118: Württemburg Interior Ministry to Prussian Ministry for Learning, Art, and Public Instruction, 27 July 1923. Compare Clark's *Einstein* (ref 17) p 41.

28 Paul Forman and Paul Hanle, *Einstein: A Centenary Exhibition* (Washington, DC 1979) p 14. If he had successfully completed the lower classes at his *Gymnasium*—as his father had done at the Stuttgart *Realschule*—Einstein would have qualified to spend only one year in the army as a so-called 'volunteer'. M Winteler-Einstein, 'Albert Einstein' (ref 17) pp 5, 16.

29 This is how I interpret the remark of John Plesch in *Janos: The Story of a Doctor* transl Edward Fitzgerald (London 1947) p 219.

30 A Einstein, 'Autobiographische Skizze' (ref 21) p 9. Carl Seelig claims that a friend of the Einsteins then living in Zurich, Gustav Meier, advised Albert to go to Aarau. Seelig, *Albert Einstein: Leben und Werk eines Genies unserer Zeit* (Zurich 1960) p 6.

31 Jagdish Mehra, 'Albert Einsteins erste wissenschaftliche Arbeit', *Physikali-*

sche Blätter **27** (1971) 386–91. A photocopy of the essay may be found at Princeton University, Firestone Library, Einstein microfilms, IA9.

32 Information taken from *Encyclopaedia Britannica*, eleventh edition (1911). The discussion in this and the following section departs from the remarks by Gerald Holton on Aarau in 'On Trying to Understand Scientific Genius', *Thematic Origins of Scientific Thought* (Cambridge, Mass 1973) pp 372–3.

33 Augusta Wedler-Steinberg, *Geschichte der Juden in der Schweiz vom 16. Jahrhundert bis nach der Emanzipation* ed Florence Guggenheim-Grünberg, 2 vols (Goldach, Switzerland 1966–1970) **1** 87, 100, 165, 168, 223; **2** 46–7, 112, 133.

34 T Müller-Wolfer, *Die Aargauische Kantonsschule in den vergangenen 150 Jahren* (Aarau 1952) pp 14–63.

35 August Tuchschmid, 'Die Entwicklung der Aargauischen Kantonsschule von 1802 bis 1902', in *Jubiläum der Aargauischen Kantonsschule am 6. Januar 1902: Vorträge und Reden* (Aarau 1902) pp 13–63, on p 27.

36 Christa Jungnickel, 'Teaching and Research in the Physical Sciences and Mathematics in Saxony, 1820–1850', *Historical Studies in the Physical Sciences* **10** (1979) 3–47, on p 26.

37 Wilhelm Oechsli, *Geschichte der Gründung des Eidg. Polytechnikums mit einer Uebersicht seiner Entwicklung 1855–1905*. Vol I of *Eidg. Polytechnikum Festschrift* (Frauenfeld 1905) p 281.

38 Albert Barth, *Die Reform der höheren Schulen in der Schweiz* (Basle 1919) pp 15, 21.

39 A Tuchschmid, 'Entwicklung' (ref 35) pp 47–54.

40 *Ibid* pp 61–2.

41 *Programm der Aargauischen Kantonsschule: Schuljahr 1896/97* (Aarau 1897) pp 12–16.

42 Max Flückiger, *Albert Einstein in Bern* (Berne 1974) p 26.

43 Carl Seelig, *Albert Einstein: A Documentary Biography* transl M Savill (London 1956) pp 19–21. Flückiger (*Einstein* [ref 42] pp 24–6) cites relevant manuscript material on this subject.

44 From Einstein's *Personalakte* at the cantonal school. I am grateful to Professor Dr Hans Troxler-Keller, Bibliothek der Aargauischen Kantonsschule, for having kindly made this material available to me.

45 *Programm der Aarg. Kantonsschule* (ref 41) p 17; Seelig, *Einstein* (ref 43) p 17.

46 Staatsarchiv Aarau, Departementsakten Erziehungsdirektion, Mappe Ks/ Kantonsschule, 1896, 'Abgangsnoten für die Schüler der 4. techn. Klasse (Herbst 1896)', dated 5 September 1896. Paul Forman kindly provided me with a copy of this and all other material cited subsequently as belonging in the Staatsarchiv Aarau.

47 Gustav Uhlig, in *Zur Erinnerung an die Einweihung des neuen Kantonsschulgebäudes in Aarau am 26. April 1896* (Aarau 1897) p 35; Friedrich Mühlberg in *Jubiläum 1902* (ref 35) pp 74–5.

48 T Müller-Wolfer, *Die Aargauische Kantonsschule* (ref 34) pp 120–3.

49 *Programm der Aarg. Kantonsschule* (ref 41) p 56. The natural history museum of the Aargau Scientific Society was also installed in the new building, but its collection seems not to have been unusual for the time. Friedrich Mühlberg,

32   *Einstein's education*

'Das Aargauische Naturhistorische Museum', in *Festschrift zur Feier des hundertjährigen Bestandes der Aargauischen Naturforschenden Gesellschaft* ed F Mühlberg (Aarau 1911) pp cxi–cxxviii, cxix.

50 On physical laboratories in German secondary schools at this time see Paul Bode's *Die Reform des mathematischen und naturwissenschaftlichen Unterrichts an höheren Schulen in der Gegenwart* [dissertation, University of Leipzig 1911]; E Schneider, *Reformbestrebungen im Bereich des Physikunterrichts der höheren Schule* (dissertation, University of Kiel 1953) pp 35–87. A carbon copy of Schneider's dissertation is located in the Universitätsbibliothek, Kiel. Jürgen Sievert (*Zur Geschichte des Physikunterrichts* (dissertation, University of Bonn 1967) p 218) lists only eleven German secondary schools where laboratory instruction was provided in 1896. See also Göllnitz, *Beiträge* (ref 1) pp 140–8.

51 A Hartmann, in *Jubiläum Prof. Dr. August Tuchschmid* [Aarau 1922] p 5.

52 *Zur Erinnerung* (ref 47) p 5.

53 *Ibid* pp 22–6.

54 A Hartmann, in *Jubiläum Prof. Dr. August Tuchschmid* (ref 51) pp 4–9.

55 *Ibid*.

56 *Prof. Dr. Friedrich Mühlberg: Separatabdruck aus dem Jahresbericht der Aargauischen Kantonsschule für 1915/16* (Aarau 1916).

57 C Seelig, *Einstein* (ref 43) p 19.

58 According to Tuchschmid's report on the excursion in *Programm der Aarg. Kantonsschule* (ref 41) pp 19–21.

59 C Seelig, *Einstein* (ref 43) p 13.

60 *Prof. Dr. Heinrich Ganter: Separatabdruck aus dem Jahresbericht der Aargauischen Kantonsschule für 1915/16* (Aarau 1916).

61 Cited in *ibid* p 8.

62 Heinrich Ganter and Ferdinand Rudio, *Die Elemente der analytischen Geometrie der Ebene, zum Gebrauch an höheren Lehranstalten sowie zum Selbststudium: 1 Die analytische Geometrie der Ebene* (2nd ed, Leipzig 1894).

63 *Prof. Dr. Heinrich Ganter* (ref 60) p 7.

64 *Ibid*.

65 C Seelig, *Einstein* (ref 43) p 21.

66 Staatsarchiv Aarau. Einstein to Titl. Erziehungsdirektion des Kantons Aargau, 7 September 1896.

67 Aargauische Kantonsschule, *Programm für die Maturitätsprüfung an der technischen Abteilung im Herbst 1896* [Aarau 1896].

68 *Programm der Aarg. Kantonsschule* (ref 41) p 16.

69 Staatsarchiv Aarau, 'Maturitätsprüfung der Gewerbeschule im Herbst 1896'.

70 Surveys of questions asked on *Maturitätsprüfungen* in Prussia, Hamburg, and the rest of Germany during this time are given in Walter Lietzmann, *Die Organisation des mathematischen Unterrichts an den höheren Knabenschulen in Preussen* (Leipzig 1910) pp 42–93; John William Albert Young, *The Teaching of Mathematics in the Higher Schools of Prussia* (London 1900) pp 89–92; Francisque Marotte, *L'Enseignement des sciences mathématiques et physiques dans l'enseignement secondaire des garçons en Allemagne* (Paris 1905) pp 53–60. Marotte provides samples of questions in mathematics, physics, and chemistry.

71 Staatsarchiv Aarau. Examination paper headed: 'Aufgabe I. Albert Einstein'.
72 *Ibid.*
73 Staatsarchiv Aarau. Examination paper headed: 'Albert Einstein'.
74 *Ibid.* 'Tangentenbussole und Galvanometer. Albert Einstein'.
75 *Ibid.* 'Aufgabe. Albert Einstein'.
76 *Ibid.* 'Nachweis der früheren Vergletscherung . . . Albert Einstein'.
77 *Ibid.* 'Inhaltsangabe von Goethes Götz von Berlichingen. Albert Einstein'.
78 Bibliothek der Aargauischen Kantonsschule, Einstein's *Personalakte.*
79 Staatsarchiv Aarau. 'Mes projets d'avenir. Albert Einstein'.
80 The latest and best discussion is given in Russell McCormmach's 'Editor's Foreword', *Hist. Stud. Phys. Sci.* **7** (1976) xi–xxxv.
81 Jules T Muheim, 'Die ETH und ihre Physiker und Mathematiker. Eine Chronologie der Periode 1855–1955', *Neue Zürcher Zeitung: Beilage Forschung und Technik* 9 April 1975.
82 R McCormmach, 'Editor's Foreword' (ref 80).
83 A Einstein, 'Autobiographical Notes' (ref 16) p 17.
84 Maurice Solovine, 'Introduction', in Albert Einstein's *Lettres à Maurice Solovine* (Paris 1956) p vii.
85 Cited in McCormmach's 'Editor's Foreword' (ref 80) p xiv.
86 Copies of Einstein's, Grossmann's, and Kollros' matriculation records are available in the Wissenschaftshistorischen Sammlung of the ETH-Bibliothek, Zurich.
87 W F Meyer, *Arithmetik und Algebra* (Leipzig 1898–1904), vol I of *Encyklopädie der mathematischen Wissenschaften mit Einschluss ihrer Anwendungen.*
88 Eugen Netto, *Vorlesungen über Algebra* (Leipzig 1896).
89 Heinrich Weber, *Lehrbuch der Algebra*, 2 vols (Brunswick 1895–6) 'Vorwort'.
90 Hermann Minkowski to David Hilbert, 31 January 1897. Lili Rüdenburg and Hans Zassenhaus, eds, *Hermann Minkowski: Briefe an David Hilbert* (Berlin 1973) p 94. Minkowski commented that attendance in his course on analytical mechanics was declining drastically, even among the cleverest students. This he attributed to his demanding lecture style. Hermann Weyl contrasted Hilbert's 'fairly fluent' speech to Minkowski's 'hesitant' speech in 'David Hilbert and His Mathematical Work', *Bulletin of the American Mathematical Society* **50** (1944) 654.
91 A Einstein, 'Autobiographische Skizze' (ref 21) p 11.
92 Minkowski papers, box V, folder 11, Niels Bohr Library, American Institute of Physics, New York (henceforth AIP).
93 Einstein Archives, box 38, Princeton University Library.
94 Grossmann's notebooks for five of Minkowski's courses survive in the library of the Federal Institute of Technology. Einstein registered for the same courses: 'Geometrie der Zahlen, WS 1897/98', vols I and II; 'Potentialtheorie, SS 1898', 2 vols; 'Funktionentheorie, SS 1898', 1 vol; 'Elliptische Funktionen, WS 1898/99', 1 vol; 'Algebra, SS 1899', 1 vol. Handschriftenabteilung, Bibliothek der ETH, Zurich, Hs 421:27–Hs 421:31.
95 Hermann Minkowski, *Geometrie der Zahlen* (Leipzig 1896).
96 AIP. Minkowski papers, box V, folder 13. 'Wintersemester 1897/98. Geometrie der Zahlen'.
97 H Minkowski, *Diophantische Approximationen* (Leipzig 1907). Minkowski

noted in the foreword that the text was based on lectures given at the University of Göttingen during the winter semester 1903/04.

98 Minkowski, 'Geometrie' (ref 96) 'I. Vorles. d. 28.10.97'.

99 H Minkowski, *Diophantische* (ref 97) ch 2. See G H Hardy and E M Wright, *An Introduction to the Theory of Numbers* (Oxford 1945) pp 26–31; Hermann Weyl, *Algebraic Theory of Numbers* (Princeton 1940) p 141; Jean Dieudonné, 'Minkowski, Hermann', *Dictionary of Scientific Biography* 9 (New York 1974) 411–14.

100 Felix Klein, 'Ausgewählte Kapitel der Zahlentheorie, I: Vorlesung, gehalten im Wintersemester 1895/96', mimeographed (Göttingen 1896) p 1.

101 Bibliothek der ETH, Notebook of Louis Kollros, Hs 105:1. 'Mechanik. Herzog. 1. Semester 1897–98'.

102 AIP. 'Wintersemester 1898/99. Mechanik'.

103 Felix Klein and Arnold Sommerfeld, *Ueber die Theorie des Kreisels* (Leipzig 1897). Vol 1 of four vols.

104 Edward John Routh, *Die Dynamik der Systeme starrer Körper* transl A Schepp (Leipzig 1898), from the sixth (1892) English edition.

105 F Klein and A Sommerfeld, *Ueber die Theorie* (ref 103) 'Anzeige des Buches'.

106 AIP. 'Wintersemester 1898/99. Mechanik'.

107 H Minkowski to D Hilbert, 22 December 1890, in *Briefe* (ref 90) pp 39–40.

108 AIP. 'Wintersemester 1898/99. Mechanik'.

109 L Kollros, 'Erinnerungen eines Kommilitonen', in Seelig, *Helle Zeit* (ref 21) pp 21, 23.

110 A Einstein, 'Folgerungen aus den Kapillaritätserscheinungen', *Annalen der Physik* 4 (1901) 513–23, received 16 December 1900. By Einstein's account this paper must have been completed in the year of 'intellectual depression' that followed his having successfully passed the final examinations at the Polytechnic. Einstein, 'Autobiographische Skizze' (ref 21) p 12.

111 The standard reference is Paul Forman's 'Weimar Culture, Causality, and the Quantum Theory, 1918–1927: Adaptation by German Physicists and Mathematicians to a Hostile Intellectual Environment', *Hist. Stud. Phys. Sci.* 3 (1971) 1–115. Forman has elaborated his views in 'The Reception of an Acausal Quantum Mechanics in Germany and Britain', in *The Reception of Unconventional Science* ed Seymour H Mauskopf (Boulder, Colo 1978) pp 11–50.

112 J Plesch, *Janos* (ref 29) p 208.

113 Leopold Infeld, *Quest: The Evolution of a Scientist* (Garden City, NY 1941) p 279.

2 Audacious enterprise: the Einsteins and electrotechnology in late nineteenth-century Munich

It is well known that Albert Einstein's father Hermann and uncle Jakob operated a factory in Munich for producing electrical apparatus. In the present chapter I discuss this enterprise, the climate surrounding it, and the innovative approach to electrotechnology taken by Jakob Einstein. Uncle Jakob published with leaders of the profession. He took out no fewer than six patents during the Munich years, and his inventions received recognition by colleagues. In his business dealings he challenged powerful and wealthy industrialists, and for a brief moment the Elektro-Technische Fabrik J Einstein & Co verged on becoming a major force in Munich industrial circles. Lessons from the ambitions and fate of Jakob's German endeavours, I shall contend, were not lost on his nephew.

Electrotechnology in late nineteenth-century Germany

In reviewing the geography of industrialising Germany, one cannot fail to be struck by the tardy emergence of Bavaria. It was the second largest German state, a land of great agricultural and natural wealth. Yet in the unification of Germany, Bavaria came, like Polish-speaking Prussia and perhaps Alsace–Lorraine, as an uncooperative partner. Munich saw itself as a centre of German culture outshining the newly-arrived Berlin; Bavaria was, and remains, tradition-bound, conservative, and insular. When Germany industrialised with Ruhr coal and iron, with Hamburg and Frankfurt commerce, and with Berlin and Leipzig patronage, Bavaria stood aloof. Bavarian entrepreneurs hesitated as their German *confrères* launched into the earliest phase of the Second Industrial Revolution, that of electrification.

The first of the electrical industries to develop were related to the telegraph, and among these, around 1880, the firm of Siemens & Halske predominated. In the late 1840s the task of setting up a telegraph line for the Prussian army had been entrusted to Lieutenant Werner Siemens. Upon developing a serviceable cable, he collaborated with a mechanic, Johann Georg Halske, to establish a firm for producing the communications system. In 1849 he connected Berlin and Frankfurt by underground wire. The young company distinguished itself from smaller competitors only by the number of its employees. In form, it was still a handicraft shop. By the middle 1870s, the guiding light of the operation, Siemens, found himself recipient of a doctor of philosophy degree *honoris causa*, a member of the Berlin Academy of Sciences, and director of a near-monopoly in Europe over telegraphic communication, a position of power shared with the British branch of the firm directed by his brother Wilhelm. At the time of the constitution of the German Empire in 1870, Siemens controlled the London–Calcutta telegraph line. He employed around 3000 workers, mostly in the vicinity of Berlin. In Prussia alone there were well over 50 000 km of telegraph lines, and more than 1200 telegraph officials.[1]

The first telegraphs functioned with low-voltage, low-intensity, direct current, generated by chemical means. A revolution in the electrical industry followed the invention of the dynamo, a machine for generating high intensity current—*Starkstrom* in contrast to *Schwachstrom*. As one of those to whom credit for the dynamo has been assigned, Werner Siemens immediately recognised the 'colossal' implications of the new machine. It would, he wrote to brother Wilhelm in London in 1866, open a 'new era in electromagnetism'.[2] It heralded cheap electrical lighting and distribution of electrical power. With the establishment of central generating stations, electricity began to flow in great quantities into the electrochemical industry, which until then had limited much of its activity to gold and silver plating. Around the middle 1880s, stimulated by an American model, commercial electricity was used for incandescent lighting. A decade or so later, electrical power from central stations drove both stationary motors and traction motors for transportation. The new electrotechnical industry depended on skilled and semi-skilled workers for turning out countless kilometres of wires and cables, and myriad lamps and bulbs. It also required skilled mechanics for such items as measuring instruments, telephone receivers, counters, electrodes, and specialised motors. By the early 1880s Siemens had stretched his reach from telegraphy and power generation to transportation. He constructed the first electrical tramway in a suburb of Berlin.

Siemens was at heart a technical innovator and engineer, not an entrepreneur; and he did not rush to acquire German patent rights to the inventions of others, for example, to Edison's light bulb. This plum fell to Emil Rathenau for 350 000 M; with five million more marks, Rathenau set up the German Edison Company. The Allgemeine Elektrizitäts-Gesellschaft—or AEG, as Rathenau's firm subsequently became known after a reorganisation in 1888—worked closely with Siemens to manufacture dynamos. It was Rathenau, not Siemens, who won the contract to light the streets of Berlin by electricity. By the late 1880s, Rathenau had nearly 2000 employees. Capitalisation increased many-fold to cover the new initiatives. AEG expanded into the field of high-intensity current, while Siemens, heavily engaged in telegraphy, ranged over the entire field of electrotechnology.[3]

The central place occupied by AEG—one that had an impact on the careers of the Einsteins—forced German competitors to restrict their interests geographically. The Nuremberg mechanic Sigismund Schuckert, for example, had begun manufacturing dynamos of his own design in 1874 and rapidly established a name in Bavaria and neighbouring areas. Although Schuckert expanded outside Germany, AEG beat him to the Nuremberg streetcar contract. Yet during the 1880s and early 1890s, the market was insatiable, at least until the crisis of 1900–2 which led to the great German electrical trusts, and dozens of firms occupied various 'ecological niches' in it. A branch office of the American Thompson–Houston Company evolved at Berlin into Union Electric and prospered by converting horse-drawn streetcar systems into electrical ones. Other companies worth millions of marks included Frankfurt's Lahmeyer, Cologne's Helios, and Dresden's Kummer. During the great depression of 1875–96, the German electrical industry—first in the manufacturing sector and then in utilities—expanded and consistently provided a return on investments.[4]

The crisis of the late 1890s followed enormous growth. From a mere 18 public, electrical generating facilities in 1888, there came 269 in 1896 and 805 in 1900; 15 000 electrical workers in 1890 multiplied into 54 417 eight years later. In view of such an expanding market, it is not surprising that, although the giant firms hired thousands of workers, the average manufacturer of electrical products employed, in 1895, only 25 people. Berlin and its surroundings hosted 158 companies with 8551 employees, and a number of these were classified as small (with between 1 and 5 employees) and medium-sized (between 6 and 50 employees).[5] Few foresaw, around 1890, that many of the small firms—that of the Einsteins included—would not survive the decade.

Bavaria was slow to take to the field of electrotechnology. As late as 1895, it had only one factory employing more than 200 people for producing electrical motors and two of the same size for turning out other electrical products; none of these was located in Munich. There were 13 Bavarian electrical factories employing between 6 and 50 people, and 9 employing 5 or fewer. Bavaria had only 38 of the more than 200 German electrical generating plants, and all of these employed 50 or fewer workers; 28 of them were run by crews of no more than 5 persons.[6] Munich was a large metropolis, one ripe for electrification. Jakob and Hermann Einstein's resettlement in 1880 from Ulm to Munich placed them in an environment that would reward innovation and business acumen.

The Einsteins were not alone in seeing possibilities for electrical enterprise in Munich. When they were setting their fledgling operation on its feet, the engineer Oskar von Miller threw himself into promoting electrical power for his native city.[7] Miller was the son of the director of the royal Bavarian foundry, a world-famous institution that had constructed the door for the Capitol in Washington. In 1882 he organised in Munich the first German electrotechnical exhibition. Two years later he opened Munich's first central electrical generating station, a small coal-burning operation supplying direct current to nearby subscribers.[8] Between 1884 and 1890 Miller worked by the side of Emil Rathenau, directing the ancestor of the AEG in Berlin. With this experience under his belt, he returned home to set up his own office as a consulting engineer. By virtue of his connections, he was appointed technical director of an ambitious electrotechnical exhibition to be held at Frankfurt during the spring and summer of 1891. Whereas previous exhibitions had been designed to stimulate interest in electrical lighting, Miller wanted the Frankfurt one to examine the feasibility of high-tension, polyphase transmission through the use of transformers, and so undermine the practice of erecting numerous small, local generators. Although his demonstration by no means constituted the first successful long-distance system, Miller dramatically brought hydroelectrically generated current to the fair grounds from Lauffen, 178 km away.[9]

While Miller was first at Berlin and then preoccupied with his schemes for Frankfurt, electrification in Munich proceeded at a slow pace. In 1882, the same year that Miller erected Munich's first generator and organised the Munich exposition, the city formed a commission to study whether electricity could be produced from the local river, the Isar. The commission met with hostility from gas-lighting interests; they opposed the project and were successful in retaining their monopoly on street illumination into the 1890s. As a result, the city was for some time unable to allow private contractors the use of public thoroughfares for distributing electrical current. The system favoured small generating plants. In 1883 the Residenztheater with 706 outlets became Munich's first electrically-lit building. Then came the Hoftheater, the Odeon, the parliament, various shops and restaurants, and a small railway to nearby Ungerer-Bad. By 1889 Munich had 588 arc lamps and 23 000 incandescent bulbs on 116 sites. Steam generators produced 60% of the power, gas 30%, and water 10%. All these were direct-current systems. The city finally agreed to give limited lighting rights to electrical utilities in 1891. In 1893 Munich granted Schuckert the contract for building the first generator to light the city core; it, too, produced direct current.[10]

Having entered the electrical lighting business, in 1894 the city of Munich created a municipal office to oversee it. For ten years the city had been financing a hydroelectrical research station under Professor Ernst Voit of the local institute of technology, and so its councillors had before them the basis for making an intelligent choice to head the new office. For this post they called Friedrich Uppenborn, perhaps the best known electrical engineer in Munich. He was above all an aggressive spokesman for municipal lighting.[11] Beginning in 1881 Uppenborn edited several electrical journals, finally creating the *Elektrotechnische Zeitschrift* in 1889.[12] The latter, published jointly by Oldenbourg in Munich and Springer in Berlin, led the field.

The story of the electrification of Munich has so far been told from the point of view of men at the top, those who, by circumstances of birth and fortune, came to occupy positions of influence and power. Yet the forces guiding change are revealed as clearly in the aspirations of men and women bereft of political and economic leverage as in the resolutions of councillors and captains. We now consider several minor actors who were compelled to retire from the scene by the designs of their better-heeled competitors.

The Einstein business

The Einsteins began their Munich business after the introduction of the first general patent regime in Germany, a system designed to encourage invention and stimulate technology. It was long overdue. During the first two-thirds of the nineteenth century, separate patent laws existed in the various German-speaking states. None especially encouraged the exploitation of invention. At the urging of Werner Siemens and the Association of German Engineers, in 1877 the new Empire enacted a uniform patent code. According to the law, a licensee paid thirty marks for the first year of his patent, fifty for the second, and each year thereafter a fee increasing by fifty marks, until the patent expired after fifteen years. If the licensee kept patent rights for the maximum length of time—most let their patent expire long before then—he would have paid the state a total of 5280 M. The new law brought order to a chaotic situation, but proved cumbersome and inefficient. Between 1878 and 1889, the number of annual patent grants remained relatively stable at around 4200, but the annual number of patent applications doubled from 6000 to 12 000; the annual number of complaints regarding infringement increased from 600 to 2800. To rectify some of these shortcomings, the licensing procedure was streamlined in 1891.[13]

The patent laws were to some extent agents of democratisation, for they held out the promise of rewarding inventive activity on the part of small and medium-sized firms. The Einsteins' high-technology enterprise, of modest proportions but harbouring the possibility of rapid expansion, was one of many smaller firms spurred on in this way to take out electrical patents. Every invention has an inventor, and Jakob Einstein was his firm's technical genius. In the years between 1886 and 1893 he took out six patents in the name of his company.[14]

The earliest and the latest of Jakob Einstein's patents concerned improvements in arc lamps. The middle four were filed between November 1889 and February 1890. One was an automatic circuit breaker for arc lamps. The remaining three consisted of devices for measuring electrical current flow. An unusual feature of Jakob Einstein's inventive spirit was his propensity to collaborate with others on the patents. The co-proprietor of the first one was a certain J A Essberger. Two of the middle four dealing with an electricity meter were filed with another little-known figure, Sebastian Kornprobst. At least in the latter cases, the idea came from the collaborator, and Jakob saw to its implementation and manufacture. We know about the division of labour from a report by C L Imhoff of the Munich electrotechnical research station, for Imhoff referred to the device as an 'electricity meter of the firm J Einstein & Co, Munich, Kornprobst System'.

The instrument in question was a clock meter, suitable for measuring ampere-hours as well as watt-hours. Meters of this kind employed a pendulum clock with the pendulum designed as a shunt coil. Fixed below or near to the shunt coil was a coil with the current to be measured. The rate of the shunt-coil pendulum clock would obviously depend on the current, and its changing rate could be compared and counted relative to a standard clock. The counting mechanism could be made directly to register the power in the circuit. If the shunt-coil pendulum were replaced by a permanent magnet, the meter recorded ampere-hours. The Einstein–Kornprobst meter was meant principally to measure either direct or alternating current, not power. Imhoff gave high marks to the apparatus: 'The construction itself is very ingenious, the execution of the work perfectly satisfactory.' In Imhoff's tests, the meter was extraordinarily accurate over the range from five to fifty amperes.[15]

Two clocks keeping different time, each in what might be called its own frame of reference, lay at the centre of the Einstein–Kornprobst meter. The idea of synchronising and comparing clocks in moving frames of reference plays such an important role in the special theory of relativity that these patents fairly call out for further comment. Some writers have claimed to see intimations of relativity in an essay written by Einstein when the fifteen-year-old émigré lived in Italy; and it has recently been suggested that Jost Winteler's doctrine of relativistic linguistics had an impact on Einstein when the sixteen-year-old boarded for a year with him.[16] One can also imagine Jakob spreading out his patent plans on the kitchen table and explaining them to his eleven-year-old nephew Albert, and in this way locate the germ of relativity at an even earlier date.

It is a mistake to use such conjectures for constructing a causal argument in intellectual history. No more importance can be ascribed to Einstein's essay or to Winteler's linguistics or to Jakob's clocks than to Einstein's vague exclamation to his friend Marcel Grossmann, in 1901, about interference experiments and matter moving relative to the light ether.[17] *Qui haeret in litera haeret in cortice.* The value of documents like the Einstein–Kornprobst patent descriptions and the letter to Grossmann lies in their contribution to establishing an environment or a frame of mind. To the extent that we are interested in Albert Einstein's intellectual development, we must try to examine the full range of his uncle's and his father's business activities.

At the time that Jakob Einstein was giving expression to his inventive urge, he pushed ahead in other areas. Munich and points south were wide open for entrepreneurs who could set up electrical generating plants and from them string a network of arc lamps. Yet plants required substantial capital, and capital flowed to firms that had demonstrated technical competence and commercial aptitude. At least through the middle 1880s, the Einsteins concentrated on manufacturing dynamos. Friedrich Uppenborn, during his time as editor of the Munich-based review *Zentralblatt für Elektrotechnik*, chose the first page of his tenth volume, in 1888, to comment on dynamo construction in general and on the Einsteins' contribution to the field in particular. Uppenborn noted how dynamo construction had just undergone major transformations. He remarked on the patents taken out by English firms, by Siemens & Halske, and by Schuckert. But instead of providing his readers with a picture of any of the machines produced by these well-known firms, he featured an engraving of the Einsteins' newest dynamo. It was designed to supply arc lamps. Originally, Uppenborn reported, the Einsteins had constructed a dynamo with a discoidal, or flat-ring, armature. This method differed from Siemens' original shuttle-wound armature in that it employed two sets of poles with the radial depth of the armature greatly exceeding its length. Following up on an article in the *Zentralblatt* for 1886, Uppenborn continued, the Einsteins changed their armature to a bipolar winding with several wire loops wound side-by-side around a drum. In this way, the drum could contain dozens of identical windings, making the dynamo multipolar.[18] The latter design was easier to manufacture and more efficient to operate, and it dominated the market for the next generation.

It has sometimes been claimed that technology leaves fewer traces for the historian than does science. Police and commercial registers, however, can be made to reveal technological information that would never have been recorded in print. From indications about the Einsteins' business endeavours preserved in such archives, we know that at the time of

Albert's birth and for a year thereafter, Hermann worked in the Ulm bedding shop of Israel & Levi. In June 1880 he moved with his family to Munich. There, five months later he, together with his brother Jakob, opened a shop specialising in gas and water installations; at the same time, the Einsteins had a two-thirds interest in the mechanical-engineering and repairs shop of the Kiessling firm. The brothers struck out on their own in May 1885, founding the Elektro-Technische Fabrik J Einstein & Co; Hermann handled the commercial side of the factory, and to Jakob fell technical matters. Having inaugurated a new enterprise, the Einsteins moved their home away from the city core to a larger house or houses in the Munich suburb of Sendling.[19]

Evidence suggests that the new firm aimed to enter the field of electrical power generation. In 1885 it received a contract to install electric lights for the first time at the Munich *Oktoberfest*.[20] The Einstein brothers could well have used a dynamo of their own design to supply current. Within five years, the company was on the verge of landing a substantial contract to provide an electrical generating plant for a town in northern Italy. According to a letter from Jakob Einstein to Theodor Peters, the director of the Association of German Engineers in Berlin, an Italian company agreed to call in the Einsteins to construct the facility. Because the record of the Einsteins was 'not widely known', Jakob wrote to Peters, the Italians required that the plans and price schedule be scrutinised and certified by Peters' Association. Jakob asked that Peters send along a statement that the firm's fees fell in line with the Association's conventions, and, as well, a statement that Jakob was a member in good standing of Peters' engineering brotherhood. Peters immediately complied, and for his help received a fee of 55 M.[21] The contract in Italy went through, followed by another one; within a year the Einsteins also had a plant in Munich. The company had grown important enough to make an appearance at a major symposium of the German electrical industry at Frankfurt in 1891.

The Einsteins exhibit at Frankfurt

The Frankfurt exhibition, more ambitious than anything similar previously mounted in Germany, followed in the best tradition of middle nineteenth-century world's fairs. Supported by both local and imperial treasuries, it cost well over 1.3 million marks, a sum 50% greater than initially foreseen. The overrun was more than compensated by popular reception; visitors left more than 1.4 million marks for the price of admission, to buy food and spirits, and to enjoy such standard amenities as balloon rides and telephone calls. More than 1 016 000 admission tickets were sold. On a typical Sunday, 11 101 people would have entered the fair grounds, although a special day featuring reduced admission prices could draw three times this number. Imperial Finance Minister Johannes Miquel opened the exhibition by invoking the useful and practical ends that electricity served. To provide imperial recognition of the exhibition's success and also to bask in its glory, the Kaiser himself spent a day touring the grounds in early autumn. The imperial visitors from Berlin would have surveyed electrical tramways and an enormous artificial waterfall. Large halls were given over to all manner of electrical equipment. Polite culture even bent to serve the ends of the exhibition with the staging of a ballet, a classical allegory of electricity featuring people representing Prometheus, Alessandro Volta, and Luigi Galvani.[22] The stunning success of the exhibition reflected the efforts of the progressive mayor of Frankfurt, Franz Adickes, a champion of scientific education and the motive force behind the creation, twenty years later, of his city's university.

Any German contender in the competitive world of electrotechnology would have been strongly advised to exhibit his wares at the fair. Jakob and Hermann Einstein acted in the expected manner and showed the complete line of their products and services: dynamos, arc lamps, and electricity meters. From the pages of the voluminous official transactions of the Frankfurt exhibition emerges a detailed record of the technological ambitions of Albert Einstein's father and uncle.

Near the middle of the large machine hall, by far the most expensive and impressive building on the grounds, the brothers Einstein exhibited their dynamos. Among eight featured models, three were in service. The first of these, with a cast-iron magnetic core, could supply motors drawing up to 1200 watts. The second working dynamo had a horseshoe-shaped magnet with two exciter coils and produced from 7000 to 30 000 W. Machines of the first and second types had been sold to the glass-cutting company of von Praag and to the Blackman Ventilating Co, both in London. The third and largest dynamo, one coupled directly to a steam engine, delivered 75 000 W at 120 volts. It was rated at 100 horsepower. It had six electromagnets set radially on a drum of 70 cm external diameter. Each winding had 59 coils set in grooves. This dynamo was undoubtedly the one that Friedrich Uppenborn described in his *Zentralblatt* three years previously. At the fair it provided power to a number of buildings, including the Pfungstädter tavern and the Irrgarten, an outdoor park. Beyond the machine hall, the Einsteins used a small, 8 hp gas dynamo to run electrical measuring instruments, and a compound dynamo, probably one of 15 hp, providing current for a Höpferner copperplating apparatus.[23]

The Einsteins also displayed several of the arc lamps that Jakob patented. At the centre of nineteenth-century arc lamps were two carbon rods separated by a small distance; when the rods were placed at different potentials, such as those of an electrical circuit, a spark would arc between them and the two would glow. By 1890 high-quality rods were readily available. The major technological problem concerned designing a self-regulating mechanism to maintain the proper arc gap as the carbon rods burned away. In Jakob Einstein's lamp, two rods were mounted vertically to produce a light point. The top one remained fixed, while the bottom one advanced upward, guided by what would later be called an electro-servomechanism mounted above the arc. In lamps of this kind, hot gases heated up the electromagnet in the regulating mechanism, resulting in an increasingly larger current crossing a wider and wider gap; at a certain point, the lamp would cease to function. Jakob cleverly solved this problem by introducing a correcting mechanism to ensure that the arc length and current strength remained constant. During the exhibition, Professor Ernst Voit of the Munich electrotechnical testing station compared various of Jakob's arc lamps against those of competitors. His were neither the best nor the worst in terms of drawing current and power at a constant rate.[24]

In the hall for measuring instruments, the Einsteins exhibited Jakob's patented electricity counter. It, like the dynamos and arc lamps, was one of a number of models present. At the time there was great interest in metering electricity. In 1889, the city of Paris had conducted a competition for the best meter. There was no first prize, but Professor Dr Aron of Berlin received 2000 francs for his patented design. The French electricians called for submissions again in 1891. This time they awarded first prizes to both Aron and to the American Elihu Thomson; each electrical engineer received 5000 francs.[25] Jakob Einstein and Sebastian Kornprobst had undoubtedly been aware of the Paris competitions. Even if they did not submit a design, they would have realised that a superior meter could net them a small fortune.

The Frankfurt exhibition offered entrepreneurs the opportunity to place all their machines and appliances in working order. The buildings and grounds were electrified by a number of participating exhibitors. With their dynamos, lamps, and meter, the Einsteins chose to supply several concessions: the Café Milani, the Pfungstädter Bierhalle, the Shooting Stand, and the multi-coloured lights of the Irrgarten. In all, the brothers supplied direct current for 42 arc lamps and 500 incandescent bulbs.[26]

At the end of the summer, two notable gatherings took place on the fair grounds. One was an international electrotechnical congress, at which Siemens, Rathenau, and Uppenborn spoke, along with the British engineers Sylvanus P Thompson and W H Preece. Heinrich F Weber travelled from the Zurich Institute of Technology to lecture on the theory of the electric light; in five years he would teach experimental physics to Albert Einstein. More than 650 people turned out to hear the distinguished men of industry and learning.

Immediately preceding this congress was another, and more significant assembly. Official delegates from scores of cities in Germany and abroad met for three days to consider the state of municipal electrical lighting and power transmission. They and hundreds of other participants heard presentations by Uppenborn and Oskar von Miller and were generally regaled with the prospects of a rosy, electrical future.[27] Twenty-one companies contributed to the published proceedings of the second congress, including some from Basle, Vienna, Rotterdam and Boston. Two of the firms were based in Munich. One was the recently established office of Miller, the engineer who served as technical adviser to the Frankfurt exhibition. The second Munich firm that published a text—a firm many years senior to Miller's—was owned by Jakob and Hermann Einstein.

The Einsteins' text, undoubtedly written by Jakob, described the electrical distribution system that the company had set up in the Munich quarter of Schwabing, as well as in the small, northern Italian towns of Varese and Susa. The Einsteins generated direct current using a so-called three-conductor system. In this system, a number of generators were generally wired in parallel to the same earth so that any one of them could be removed from service without breaking the supplying circuit. The positive poles of the generators fed into one line, and the negative poles into another. A third line was kept at a potential midway between the potentials of the positive and negative pole lines. Three wires went out to subscribers, who drew current from a circuit formed by the middle wire and either the negative or the positive one. To correct for different loading on the positive and negative sides of the system, small dynamos—balancing machines—were placed in the main circuit between the middle line and both the negative and positive lines. To maintain power without continuously running the large dynamos, it was usual to connect a set of storage batteries between the middle line and each of the two outer ones; the batteries would often be charged by booster generators, connected in tandem with the balancing generators. Such a system, with its several correcting devices, allowed the main dynamos to be worked at their maximum efficiency regardless of varying loads.[28]

The three-conductor system was the dominant method of distribution at the end of the nineteenth century, and Jakob Einstein's description conformed to accepted practice. In his short essay, he emphasised economics. He noted that a less ambitious generating plant could dispense with electrical batteries, especially when demand occurred without oscillation at a fixed time of the day, as was the case for street lighting. He observed that the generating plant for such a system lay at the geographical centre of its subscriber network. The distribution network—either linear or ring-shaped—extended from several nodes so that the lines to users sustained a maximum voltage loss of only around 1.5%. Feeder lines from the dynamo to the nodes could suffer a much greater drop in voltage, up to around 15%, so one needed continuously to adjust the dynamo output to correct for voltage readings taken at the nodes. The Einsteins' plant in Schwabing employed two dynamos in series, rather than in parallel, although a switch could disengage either dynamo for repairs during periods of slack demand. From their plant issued a linear network with four nodes. Feeder lines 12 mm in diameter connected the dynamos to the nodes. Each line had a current meter of physicist Friedrich Kohlrausch's design so that a machinist could regulate output from the powerhouse.

The switchboard from which Jakob monitored his station was an uncomplicated affair. It enabled him to work his dynamos in series or in parallel; if one dynamo were placed out of action, the other could then continue to provide partial power to the system. Jakob installed special conductors and breakers for the arc lamps in his network so that they could function with the lower current delivered by only one dynamo. Provision was made to guarantee that the incandescent lights would also function on reduced current.

The dynamos generated direct current. Presumably coal provided power. From Jakob's description, the plant would have required in attendance at least one stoker and one machinist on the switchboard. Assuming two working shifts implies a minimum of four employees, although such a skeleton arrangement would have meant much work for the owners. We may suppose that the plants were small ones, designed to supply electricity to a limited number of subscribers—as was the case at the Frankfurt exhibition.[29] Yet whatever the scale of these initiatives, and whatever their operating procedures, we may be confident that all facets of electrical generation, distribution, and utility were topics of daily conversation in the Einstein household just when Albert was undergoing an intellectual awakening.[30]

Financing a problematic expansion

In 1890 the Einsteins' company found itself on the verge of a major expansion. It had moved from manufacturing dynamos and supplying temporary power to setting up permanent power stations in Munich and northern Italy. Jakob Einstein was experimenting with new electrical meters and lighting apparatuses, and he had participated in the Frankfurt meeting on municipal illumination. The Einsteins were poised to act just when the authorities in Munich, faced with a burgeoning population, moved to electrify their city.

The enterprising brothers nonetheless faced difficulties. One problem concerned the format of power distribution. The Einsteins had experience only of small stations that distributed direct current locally. The Frankfurt–Lauffen line engineered by Oskar von Miller, however, had demonstrated the feasibility of long-distance, alternating-current transmission. It raised new possibilities of economical electrical generation at large central plants. Then, too, the Einsteins were familiar with coal-burning, steam technology, whereas water and gas had to be considered as competing power sources. The biggest problem, though, concerned scale. If they did not want to be driven out of the Munich market by such giants as AEG and Schuckert, Jakob and Hermann Einstein had to raise a great deal of capital.

The money required by successful entrepreneurs in electrical-power generation was substantial. Around 1890 most electrotechnical companies in this area had over a million marks in operating capital. Smaller, specialised firms were able to take advantage of expansion in the electrical industry during the early 1890s: the Akkumulatorenwerke System Pollak AG Berlin could in 1894 run on an investment of 565 000 M; the Saarbrücker Elektrizitäts AG in St Johann, with 500 000 M capitalisation, emerged from the factory of engineer Hugo Bartels, which had been backed by only 150 000 M.[31] To place these figures in perspective, we have only to recall that between 1891 and 1895 annual per capita income in Germany was around 600 M.[32] A distinguished university professor lived handsomely on ten times that amount.[33]

The Einsteins did not succeed in raising the necessary capital. Their company failed in 1894, and the brothers relocated in northern Italy. Two world wars and various calamities have claimed the successor company's records.[34] While neither bankruptcy proceedings nor company ledgers have yet surfaced, a trace remains in the Munich notarial archives of a number of financial transactions in the years before 1894. It appears that the directors of the firm, unable to attract many outside investors, borrowed money against their home.

Two documents provide unmistakable evidence of the financial straits that, by August 1893, the Einstein company had entered. They are loans taken out by Hermann Einstein, on behalf of the firm J Einstein & Co, with the Bayerischen Hypotheken- und Wechselbank in Munich. The first note was for 38 000 M; half of it was guaranteed by a mortgage on the Einsteins' residence, no 14 Adlzreiterstrasse. Interest on the loan was pegged at ten per cent. Semiannual repayment, over twenty years, was to begin on 1 January 1894. The second loan came on the same day as the first. According to its terms, Hermann Einstein signed for 26 000 M, also guaranteed by his home; interest and repayment were identical to the first mortgage.[35] A year before its demise, then, the Einsteins' operation obtained around 60 000 M at ten per cent interest. It must have been a debt of desperation, for an entrepreneur would reserve his home as the ultimate collateral. Ten per cent was a high rate of interest at the time. Still, during the great electrical boom beginning in 1893 and lasting until the crash of 1900, dividends from all the giant electrical companies soared to ten per cent and even fifteen per cent.[36] The brothers correctly gauged

Figure 1 Advertisement for J Einstein & Co, 1891. *Elektrizität: Offizielle Zeitung der Internationalen Ausstellung Frankfurt am Main 1891*, printed in several issues.

that even borrowing at ten per cent they stood a chance to turn a handsome profit.

The sum of 60 000 M could surely not have been the Einsteins' total indebtedness. A firm of the kind that they sought to establish needed at the very least three or four times that amount in operating capital. On this point the archives are obliging. Christian Fertig, the same notary who recorded the loans of 1893, reported three years earlier a mortgage of 35 000 M to Hermann Einstein; the lending institution was again the Bayerische Hypotheken- und Wechselbank. The mortgage carried ten per cent interest and ran for twenty years. It was held against no 47a Kanal-strasse, a property several score metres east of the Isartor just outside the city core, not far from the Einsteins' previous residence on Müllerstrasse.[37] That Hermann Einstein might have owned such a costly building is in itself not surprising, for in the 1880s he had enjoyed access to substantial funds—Albert was, after all, attending the elite and expensive Luitpold Gymnasium, an unusual course for a manufacturer's son.[38] Yet the notary's description of Hermann Einstein's occupation as 'Antiquitäten-händler' gives us pause. It being unlikely that two different men with the name Hermann Einstein would have frequented the same notary within several years of each other to take out a mortgage with the same bank, we are led to conclude that Albert Einstein's father ran an antiques shop in addition to his role in Jakob's electrical company.

There is more. In 1892 Hermann Einstein again appears in the records of Christian Fertig. This time his occupation is given as 'Antiquitäten und Kunsthändler', and in an unusual step his location (presumably his shop) is indicated as no 37 Maximilianstrasse. Hermann was receiving 10 000 M in earnest-money from Karl Waiderlich, a Munich businessman, for a mortgage on a property in the Untersendling suburb near the Einsteins' residence.[39] Although the final settlement (if there was one) does not appear in Fertig's chronicles, the agreement with Waiderlich would well testify to the Einsteins' desire to raise capital for their electrotechnical .ambitions.

The loans obtained between 1890 and 1893—some 100 000 M—may represent only a part of the capital that the Einsteins were able to gather, but the sum was arguably at least a substantial fraction of the total. By 1893 the Einsteins would have learned that the Nuremberg firm of Schuckert had obtained the street-lighting contract for Munich. No doubt they, too, had sought to place a tender for it. Unable to share in Schuckert's good fortune, the business went under in 1894. As Oskar von Miller and Ernst Voit emphasised eighteen years later, it was 'driven out by branches of more efficient, out-of-town factories' which sprouted in the Bavarian capital.[40] With the Einsteins' exit from the scene, Munich lost its only manufacturer of dynamos.[41]

We do not yet know a great deal about the fortunes of the Einsteins in

Milan, whither they initially travelled and where after 1896 they sank roots, but Elena Sanesi has recently constructed a picture of their business dealings in Pavia.[42] There, between early 1894 and late 1896, the Einstein brothers ran a company similar to the one that they had left in Munich. Their first major business partner was Lorenzo Garrone, an engineer living in Turin, who would have known of the Einsteins' capabilities from his interest in the electrification of Susa. In March 1894, the Einsteins contributed 60 000 L (48 000 M) to form a company with 105 000 L (84 000 M) capital, their other major associate being Garrone. The working arrangement specified that Jakob and Garrone would handle the technical part of the business, and Hermann the administrative part. The Einsteins completed the necessary paperwork, part of which required a return visit to Munich for the approval of the Italian consulate there.

Properly constituted, the Società Einstein, Garrone e Cia drew up plans for an impressive office building to direct its manufacture of dynamos and other electrical devices. Until late in 1894, the Einstein brothers remained in Milan while placing the Pavia company in working order. By October 1894 they required more capital for their new building, and to this end they borrowed 50 000 L at four per cent per annum from a Turin engineer. July 1895 found the Einsteins again short of liquid assets, and they kept going by taking in another associate, this time an engineer from Milan. The refurbished company lasted a year longer. In June 1896 the owners decided to liquidate. They sought 250 000 L for the assets of their enterprise; it appears as if, over the next six months, Einstein, Garrone & Co were unable to bring in even three-quarters of that sum. Most of the incoming cash went to pay off creditors and the subsequently acquired silent partners, the latter of whom found it necessary to engage solicitors on their behalf. Jakob Einstein then took up a position in a large, Italian engineering firm. His brother Hermann tried, once more, to set up an electrotechnical firm in Milan.[43]

The impact of the enterprise

The process of ending a business is not pleasant. An entrepreneur is forced to inventory the total extent—even the wreckage—of his labour and aspirations. His family often shares the uncertainty and anguish. The insolvency of Jakob and Hermann Einstein's firm would have been especially disturbing to a sensitive and precocious fifteen-year-old youth who had grown up enjoying some of the *Gemütlichkeit* that characterised bourgeois life in *fin-de-siècle* Munich. Small wonder that, left behind as a boarder when his closely-knit family moved to Italy, Albert Einstein lost interest in his progressive, if unbending, school curriculum and in the rigid conventions of German society that had severed him from his parents.

His decision to renounce German citizenship, made at this time, can be seen as a reprisal against an entire society that had taken away his family's livelihood.[44]

A letter of Einstein's affords insight into his feelings regarding the misfortune that his family had suffered. Then in the middle of his studies at the Zurich Institute of Technology, Einstein wrote to his sixteen-year-old sister, two years his junior:

> If it had gone according to me Papa would have already sought a [that is, another] position two years ago, and so he and we would have been spared vexation. . . Most of all I have been struck by the misfortune of my poor parents, who for so many years have not had a happy minute. I am deeply saddened too, that I, as a grown man, must look on inactively, without being able to do the least little thing.

Young Albert Einstein was then being supported by the generosity of a relative. So acutely did he feel his powerlessness that he lamented: 'I am nothing but a burden for my kin . . . It would really be better if I had not lived at all.' The picture that has come to us of Einstein's student days in Zurich is one of a free-spirited youth unconcerned with attending his lectures regularly. Here we see a darker side to his life: a man grimly dedicating himself to learning and, as we know, by no means limiting himself to the existing curriculum; a man always aware that his freedom as a student was dearly purchased. Einstein confided to his sister: 'I have always done everything my small powers allowed and . . . year after year not once did I amuse or divert myself unless my studies permitted [*bietet*]. I remain upright and must often guard myself against despair.'[45] Einstein's lifelong code of social justice was forged, it appears, in the heat of personal misfortune. From an early age he had first-hand experience of the cruel and hypocritical chase to earn a living that is condemned on the first page of his autobiographical notes.[46]

A practical profession in engineering or law might have held out more certain possibilities for financial rewards, but while at Zurich Einstein never swerved from devoting himself to physics and mathematics. That the young theoretical physicist—first as a duly certified schoolteacher with no permanent post and then beginning as a minor functionary in the state patent office—could not provide much material support for his parents and sister, must have been a continuing, if latent, source for self-recrimination. At the same time, Einstein may well have felt that, by virtue of his family experience with electrotechnology, his instruction in the subject at Aarau and Zurich, and his extensive reading, he would naturally have been able to succeed at the tasks of an electrical engineer.

So it was that Einstein, whom the public views as an absentminded and impractical seer, in his youth succeeded at an exacting, governmental post that demanded a sense for the practical. For most of his working day, the young theoretical physicist filed reports on patent applications in the field of electrotechnology. In 1908, even after he had become *Privatdozent* at the University of Berne and when his scientific publications brought him into personal contact with Germany's leading theorists, Einstein continued to put in eight hours of what he called 'fatiguing work' every day at the patent office.[47] His labour was meticulous and disciplined. It required attention to detail and to precedent.

While Einstein the theorist always sought to clarify basic principles, he was also sympathetic to physical instrumentation. As a last-year pupil in the cantonal school at Aarau, his grades improved at the time that a splendid new physical laboratory opened there. During his student years in Zurich, he was most strongly attracted to the laboratory of his professor of experimental physics, Heinrich F Weber. As a patent examiner, and just when his work on relativity and the quantum theory of radiation had brought him to the attention of physicists around the world, Einstein laboured on the construction of an electrostatic machine for making small electrical measurements; the practical theorist hoped to be able to achieve a sensitivity of 10^{-5} volts, and thereby verify his own theory of Brownian movement. He accordingly travelled several times from Berne to Fribourg in Switzerland, in order to test his apparatus in the laboratory of associate professor Albert Gockel. He pursued his quest for two years, collaborating with his friends, the brothers Conrad and Paul Habicht, on refining the instrument's design.[48] Later in life, Einstein took out patents on other devices with several colleagues.

Without considering the circumstances of the Einstein family business, such proclivity on the part of the young theoretician would seem contrary, and even paradoxical. The requirements for success as a patent clerk disallow the rebellious temperament displayed by Einstein during the years before he arrived at Berne. Always unconventional, Einstein had resisted authority and established procedures. Although he was an excellent pupil, he left a fine and liberal *Gymnasium* in Munich for schoolless days in Italy. A few years later, while a student at the Institute of Technology in Zurich, Einstein skipped lectures for most of his courses; as a result, none of his professors invited the young graduate to become an assistant. By his own admission, Einstein succeeded in his final examinations only by cramming for two months from the lecture notes of his classmate Marcel Grossmann. A patent examiner scrutinises inventions according to fundamental scientific principles and historical precedent, but in his first scientific papers (and throughout his life) Einstein consistently neglected to refer to pertinent work by his predecessors.

When he took up his place at the patent office, Einstein had reason to want to succeed at a conventional employment: after flitting from one temporary job to another, he was newly married and soon to become a father. Such circumstances have awakened in countless young men dormant qualities of regularity and responsibility. We see the effects of something other than maturation, however, in Einstein's careful work as a patent clerk. His appointment at Berne was something in the nature of a spiritual homecoming. Albert Einstein's affinity for patent work and his correlative interest in electrical instrumentation had been prepared in the environment of his youth in Munich.

Notes and references

1 Among the many sources describing the events discussed in this and following paragraphs are: Emil Kreller, *Die Entwicklung der deutschen elektrotechnischen Industrie und ihre Aussichten auf dem Weltmarkt* (dissertation,University of Griefswald 1903); David S Landes, *The Unbound Prometheus: Technological Change and Industrial Development in Western Europe from 1750 to the Present* (Cambridge 1969) pp 281–90; W O Henderson, *The Rise of German Industrial Power, 1834–1914* (Berkeley 1975) pp 191–8; Thomas Parke Hughes, 'Siemens, Ernst Werner von' *Dictionary of Scientific Biography* **12** (1975) 424–6. See also Otto Mahr's *Die Entstehung der Dynamomaschine* (Dr Ing dissertation, Berlin Institute of Technology 1941).
2 E Kreller (ref 1) p 7.
3 *Ibid* pp 14, 21.
4 *Ibid* p 25, and accompanying chart.
5 Waldemar Koch, *Die Konzentrationsbewegung in der deutschen Elektroindustrie* (dissertation, University of Berlin 1907) p 34; Hans Gutenberg, *Die Aktiengesellschaften der Elektrizitätsindustrie* (dissertation, University of Berlin 1912) pp 1, 6, 70.
6 H Gutenberg (ref 5) p 70.
7 Walther von Miller, *Oskar von Miller nach eigenen Aufzeichnungen, Reden und Briefen* (Munich 1932); Eugen Kalkschmidt, *Oskar von Miller: Ein Führer deutscher Technik* (Stuttgart 1924); Ludwig Nockher, *Oskar von Miller: Der Gründer des Deutschen Museums von Meisterwerken der Naturwissenschaft und Technik* (Stuttgart 1953); Wilhelm Lukas Kristl, *Der weiss-blaue Despot: Oskar von Miller in seiner Zeit* (Munich [1967]).
8 W von Miller (ref 7) p 48.
9 *Ibid* p 57.
10 C Zell, *Geschichte der Elektrizitätsversorgung Münchens* (Munich 1949) pp 7–15. Zell's monograph, bound together with K Hencky, *Die Erweiterung des Uppenborn-Kraftwerkes der Stadt München (Eichingerstufe)* (Munich 1949), is available in the library of the Deutschen Museum, Munich. A useful source is the *Festschrift* of the 71st meeting of the Association of German Scientists and Physicians, presented by the city of Munich: *Die Entwicklung Münchens unter dem Einflusse der Naturwissenschaften während der letzten Dezennien* ed F von Winckel and W Dyck (Munich [1912]). Two articles in the *Festschrift* are noteworthy: Oskar von Miller and Ernst Voit, 'Elektrotechnik in München: Historisches', pp 125–45; Friedrich Uppenborn, 'Die Versorgung Münchens mit elektrischer Energie', pp 146–71.

11 Friedrich Uppenborn, *Der gegenwärtige Stand der Elektrotechnik und ihre Bedeutung für das Wirtschaftsleben* (Berlin 1892), which gives historical sketches of the most important electrical generating stations in 22 German towns. Munich is not included.

12 C Zell (ref 10) pp 13–15.

13 Alfred Heggen, *Erfindungsschutz und Industrialisierung in Preussen 1793–1887* (Göttingen 1975); Rudolf Nirk, '100 Jahre Patentschutz in Deutschland', in the centenary *Festschrift* for the German patent office, *Hundert Jahre Patentamt* (Munich 1977) pp 345–402; Ulrich C Hallmann and Paul Ströbele, 'Das Patentamt von 1877 bis 1977', *ibid* pp 403–41.

14 The patents were: no 41828, J A Essberger and J Einstein & Co, 'Neuerung an elektrischen Bogenlampen', 31 Dec 1886; no 53207, J Einstein & Co, 'Ausschaltvorrichtung für die Selbstunterbrechung bei elektrischen Bogenlampen', 30 Nov 1889; no 53546, Einstein & Co and Sebastian Kornprobst, 'Vorrichtung zur Umwandlung der ungleichmässigen Zeigerausschläge von Elektrizitätsmessern in eine gleichmässige, gradlinige Bewegung', 26 Feb 1890; no 53846, Einstein & Co and Kornprobst, 'Neuerung an elektrischen Mess- und Anzeigevorrichtungen', 21 Nov 1889; no 60361, Einstein & Co and Kornprobst, 'Federndes Reibrad', 23 Feb 1890; no 74429, J Einstein & Co, 'Führungsvorrichtung für die Kohlenträger bei Bogenlampen', 10 Oct 1893. The patent descriptions may be consulted at, among other places, the German patent office in Munich.

   According to the 'Schülerverzeichnis ab 1829' kept in the Stuttgart Universitätsarchiv, Jakob Einstein, a manufacturer from Munich, attended the Institute of Technology at Stuttgart as student no 252. Although other records from the period have been destroyed, it is probable that Jakob acquired many of his engineering skills at the Stuttgart 'Polytechnic'.

15 C L Imhoff, 'Elektrizitätszähler d. Firma J Einstein & Co, München, System Kornprobst', *Elektrotechnische Zeitschrift* **12** (1891) 278–9.

16 Jagdish Mehra, 'Albert Einsteins erste wissenschaftliche Arbeit', *Physikalische Blätter* **27** (1971) 386–91; Ronald W Clark, *Einstein: The Life and Times* (New York 1971) pp 30, 42; Elmar Holenstein, 'Albert Einsteins Hausvater in Aarau: Der Linguist Jost Winteler', *Schweizer Monatshefte* **59** (1979) 221–33.

17 Albert Einstein to Marcel Grossman [summer 1901], analysed by Russell McCormmach in 'Einstein, Lorentz, and the Electron Theory', *Historical Studies in the Physical Sciences* **2** (1970) 41–87, on p 52.

18 'Rundschau', *Zentralblatt für Elektrotechnik* **10** (1888) 1–2.

19 Documents from the commercial registers of the Stadtarchiv Ulm and from the police and commercial registers of the Stadtarchiv München are cited in *Einstein und Ulm: Festakt und Ausstellung zum 100. Geburtstag von Albert Einstein* ed Hans Eugen Specker (Stuttgart 1979) pp 54–5, 65 [*Forschungen zur Geschichte der Stadt Ulm, Reihe Dokumentation* **1**]. The evidence here revises the account in the standard biographies of Albert Einstein, cf Clark (ref 16) pp 23–5, 39. Clark has suggested that Hermann's in-laws, who were wealthy provisioners, contributed to his domestic upkeep. The in-laws have been identified in Paul Sauer's *Die jüdischen Gemeinden in Württemberg und Hohenzollern: Denkmale, Geschichte, Schicksale* (Stuttgart 1966) p 173. Max

Talmey described the Sendling house as large and set back from the road, with a number of trees in the yard; he recalled the Einsteins' factory adjacent to their residence. M Talmey, *The Relativity Theory Simplified and the Formative Period of Its Inventor* (New York 1932) p 161, cited in Paul Forman's 'Introduction: Einstein and Research', in *The Joys of Research* ed Walter Shropshire Jr (Washington 1981) pp 12–24, on p 13.

20 Erich Kiesel, 'Im Alter von 12 bis 16', *Münchner Stadtanzeiger, Süd* **35**:22 (1979) 8.

21 J Einstein to Theodor Peters, 11 and 19 April 1980, in Darmstaedter Collection, 7ie, 1909 (7), Staatsbibliothek Preussischer Kulturbesitz, Berlin.

22 Frankfurt am Main, Internationale elektrotechnische Ausstellung, *Offizieller Bericht über die internationale elektrotechnische Ausstellung in Frankfurt am Main 1891* **1**: *Allgemeiner Bericht* (Frankfurt 1893) pp 31–3, 67–9, 546–50. Complete statistics are provided on expenses and numbers of visitors. Special features of the exposition are recorded in the *Elektrotechnische Zeitschrift* **12** (1891) 73, 118, 131, 169, 185, 249–50, 261, 287, 358, 393–4, 494–5, 507.

23 *Bericht* **1** (ref 22) 142–4, 302–3, 353, 462. *Elektrizität: Offizielle Zeitung der Internationalen Elektrotechnischen Ausstellung Frankfurt am Main 1891* no 3 (29 April 1891) p 55; no 14 (18 July 1891), 'Dynamo-Maschinen der Elektrotechnischen Fabrik J Einstein & Cie, München', 410–11. Jakob Einstein probably wrote the short articles describing his company's product line.

24 *Bericht* **1** (ref 22) pp 305–6; *Offizieller Bericht . . .* **2**: *Bericht über die Arbeiten der Prüfungs-Kommission* (Frankfurt 1894) 130–55; *Elektrizität* no 17 (8 August 1891), 'Nebenschlusslampe der Elektrotechnischen Fabrik J Einstein & Co in München', pp 531–2.

25 *Elektrizität* no 10 (20 June 1891) p 275.

26 *Bericht* **1** (ref 22) pp 58, 302–4; *Elektrizität* no 30 (31 October 1891) p 1028.

27 'Versammlung deutscher Städtverwaltungen in der elektrischen Ausstellung in Frankfurt a. M.', *Elektrotechnische Zeitschrift* **12** (1891) 441; 'Städetag in Frankfurt a. M. vom 27. bis 29. August 1891', *ibid* 601–29.

28 F Uppenborn ed, *Die Versorgung von Städten mit elektrischem Strom nach Berichten elektrotechnischer Firmen über die von ihnen verwendeten Systeme* (Berlin 1891) pp 63–6.

29 That no trace of the Schwabing, Varese, or Susa plants remains in German and Italian archives suggests that the Einsteins may have supplied few enough subscribers so as not to require municipal authorisation.

30 A Einstein, 'Autobiographical Notes', in *Albert Einstein—Philosopher-Scientist* ed P A Schilpp (La Salle, Ill 1949) pp 3–5, 9–11, 15.

31 H Gutenberg (ref 5) p 13.

32 Frank B Tipton Jr, *Regional Variations in the Economic Development of Germany during the Nineteenth Century* (Middletown, Conn 1976) p 83.

33 Rep 92, Althoff, AI no 50, pp 98–9, p 226, Zentrales Staatsarchiv, Merseburg. According to a Prussian survey dated 27 September 1890, average salaries of *ordentlichen* and *ausserordentlichen* professors ran from a high of 7411 M and 2644 M at Berlin to a low of 3788 M and 2295 M at Braunsberg and Münster. In March 1892, salaries of full professors at two of the most important Prussian universities were distributed in the following way:

		Salary in 1000 marks				
		0–5	5–6	6–8.4	8.4–12	12
Number of professors receiving the salary	Berlin	10	1	12	19	3
	Göttingen	5	6	8	0	1

34 Jakob Einstein's son Robert committed suicide after having learned that the fascists had killed his wife and sons. Elena Sanesi, 'Three Letters by Albert Einstein and Some Information on Einstein's Stay at Pavia', *Physis* **18** (1976) 174–8.

35 Not. München V, 1893/1881 and 1893/1883, Staatsarchiv, Munich. The property specified on the first mortgage was plan no 10 275, that on the second plan no 10 275 $^1/_3$, indicating in all probability two adjacent properties. The Adlzreiterstrasse address is given as the Einsteins' domicile in Werner Meyer's 'Die Geistesreise vom Hinterhof: Albert Einstein lebte acht Jahre in München in der Adlzreiterstrasse', *Münchner Stadtanzeiger, Süd* **35**:21 (1979) 3. On lending money against real estate a bank would immediately collect its interest. A mortgage of 26 000 M would thus furnish working capital of a bit over 20 000 M.

36 E Kreller (ref 1), chart opposite p 25.

37 Not. München V, 1890/3453, Staatsarchiv, Munich.

38 According to Jürgen Kocka, sons of manufacturers in the Rhineland were generally educated at first privately and then sent to *höheren Bürgerschulen* or *Oberrealschulen* until the age of fifteen or sixteen; few went to the classical *Gymnasien*. Kocka, *Unternehmer in der deutschen Industrialisierung* (Göttingen 1975) p 62.

39 Not. München V 1892/2612, Staatsarchiv, Munich.

40 O von Miller and E Voit (ref 10) p 132.

41 H Gutenberg (ref 5, p 70) indicates that in 1895 Bavaria had only one manufacturer of dynamos, electric motors, and transformers; this firm, which employed more than fifty people, was undoubtedly Schuckert of Nuremberg.

42 Elena Sanesi, 'L'Impresa industriale di Hermann e Jacob Einstein a Pavia (1894–1896)', *Bollettino della Società Pavese di Storia Patria* **34** (1982) 198–210.

43 Maja Winteler-Einstein, 'Albert Einstein: Beitrag für sein Lebensbild' (Florence 1924) p 8. The text is a 39-page typescript, a copy of which is available in the Einstein Archives, Princeton.

44 See chapter 1.

45 Albert Einstein to Maja Einstein, 1898, Princeton University Library. The letter is cited in Winteler-Einstein's 'Albert Einstein' (ref 43) p 18. My translation of the letter differs substantially from that in *Albert Einstein, the Human Side: New Glimpses from his Archives* ed Helen Dukas and Banesh Hoffmann (Princeton 1979) pp 14, 123.

46 A Einstein (ref 30) p 3.

47 Albert Einstein to Johannes Stark, 14 Dec 1908; Nachlass Johannes Stark, Staatsbibliothek Preussischer Kulturbesitz, Berlin.

48 Albert Einstein to Albert Gockel, n.d. and 3 Dec 1908; Autogr. 1/111 and 112, Staatsbibliothek Preussischer Kulturbesitz, Berlin; Jakob Laub, 'Albert Einstein und Albert Gockel', *Academia Friburgensis* **20**:1 (1962) 30–3; A Einstein, 'Neue elektrostatische Methode zur Messung kleiner Elektrizitätsmengen', *Physikalische Zeitschrift* **9** (1908) 216–17. In their subsequent article describing the apparatus, the brothers Habicht indicated that they tested it together with Einstein in the physics laboratory of the University of Zurich. Conrad Habicht and Paul Habicht, 'Elektrostatischer Potentialmultiplikator nach A Einstein', *Phys. Z.* **11** (1910) 532–5. Related issues have recently been addressed in an unpublished manuscript of Horst Melcher's 'Albert Einstein in der Deutschen Physikalischen Gesellschaft', as well as in Melcher's 'Albert Einsteins Patente', *Spektrum* **9** (1978) 23–6.

3 Einspänner: the social roots of Einstein's world view

Einstein was a man set apart. Given to easy laughter, devoid of vanity or pretense, gentle and kind, he was, nevertheless, in his own words, an *Einspänner*, a man who goes by himself, drawing strength from solitude.

Otto Nathan and Hans Norden, eds,
Einstein on Peace (New York 1961) p v.

Adjusting to the circumstances of failure

Rewarded at an early age by the most prestigious physics chair in the world, Albert Einstein emerged triumphantly from a series of failures.[1] He failed to complete *Gymnasium* in Munich; he failed in his first attempt to enter the Zurich Polytechnic and he failed to land an assistantship upon finally graduating from the school; at least once he failed to obtain a doctorate from the University of Zurich.[2] He could not manage to find a regular teaching post in the Swiss schools. His first marriage was not a success. Failure remained his companion at the height of material success. He was unable to advance a reasonable pacifist alternative during the First World War, just as little of substance came from his science diplomacy during the 1920s. In the United States, Einstein exerted virtually no influence on the course of physics. He could not stop the race to develop nuclear arsenals. The unified field theory forever eluded him.

Einstein emerged unscathed from the circumstances of failure because he had come to each one consciously and willingly. He himself chose to leave secondary school in Munich. He elected to sit for the entrance examination at Zurich without having undergone the usual preparation. He preferred to skip the lectures of his professors and to depart from their advice in the laboratory. Upon graduation, he wanted to remain relatively close to Zurich, his adopted homeland, when he might well have found a permanent teaching position elsewhere in German- or French-speaking Switzerland. For the subject of his early and unsuccessful doctoral thesis, he avoided a safe and straightforward exercise and worked without consulting a faculty adviser. Einstein devoted much time to unpopular pacifist causes instead of cultivating more intensively the confidence of decision makers. In later life he might have directed his energies to elaborating quantum mechanics or honing new mathematical techniques for the theoretician's possible use, instead of to pursuing a non-quantised general relativity.

When interacting with people, Einstein seemed resilient and optimistic. A quiet, slow-burning, and intense fire animated and guided his activity. Yet the fire cast long shadows. Einstein, whom his distinguished contemporaries characterised as the most 'genial' of men, remained a brooding spirit with a sarcastic tongue. His schoolmates saw him as pedantic. The close friends of his youth found him a source of peculiar personal advice. As a young theoretical physicist, he berated harmless critics with overly powerful strokes of his pen. In the Berlin physics seminar, he is reported to have sat near the front of the audience and cracked dirty jokes. When irony left him, at the end of his life, Einstein's lined expression came to symbolise wisdom's immense sadness at having provided humanity with awesome instruments of destruction. At once warm and distant, *sachlich* and abstract, mocking and serious, Einstein's temperament excluded the pretension, pomposity, and jealousy that often radiated from his physicist colleagues.[3]

Einstein's emotional distance from even his immediate family and his cheerful accommodation to failures in the realm of human affairs suggest that, though his published work became seminal for the physics discipline and though he was friendly with royalty and rulers, the man remained an outsider. In his youth and young manhood, Einstein's station was certainly at odds with his career plans. We see this as the sixteen-year-old youth, beginning his year at the Aarau cantonal school, was waiting to hear from the state of Württemberg about his request to be released from German citizenship. The order came through early in January 1896. Authorities considered the émigré, who had stated his desire to make Italy his home, as someone 'without confession and without means'. The future theoretical physicist carried the designation of 'trade and commercial helper and factory worker', a natural category for an officially unskilled school drop-out and the son of a manufacturer whose business had just failed. By such reckoning, even though his parents and close relatives had special talents as entrepreneurs, Einstein became one of the first 'members' of the German working class to enter the Berlin Academy of Sciences.

When he wrote the earliest of his texts in physics, Einstein stood outside the convocation of his discipline. In a handwritten *vita* from the Berlin period, he indicated that between 1902 and 1909, he had worked as an 'engineer'—not as a patent examiner—despite his certain knowledge that the engineering profession enjoyed ambiguous status in the scholarly and scientific world of Central Europe.[4] As a Jewish pacifist with a Swiss passport, Einstein became Germany's *outré* scientific envoy to the Allied nations during the cold war that continued after 1918. Later, choosing to live in an inadequate house at the centre of a wealthy university town, Einstein, Cassandra-like, exercised no leverage at all in his scientific discipline; his friend and close collaborator, Leopold Infeld, reported how Einstein suffered good-naturedly when Princeton physicists took unconcealed delight in attempting to ridicule his scientific principles.[5] While most distinguished physicists sought to retire from active research as they approached their sixtieth year, until the very end of his life, Einstein worked on *physics* with the intensity of a postgraduate student.

In summing up Einstein's character, his former colleague Banesh Hoffmann and his former secretary Helen Dukas have described him as a 'creator and rebel'.[6] Einstein contributed to the image of rebel by continually emphasising individual achievement and by remaining indifferent to historical reconstruction. Miss Dukas insisted that Einstein owed little to any of his *milieux*, that he would have arrived at his epoch-making discoveries even if he had lived 'at the North Pole'.[7] Einstein certainly resisted a number of established authorities and governing powers, and in this sense he was a rebel as surely as John Milton, Thomas Jefferson, and Rosa Luxemburg were rebels. Einstein had, however, little in common with political or social malcontents. He associated eclectically with many anti-establishment groups, both large and small, but he never questioned the rule of civil law, and he readily accepted money and distinctions from various distasteful political regimes. In his field of research, Einstein resisted changes in fashion, continually appealing instead to higher authority. When indeterminist quantum mechanics and the notion of acausality swept through the world of physics, Einstein kept faith in a traditionalist, causal scheme of things.

The point is unambiguously made in his 1938 collaboration with Leopold Infeld, *The Evolution of Physics*. The book's very title indicated to a reader that the development of physics was cumulative and orderly—not at all punctuated by revolutions. When Einstein and Infeld referred to relativity (in Einstein's own eyes his most original achievement was general relativity), they stressed how the theories had emerged naturally and slowly from James Clerk Maxwell's formulation of the electromagnetic field. At a time when scores of researchers issued calls for a revolutionary solution to the problems facing physics, Einstein carefully proceeded by building on traditional principles.[8]

One may rebel once and then become part of a new regime, or one may continually rebel against any hint of authority. To identify Einstein with rebellion is to make one of two assumptions: either he, initially raised under a cultural or political regime, came to doubt the legitimacy of received truths and established power; or he continually resisted all authority. Einstein's character fits well with neither assumption. Indeed, the remarkable circumstance about the life of the great theoretical physicist is the extent to which his character, while growing richer, always offered the same aspect—valuing intellectual honesty, graciousness and perseverance. The experiences of the twentieth century eroded only his optimism.

If he was not a rebel, might Einstein have been a bohemian of science? Late in the nineteenth century, the compilers of the *Oxford English Dictionary* referred to a bohemian as 'a gipsy of society', someone who cut himself off from, or whose habits drove him away from, his society. The term applied especially to an artist, writer, or actor who led 'a free, vagabond, or irregular life, not being particular as to the society he frequents, and despising conventionalities generally'. Even this formulation of bohemianism, however, (which leaves aside connotations of licentiousness, impulsiveness, and flamboyance) does not easily conform to the character of the theoretical physicist. Einstein certainly moved easily through central and southern Europe, but his habits—innocuous enough to offer no offence—served to focus attention on his highly prized thoughts; Einstein, who held down regular employment from the age of twenty-three until his death, was hardly a vagabond. He worked at theoretical physics more assiduously than did almost all of his colleagues. He despised no one for following the conventions that he avoided.[9]

Einstein's consistent strength of purpose and fixed ethical principles suggest that, rather than a bohemian or a rebel, he comes close to what Gordon Wright has identified as an 'outlier'.[10] He did not fit the majoritarian mould. His style and his temperament remained apart from those typical of the environments where he lived—in Munich, Italy, Switzerland, Berlin, and Princeton. In 1913, he came to the imperial German capital as a foreign sage, and he remained a foreigner there for the next twenty years.[11] He fitted into Weimar society no better than he had fitted into its Wilhelmian predecessor. An outlier, in Wright's view, is simply an individual who behaves differently from most people. Einstein was more than a nonconformist. His life bears striking resemblance to the pattern that has been attributed to 'stranger' or 'marginal man'.

The notion of a 'stranger' may be traced to the writings of Georg Simmel, a German sociologist whose academic career was impeded by anti-Semitic prejudice. In his general treatise on sociology, published in 1908, Simmel devoted a number of pages to the 'stranger', the individual who lives in a culture but finds himself, by virtue of his previous experience, spiritually or temperamentally removed from it. The stranger's internal values keep him apart from other people. He is remote, even in his most intimate relationships. Simmel argued that, because of his separate status, the stranger brings abstractness and generality to his perceptions and judgments. Freed from commitments that could prejudice his perception and understanding, the stranger views his cultural surroundings with detachment and objectivity. He surveys the world from a privileged vantage point.[12]

A generation after Simmel published his *Soziologie*, the American sociologist Robert Ezra Park elaborated the notion of stranger into that of 'marginal man'—an individual living on the interface between two cultures. Although allegiance to two systems of values produced tension and conflict, Park emphasised the fecundity of the hybrid:

> The fate which condemns him [the marginal man] to live, at the same time, in two worlds is the same which compels him to assume, in relation to the worlds in which he lives, the rôle of a cosmopolitan and a stranger. Inevitably he becomes, relatively to his cultural milieu, the individual with the wider horizon, the keener intelligence, the more detached and rational viewpoint. The marginal man is always relatively the more civilized human being.

For Park, the marginal individual had an archetype: 'He occupies the position which has been, historically, that of the Jew in the Diaspora. The Jew, particularly the Jew who has emerged from the provincialism of the ghetto, has everywhere and always been the most civilized of human creatures.' The Jew, as a marginal man, was forever only partially assimilated into the culture where he lived.[13]

To Park's protégé Everett V Stonequist fell the task of elaborating his master's thought. In 1937, Stonequist published *The Marginal Man*. His book, as he announced in the subtitle, would be an enquiry into personality and cultural conflict. What the book lacked in analytical precision and clarity it made up in speculative verve. Along with Park, Stonequist believed that cultural conflict engendered a condition of psychological tension. Marginality became manifest when incomplete acculturation produced an individual with conflicting cultural ties. The result was a dual personality, an underlying uneasiness and sense of isolation. Marginality appeared in people with mixed racial ancestry, although it was also common among members of cultural minorities, such as American Blacks and Jews. In surveying autobiographies of people caught between two cultures, Stonequist extracted impressionistic evidence to lend support to his notion.[14]

Stonequist's 'marginal man' sustained criticism and suffered modification in the following two decades. The sociologist Milton M Goldberg argued that the marginal man appeared frequently among adult immigrants, people forced to adapt but too old to accept all features of the new culture. In Goldberg's view, a young person could become integrated into a 'marginal culture' if he received proper encouragement from family and friends.[15] During the 1940s and 1950s the notion dominated discussions about Jews and the problems that they faced in assimilating.[16] Jews were likely to be marginal men, psychologist Kurt Lewin wrote, because of the uncertain and unpredictable acceptance that greeted them in non-Jewish society.[17] In many sociological treatises, the marginal man received a short excursis.[18] He was held to be capable of great achievements, but only at the cost of pain and suffering.[19] In the view of one sociologist, Alfred Schuetz, the stranger's objectivity 'lies in his own bitter experience of the limits of the "thinking as usual", which has taught him that a man may lose his status, his rules of guidance, and even his history and that the normal way of life is always far less guaranteed than it seems.' As a result,

> the stranger discerns, frequently with a grievous clear-sightedness, the rising of a crisis which may menace the whole foundation of the 'relatively natural conception of the world', while all those symptoms pass unnoticed by the members of the in-group, who rely on the continuance of their customary way of life.[20]

The marginal man groaned under a heavy burden. For the most part writers seem not to have come back to Simmel's and Park's thought that the marginal situation produced well-balanced, dispassionate thinkers. 'To be a stranger', Simmel wrote, 'is naturally a very positive relation.'[21] The stranger's objectivity, in Simmel's view, underwrote his freedom.

I have discussed the large literature on the 'stranger' at some length, because I shall argue that Simmel's original notion contributes to unravelling Einstein's character. This is not to deny that, at some level, by virtue of maturation, everyone is a stranger in his world. Coming to terms with the beliefs of one's parents and forebears, even within a relatively homogeneous culture, is a subtle psychological process. It lies at the base of the tension between tradition and innovation. Every adult bears the gifts and burdens of his parent's legacy. Among these he may carry letters of marque, swiftly empowering him to acquire the trappings of a successful career; other items in the legacy are quickly jettisoned, enabling rapid progress in a chosen direction. Some of the legacy is borne uncomfortably as unwanted baggage that, while not entirely dysfunctional, never fits well with the rest of the person's character. Elaboration of questions such as these provides the substance for countless psychological monographs and *Bildungsromanen*.

The initial parameters for evaluating the issue of tradition and innovation are complex, but they may be specified with some confidence in the usual cases when parents and offspring shared many of the values held by the majority culture. When addressing immigrants or strangers, however, the situation is less tractable. More is required than simply describing a number of salient features in the native culture of the parents and in the host culture where they raised their child. One needs to characterise the interaction between the two worlds of the parents—the instabilities and critical points of the mixture. One needs to know whether a new synthesis emerged or whether, as in carrying out so many daily tasks, distinct levels of activity coexisted with each other in dynamic tension or in equilibrium. The chemistry governing the several cultures of parents is critical for understanding intellectual development in an ethnic child. Raised either in ethnic seclusion or as part of a majority, a young adult may quite reasonably regard his heritage as an accidental artifact without intrinsic value. He may seek a new identity to replace the one that was either impressed on or denied him. He may dedicate himself either to upholding the family tradition or to rediscovering its buried roots.

That Einstein was an irreligious Jew who in later life strongly identified with Zionism, that he was an outlier who always saw himself as an internationalist, that, unfettered by convention, he followed the 'free dictates of thought' in whichever direction reason pointed, suggest the senses in which the theoretical physicist shared the attributes of Simmel's stranger and Park's marginal man. The strongest argument in favour of viewing Einstein as a twentieth-century stranger comes from his having grown up in a special environment, the one surrounding emancipated, urban Jews in Württemberg and Bavaria. Associated with this environment, which would qualify as Goldberg's 'marginal culture', are a number of Einstein's habits of thought and intellectual preferences.

The Jewish heritage and ethical predisposition

Although Einstein was a city-dweller by birth and upbringing, his immediate ancestors had their roots in the Württemberg countryside. Buchau, the birthplace of Einstein's father Hermann and uncle Jakob, was in mid-century a small bucolic town. Storks nested on the town roofs and fished in the nearby marshes of the Federsee, the environment that in the 1870s would yield evidence of stone-age civilisation. Most of Buchau's residents engaged in agriculture, although after 1858 small knitting factories sprouted, providing work for several score people. In Buchau, as in most other small towns in southern Germany, Jews cleaved to the visions and traditions of their ancestors. Within an elaborate synagogue they sat through disorderly and informal religious services, where a scholar attempted to connect each member of the congregation to the well-spring of knowledge.[22]

As Jews, Einstein's parents and grandparents set themselves apart not only by the way that they worshipped their god. They maintained a distinct appreciation of life. Especially striking are the Jewish views at this time on labour, education, and material progress. With regard to labour, the traditional Swabian approach to earning a livelihood emphasised work: the end result mattered less than dedication to the task at hand. For a Jew in southern Germany, however, work was merely a means to an end: one worked to earn money, but work in itself had no special dignity. Moving to matters of learning, among Christians in rural Swabia, education was either a privilege of the upper classes or a figure of speech for laziness. Among Jews, one finds quite a different notion: erudition implied a state of grace. Finally, small towns in southern Germany, among the last parts of the Empire to receive the fruits of industrialisation, remained rural in character throughout the nineteenth century. Their inhabitants were slow to embrace many of the external features of the modern world. In such a climate of conservatism, Jews were seen as belonging to the industrial culture of the metropolis. Available evidence indicates that Jews appropriated modern technologies more rapidly than their Christian countrymen did; Jewish women were among the first to use facial cosmetics, and Jewish households the earliest to subscribe to a telephone.[23]

The three traditional sensibilities of South German Jews—adaptability with regard to earning a living, respect for learning, and desire for progress—recur in the stories of Albert Einstein's ancestors. One of the physicist's forebears, Martin Einstein, earned a doctorate of medicine in 1842 and practised in Buchau from 1862 until at least 1884. Julius Einstein from Buchau practised medicine in Hohentengen and Ulm. Flexibility and receptivity to state-of-the-art technology are evident in the careers of the brothers Joseph Leopold Einstein and Salomon Einstein, who founded a weaving firm in Jebenhausen in 1842. From there, these Einsteins moved to Göppingen, back to Jebenhausen, and on to Stuttgart.[24] The geographical itinerary of Einstein's parents also suggests a flexible and optimistic approach to the working world: between 1880 and 1900 his father ran various electrical concerns in Munich, Milan, and Pavia. At least while he was in Munich, Hermann Einstein experimented, too, with employment in the world of antiques and art.

In the future theoretical physicist, two generations removed from the German countryside, we can detect a tension between the traditional Swabian and the traditional Jewish approaches to life. Conforming to the Swabian work-ethic, the young man seems always to have been earnest and serious about the undertakings at hand. Einstein was not, however, an omnivorous intellectual of the traditional Jewish kind, for whom all learning is sacred. He expressed little interest in either the social sciences or liberal arts, and he held formal schooling in no special regard.[25] Indeed, he occupied a regular teaching position for fewer than six years. He was, from almost the beginning of his career, an independent wise man, adorning the Berlin Academy of Sciences, and later, a prophetic figure circulating around an analogous academy erected by New York financiers at their bedroom retreat in Princeton. The blend of Swabian and Jewish values made Einstein appear at once both intimate and distant, a spiritual adviser quite out of place in modern factories for producing knowledge.

Though his parents had their roots in small towns, they were from an early age swept up in the flood of Jews heading for urban centres when the last of the laws restricting their mobility and citizenship rights disappeared. The middle third of the nineteenth century witnessed a revolution in Jewish culture. In 1832, 93% of Württemberg's 10 000 Jews followed their customs and traditions in sixty rural communities. Within two generations this way of life disappeared as Jews—Albert Einstein's relatives among them—forsook small towns for the cities. The most successful of Einstein's early nineteenth-century ancestors, the textile manufacturer Salomon Einstein, left Jebenhausen in 1849 for Göppingen, a city with rail connections and commercial possibilities. Hundreds followed in his wake. The Jewish population of Jebenhausen declined from around 550 in 1843 to 85 in 1880. Smaller towns lost all their Jewish residents as, between 1856 and 1863, 5% of all Württemberg Jews (some 540 people) left the state entirely.[26]

With their migration to the cities, rural Jews in southern Germany came into contact with experiments that had been conducted in the north, over the first half of the nineteenth century, to modify traditional Judaic practice. Before this time, the Jewish concept of man's place in nature was a teleological one: the individual sought to know God and waited for the Messiah. With the beginnings of emancipation came, in the words of one historian, 'a rejection of traditional Judaism bordering on nihilism and self-hatred'. Relaxed study preparing one for direct communion with God deferred to rigid rules for parcelling out a religious identity. Synagogue services became precise and orderly, following the model of Lutheran ones, and the rabbi became a spiritual leader rather than a man of learning. Following the innovations of Hamburg religious reformer Eduard Kley, synagogues increasingly bore the new name of 'Tempel', and they gave abbreviated services in German.[27]

The religious outlook of the first generation of emancipated Jews in southern Germany is recorded in a questionnaire administered during the late 1880s by Daniel Einstein, a rabbi at Karlsruhe who had taught in Bavaria and a relative of the physicist Albert. Most Jewish communities in Baden, Daniel Einstein reported, conducted religious services with little deviation from tradition. The procedure for apprising young people of their religious obligations, however, underwent a major change. Many communities no longer required Torah reading for the bar mitzvah, and larger cities introduced confirmation for girls. Respondents from many places objected to the excessive length of holiday services; they noted how the Hebrew prayers were not understood by most of the worshippers. As Hebrew fell by the wayside, so emancipated Jews abandoned their creole,

Yiddish. '*Not* to speak Yiddish', historian Peter Gay has underlined, 'was one thing a German Jew, as a good German, did.'[28]

Reflecting on fifty years of Jewish life in Munich, Ludwig Feuchtwanger emphasised, in 1937, how late nineteenth-century Munich Jews for the most part left traditional customs behind in the small town where they had originated. They pushed the religious and cultural values of their parents to the periphery of their lives, embracing instead a modernist worldview. Theirs was an optimistic vision of the future, one strongly coloured by humanitarian impulse. They sought material success in their trades and careers, and looked forward to attaining respect from the community at large. They sent their children to the best non-secular educational institutions as preparation for commercial, industrial, or academic careers. While not especially devout, they valued donating time and money to social causes, especially Jewish charities.[29]

Feuchtwanger's commentary, intended as part of a *Festschrift* for the fiftieth anniversary of the Munich synagogue, may be read as a defence of assimilationism, an ethic propelling German Jews toward integrating themselves fully in the surrounding, majoritarian culture. This was the view embraced by Einstein's close relatives. Although his parents were married in a religious ceremony, they seem to have expressed little interest in maintaining the rituals associated with the Hebrew faith.[30] Their home was not kosher. Einstein's father Hermann was outward looking and progressive. He appears among a handful of Ulmese Jews who paid to donate a statue of the prophet Jeremiah to the Ulm minster in celebration of its five-hundredth anniversary. Hermann, in signing the birth certificate of his first child Albert, chose to write in modernist French script instead of traditional Gothic.[31] From all reports, Hermann remained cheerful and optimistic, even in the dark days after 1894, when his various electrotechnical enterprises were floundering. Hermann's cultured wife Pauline, too, retained her optimism even when the family's livelihood came into question. Both parents modified certain features of Jewish tradition into humanitarian gestures. They regularly invited indigent acquaintances, such as the medical student Max Talmey, to share one of their weekly meals. And they remained proud of their heritage, for they arranged to give their son private instruction in the tenets of Judaism.[32]

In addition to upholding the assimilationist creed, the Einstein families shared other characteristics of the Munich Jewish community, a community playing a decreasing role, as time went on, in the life of the city. At the time of the constitution of the Empire, Jews made their presence felt most strongly in Berlin. After the 36 000 Berlin Jews came some 13 000 in both Hamburg and Breslau, and 7500 in Frankfurt am Main; Cologne, Leipzig, and Munich each had Jewish communities of around 3000. Jews continued to flock to Berlin and Frankfurt, coming to dominate many aspects of life in these two cities.[33] In Cologne, Leipzig, and Munich, however, the Jewish populations, doubling every 25 years, increased at a rate slower than that of the population as a whole; they were a declining minority.[34] Jews saw Bavaria, in general, as an inhospitable environment. Unlike the dramatic growth in the Jewish population of Prussia, the number of Jews in Bavaria remained constant at somewhat more than 50 000 across the nineteenth century, natural increase and immigration almost exactly balanced by emigration. Over the thirty years preceding the foundation of the German Empire, in 1871, some 25 000 Jews migrated out of the kingdom.[35]

Jews constituted around 2% of the population of Munich during the years when Einstein lived there, from 1880 to 1894. The ethnic minority clung to the old city core as the urban municipality absorbed one suburb after another to comprise, in 1895, 397 881 people. When in 1885 the Einstein household moved to the newly integrated quarter of Sendling, they would have found themselves in an almost entirely Christian environment. Less than a decade before then, when Sendling became part of Munich, it had only 8 Jews in a population of 5805.[36] Between 1880 and 1895, two out of every three Munich Jews had not been born in the city. Because there were relatively few Jews in the countryside around Munich, many recent arrivals came from distant parts (table 1). In 1895, one in seven had been born outside Germany, a large number in this category stemming from Eastern Europe; when the Einsteins left Munich in 1894, more than one Jew in five was born in Germany beyond Bavaria, as was the case for young Albert. By 1895, he would have been one among fifty-one German–Jewish boys in Munich between 6 and 15 years of age who had been born outside Bavaria.[37]

Table 1 Birthplace of Jews residing in Munich, by lustrum†.

Year	Munich	Elsewhere in Bavaria	Elsewhere in Germany	Abroad	Total Jewish population
1880	1483	1552	742	367	4114
1885	1729	1736	918	471	4854
1890	1989	2024	1301	794	6108
1895	2308	2186	1602	1076	7167

†J Segall, *Die Entwickelung der jüdischen Bevölkerung in München 1875–1905: Ein Beitrag zur Kommunalstatistik* (Munich 1910) pp 2, 40.

The Einsteins' decision to enter the industrial world was also taken by a number of their Jewish contemporaries in Bavaria. In 1882, commerce claimed somewhat more than half of all employed Jews, while around one in ten worked in industry. For those of other religions, only 16% worked in commerce while one in four belonged to the industrial world (table 2).

In 1882 Munich counted 241 Jews in industry—one eighth of its Jewish workers. When the Einstein brothers arrived in the southern German city, then, they formed one per cent of the Jewish industrial workforce.[38] In 1894, when around 550 Jews worked in Munich industry, somewhat more than one hundred had been educated as supervisory personnel. Jakob Einstein, a talented engineer and inventor, was one of this corps (table 3).[39] Finer precision about the Jewish industrial workforce in the 1880s and 1890s is difficult to obtain, but statistics from 1907 provide an upper bound on the earlier situation. In 1907, when 713 Jews were active in Munich industry, 57 worked with machinery and apparatus of various kinds. Placing aside 12 watchmakers, only 23 among the 57 engaged in *constructing* mechanical objects.[40] Notwithstanding the large number of Jews working in industry, then, it is reasonable to assume that in the early 1890s the Einstein brothers constituted at the very least 10% of all Jews engaged in mechanical or electrical engineering. They belonged to a select fraternity.

Table 2 Occupations of Bavarian residents, in percentages†.

Nature of employment	1882		1895	
	Total population	Jewish population	Total population	Jewish population
1 Agriculture	53.36	9.39	44.24	3.73
2 Industry	22.30	11.37	26.73	12.93
3 Commerce/ transportation	6.09	52.55	8.13	53.40
4 Lending/exchange	0.8	0.15	9.92	1.14
5 Government/liberal professions	4.32	4.04	5.07	5.43
6 Self-employed or unemployed	9.73	19.15	10.35	21.31
7 Domestic service	3.40	3.36	4.56	2.06
	100.00	100.00	100.00	100.00

†J Segall, *Die Entwickelung der jüdischen Bevölkerung in München 1875–1905: Ein Beitrag zur Kommunalstatistik* (Munich 1910) p 30.

External forms and deep structure

Fashions in scientific thought are central for understanding the reception of Einstein's work because, on the level of experimental results or predictions, there is very little difference between Einstein's etherless special theory of relativity and Lorentz's electron theory, and none at all between

Hilbert's theory of gravitation and Einstein's general theory of relativity. It has been suggested that Einstein's early work on the theories of relativity was in the vanguard of fashion, and for this reason it received rapid approbation in wider circles. Einstein's thought, however, was that of a classical theoretical physicist, much in the style of his mentors Lorentz and Boltzmann. Einstein energetically resisted, as long as he was able, participating in the vogue of abstract mathematisation advanced by researchers at Göttingen and Paris. He judiciously weighed the importance of his discipline's traditions.

Table 3 The Jewish workforce of Munich in 1895, in absolute numbers†.

Nature of employment	Employee background			Total
	a	*b*	*c*	
1 Agriculture	5	1	2	8
2 Industry	271	124	161	556
3 Commerce/transportation	1020	398	346	1764
4 Lending/exchange	—	—	5	5
5 Government/liberal professions	185	73	1	259
6 Self-employed or unemployed	51	4	1	56
7 Domestic service	973	—	—	973

Key: *a* Independently employable.
　　b Technically and commercially educated supervisory and clerical personnel.
　　c Helpers, apprentices, and uneducated workers.

†J Segall, *Die Entwickelung der jüdischen Bevölkerung in München 1875–1905: Ein Beitrag zur Kommunalstatistik* (Munich 1910) pp 31, 33.

　　Yet if Einstein avoided fashion, he cultivated a characteristic style in his publications. The dominant quality in this style, many commentators have argued, is simplicity. The theoretical physicist sought to eliminate from his personal life and thought all that was inessential for the task at hand. Until the arrival of a secretary in the 1920s, he kept neither incoming correspondence nor copies of his own letters; while teaching, Einstein would not write out his lectures or designate a student to serve as scribe. When nominal head of an institute at Berlin, he expressed no interest in administrative matters. Simplicity, however, has many guises, and it is not clear that in his social dealings or in his non-technical publications—much less than in his scientific research—Einstein always pursued the least complicated path. Rather than following simplicity, in the abstract sense, he obeyed the rules of a special cosmology. To explore Einstein's cosmology, it is well to consider how, in his view, external form related to deep structure. The relationship is apparent in both the physicist's personal appearance and his scientific thought.

Einstein's appearance

The familiar picture of Einstein is that of a man in dishevelled, undistinguished apparel. From the time of his twenties, Einstein 'preferred old clothes—a mended sweater, an ancient waistcoat—to any material strange to the touch'.[41] Even after he had become a rich man and could well have dressed elegantly without investing time or energy in making sartorial decisions, he deliberately cultivated an image of casualness. His trousers and shirts were loose and comfortable. He never donned a disguise, as a bohemian might. His raiment was only as presentable as his mother, wife, maid, or other housekeeper would arrange for. Einstein was unhappy in putting on stiff, new clothes that had not yet adapted to his body. Like metal jewellery—which Einstein similarly avoided—new clothes are cool and impersonal. They stand out, as Georg Simmel has emphasised, 'above the singularity and destiny' of their wearer. To reject new clothes was to assume the role of a stranger, Simmel continued, to indicate that the conventions of majoritarian culture were unimportant:

> A long-worn piece of clothing almost grows to the body; it has an intimacy that militates against the very nature of elegance, which is something for the 'others', a social notion deriving its value from general respect.[42]

Raised in the culture of emancipated Jewry, Einstein sought recognition (to the extent that he did) from among those rare physicists who judged a person by his publications. From others he asked tolerance. Respect was a quality that he found within himself.

Later in life, Einstein became fond of wearing shoes without socks. Socks, he is said to have claimed, only developed holes, and in rejecting them he simplified his life. Yet socks are practical. They cushion the feet, absorb moisture, and impede the growth of dangerous bacteria. They protect shoe linings. Having taken account of these functions, we are reasonable to suppose that Einstein liked the feel of leather. At Princeton, he frequently wore a leather jacket. Absorbing body oils, leather becomes supple and fragrant. It moulds to the person of the wearer. Here is a preference similar to the one favouring old clothes. It values objects attuned to an individual.[43]

Einstein's personal style is especially interesting on the level of cosmetics. An oversensitivity to organic odours, reflecting a puritanical or scientific heritage, is not characteristic of European culture. The smells on a crowded bus in Philadelphia or Cambridge differ greatly from those on one in Milan or Munich. Einstein preferred a traditional, masculine aura of sweat and tobacco. There is no testimony from the years before Einstein moved to America to suggest that he did not bathe regularly;

certainly his nightshirt, during the Berlin days, was kept clean and fresh.[44] But in Princeton, especially after the death of his wife, he grew tired of nightclothes and the washing ritual.[45] Regarding other matters of personal health, Einstein appeared less diffident. He by no means neglected basic dental hygiene, keeping his teeth to the end of his life.

Einstein wore his hair moderately long—it generally never passed his shoulders—and he cultivated an unpretentious moustache. In this aspect, his style is a compromise between hirsute predecessors like Lorentz, Boltzmann, and Poincaré, and the relatively hairless generation of physicists who matured after the use of the safety razor had become fashionable early in the twentieth century. Much latitude of judgment is exercised in the matter of men's facial hair. A fringe beard frames the unity of the facial senses; a vandyck beard accentuates orality; a full beard is a screen, discouraging others from approaching. But a moustache only creates a barrier between the primary passive sense, vision, and the active functions of the mouth—ingestion and speech. The barrier may be only a faint, pencil-thin suggestion; it may be made hostile by shaping it with wax into a point; or it may be vaguely narcissistic, when trained to a sinuous curve. It can also be unassuming and unambiguous, signalling that in its wearer there is a privateness and pensiveness which is inaccessible through conversation, however animated and intimate. The latter is what Einstein chose.

Who does not seek simplification, to abandon everything not of central importance? Yet the overwhelming majority of people have no control over how they shall appear to the world. Non-conformity, or slovenliness, is interpreted as disrespect to one's superiors. This is true even in America, where dress codes have always appeared capricious to European observers. Most social occasions feature people wearing a wide spectrum of shapes and colours—so different from the muted tones dominating Central Europe. Americans avoid formal attire, even when a situation calls for solemnity. How natural it was, then, for Einstein to dress informally, after he moved to Princeton, in the sense of informality familiar to early twentieth-century intellectuals. In so doing, he accentuated his image as a stranger.

Mathematics and physics

Einstein's approach to physics—his *method*—underwent substantial change over his scientific career of sixty years. Einstein's early work radiates a refreshing directness, where physical reasoning speaks while mathematical elaboration and digression wait in the wings. It is not surprising that an early aversion to both idealism and sentimentality led him to find in Ernst Mach a congenial writer. With his work towards general relativity beginning around 1908, Einstein became inextricably enmeshed in complicated mathematics, which he desperately sought to unravel and then dominate. By the end of the First World War he had discovered Immanuel Kant's idealism, and soon affirmed that truth about the physical world could be divined, Leibniz-like, from the aesthetics of mathematical expressions. When, more than a decade later and in a new land, Einstein collaborated with Leopold Infeld on *The Evolution of Physics*, the aging theoretical physicist continually emphasised how all physical theories, though free creations of the mind, arose from weighing experimental and observational evidence.

In view of this complicated evolution, then, can it be said that Einstein's scientific thought consistently followed fundamental principles or prejudices? Beyond strength of purpose and honesty in exposition, are there constants appearing at all points in his work? Or did Einstein's scientific sensibilities develop in unexpected ways, unconstrained by the accidents of his birth and upbringing? Did Einstein approach each scientific problem uniquely, did he continually forge analytical tools anew? Was there one physicist Einstein, or was there one man who studied many different physical problems?

Only a shallow historian would attempt to sketch Einstein's single 'method'. (Would one give serious attention to an analogous attempt at fathoming Goethe or Tolstoy?) Yet a case can nevertheless be made for the continuing presence, in Einstein's work, of a special vision concerning the representation of physical laws in mathematical form. Mathematics described the external form of reality. Einstein always sought to penetrate beneath external forms, to apprehend a deeper structure. Although, for Einstein, mathematics offered useful tools for physical research, the laws of nature had ultimately to be described in words. Einstein valued ordinary conversation and dialogue as a means of clarifying his ideas. He favoured the give and take of discussion over formal presentations. Nature's language was man's language. Even if one needed to summon the Deity by writing abstract cyphers, one reserved the right to address Him directly in human speech.[46]

Language serves to prevent knowledge from circulating as surely as it does to communicate understanding. Polite conventions keep conversation distant and impersonal, and they above all present a barrier to *parvenus*. The use of frank language, the view that politeness in speech is tantamount to lying, was one hallmark of emancipated German Jews. This preference is overwhelmingly present in Einstein's writings, where it has usually been misidentified as *fetching* simplicity. Einstein knew how devastating honesty could be—to himself and to others. (As a schoolboy his honest character caused him to be derided as *Biedermeier*—ploughboy or 'honest Abe'.[47]) For this reason, he tempered his frankness with earthy levity. Frankness, expressed entirely without malicious intent, is a rare enough occurrence to merit comment, and the phenomenon was continually remarked o. those who knew Einstein.

Just as Einstein avoided the obscuring tessellations of language in favour of forthright expression, so he continually strove to bring the deep structures of nature into full view. He never lost faith that one could synthesise nature's various laws according to nineteenth-century canons of reason. Einstein's was an optimism that, as the twentieth century advanced, became anachronistic. It was of a piece with older, progressivist views on the forward advance of civilisation and the material promises extended by scientific activity; it was an optimism predicated on democracy.

Various interpreters have elaborated the methodological outlook of the mature Einstein. The most perplexing feature of this outlook has been seen as Einstein's insistence that, whereas scientific theories were the free inventions of the human spirit and whereas mathematical abstractions mirrored physical reality, experiment still formed the basis for advances in science and physical intuition still remained essential to divine which of many possible mathematical harmonies in fact corresponded to affairs in the real world. It would serve little purpose to attempt to restrain Einstein's later methodological preoccupations within the confines of one or another philosophical school. Yet a remark of Einstein's in a 1949 omnibus reply to his critics provides a concise summary of his position. Einstein cited the 'truly valuable insight' of Immanuel Kant:

> The real is not given to us, but put to us (*aufgegeben*) (by way of a riddle). This obviously means: There is such a thing as a conceptual construction for the grasping of the inter-personal, the authority of which lies purely in its validation.[48]

In Einstein's view, public knowledge was possible, and its content was determined by experiment and observation. This does not conflict with the circumstance that visions of the world arise in the human mind from among many possibilities; creating new scientific ideas depended on character traits, moral imperatives, and psychological predilections—all things that Einstein believed could best be understood by only the individual creator himself.[49]

Einstein's close collaborator and friend Leopold Infeld described Einstein as a materialist, in the sense that he believed in the reality and understandability of an external world. Trying to understand the world was much like trying to fathom the mechanism of a pocket watch that was forever sealed.[50] Yet Einstein believed that, for each person, there was a realm of private thought. In this realm, Einstein saw himself thrashing out the fundamental matters of theoretical physics. The theoretical physicist could not have been clearer about 'my strict adherence to logical simplicity and my lack of confidence in the merit of ever impressive confirmations of theories, whenever questions of principle are involved'.[51] When Einstein insisted that arriving at new scientific ideas was 'mainly a matter of character', he meant that it took place in a private realm inaccessible to scientific verification, but one that was somehow conditioned by moral virtues.[52] In this view, Einstein came perilously close to asserting an indeterminacy for human creativity.

Here, then, is a basis for Einstein's steadfast refusal even to consider the Copenhagen interpretation of quantum mechanics. The new theory of quanta threatened to remove the barrier between individual thought and public knowledge by calling traditional validation into question. Social commentators have often located in this integration a new vindication of free will. For Einstein, however, such a new approach to knowledge offered no special place for a person's private, inchoate, and unpredictable thoughts. With creativity placed on exactly the same footing as public discussion of personal creations, there would be no escape from the public view; all features of life would be exposed to prying and unsympathetic scrutiny. The creative spirit—permitted to exist only as something unmentionable beyond discussion—would wither and die. There would be no *Einspänner* in such a world.

After the death of his second wife, Einstein characterised his *habitus* as that of a solitary bear, pacing in his lair. In view of Einstein's solitude as a fundamental character trait, his early attraction to Ernst Mach's thought assumes a new aspect. Einstein was attracted to Mach because of the latter's iconoclastic approach to epistemology, his view that observable evidence provided the only basis for discussing the merits of a theory. Einstein liked, as well, Mach's call for simplicity. It was a call that demanded the free exercise of physical intuition in selecting which among many possible, simple ideas were to be proposed as physical principles. Following this scheme of things, Einstein would naturally have seen mathematics as providing useful tools, but as offering an insufficient basis for determining nature's laws intuitively. In the decade before 1918 Einstein wrestled with the mathematics of general relativity. During the twilight of imperial Germany he vigorously argued with mathematicians such as David Hilbert and Felix Klein against allowing physical laws to emerge directly from beautiful mathematical formalism. Following this strenuous exercise, Einstein came, as he approached his fiftieth year, to venerate mathematics, holding it to be of interest for its own sake. The great theoretical physicist for the first time published in a mathematical journal.[53] At just the time when it became normal for highly abstract, mathematical digressions to appear in German physics periodicals, Einstein deliberately set himself apart from his colleagues by assuming a place as an editor of the *Mathematische Annalen*. Having been lionised by his colleagues and the world at large, Einstein re-established his place as an outsider.

Notes and references

1 In this chapter, references are omitted for generally accepted circumstances in Einstein's life and for points documented elsewhere in the present book. Although his approach differs from the one used here, Erik H Erikson provides a related evaluation in 'Psychoanalytical Reflections on Einstein's Centenary', in *Albert Einstein: Historical and Cultural Perspectives* ed G Holton and Y Elkana (Princeton 1982) pp 151–73.

2 When on 18 December 1901 he applied to the Swiss patent office for a position as engineer, second class, Einstein wrote that he had just sent his doctoral dissertation to the University of Zurich. It concerned the kinetic theory of gases, and though rejected by the physicists at Zurich, the text undoubtedly turned up as one of Einstein's early papers in the *Annalen der Physik*. Max Flückiger, *Albert Einstein in Bern* (Berne 1974) pp 53–4. A little more than a year later, Einstein wrote to Michele Besso that he would try to become *Privatdozent* without taking a doctorate, as the latter procedure had become a tiresome 'comedy'. Einstein to Besso, January 1903, in *Albert Einstein – Michele Besso, Correspondance 1903–1955* ed Pierre Speziali (Paris 1972) pp 3–6.

3 In his writings, Leopold Infeld provided the finest first-hand account of Einstein's thinking process. Of signal importance is Infeld's discussion in *Quest: The Evolution of a Scientist* (Garden City, NY 1941), reissued as *Quest: An Autobiography* (New York 1980), esp pp 246–321. In referring to Einstein as 'genial', his German-speaking colleagues meant that he was 'gifted with genius'. Einstein's North American admirers repeated the word and found that it extended, in English, to cover the attributes of cheerfulness, joviality, and kindliness. Einstein's childhood governess called him *Pater Langweil*—'Johnny One-Note'. Anton Reiser[Rudolf Kayser], *Albert Einstein: A Biographical Portrait* (London 1931) p 29.

  Einstein's advice to Julia Niggli of Aarau, in 1899, about the sins of all men is at the very least odd. Carl Seelig, *Albert Einstein: A Documentary Biography*, transl Mervyn Savill (London 1956) p 20. Einstein needlessly pilloried Dimitri Mirimanoff in 'Bemerkung zur Arbeit von D Mirimanoff, "Ueber die Gleichungen der Elektrodynamik bewegten Körper von Lorentz und das Prinzip der Relativität" ', *Ann. Phys.* **28** (1909) 885–8, a text that the coeditor of the *Annalen*, Wilhelm Wien, asked Einstein to clarify before publication. Wien to Einstein, 19 January 1909, Einstein Archives, Princeton. Enrique Gaviola, a physics student at Berlin in the middle 1920s, relayed to me his observations on Einstein's comportment in the physics seminar there.

4 Hans Eugen Specker, ed, *Einstein und Ulm: Festakt und Ausstellung zum 100. Geburtstag von Albert Einstein* (Stuttgart 1979) [*Forschungen zur Geschichte der Stadt Ulm, Reihe Dokumentation* 1] pp 71–2, 77.

5 Eugene P Wigner recalled Einstein's isolation at Princeton in 'Erinnerungen an Albert Einstein' in *Gedächtnisausstellung zum 100. Geburtstag von Albert Einstein, Otto Hahn, Max von Laue, Lise Meitner* ed Friedrich Beck *et al* (Bad Honnef 1979) pp 133–6. Leopold Infeld described attempts to ridicule Einstein in *Why I Left Canada: Reflections on Science and Politics* transl Helen Infeld, ed Lewis Pyenson (Montreal 1978) pp 156–8.

6 Banesh Hoffmann, with the assistance of Helen Dukas, *Albert Einstein: Creator and Rebel* (New York 1972).

7 Helen Dukas used these words in a conversation with me.

8 That Einstein was no rebel has been emphasised in a remarkable essay by Paul Forman, 'Introduction: Einstein and Research', in *The Joys of Research* ed Walter Shropshire Jr (Washington, DC 1981) pp 13–24, as well as in Lewis Pyenson's 'Introduction' in Infeld's *Why I Left Canada* (ref 5) pp 1–13, on p 9. Compare: Stephen G Brush, 'Scientific Revolutionaries of 1905: Einstein, Rutherford, Chamberlin, Wilson, Stevens, Binet, Freud', in *Rutherford and Physics at the Turn of the Century* ed Mario Bunge and William R Shea (New York 1979) pp 140–71. Infeld reported Einstein's emphasis on general relativity in *Why I Left Canada* (ref 5) p 152.

9 Helen Dukas was quite definite that Einstein and his circle of friends in Zurich and Berne were 'anything but "bohemian" '. She continued: 'They may look so to "American eyes" but not to European ones.' Helen Dukas to Lewis Pyenson, 16 September 1974. Miss Dukas was responding to the argument advanced by Lewis Feuer in *Einstein and the Generations of Science* (New York 1974). Compare Einstein's reproach to his good friend Michele Angelo Besso, when Einstein learned that Besso's son was not attending school: 'You, yourself, are a bit of a bohemian in this way, too. Pity!' Einstein to Besso, 13 May 1911. *Einstein–Besso Correspondance* (ref 2) pp 19–22.

10 Gordon Wright, *Insiders and Outliers: The Individual in History* (San Francisco 1981).

11 Significant in this regard is the barest mention of Einstein in Peter Gay's *Weimar Culture: The Outsider as an Insider* (New York 1970).

12 Georg Simmel, 'Exkurs über den Fremden', in his *Soziologie: Untersuchungen über die Formen der Vergesellschaftung* (Leipzig 1908) pp 658–91, translated in Kurt H Wolff's *The Sociology of Georg Simmel* (Glencoe, Ill 1950) pp 402–8, from the third (1923) edition of Simmel's book.

13 Robert E Park, 'Introduction', in Everett V Stonequist's *The Marginal Man: A Study in Personality and Culture Conflict* (New York 1937, 1961) pp xvii–xviii.

14 E V Stonequist (ref 13).

15 Milton M Goldberg, 'A Qualification of the Marginal Man Theory', *American Sociological Review* 6 (1941) 52–8.

16 Julian L Greifer, 'Attitudes to the Stranger: A Study of the Attitudes of Primitive Society and Early Hebrew Culture', *American Sociological Review* 10 (1945) 739–45. David I Golovensky, 'The Marginal Man Concept: An Analysis and Critique', *Social Forces* 30 (1952) 333–9.

17 Kurt Lewin, *Resolving Social Conflicts* (New York 1948) pp 178–82.

18 E Franklin Frazier, *Race and Culture: Contacts in the Modern World* (New York 1957) pp 311–18; Brewton Berry, *Race and Ethnic Relations* (Boston 1958) pp 259–61; James W Vander Zanden, *American Minority Relations: The Sociology of Race and Ethnic Groups* (New York 1966) pp 313–19.

19 George Eaton Simpson and J Milton Yinger, *Racial and Cultural Minorities* (New York 1965) pp 143–7.

20 Alfred Schuetz, 'The Stranger: An Essay in Social Psychology', *American Journal of Sociology* 49 (1944) 499–507, on p 507.

21 K H Wolff, *Simmel* (ref 12) pp 402, 405.

22 Johann Evangelist Schöttle, *Geschichte von Stadt und Stift Buchau* (Waldsee 1884); Anton Schuhmacher, *Wirtschaftliche Entwickelung der Stadt Buchau am Federsee* (dissertation, University of Tübingen 1912); Walter Staudacher, *Führer durch Buchau und das Federseeried* (Buchau [1925]) pp 36, 76.

23 Utz Jeggle, *Judendörfer in Württemberg* (Tübingen 1969) pp 158–64, 225–7.

24 Schöttle, *Geschichte* (ref 22) pp 180, 196; Aron Tänzer, *Die Geschichte der Juden in Jebenhausen und Göppingen* (Berlin 1927) pp 145–6, 148–9; Reinhold Adler, *Beiträge zu einer Geschichte der israelitischen Gemeinde Buchaus: Von den Anfängen bis zum Beginn des Hitlerreiches* [Zulassungsarbeit zur 2. Reallehrerprüfung, Pädagogische Hochschule Weingarten, 1973] p 139. A copy of the last document is available at the Leo Baeck Institute Library, New York. Aron Tänzer, 'Der Stammbaum Prof. Albert Einsteins', *Jüdische Familien-Forschung: Mitteilungen der Gesellschaft für Jüdische Familien-Forschung* **28** (1931) 419–21, a copy of which is located in the Einstein Archives, Princeton.

25 In urging Besso to send his son to school, Einstein emphasised that from formal education one learned how 'to adapt oneself to an organisation, something so very important for everyone'. He was silent about other benefits accrued. Einstein to Besso, 13 May 1911. *Einstein–Besso Correspondance* (ref 2) pp 19–22.

26 U Jeggle, *Judendörfer* (ref 23) pp 191–7.

27 Heinz Moshe Graupe, *The Rise of Modern Judaism: An Intellectual History of German Jewry, 1650–1942* transl John Robinson (Huntingdon, NY 1978) pp 143–6, 168–71.

28 Bernhard Rosenthal, *Heimatgeschichte der badischen Juden seit ihrem geschichtlichen Auftreben bis zur Gegenwart* (Bühl/Baden 1927) pp 387–8. Peter Gay, 'Encounter with Modernism: German Jews in German Culture, 1888–1914', *Midstream* **21** no 2 (1975) 23–65, citation on p 31.

29 Ludwig Feuchtwanger, 'Neuere Geschichte', in: Munich, Israelitische Kultusgemeinde, *Festgabe: 50 Jahre Hauptsynagoge München 1887–1937* (Munich 1937) pp 30–42, on pp 34–7.

30 H E Specker, *Einstein und Ulm* (ref 4) p 55.

31 *Ibid* pp 57, 61.

32 P Forman, 'Einstein and Research' (ref 8) p 14.

33 Jakob Segall, *Die Entwickelung der jüdischen Bevölkerung in München 1875–1905: Ein Beitrag zur Kommunalstatistik* (Munich 1910) p 6.

34 Jakob Lestschinsky, *Das wirtschaftliche Schicksal deutschen Judentums: Aufstieg, Wandlung, Krise, Ausblick* (Berlin 1932) [*Schriften der Zentralwohlfahrtsstelle der deutschen Juden und der Hauptstelle für jüdische Wanderfürsorge* no 7] p 63.

35 L Feuchtwanger, 'Geschichte' (ref 29).

36 J Segall, *Entwickelung* (ref 33) pp 2–3.

37 *Ibid* p 65. The corresponding figure for the male population of Munich as a whole, in this age span, was 791.

38 *Ibid* p 31.

39 *Ibid.*

40 Paula Weiner-Odenheimer, 'Die Berufe der Juden in München', *Zeitschrift für Demographie und Statistik der Juden* **11** nos 10/11/12 (1915) 85–96, on p 88.

41 Antonina Vallentin, *The Drama of Albert Einstein* transl Moura Budberg

(Garden City, NY 1954) p 27. Although when discussing physics Vallentin is not to be trusted, her description of Einstein's personal characteristics seems right on the mark.

42 G Simmel, 'Exkurs über den Schmuck', in his *Soziologie* (ref 12) pp 365–72, on p 368; K H Wolff, *Georg Simmel* (ref 12) p 341.

43 For Einstein's rejection of socks and love of leather see A Vallentin, *Einstein* (ref 41) p 28, and L Infeld, *Quest* (ref 3) p 293.

44 The clean nightshirts, and then their absence, are reported in conversations between the Einsteins' Haberlandstrasse maid and Friedrich Herneck, in Herneck, *Einstein privat* (Berlin 1978) p 59.

45 Einstein's infrequent baths during the 1940s were relayed to me by Derek J de Solla Price, who sat next to him at a Princeton colloquium.

46 Einstein insisted that expressing ideas in words was the ultimate goal in: Jacques Hadamard, *An Essay on the Psychology of Invention in the Mathematical Field* (Princeton 1945) p 142.

47 P Forman, 'Einstein and Research' (ref 8) p 14, has rendered 'Biedermeier' as 'straight arrow'. (The American expression 'honest Abe' recalls Abraham Lincoln.) The reference to Einstein's moniker is found in F Herneck, *Einstein privat* (ref 44) pp 14–15. Herneck reports that Einstein called his salon on Haberlandstrasse in Berlin, the *Biedermeierzimmer*. Cf Alexander Moszkowski, *Conversations with Einstein* transl H L Brose (New York 1970) p 222.

48 A Einstein, 'Remarks to the Essays Appearing in this Collective Volume', in *Albert Einstein—Philosopher-Scientist* ed P A Schilpp (La Salle, Ill 1949) pp 665–88, on p 680.

49 A Einstein, 'Foreword', in A Reiser, *Einstein* (ref 3) p 11.

50 L Infeld, *Why I Left Canada* (ref 5) pp 70–2.

51 A Einstein to L Infeld, 20 September 1949, in *ibid* p 142.

52 L Infeld, *ibid* p 180.

53 In a letter to Elie Cartan of 25 August 1929, Einstein wrote about his first *Mathematische Annalen* paper, where 'only the mathematical implications are explored and not their application to physics'. Robert Debever, ed, *Elie Cartan–Albert Einstein: Letters on Absolute Parallelism* (Princeton 1979) pp 18–19.

4   Hermann Minkowski and Einstein's special theory of relativity

Introduction

With his work on the general theory of relativity in the period 1912–16 Einstein thought that he was introduced for the first time to the heuristic power of mathematics for formulating new physical theories. Before 1912 he avoided complicated or innovative mathematics.[1] In particular, unlike many other mathematicians and physicists, Einstein remained unimpressed with the physical ideas in Hermann Minkowski's theory of matter and four-dimensional space–time, developed during the period 1907–8. Einstein believed instead that Minkowski had introduced a useful mathematical formalism that was not of central importance for understanding the fundamental ideas of the special and general theories of relativity.[2]

Hermann Minkowski was Einstein's most important mathematics teacher at the Federal Institute of Technology in Zurich. Einstein took nine courses from him.[3] By the time that he graduated in 1900, however, Einstein had become indifferent to Minkowski's approach to mathematics and physics.[4] Minkowski remembered Einstein's lack of enthusiasm a decade later when he modified Einstein's special theory of relativity.[5] Minkowski thought that by mathematising special relativity he clarified the essential physical features of Einstein's theory. Although Einstein accepted Minkowski's mathematisation as only a technical improvement on his own work, many other physicists and mathematicians attempted to extend Minkowski's formulation of matter and electromagnetism. Few realised that there were major differences between Minkowski's and Einstein's approaches to the principle of relativity.

In this chapter I examine Minkowski's interpretation of Einstein's principle of relativity, emphasising Minkowski's views on the relations between mathematics and physics as well as his speculations concerning a possible unification of electromagnetism and gravitation. I conclude by suggesting how the different approaches of Minkowski and Einstein to the role of mathematics in physics illuminate the reception of Einstein's thought.

Minkowski's interpretation of special relativity

If Einstein was not favourably impressed with Minkowski's mathematics lectures, Minkowski later thought that his own interpretation of the principle of relativity was superior to Einstein's because of Einstein's limited mathematical competence. He is reported to have told his students that Einstein was a 'lazy dog' at Zurich, and he was surprised that Einstein had been able to formulate the special theory of relativity.[6] Indeed, during a series of lectures on the electrodynamics of moving bodies delivered before an audience of physicists in the spring of 1908, Minkowski argued that he was privileged to judge Einstein's incomplete mastery of mathematics because 'Einstein drew his mathematical development from me. Though he was one of the best of his time, the mathematical knowledge that he could acquire from the Polytechnic in Zurich, where mathematics was not the strongest subject, was incomplete.'[7] Minkowski insisted that he was only mentioning Einstein's mathematical limitations to lend credibility to his criticism of Einstein, especially in view of the uncertain authority he commanded in his present audience with respect to 'physical things', into which he would not go. His own view, in contrast to Einstein's, was based on 'a natural law of the most general rank, I would even willingly call it the first general natural law'. This law, later identified as the principle of the absolute world, was of central importance because it based all natural knowledge concerning space and time on original concepts, and because the extraordinary consequences of the law treated 'super-real things which have not really been mentioned until now'.

For his part, Einstein was sceptical about the physical consequences of Minkowski's approach. As soon as Minkowski's first published statement on relativity appeared, Einstein turned to the only part of Minkowski's paper that contained a physical prediction, specifically, the formulation of the ponderomotive electromagnetic force. In a short paper written with his collaborator Jakob Johann Laub, Einstein observed that Minkowski required the electromagnetic force on a particle in motion always to be normal to the particle's path in four-dimensional space, a formulation that did not account for the polarisation current produced by a current flowing through a wire in the presence of a magnetic field.[8] The required polarisation current was a natural outcome of Einstein's special theory of relativity. Einstein and Laub's objections reflected a more basic disagreement with Minkowski concerning the general expression for a relativistic analogue to Newton's second law. As a result, Einstein and Minkowski arrived at different expressions for the transverse and longitudinal electron masses, although the ratio of the two components remained the same in both theories.

Minkowski's covariant formulation for Newton's second law of motion, as Philipp Frank observed at the time, carried a different physical interpretation from that of Einstein and Laub.[9] Minkowski's choice is, indeed, the choice that is taught today. In part for this reason, some contemporary observers considered Minkowski's physical, as well as his mathematical, results to be a significant improvement on Einstein's work. The latter, in their view, was nothing more than a contribution to the electron theory. Minkowski interpreted his own work in this way. He did not realise that Einstein had developed a theory of physical measurement, a new synthesis of classical mechanics and Maxwellian electrodynamics. Minkowski believed that, whereas Einstein was concerned only with electrodynamics, he himself was formulating a new theory of matter that revealed the true mathematical harmony of the physical world.

Minkowski's first public statement on Einstein's principle of relativity was delivered as an address to the Göttingen Mathematical Society in the autumn of 1907. Minkowski did not believe that his ideas were in publishable form. In 1915, six years after Minkowski's death, Arnold Sommerfeld transcribed and edited the text for publication.[10] Occasionally Sommerfeld thought that Minkowski's terminology was ill-chosen. Annotating a typescript of Minkowski's manuscript, Sommerfeld expressed opposition to Minkowski's use of the ether and would have liked to eliminate the archaic 'ponderomotive force' in favour of 'electromagnetic force'.[11] Sommerfeld was unable to resist rewriting Minkowski's judgment of Einstein's formulation of the principle of relativity. He introduced a clause inappropriately praising Einstein for having used the Michelson experiment to demonstrate that the concept of absolute rest did not express a property of phenomena.[12] Sommerfeld also suppressed Minkowski's conclusion, where Einstein was portrayed as the clarifier, but by no means as the principal expositor, of the principle of relativity.[13] With the exception of these changes, it seems that Sommerfeld printed Minkowski's manuscript substantially as he found it.

In his address to the Göttingen Mathematical Society, Minkowski interpreted Einstein's principle of relativity as a prelude to his own radical interpretation of space and time. He incorrectly understood Einstein's work as a contribution to electrodynamics. At the same time, he thought that he revealed Einstein's work in its true generality because he applied ideas from pure mathematics to Einstein's electromagnetic content:

> An ideal transformation of our presentation of space and time, which we have long wanted to carry out, recently seems to have come out of the

electromagnetic theory of light. This is something the mathematician should be keen to know. He is, moreover, particularly predisposed to internalise the new intuitions, as they consist in adapting concepts with which he is long since conversant. To some extent, the physicist needs to invent these concepts from scratch and must laboriously carve a path through a primeval forest of obscurity; at the same time the mathematician travels nearby on an excellently designed road. In any event, the new approaches—provided they account correctly for the observed phenomena—mark possibly the greatest triumph that the application of mathematics has recorded: the position that the world in space and time is in a certain sense a four-dimensional, non-Euclidean manifold. It will become apparent, to the glory of mathematicians and to the boundless astonishment of the rest of mankind, that the mathematicians have created purely within their imagination a grand domain that should have arrived at a real and most perfect existence, and this without any such intention on their part.[14]

Minkowski emphasised the usefulness of unconventional mathematics for the physicist. Although experiment appeared as the final arbiter of the theory, Minkowski felt that physicists had recently verified the actual existence of truths that mathematicians had already established.

Minkowski's 'Principle of Relativity' was divided into four sections: electricity, matter, dynamics, and gravitation. The first two sections served to reformulate an interpretation of electrodynamics that David Hilbert had proposed several weeks earlier in a seminar that he and Minkowski were conducting on the partial differential equations of electrodynamics. According to lecture notes recorded by Hermann Mierendorff, Hilbert introduced the seminar by describing the three continua—ether, electricity, and matter—that filled geometrical space.[15] The ether was an immovable continuum, and its state was given by the electric (E) and magnetic (H) field intensities. Electricity was a continuum subject to motion, and it was characterised by a scalar charge density ϱ and a vector current density. In traditional mechanics, determination of motion resulting from known forces was one of the standard problems, Hilbert continued. In electrodynamics, however, one generally sought the charge and current densities in the presence of external forces. To do this, one defined as electromagnetic force the vector $\Lambda = \varrho \, (E + v \times H)$, and equated this force to $\Lambda = m \, \mathrm{d}^2K(t)/\mathrm{d}t^2$, where $K(t)$ was the radius vector of a moving particle of mass m and velocity v. For matter at rest, it was necessary to specify three contributions to $K(t)$ from the nature of matter. The first was defined as the curl of a new quality, the magnetisation of matter. Second was the partial time derivative of the electrical polarisation of matter. The third contribution to $K(t)$ came from the motion of charges. Hermann Mierendorff recorded that Hilbert felt that this formulation of electromagnetic force did not hold, however, for matter in motion. Hilbert simply observed without being specific that it remained to be seen whether

Lorentz's equations for the electrodynamics of moving bodies were correct.[16]

In the first two sections of the 'Principle of Relativity', Minkowski elaborated Hilbert's formulation of electricity and matter in terms of four-dimensional space–time vectors. He underlined the necessity of a distinction between electricity and matter because, though a purely electromagnetical basis might someday be provided for mechanics, the Michelson experiment argued against the existence of an absolute state of rest. This point could be cleared up, Minkowski suggested, if one assumed that the equations of the electrodynamics of matter remained unchanged by a coordinate transformation under the Lorentz rotation group. In this sense, the principle of relativity became a new physical law. Minkowski, then, substantially revised Einstein's two postulates of the special theory of relativity and ignored Einstein's rejection of the ether. The second half of Minkowski's paper made little use of his four-dimensional machinery. Part 3 was entirely devoted to showing that the principle of relativity, as he defined it, did not contradict the energy of radiation calculated from Max Planck's quantum theory. Minkowski glossed a paper by Planck showing that the second law of thermodynamics could be formulated in a relativistically covariant manner,[17] and he suggested how Planck's argument could be recast in four-dimensional space–time. The final section of Minkowski's paper was a brief paragraph on Henri Poincaré's investigation in 1906 of possible formulations of a non-Newtonian gravitational law which were invariants of the Lorentz group.[18]

It should be emphasised that all the physical propositions in Minkowski's early approach were derivative. His original contribution concerned the requirement that valid physical laws had to be invariants of the Lorentz group in four-dimensional space–time. Minkowski's orientation is succinctly revealed in an unpublished lecture on complex analysis probably delivered just before the 'Principle of Relativity' paper.[19] Mathematics was his main concern; allusions to physics expressed basic confusions. 'The glory and reward' of complex analysis, he stated, was to be found in an application that reflected 'a pre-established harmony among contemporary mathematical branches of knowledge, specifically the formation of concepts and problems that are useful for extending [this] theory and for the development of physical theories'. He had in mind 'a recent triumph of mathematics . . . that perhaps will number among the greatest successes that the application of mathematics to science has yet shown'. This was the recently formulated principle of relativity, which, 'if it really is shown to have succeeded, totally upsets all previous conceptions of mechanics'. The principle replaced the classical principle of inertia that required the existence of an absolute frame of reference and in which the laws of mechanics were in no way changed by a uniform spatial transformation.

(This evaluation is at best unclear; the classical principle of inertia is not related to absolute space.) The new principle arose from a defect in Maxwell's optics, which had raised the theoretical possibility of detecting the influence of the earth's motion on the velocity of light. All experiments attempting to do this gave a negative result. The problem was cleverly solved, Minkowski suggested, by Hendrik Antoon Lorentz who modified Maxwell's electrodynamics to exclude the influence of uniform motion on the propagation of light. This idea led to the Lorentz transformation law, which, in turn, developed into the principle of relativity. Neither Einstein nor any agent in this development other than Lorentz was mentioned.

The new principle governed all of physics and glorified mathematics to the highest degree. It expressed the fact that the laws of mechanics were covariant under the Lorentz group. Implications of the principle of relativity were being worked out by several physicists; Minkowski mentioned that Planck's relativistic dynamics had revolutionised the concept of mass, although this inappropriate remark leaves the impression that he had not yet studied Planck's paper. The most important result of the principle of relativity followed a long tradition in mathematics. This was the realisation that time had to be considered as an imaginary length. As a result, the world was in reality a four-dimensional, non-Euclidean manifold. This was an enormous triumph for pure mathematics because 'the mathematician has revealed great domains purely by his imagination without ever expecting that they would come to enjoy a real existence in nature'. Minkowski observed that these recent results were extraordinary because they revealed a dramatic revision of the physical world picture. He implied that it was hardly surprising, however, that pure mathematics provided such a radical interpretation of physical reality.[20]

One month after the 'Principle of Relativity' lecture, Minkowski presented a paper to the Göttingen Scientific Society on the basic equations of electromagnetic processes.[21] This was the work to which Einstein responded in 1908. It remained the only one of Minkowski's papers to appear in print before he died in January 1909, and it is the most mathematically sophisticated of all his writings on relativity. The underlying aim was to provide the foundation for a theory of matter by reinterpreting the electron theory. The paper was not concerned, as Einstein's work had been, with the principles of measuring physical quantities, nor for the most part with contradictions between the mechanical and electromagnetic world pictures.

In his paper, Minkowski elaborated the tripartite division of physical space that Hilbert had introduced in their seminar. Minkowski defined three uses of the word relativity, each identified to some extent with Hilbert's three continua. The *theorem* of relativity was the 'purely mathematical fact' that equations describing systems in uniform motion relative to each other were covariant under Lorentz transformations. The theorem of relativity was a direct consequence of Maxwell's equations. The *postulate* of relativity was the hypothesis that the theorem of relativity described the motion of ponderable—that is, electromagnetic—matter. It was not concerned with defining measurable quantities derived from laboratory matter, and Minkowski pointed out that it specified no particular relation between electricity and matter. The postulate of relativity was to be used for matter in the same way that the conservation of energy was introduced when specific expressions for energy were not known. The *principle* of relativity formulated the notion that Lorentz covariance held among genuine, material quantities in moving bodies. It asserted that appropriate measurable quantities existed for all physical phenomena involving matter in motion. Minkowski credited Lorentz with discovering the theorem and the postulate of relativity, and Einstein with proposing an early version of the principle of relativity.[22]

The first part of the paper concerned the pure electromagnetic field, that is, electromagnetism when only the ether was present. Minkowski expressed Lorentz's reformulation of Maxwell's equations in terms of a four-dimensional vector space where three dimensions had unit vector 1 and the fourth dimension had an imaginary unit vector $\sqrt{-1}$. The vector space was chosen, of course, so that the first three dimensions would correspond to ordinary physical space and the fourth dimension to time. Minkowski did not, however, motivate his choice for the reader in this way. On the contrary, in deriving the theorem of relativity he sought to indicate how pure mathematics could furnish the basis for physical laws.

Minkowski began by considering a coordinate rotation such that:

$$x_1' = x_1 \qquad x_2' = x_2$$
$$x_3' = x_3 \cos i\psi + x_4 \sin i\psi$$
$$x_4' = -x_3 \sin i\psi + x_4 \cos i\psi.$$

As an angle of rotation in four-dimensional space, ψ was a purely imaginary quantity. Minkowski next set

$$q = -i \tan i\,\psi = (e^\psi - e^{-\psi})/(e^\psi + e^{-\psi}).$$

This notational substitution allowed him to write the relations

$$\cos i\,\psi = (1 - q^2)^{-1/2} \qquad \sin i\,\psi = i\,q(1 - q^2)^{-1/2}$$

where q was a quantity between -1 and 1. Making an algebraic substitution, Minkowski put the original angular rotational transformation in the form

$$x' = x \qquad\qquad y' = y$$
$$z' = \frac{z - qt}{\sqrt{1 - q^2}} \qquad t' = \frac{-qz + t}{\sqrt{1 - q^2}} \ . \tag{1}$$

From this step, it was apparent that q was a normalised velocity of some sort. The linear transformation of determinant +1 characterised by equations (1) was called a special Lorentz transformation. Minkowski considered the quantity $\varrho \sqrt{1-w^2}$, where w was the velocity of a particular coordinate system, and ϱ was an invariant with respect to the special Lorentz transformation, and he showed that ϱ was identical to the rest density of electricity in the presence of matter. Minkowski extended his results to demonstrate that Maxwell's equations were covariant under space-like rotations.

The second and larger part of Minkowski's paper concerned electromagnetic processes in the presence of matter. As in the first part, Minkowski initially presented axioms that formed the basis of his analysis. (i) When matter was at rest, all basic electromagnetic quantities were also assumed to be at rest. In other words, the results of the first section of the paper were a necessary limiting case for what would follow. (ii) Any velocity attained by matter had to be less than the velocity of light in empty space. (iii) When the magnetic and electric fields transformed as a space–time vector of the second kind (that is, as a second-rank, antisymmetric tensor) under a Lorentz transformation, then the current and charge density necessarily transformed as a space–time vector of the first kind (that is, as a four-dimensional space–time vector). This requirement was equivalent to asserting that equations for moving bodies had to be covariant with respect to a Lorentz transformation.

Minkowski's axioms reveal how his approach differed from Einstein's special theory of relativity. Minkowski's first axiom was contrary to the spirit of Einstein's principle of relativity, which implied that an absolute state of rest could not be achieved. (One might say that it is not a serious provocation because Einstein also spoke of rest systems without the qualification, which was to be understood, that he meant a state of rest relative to a particular frame of reference.) Minkowski had previously introduced the second axiom in his lecture on complex analysis. It corresponded to a proposition that Einstein had *deduced* as a consequence of his own second postulate of relativity, which stated that the velocity of light in empty space was a constant independent of the velocity of the emitting body. Minkowski called his third axiom the principle of relativity, a completely new definition of the term, and certainly one that Einstein had not used. Although he made no use of four-dimensional space–time, Einstein had derived the transformation laws for the electromagnetic field after he had postulated that it was not possible to distinguish whether a system moving with constant velocity relative to another system was indeed at rest or actually in motion.

Extending special relativity: Minkowski's theory of gravitation

In the appendix to his paper of 1908 on the basic equations for electro-magnetic processes, Minkowski sought to formulate relativistic mechanics. The appendix closed with an attempt to treat gravitation. Minkowski's interest in gravitation reflected a long-standing concern for many Wilhelmian scientists.[23] It was clear by 1900 that small discrepancies in the perihelion precessions of the four inner planets as well as in several short-period comets could not be resolved by Newton's laws of mechanics and gravitation.[24] This persistent anomaly, together with other considerations based on the size and physical properties of the universe as a whole, led the widely respected Munich astronomer Hugo von Seeliger to question the exact inverse-square nature of Newton's gravitation law.[25] Examination of the assumed equivalence in Newtonian mechanics between inertial and gravitational mass led to several attempts, such as those by Ernst Mach in 1889[26] and by Roland von Eötvös in 1896[27], to arrive at a more precise mechanical notion of gravitational mass. Of most interest in Germany after 1900, however, were investigations of electrodynamics as an analogy for or as the source of gravitational phenomena. Between 1900 and 1905, Lorentz[28], Wilhelm Wien[29], Richard Gans[30], Fritz Wacker[31], and Alexander Wilkens[32] examined whether gravitation could be treated according to the electromagnetic view of nature.

Far from an afterthought, Minkowski's appendix on gravitation served to indicate his plans for future work.[33] He sought to unify electro-magnetism and gravitation by introducing a new, geometrical mechanics. The appendix showed how gravitation might plausibly be expressed in the same four-dimensional space–time geometry used for electromagnetic processes.

Minkowski began by defining a ray structure (*Strahlgebilde*) for a fixed space–time point B* (x^*, y^*, z^*, t^*) as the set of all space–time points B (x, y, z, t) such that, for $t-t^* \geq 0$,

$$(x-x^*)^2 + (y-y^*)^2 + (z-z^*)^2 = (t-t^*)^2. \tag{2}$$

Minkowski fixed the velocity of light as unity for ease in calculation. B* was called the light point (*Lichtpunkt*) of all points located on the concave side of the three-dimensional surface described by relation (2). Inversely, the point B could be considered fixed, and the point B* could be varied. Seen in this way, for any point B in space–time, light points represented the boundary of all other points with which B could communicate during the past.

Minkowski considered a material point F of mass m and a material point F* of mass m^*. He located F at point B, and identified the line segment BC as an infinitesimally small part of the space–time line of F, calling the latter the principal line (*Hauptlinie*) of F. B* was constructed as the light point of B on the space–time line of F*, and it was given the coordinates (0, 0, 0, τ^*). C* was constructed as the light point of C, again on the space–time line of F* (see figure 2). Minkowski defined as coordinates (0, 0, 0, 0) the centre of curvature of the space–time line of F* at point B*, since this entailed no contradiction with his previous definitions. He then constructed line OA' parallel to B*C* as the radius vector on the hyperbolic shell $-x^2 -y^2 -z^2 -\tau^2 = 1$ having coordinates (0, 0, 0, t), $t \geqslant 0$. Point D* was located as the intersection of the extension of line B*C* with the space which was normal to OA' through the point B. The point A', at first left indeterminate, was finally fixed at the line BD*.

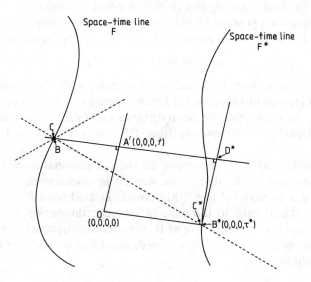

Figure 2 Geometrical reconstruction for Minkowski's treatment of gravitation in the 'Basic Equations for Electromagnetic Processes'.

Minkowski assumed that the new relativistic law of gravitation was of the same general form as the Newtonian one. That is, it had the appearance

$$-mm^*r/r^3. \tag{3}$$

Here m and m^* were two masses, and r was the three-dimensional vector separating them. Offering no explanation to his readers, Minkowski postulated that the gravitational force on the mass point F at space–time point B could be expressed by a four-dimensional space–time vector,

$$m\,m^*\left(\frac{\text{OA}'}{\text{B*D*}}\right)^3\text{BD*} \tag{4}$$

where OA', B*D*, and BD* were themselves four-dimensional space–time vectors, and Minkowski's notation (OA'/B*D*) indicated the vector difference, OA' − B*D*. (Here one must make the additional assumption, for which Minkowski did not alert the reader, that point A' was actually on the line BD*.) Since BD* was normal to the time-like vector OA', vector BD* would be a space-like vector in the instantaneous rest frame of B*. BD* measured the 'spatial' distance (the four-dimensional vector with time held constant) between B and B*. The only non-zero component of OA' was time. Since OA' was defined to be parallel to B*D*, B*D* was also purely time-like in character. Therefore, the vector (OA'/B*D*) had magnitude $(t - \tau^*)$. Thus, all the quantities in equation (4) had counterparts in the classical equation (3). The vector BD* in equation (4) played a role analogous to the ordinary three dimensional spatial vector *r* in equation (3). Because of the relation

$$x^2 + y^2 + z^2 = (t - \tau^*)^2 \tag{5}$$

the magnitude $(t - \tau^*)^{-3}$ could be associated with the magnitude r^{-3}. (Relation (5) was just relation (2) for the special case represented in figure 2. It gave the connection between distance and time on the wave front of a gravitational wave emanating from B* with velocity equal to that of light.)

Minkowski sought an expression for the gravitational force at F due to F*, for any mass at F; that is, he wanted to calculate the gravitational field at F due to mass m^* at F*. Minkowski located point F at coordinates B(x, y, z, t) and gave to the mass m^* the coordinates $(0, 0, 0, \tau^*)$. If *t* was the proper time coordinate at B, then the acceleration at point F due to mass m^* at point F* was determined, according to equation (4), by the four equations:

$$\frac{d^2x}{d\tau^2} = \frac{-m^*x}{(t - \tau^*)^3} \qquad \frac{d^2y}{d\tau^2} = \frac{-m^*y}{(t - \tau^*)^3}$$

$$\frac{d^2z}{d\tau^2} = \frac{-m^*z}{(t - \tau^*)^3} \qquad \frac{d^2t}{d\tau^2} = \frac{-m^*}{(t - \tau^*)^2} \frac{d(t - \tau^*)}{dt} \tag{6}$$

where

$$\left(\frac{dx}{d\tau}\right)^2 + \left(\frac{dy}{d\tau}\right)^2 + \left(\frac{dz}{d\tau}\right)^2 = \left(\frac{dt}{d\tau}\right)^2 - 1. \tag{7}$$

Equation (7) expressed the differential relation of the Lorentz metric.

Minkowski observed that, according to Newtonian mechanics, the first three equations in expression (6) were of the same form as the equations of motion of a mass point under the acceleration of a fixed centre. He recalled the classical equations for a spatial orbit with semi-major axis *a*, eccentricity *e*, and eccentric anomaly E.[34] If *T* was the difference between the proper time for a complete revolution in a real, Keplerian elliptical orbit with semi-major axis a and a circular orbit of radius a, and if n was the fractional excess defined by $n = 2\pi/T$, then the mean anomaly $n\tau$ was expressed by the Kepler equation

$$n\tau = E - e \sin E. \tag{8}$$

Further, the radius of an elliptical orbit was given by $r = a(1 - e \cos E)$. By transforming equation (7) to planar, polar coordinates, then, and explicitly reintroducing the velocity of light c that was assumed equal to unity until this point in the calculation, Minkowski obtained the equation

$$\left(\frac{dr}{d\tau}\right)^2 = \left(\frac{dt}{d\tau}\right)^2 - 1 = \frac{m^*}{ac^2}\left(\frac{1 + e \cos E}{1 - e \cos E}\right). \tag{9}$$

Solving equation (9) for dt, and expanding the result to terms in c^{-2}, Minkowski arrived at the expression:

$$dt = d\tau\left(1 + \frac{1}{2}\frac{m^*}{ac^2}\frac{1 + e \cos E}{1 - e \cos E}\right). \tag{10}$$

Multiplying both sides of equation (10) by n gave the differential mean anomaly $n\,dt$. Equations (8) and (10) yielded

$$n\,t + \text{constant} = \left(1 + \frac{1}{2}\frac{m^*}{ac^2}\right)n\tau + \frac{m^*}{ac^2}\sin E. \tag{11}$$

Minkowski computed that if m^* were the mass of the Sun, and a were the semi-major axis of the Earth's orbit, then m^*/ac^2 would be of the order of 10^{-8}. Without additional assumptions, the periodic anomalies in the planetary orbits were thus computed to be much smaller than the observed quantities.

Minkowski's geometrical approach to gravitation as an analogy to the attraction of two oppositely charged particles was not convincing for many physicists and mathematicians. In comparing Minkowski's work with Poincaré's formulation in 1906 of covariant, non-Newtonian gravitational laws, Arnold Sommerfeld considered Minkowski's approach no more fruitful than that of Poincaré.[35] Max Bernhard Weinstein, a physical scientist respected for his knowledge of mathematics, found the last part of Minkowski's calculation unintelligible.[36]

Extending special relativity: Nordström's defence of Minkowski

Although Minkowski's gravitational speculations merited little discussion, his formulation of electrodynamics was nonetheless used as the basis for attempts to explain gravitation. The route most frequently followed was an attempt to formulate 'relativistic' analogues for classical physical notions such as force, inertia, rigidity, and heat. Former colleagues, admirers, and students of Minkowski's, notably Gustav Herglotz, Jun Ishiwara, Max von Laue, Max Born, and Gunnar Nordström, as well as detractors of Minkowski, such as Max Abraham, attempted to elaborate the mathematician's electrodynamical formalism. Gunnar Nordström's work in the period 1909–15 may be taken as representative of the extent to which many physical theorists accepted Minkowski's mathematics and electrodynamics as the basis for constructing new world pictures.

In 1909, the well-known critic of the Lorentz electron theory Max Abraham challenged Minkowski's expression for the electromagnetic energy of matter.[37] In his paper on the basic equations of electrodynamics, Minkowski had postulated an asymmetric form for the electromagnetic force, and he had not included mechanical or elastic energy terms within the electromagnetic energy. Abraham assumed, on the contrary, that the electromagnetic force could be obtained by calculating the four-dimensional divergence of a symmetric tensor quantity. Abraham thought that this formulation implied that Minkowski's theory would give rise to mechanical torques which could not be eliminated by a coordinate transformation of electromagnetic momentum. Making use of his theory of the rigid electron, Abraham argued that Minkowski's electromagnetic force implied the existence of forces not of electromagnetic origin.

Abraham's approach was challenged by Gunnar Nordström, who had studied under Minkowski during the years 1906 and 1907 and who since that time had published several summaries of Minkowski's ideas on space–time in Finnish journals.[38] Nordström offered the opinion that Minkowski's formulation was indeed self-consistent.[39] He followed Minkowski in considering as the complete electromagnetic force a quantity that was normal to the four-dimensional velocity. Abraham objected that even if one believed in the principle of relativity, Minkowski's formulation for the electromagnetic force was incorrect because, in relativistic mechanics, the inertial mass had to depend upon all energies.[40] In particular, if Joule heat developed in the course of moving a material object, the object's rest mass density would have to change. Abraham observed that his formulation of the electromagnetic force should have been the more reasonable one: 'An experimental decision between them seems at present impossible. Hence, the choice that one makes is, in part, a matter of personal taste. Nonetheless, I would not be completely mistaken if I believed that the majority of all physicists who have watched the development of electrodynamics attentively would prefer the second interpretation [Abraham's own].'[41]

As an answer to Abraham, Nordström attempted to generalise his previous argument by demonstrating that Abraham's electromagnetic force contradicted the conservation of energy.[42] After a communication from Abraham, however, Nordström withdrew his argument.[43] Abraham

restated his case in favour of a symmetrical expression for the electromagnetic energy by revealing an apparent contradiction in Nordström's
exposition.[44] Abraham argued that Minkowski's expression for energy
conservation did not deal with the Joule heat phenomenon. He observed
that Nordström's attempt to add a Joule heat term to Minkowski's formulation of energy conservation in a non-covariant fashion was self-contradic-
tory. The difference between the two formulations of the Joule heat,
Abraham argued, was

$$Q_{\text{Nordström}} = \frac{Q_{\text{Abraham}}}{1 - (v/c)^2} .$$

Abraham appealed to Planck's argument that both entropy and the quantity $T(1 - v^2/c^2)^{-1/2}$ (where T was absolute temperature) were invariant
for a moving body.[45] According to the second law of thermodynamics, the
quantity $Q_{\text{Abraham}} (1 - v^2/c^2)^{-1/2}$ would accordingly have to be a scalar.
Nordström, however, arrived at a value for the Joule heat that was not
invariant. Abraham observed that Nordström's value contradicted
Planck's relativistic thermodynamics. Even within the theory of relativity,
then, Abraham's formulation of the electromagnetic force—not
Minkowski's—was consistent.

By 1911 Nordström was forced to agree with Abraham.[46] Nevertheless,
at around this time Nordström began to investigate the possibility of
reformulating the Newtonian law of gravitation by using Minkowski's
electrodynamics.[47] Several gravitational theories emerged from his attempt
to extend Minkowski's notion of an absolute continuum of matter in
space–time.[48] Following Minkowski's suggestions, Nordström did not
attempt to couple electromagnetic and gravitational interactions: Nordström insisted that the velocity of light remained uninfluenced by gravitational phenomena and kept rigorously constant in a vacuum. To obtain
the gravitational equations of motion, Nordström simply replaced
Minkowski's four-dimensional electrodynamic potential with a hypothetical, gravitational potential. As an unexpected consequence of his
theory, gravitational mass depended exponentially on the gravitational
potential ϕ : $m = m_0 \exp (\phi/c^2)$.

Deeply involved in general relativity, Einstein thought that Nordström's
theory led to the unsatisfying result that a 'rotating system in a gravitational field undergoes a smaller acceleration than a non-rotating system'.[49]
Since the equations of motion would therefore depend on the internal
structure of mass systems, the principle of equivalence (whereby physical
processes had to occur identically in an accelerating frame of reference
and in a gravitational field) could not be satisfied. Nordström did not
dispute Einstein's argument. He continued to examine the equivalence
principle in the light of relativistic mechanics of deformable bodies. He
wanted to reintroduce the notion of mass into the discussion of Max von

Laue and Gustav Herglotz, who had both considered relativistic rigid-body mechanics without ever questioning the 'concept of inertial mass'.[50] During July 1913, while vacationing in Zurich, Nordström substantially modified his original theory.[51] He attempted to eliminate the unusual exponential behaviour of mass by allowing the gravitational constant to depend on the potential. In order to determine the form for the gravitational potential, Nordström first considered the limited case where mass executed only time-independent motion and where the total impulse for the system was zero. His entire theory could be summarised in two sets of equations:

$$\Box \phi = c^2 v \qquad F_x = - c^2 v \log \phi_x \quad \text{etc}$$

where c was a universal constant, the velocity of light, and where v was the relativistic mass. In addition, Nordström showed by a method similar to one employed in constructing his first theory that the inertial mass of a body varied directly with the gravitational potential, whereas the gravitational mass of a body remained a constant. He demonstrated that both clock rates and measuring rods varied inversely with the scalar gravitational potential, and he recovered Abraham's results for the classical electromagnetic mass of the electron and for the energy of the electron's electric field. In 1914 he showed that the new theory did not contain the same flaw that Einstein had pointed out in the old one: in the new theory the behaviour of mass in a uniform gravitational field was not structure-dependent. Nordström concluded that his theory gave a retardation instead of the observed advance in the anomalous perihelion shift for planetary orbital precessions.[52]

Einstein considered Nordström's second theory more favourably than that of any other competitor.[53] In February 1914 Einstein and Adriaan Daniel Fokker reformulated Nordström's second theory by using differential geometry.[54] One month later, in March, Nordström admitted the insufficiency of his results. He began looking for direction to Gustav Mie's electrodynamical field theory rather than to general relativity.[55] At the time, Nordström, like David Hilbert, thought that Mie's work embodied the legacy of Minkowski's physics. Throughout 1914 and 1915 Nordström was intensely occupied with the search for a theory to unify gravitation and electromagnetism. Finally, in 1916, he accepted Einstein's covariant formulation of general relativity and the intimation of a future unified field theory.[56]

Conclusion

In the period after 1912, Nordström was only one of many physicists and mathematicians who attempted to extend Minkowski's ideas to phenomena involving matter and gravitation. He was, nevertheless, one of the interpreters most sensitive to the physical consequences of Minkowski's theories. Some mathematicians thought that it was entirely reasonable to base theories of electrodynamics and gravitation on mathematically convenient hypotheses concerning physical structure. Minkowski's close friend and colleague Hilbert saw his own axiomatic exposition of general relativity as equivalent to Einstein's, anticipating 'a general reduction of all physical constants to mathematical constants' that would make physics 'a science the same as geometry'.[57] In Einstein's view Hilbert's work was childlike, 'in the sense of children who know no malice in the world'.[58] Hermann Weyl formulated a field theory for electromagnetism and gravitation by requiring that four-dimensional lengths depend on their past movements;[59] Einstein replied:

> Could one really accuse the Lord God of being inconsistent if he passed up the opportunity discovered by you to harmonize the physical world? I think not. If he had made the world according to your plan [I would have said] to him reproachfully: 'Dear God, if it did not lie within Thy power to give an objective meaning to the [equality of sizes of separated rigid bodies] why hast Thou, Oh Incomprehensible One, not disdained . . . to [preserve their shapes]?'[60]

Interventions by Hilbert, Weyl and other mathematicians in the theories of relativity exerted a profound influence on theoretical physics after the First World War. Canons of aesthetics, consistency, completeness, and meaningfulness that were current in the discipline of pure mathematics found a receptive audience in physicists who were confronted with a picture of microscopic reality that seemed increasingly incompatible with physical world views formulated according to established principles in theoretical physics. Einstein's friend and collaborator Erwin Finlay Freundlich exaggerated when, in 1920, he wrote that general relativity, a great triumph for pure mathematics, was developed 'by sheer mathematical skill'.[61]

Einstein's and Minkowski's views on the special theory of relativity reflected the methodological preferences of others who were formulating physical theories in the late Wilhelmian period. Einstein self-consciously adhered to and came to exemplify the views of classical physics.[62] Minkowski, gifted with a pure mathematician's insight, provided inspiration for mathematicians who were less concerned with synthesising new physical world pictures than with formulating a mathematically elegant exposition of known physical laws according to established physical understanding. During the period before the First World War mathematicians increasingly thought, along with the historian of mathematics Wilhelm Lorey, that *mathematical physics*—the field that included all mathematical treatments of physical reality—lay halfway between mathematics and physics. Theoretical physics in Lorey's view was a subset of mathematical physics. He noted in 1916 that Minkowski and Hilbert had shown how pure mathematics was related to mathematical physics.[63] 'The end of mathematical physics is not merely to facilitate the numerical calculation of certain constants or the integration of certain differential equations', noted Henri Poincaré, a mathematician whose work Minkowski followed closely. 'It is above all to disclose to the physicist the concealed harmonies of things by furnishing him with a new point of view.'[64] As understood by Poincaré, mathematical physics was a subdiscipline of mathematics. In this perspective the Einstein–Minkowski difference illustrates how a scientific theory is received by branches of two different disciplines.[65]

Minkowski's physics was the prism through which many researchers saw Einstein's special theory of relativity in the late Wilhelmian period, and from which many tried to interpret and extend gravitational theory in the light of Einstein's general relativity. By the end of the First World War, Minkowski's work came to be seen by mathematicians such as Klein, Hilbert, and Weyl not merely as a geometrical expression of Einstein's ideas but as something more: an example of how pure mathematics might successfully resolve problems in physical theory.

Notes and references

1 Russell McCormmach discusses the early attitudes of Einstein toward mathematics in his 'Editor's Foreword' to volume 7 of *Historical Studies in the Physical Sciences* (1976) pp xi–xxxv.
2 A Einstein, *Relativity: The Special and General Theory*, transl R W Lawson (New York 1920) p 68; Einstein, *The Meaning of Relativity* (Princeton 1931) p 31.
3 As recorded in Einstein's matriculation record, Wissenschaftshistorische Sammlung of the ETH-Bibliothek, Zurich.
4 A Einstein, 'Autobiographical Notes', in *Albert Einstein—Philosopher-Scientist* ed P A Schilpp (Evanston, Ill 1949) p 16.
5 Historical treatments of Minkowski's approach to the principle of relativity include Tetu Hirosige's 'Theory of Relativity and the Ether', *Japanese Studies in the History of Science* no 7 (1968) 37–53, esp 46–8; Stanley Goldberg's *Early Response to Einstein's Theory of Relativity, 1905–1911: A Case Study in National Differences* (dissertation, Harvard University 1968), esp chapter 2; József Illy's 'On the Birth of Minkowski's Four-Dimensional World', *Proceedings of the XIIIth International Congress of the History of Science, 18–24 August 1971. Section VI. The History of Physics and Astronomy* (Moscow 1974) pp 67–72; Gerald Holton's 'The Metaphor of Space–Time Events in Science', *Eranos Jahrbuch* **34** (1965) 33–78; Peter Galison's 'Minkowski's Space–Time: From Visual Thinking to the Absolute World', *Hist. Stud. Phys. Sci.* **10** (1979) 85–121.
6 H Minkowski, cited in *Einstein: The Man and His Achievement* ed G J Whitrow

(New York 1973) p 5; Banesh Hoffmann, assisted by Helen Dukas, *Albert Einstein: Creator and Rebel* (New York 1972) p 85; Max Born, reported in C Seelig's *Albert Einstein: A Documentary Biography* transl M Savill (London 1956) p 28.

7 Untitled manuscript, n.d., Mathematisches Archiv **60**: 4. Handschriften-Sammlung, Niedersächsische Staats- und Universitätsbibliothek, Göttingen.

8 A Einstein and J Laub, 'Ueber die elektromagnetischen Grundgleichungen für bewegte Körper', *Annalen der Physik* **26** (1908) 532–40. The issue is discussed in chapter 9.

9 P Frank, 'Die Stellung des Relativitätsprinzips im System der Mechanik und der Elektrodynamik', Vienna, Kaiserliche Akademie der Wissenschaften, Mathematisch–naturwissenschaftliche Klasse, *Sitzungsberichte* **118** (1909) 373–446.

10 H Minkowski, 'Das Relativitätsprinzip', *Ann. Phys.* **47** (1915) 927–38.

11 'Das Relativitätsprinzip, von H Minkowski. Abgedruckt in den Ann. d. Phys. 1915, Correktur nach dem anderen Exemplar teilweise ergänzt. A.S.' Math. Archiv. **60**: 3. Handschriften-Sammlung, Niedersächsische Staats- und Universitätsbibliothek, Göttingen.

12 *Ibid* p 6.

13 *Ibid* p 16.

14 H Minkowski, 'Relativitätsprinzip' (ref 10) pp 927–8.

15 H Mierendorff, 'Die partiellen Differenzialgleichungen der Elektrodynamik', Hilbert Nachlass 570/5. Niedersächsische Staats- und Universitätsbibliothek, Göttingen.

16 In 1907 Lorentz's formulation of Maxwellian electrodynamics and his electron theory were accepted by most physical scientists and mathematicians at Göttingen. Exceptions were the theoretician Max Abraham and the experimentalist Walter Kaufmann (*Privatdozent* at Göttingen from 1899 to 1903). In opposition to Lorentz's electron whose shape depended on velocity, Abraham proposed a theory of the rigid electron. There is no evidence to suggest, however, that Hilbert was attracted to Abraham's theory. On Lorentz's electrodynamics see Tetu Hirosige's 'Origins of Lorentz' Theory of Electrons and the Concept of the Electromagnetic Field', *Hist. Stud. Phys. Sci.* **1** (1969) 151–209; Russell McCormmach's 'H A Lorentz and the Electromagnetic View of Nature', *Isis* **61** (1970) 469–97; on Abraham's theory see Stanley Goldberg's 'The Abraham Theory of the Electron. The Symbiosis of Experiment and Theory', *Archive for History of Exact Sciences* **7** (1970–71) 7–25.

17 M Planck, 'Zur Dynamik bewegter Systeme', *Ann. Phys.* **26** (1908) 1–34. First presented to the Prussian Academy of Sciences on 13 June 1907.

18 H Poincaré, 'Sur la Dynamique de l'électron', *Rendiconti del Circolo Matematico di Palermo* **21** (1906) 129–75. See Arthur I Miller's 'A Study of Henri Poincaré's "Sur la Dynamique de l'Electron"', *Arch. Hist. Exact Sci.* **10** (1973) 207–328; compare I Iu Kobzarev's 'Henri Poincaré's St Louis Lecture and Theoretical Physics on the Eve of the Theory of Relativity', *Soviet Physics Uspekhi* **17** (1975) 584–92.

19 Typescript of ten pages, with the struck-out title 'Funktionentheorie'. Hermann Minkowski papers, box IX, folder 4, Niels Bohr Library of the American Institute of Physics, New York.

20 *Ibid* pp 8–10.
21 H Minkowski, 'Die Grundgleichungen für die elektromagnetischen Vorgänge in bewegten Körpern', Göttingen, Königliche Gesellschaft der Wissenschaften, Mathematisch–physikalische Klasse, *Nachrichten* (1908) pp 53–111. Reprinted in *Gesammelte Abhandlungen von Hermann Minkowski* ed D Hilbert (Berlin 1911) **2** 352–404.
22 *Ibid* 352–53.
23 Three secondary sources are invaluable for understanding gravitational thought in this period. First is J Zenneck's article, 'Gravitation', completed in 1901 for the *Encyklopädie der mathematischen Wissenschaften* I 26–72. Second is Samuel Oppenheim's article, 'Kritik des Newtonschen Gravitationsgesetzes', completed in 1920, also for the *Encyklopädie* **VI** section 2.2, 80–158. The *Encyklopädie* was published by the academies of sciences at Göttingen, Munich, Leipzig, and Vienna; it appeared fascicule by fascicule between 1898 and 1935. Third is the treatment by John David North, *The Measure of the Universe* (Oxford 1965), which organises most of the sources mentioned by Zenneck into topics reflecting cosmological considerations. See also John F Woodward's *The Search for a Mechanism: Action-at-a-Distance in Gravitational Theory* (dissertation, University of Denver 1972).
24 Simon Newcomb, *The Elements of the Four Inner Planets and the Fundamental Constants of Astronomy: Supplement to the American Ephemeris and Nautical Almanac for 1897* (Washington, DC 1895). See Paul I Cohen's *Relativity and the Excess Advances of Perihelia in Planetary Orbits* (MA dissertation, University of Pennsylvania 1971) pp 84–91; J Chazy's *La Théorie de la relativité et la mécanique céleste* I (Paris 1928) 163–84. An excellent general account may be found in Antonie Pannekoek's *A History of Astronomy* (New York 1961).
25 H von Seeliger, 'Ueber das Newtonsche Gravitationsgesetz', *Astronomische Nachrichten* **137** (1895) 129–36. H von Seeliger, 'Ueber das Newtonsche Gravitationsgesetz', Munich, Königliche-bayerische Akademie der Wissenschaften, Mathematisch–physikalische Classe, *Sitzungsberichte* **26** (1896) 373–400. Einstein's comments on Seeliger's proposals are given in 'Considerations on the Universe as a Whole', in *Theories of the Universe* ed M K Munitz (New York 1957) p 276. See also Max Jammer's *Concepts of Mass* (New York 1964) pp 127–8.
26 Ernst Mach, *Die Mechanik in ihrer Entwicklung* (Leipzig 1889) pp 213–19. See Jammer (ref 25), pp 91–7; H Groener, 'Mach's Principle and Einstein's Theory of Gravitation', in *Ernst Mach: Physicist and Philosopher* ed R S Cohen and R J Seeger, volume 6 of *Boston Studies in the Philosophy of Science* (Dordrecht 1970) pp 200–215; Norman J Golden, *Some Aspects of Mach's Principle within the Theory of General Relativity* (dissertation, University of Wyoming 1971).
27 R von Eötvös, 'Untersuchungen über Gravitation und Erdmagnetismus', *Ann. Phys.* **59** (1896) 354–400.
28 H A Lorentz, 'Considerations on Gravitation', Amsterdam, Royal Academy of Sciences, *Proceedings* **2** (1900) 559–74, analysed intensively in R McCormmach's 'H A Lorentz' (ref 16) 476–8.
29 W Wien, 'Ueber die Möglichkeit einer elektromagnetischen Begründung der Mechanik', *Ann. Phys.* **5** (1901) 501–14.

30 R Gans, 'Gravitation und Elektromagnetismus', *Physikalische Zeitschrift* **6** (1905) 803–5.

31 F Wacker, 'Ueber Gravitation und Elektromagnetismus', *Phys. Z.* **7** (1906) 300–2.

32 A Wilkens, 'Zur Gravitationstheorie', *Phys. Z.* **7** (1906) 846–50.

33 Nearly twenty years later F W Lanchester treated Minkowski's ideas, although his exposition was not faithful to Minkowski's original text. F W Lanchester, *Relativity: An elementary explanation of the space–time relation as established by Minkowski, and a discussion of gravitational theory based thereon* (London 1935).

34 See, for example, Otto Dziobek's *Mathematical Theories of Planetary Motion* transl M W Harrington and W J Hussey (1892; New York 1962) pp 13–15.   ·

35 A Sommerfeld, 'Zur Relativitätstheorie: II. Vierdimensionale Vektoranalyse', *Ann. Phys.* **33** (1910) 649–89, esp 684–9.

36 M B Weinstein, *Kräfte und Spannung: Das Gravitations- und Strahlenfeld* (Brunswick 1914) p 62.

37 M Abraham, 'Zur elektromagnetischen Mechanik', *Phys. Z.* **10** (1909) 737–41.

38 The difference between Minkowski's and Abraham's expressions for electromagnetic force is considered by Wolfgang Pauli, *Theory of Relativity*, transl Henry Brose (New York 1958) pp 108–11.

39 G Nordström, 'Zur Elektrodynamik Minkowskis', *Phys. Z.* **10** (1909) 681–7.

40 M Abraham, 'Mechanik' (ref 37) p 739.

41 *Ibid* p 740.

42 G Nordström, 'Zur elektromagnetischen Mechanik', *Phys. Z.* **11** (1910) 440–5.

43 *Ibid* pp 444, 445.

44 M Abraham, 'Die Bewegungsgleichungen eines Massenteilchens in der Relativtheorie', *Phys. Z.* **11** (1910) 527–31. See Pauli's *Relativity* (ref 38) pp 106–8.

45 M Planck, 'Das Prinzip der Relativität und die Grundgleichungen der Mechanik', *Verhandlungen der deutschen physikalischen Gesellschaft* **8** (1906) 136–41.

46 G Nordström, 'Zur Relativitätsmechanik deformierbarer Körper', *Phys. Z.* **12** (1911) 854.

47 For expositions of Nordström's theory, see M Abraham's 'Neuere Gravitationstheorien', *Jahrbuch der Radioaktivität und Elektronik* **11** (1914) 484–96; A L Harvey, 'A Brief Review of Lorentz-Covariant Theories of Gravitation', *American Journal of Physics* **33** (1965) 449–60.

48 G Nordström, 'Relativitätsprinzip und Gravitation', *Phys. Z.* **13** (1912) 1126–9.

49 Nordström mentioned Einstein's scalar theory in an afterword to his paper, *ibid* 1129. Most of the afterword has been translated by G D Birkhoff, 'Newtonian and Other Forms of Gravitational Theory, II. Relativistic Theories', *Scientific Monthly* **58** (1944) 136, from which this quotation is taken. See also Eugene Guth's 'Contribution to the History of Einstein's Geometry as a Branch of Physics', in *Relativity* ed Moshe Carmeli *et al* (New York 1970) p 175.

50 G Nordström, 'Träge und schwere Masse in der Relativitätsmechanik', *Ann. Phys.* **40** (1913) 856.

51 G Nordström, 'Zur Theorie der Gravitation vom Standpunkt des Relativitätsprinzips', *Ann. Phys.* **42** (1913) 533–54.

52 G Nordström, 'Die Fallgesetze und Planetbewegungen in der Relativitäts-theorie', *Ann. Phys.* **43** (1914) 1101–10. See also M Behacker's 'Der freie Fall und die Planetenbewegung in Nordströms Gravitationstheorie', *Phys. Z.* **14** (1913) 989–92.

53 Einstein to Erwin Finlay Freundlich, 1913. Einstein Archives, Princeton University Library.

54 A Einstein and A D Fokker, 'Die Nordströmsche Gravitationstheorie vom Standpunkt des absoluten Differentialkalküls', *Ann. Phys.* **44** (1914) 321–8.

55 G Nordström, 'Ueber die Möglichkeit, das elektromagnetische Feld und das Gravitationsfeld zu vereinigen', *Phys. Z.* **15** (1914) 504–6.

56 On Nordström's later work elaborating general relativity, see, for example, H Tallqvist's 'Gunnar Nordström', *Finska Vetenskaps-Societeten Minestrecknigar och Föredrag* (1924) 14 pp separatum.

57 D Hilbert, 'Die Grundlagen der Physik. I.', Göttingen Gesellschaft der Wissen-schaften, Mathematisch–physikalische Klasse, *Nachrichten* (1915) p 407. Hilbert saw his treatment as an extension of Minkowski's work. Peter Debye, called to the chair of theoretical physics at Göttingen in 1913, believed that Hilbert's entire approach to physics was strongly influenced by Minkowski's work. Interview between Debye, T S Kuhn, and G Uhlenbeck, 3 May 1962, Archive for History of Quantum Physics, American Philosophical Society, Philadelphia.

58 A Einstein to Hermann Weyl, 23 November 1916. Einstein Archives, Princeton University Library.

59 H Weyl, *Raum–Zeit–Materie* (Berlin 1918).

60 A Einstein to H Weyl, 1918. Translated in Hoffmann's *Einstein* (ref 6) p 224. Brackets and ellipses are given by Hoffmann.

61 E Freundlich, *Foundation of Einstein's Theory of Gravitation*, transl H L Brose (Cambridge 1920) p xv.

62 The values of German theoretical physicists in the late nineteenth century have been discussed in R McCormmach's 'Editor's Foreword', *Hist. Stud. Phys. Sci.* **3** (1971) ix–xxiv.

63 W Lorey, *Das Studium der Mathematik an den deutschen Universitäten seit Anfang des 19. Jahrhunderts* (Leipzig 1916) pp 260–3.

64 H Poincaré, 'The Relations of Analysis and Mathematical Physics', transl C J Keyser, *Bulletin of the American Mathematical Society* **4** (1898) 251.

65 That mathematical and theoretical physicists take different approaches to physical laws has been suggested by T S Kuhn *et al*, *Sources for the History of Quantum Physics* (Philadelphia 1967) [*Am. Phil. Soc. Mem.* **68**] p 146; L Pyenson, 'La Réception de la relativité généralisée: disciplinarité et institution-alisation en physique', *Revue d'histoire des sciences* **28** (1975) 61–73.

5　Physics in the shadow of mathematics: the Göttingen electron-theory seminar of 1905

Introduction

How Einstein's thought differed from that of his contemporaries has been the subject of meticulous and lengthy historical discussion over the past generation. From studies by Tetu Hirosige, Stanley Goldberg, and Russell McCormmach, to mention the work of only three historians of science, we know in what ways Einstein's understanding of special relativity distinguished itself from that of Hendrik Antoon Lorentz, Max Abraham, Henri Poincaré and Max Planck.[1] Philosophers and physicists, too, have considered why Einstein's approach to electrodynamics was superior to that of his contemporaries; they have contributed some light and not a little smoke to the issue.[2]

In the present chapter I offer another way to view Einstein's unique contribution. I consider how, in the summer of 1905, a group of experts with established scientific credentials set out in an interdisciplinary seminar to solve the outstanding problems of electrodynamical theory. The group was working at one of the world's foremost centres of mathematics, the University of Göttingen. By the time that the seminar ended, eight weeks or so short of the publication of Einstein's paper, the participants had not achieved the solution that they sought. Although the seminar failed in its aim while Einstein's synthesis succeeded, the group gave expression to the way that many mathematicians and physical scientists at the time sought after nature's laws. The seminar presaged later elaborations of Einstein's theory by its leaders David Hilbert, Hermann Minkowski, Emil Wiechert, and Gustav Herglotz, as well as those by students Max von Laue and Max Born. It may also be taken as a milestone in the career paths of other Göttingen *Dozenten* and alumni, for example Karl Schwarzschild, Max Abraham, and Arnold Sommerfeld, whose work was closely analysed by the seminarists. In the scientific papers considered by the seminar many results were presented for the physics of elementary particles which were recovered and publicised widely only a generation later.

The seminar syllabus

We are fortunate in having a record of precisely the sources that Göttingen mathematicians and physicists considered essential, in 1905, for setting electrodynamical theory in order. The record is an undated one-page outline for a seminar on the basic equations of the electron theory which is preserved in the David Hilbert *Nachlass* at Göttingen.[3] From the penmanship it is almost certainly written by Herglotz and annotated by Hilbert. In this period advanced seminars on interdisciplinary topics taught by as many as four *Dozenten* were common at Göttingen. They were the pride of instruction in mathematics and the exact sciences. It was not unusual, then, that the electron-theory seminar would be conducted by professors of mathematics Hilbert and Minkowski, professor of geophysics Wiechert, and *Privatdozent* Herglotz. At least fifteen students, indicated by name, attended the seminar. Among those students who would later make their mark were physicists Max Born, Heinrich Blasius, the Glaswegian Robert Alexander Houstoun and post-doctoral auditor Max von Laue; mathematicians Heinrich Tietze and New Englander Elias Swift; and astronomer Arnold Kohlschütter.

The date of the outline can be established with certainty. According to the course listings for Göttingen provided in the *Physikalische Zeitschrift* during the period between 1899 and 1914, only one seminar, that on electron theory in the summer of 1905, was conducted by these four *Dozenten*. Furthermore, the official register of personnel and students at Göttingen for the 1905 summer semester provides positive identification for ten of the fifteen students indicated on the outline. Seminar students Meyer and Miller were no doubt in attendance in 1905, although it is not possible to choose among the several people listed in the register with these surnames. Only for three students listed on the outline does no trace remain.[4]

The aim of the electron-theory seminar was indicated by Felix Klein, originator of the interdisciplinary-seminar practice and *éminence grise* of Göttingen mathematical sciences, when Klein addressed a complementary collective seminar in electrotechnology on 3 May 1905. Taught by himself, professor of applied mathematics Carl Runge, associate professor of physics Hermann Theodor Simon, and associate professor of technical physics Ludwig Prandtl, the electrotechnology seminar would not consider difficult mathematics or physics. Klein intended there to arrive at a command of technical reality through figures, numerical calculations, and experiments. Different from his own seminar, Klein elaborated to his class, the seminar of Hilbert, Minkowski, Wiechert, and Herglotz would consider 'difficult mathematical problems' in 'theoretical physics'.[5]

The writings of Henri Poincaré and especially Hendrik Antoon Lorentz dominated the seminar syllabus. They were, in 1905, acknowledged as possibly the greatest scientists in France and the Netherlands respectively. Both were world authorities on the mathematical treatment of electromagnetism. To consider the state of electrodynamics one could have done no better than to begin with their texts. Three treatises were especially important for the seminar. First was Lorentz's study of 1895 on electromagnetic and optical phenomena in moving bodies, his *Versuch*. In it Lorentz elaborated his notion of a stationary ether and local time, and he provided a treatment of the electromagnetic field which was independent of classical dynamics.[6] The second important text consisted of Poincaré's 1901 treatise on electricity and optics.[7] Poincaré's text was a revision of an earlier work based on lectures that he gave at Paris in 1888 and 1890. In the earlier work Poincaré had discussed Heinrich Hertz's experiments in some detail. Edited by two of Poincaré's assistants, the revision added material from Poincaré's 1899 lectures where he compared the different theories relating to the electrodynamics of bodies in motion, principally the theories of Hertz, Lorentz, and Joseph Larmor. Although for Poincaré none of these theories was entirely satisfactory each had valuable parts; Lorentz's seemed the most suitable overall. Poincaré's text presented little original material. It assimilated for French readers the theoretical contributions of foreign physicists.

The final and critical guide for the electron-theory seminar came from Lorentz's 1904 article on the electron theory, written for Arnold Sommerfeld's volume on mechanics in Felix Klein's encyclopaedia of mathematical sciences.[8] It was a magisterial exposition, one that lay at the base of all subsequent work in the field. The article began with the basic equations of electron theory, passed to calculation of the field of moving electrons, and, finally, discussed electromagnetic processes in moving bodies. It closed with a treatment of approximate solutions for moving systems. Lorentz analysed nearly every paper in the field published in any language before December 1903. The leaders of the Göttingen seminar quite rightly saw Lorentz's 135-page article as an exhaustive review of electron theory. They used it as one would use an encyclopaedic text for a one-semester course today.

Upon comparing the contents of Lorentz's article with the seminar syllabus, it is evident that the article furnished the basic bibliography for sessions one to six, that is, for two-thirds of the seminar. The first three sessions directly recapitulated the first twenty or so pages of Lorentz's treatment. Here Lorentz integrated the potential wave equation, formulated the Poynting energy flux, introduced Karl Schwarzschild's electron Lagrangian or electrokinetic potential, and considered electromagnetic impulse. Lorentz then went on to form the fundamental equations of the electron theory by means of a principle of least action, deriving equations for a moving coordinate system. In particular, he showed how the scalar potential was covariant under that which Poincaré later called a 'Lorentz transformation'. (Lorentz did not, of course, use terminology from group theory.) After introducing the Liénard–Wiechert retarded potentials, Lorentz recovered Max Abraham's values for electromagnetic mass. He discussed Abraham's and Schwarzschild's results for slowly accelerated electrons, or quasistationary motion. In the second half of his article, Lorentz treated electron phenomena in ponderable bodies, appealing to his own previous work as well as that of Joseph Larmor, Gilbert T Walker and Poincaré's 1901 published lectures. Lorentz concluded with an analysis of the negative effect of the Michelson ether-drift experiments.

Which material did the seminar not pull from Lorentz's article? Primarily interested in mathematical elaborations of elementary phenomena, the Göttingen *Dozenten* paid very little attention to the extensive discussion of macroscopic processes that could be explained by the electron theory. Lorentz generously cited the work of Joseph John Thomson, but there is no indication that this research was read by the seminar. In considering the movement of electrons in metals Lorentz even mentioned, without more than passing comment, two of Planck's papers from 1901 on the law of equipartition of energy and the quantum of radiation. Of course, the seminar did not explore these seminal thoughts.[9]

Besides studying the three classic texts by distinguished foreigners, the Göttingen seminar members devoted their attention to elaborations of Lorentz's work by their own number or by their close colleagues. Although from Poincaré's earlier publications seminarists could have come into contact with his appeal to a principle of relativity, they would have missed Poincaré's elaboration in 1904 of the principle.[10] Perhaps most significantly, they would not have read the 1904 paper of Lorentz where he introduced in full grandeur the celebrated transformation that now bears his name.[11]

As one of Germany's learned academies, the Göttingen Scientific Society received the *Comptes-rendus* of Paris, the Amsterdam *Proceedings*, and the Haarlem *Archives néerlandaises* (in addition to all the usual physics journals like the *Bulletin des sciences mathématiques*), the outlets for Poincaré's and Lorentz's thought. Since three of the four seminar *Dozenten* were Society members, not to follow the progress of Lorentz and Poincaré in electrodynamics beyond 1903 was a deliberate move. Using the classic text of Lorentz as a point of departure, the seminar *Dozenten* sought to extend electrodynamical theory by means of sophisticated mathematical analysis. They wanted to provide a new structure for the formal representation of electromagnetism. To clarify this orientation it is well to consider what each of the four brought to the seminar in terms of prior commitments and intellectual capital.

The seminar's leaders

The seminar's leaders occupied special positions in the cosmology of the academic world at Göttingen. In his 1907 history treating Göttingen mathematics, Felix Klein traced three traditions of mathematical sciences back to the end of the eighteenth century.[12] The oldest tradition, that of mathematical pedagogy where mathematics was a discipline serving the needs of other specialities and future schoolteachers, began with Abraham Gotthelf Kästner and followed through the nineteenth century to Klein himself and Carl Runge. The most recent tradition, that of physics, began with Wilhelm Weber and, during Weber's self-imposed political exile in Leipzig from 1837 to 1849 as one of the 'Göttingen Seven', Johann Benedict Listing. Chairs following the physics tradition in 1905 were held by Woldemar Voigt, Hermann Theodor Simon, Ludwig Prandtl, Friedrich Dolezalek, and Eduard Riecke.

The third tradition was that of astronomy, for so Klein characterised the principal research and lecturing interests of Carl Friedrich Gauss. In the period around 1860 Gauss's chair divided into three parts. Direct heritor of Gauss was Peter Gustav Lejeune Dirichlet, and following him came, in sequence, Bernhard Riemann, Alfred Clebsch, Lazarus Fuchs, Hermann Amandus Schwarz, Heinrich Weber, and in 1895 Hilbert. Minkowski's Göttingen *ordinarius*, created in 1902, complemented Hilbert's. The two other lines traced to Gauss were in observational and theoretical astronomy. In 1905 chairs in these traditions were held by Martin Brendel, Leopold Ambronn, Karl Schwarzschild, and Emil Wiechert.

According to Klein, then, each of the professors in the 1905 electron-theory seminar followed in Gauss's footsteps. As *Privatdozent* of mathematical astronomy, Herglotz would have been placed in the same tradition. Unlike the physicists or the pedagogues, *Dozenten* in Gauss's tradition would be expected to follow his example by applying mathematics to solve outstanding problems in physical theory while at the same time cultivating an appreciation for the intrinsic value of mathematical thought. With the singular exception of Ambronn, the twentieth-century heirs to Gauss's line admirably carried out their task.[13]

Among the four seminar *Dozenten* Wiechert came closest to fulfilling the Gaussian ideal.[14] Descended from an East Prussian family in Tilsit, he received a doctorate at Königsberg in 1889 under Paul Volkmann. Wiechert's adviser was an experimental physicist of limited research ability, who, upon becoming *ordinarius* in 1894, devoted his efforts to elaborating a conventionalist and inductivist philosophy of science. For Volkmann all physical hypotheses were intuitive constructs grounded in experience, and mathematics was no more than an exact way of stating laws and propositions that were derived through imprecise observations.[15] When Wiechert was *Privatdozent* at Königsberg, he followed his mentor in seeking theoretical constructs behind observations. He argued that atoms were undoubtedly centres of force in the electromagnetic ether, and although his principal interest was the mathematical description of meteorology and geology, he directed a portion of his research energies to the electromagnetic theory of the ether.[16]

In 1897 Wiechert arrived in Göttingen as assistant to Ernst Schering at the observatory. His charge included geodesy, earth magnetism, and theoretical astronomy. A year later he became associate professor and soon began to build a new geophysical institute, completed in 1901. Wiechert then took up residence with his mother at the observatory on the hill outside Göttingen. Wiechert's mother wanted her son's restless activity to be tempered by a wife.[17] A man who kept to himself, Wiechert finally married a colleague's daughter in 1908. Despite his considerable responsibilities at the observatory, by 1905 Wiechert was an acknowledged authority on electrodynamic theory, having formulated in 1900 the 'retarded potentials' that bear his name.

Like Wiechert, the youngest *Dozent* of the seminar, Gustav Herglotz, was a polymath. Son of a notary, Herglotz distinguished himself under Ludwig Boltzmann's tutelage at the University of Vienna.[18] Fascinated by astronomy, in 1900 he moved to Munich where two years later he received a doctorate *summa cum laude* under Rudolf von Seeliger for a dissertation on the celestial mechanics of the asteroid Eros. Seeliger agreed that Herglotz should receive the *venia legendi* under Klein. In April 1903 Herglotz began to devote himself to the electron theory at the same time that he was writing a *Habilitationsschrift* on the three-body problem. Electrons were in his view amenable to the same formalism that was then used in describing celestial mechanics. Herglotz carried on a lively correspondence about his two efforts with Karl Schwarzschild, the young Göttingen astronomy professor who had also been a student of Seeliger's and was then also studying the electron theory.[19] By 1905 Herglotz and Schwarzschild had established their credentials in the field.

As the most distinguished *Dozent* in the seminar, Hilbert had a reputation resting securely on accomplishments in pure mathematics. Increasingly, though, he was tempted by mechanics. In the closing years of the nineteenth century he and Klein together had offered several advanced seminars on this subject.[20] Hilbert's approach exhibited little in the way of a physical commitment. Let us consider, as an example, the lecture that he delivered on 26 October 1905 before his class on mechanics. He emphasised there the classical point of view, citing Gustav Kirchhoff that the task of mechanics was to describe the motion of matter in the most complete and simplest way. From this definition Hilbert drew the conclusion that 'mechanics furnishes the foundation for physics and for all natural sciences'. He compared mechanics with geometry. Like mechanics, geometry in principle originated from experimenting with nature; geometry was for Hilbert a purely theoretical science that treated only the logical consequences of simple, empirically derived laws. In geometry, axiomatic systems could recover all known facts and could establish, as . well, new ones. Mechanics was not yet at this stage; its facts were quite complicated and new experimental results continually appeared. Hilbert's faith lay in geometry: 'Above all we must strive to create in mechanics a complete, axiomatised, mathematical science; this is the aim of its development.' Hilbert quoted the experimental physicist Adolf Wüllner with approval, that the success of a science depended on how well it made use of mathematics.[21]

The fourth *Dozent* for the electron-theory seminar was Hermann Minkowski, best known today, of course, for his stunning publication in 1908 of a four-dimensional formalism for Einstein's special theory of relativity. According to the recollections of Max Born, during the 1905 seminar Minkowski introduced thoughts that later appeared in his famous papers.[22] These recollections impel us to consider in some detail what Minkowski would have brought to the seminar.

Like his good friend Hilbert, Minkowski was a pure mathematician increasingly drawn to consider physical phenomena. As *Privatdozent* at Bonn in the late 1880s, Minkowski published a paper on the motion of a rigid body in an incompressible fluid not constrained by mechanical forces.[23] According to a letter sent to Hilbert in 1889, he was at the time studying Voigt's treatment of elasticity.[24] From this reference we can only speculate whether, in the course of his readings, Minkowski looked through Voigt's 1887 paper on the Doppler principle. There Voigt applied what is now known as the Lorentz transformation to wave equations (those of the form $(1/c^2) \, \partial^2 \phi / \partial t^2 - \nabla^2 \phi = 0$).[25]

In his letter of 1889 Minkowski recognised that abstract speculation was not sufficient for physical understanding; he commented that it was inconceivable to him that anyone would develop mathematical equations only with the *hope* that someone might later demonstrate their utility. Implied in the word *utility* was application to physical problems. While at Bonn, Minkowski followed physics with some interest. In a letter to Hilbert of 1890, Minkowski remarked that he had been contaminated by a physical disease requiring that he undergo a ten-day quarantine before he would be mathematically pure enough to join Hilbert and his old friend Adolf Hurwitz in Königsberg. Minkowski continued that he was swimming in 'physically navigable' water, and that he had just become a magician:

I have devoted myself for the time being totally to the magic of physics. I have my practical exercises in the physical institute. At home I study Thomson, Helmholtz, and their consorts. Indeed, starting at the end of next week, I work several days a week in a blue smock in an institute, producing physical instruments. Thus, I'm a practical man of the most disgraceful sort.[26]

The approach of the director of the Bonn physical institute, Heinrich Hertz, was undoubtedly important in Mnkowski's decision to devote his vacation to physics.[27] At this time, Hertz was well into his critique. of Maxwellian electrodynamics.

It is difficult to say when Minkowski's interest in mechanics rekindled after he left Hertz's laboratory. It is clear, however, that when he was called to the Zurich Polytechnikum as professor of mathematics, he prepared a course on analytical mechanics for the winter semester of 1896/97. As he wrote to Hilbert in January 1897, despite his efforts the course was proceeding well for neither the professor nor the students. Attendance had declined drastically, even among the most clever students. Even 'the real mathematicians, whose number is however very small, are so tied up with the other courses they have to take that they can enjoy only what has been cut up, taken apart, and accordingly funnelled into their forcibly opened mouths.'[28]

Minkowski realised that he had a difficult, demanding style of lecturing but he wondered whether this whole affair did not make him appear ridiculous in the eyes of the 'masters'. One of the masters whom he had in mind was Felix Klein. Toward the end of his letter, Minkowski asked Hilbert whether Klein's attempt to introduce technical mathematics for the first time into a German university was succeeding. Minkowski held Klein in high esteem, and he conveyed the impression that his own efforts were a more modest version of Klein's approach.[29] Writing to Hilbert during 1899, Minkowski affirmed Felix Klein's efforts to unite pure and applied mathematics: 'I always have the idea that, one day, I will help Klein against his many critics by demonstrating that the mathematician can really do something of practical value, and something better than to determine the motion of tops.'[30] Minkowski here referred to Klein and Arnold Sommerfeld's study of the motion of tops, ultimately to become a treatise that encompassed much of mechanics.[31]

Minkowski, while agreeing with Klein, felt that Klein's polemics in favour of applied mathematics were not really necessary. For Minkowski, there was no doubt that pure mathematics could contribute to practical, physical problems. Minkowski persisted with physics. In 1898, he wrote to Hilbert that he was working 'principally with mathematical physics, especially thermodynamics, which I will teach in the summer'.[32] In 1899, Minkowski wrote that he had become occupied almost completely with thermodynamics.[33] During his tenure at Zurich, between 1896 and 1902, Minkowski saw thermodynamics as a necessary extension of mechanics.

In the introduction to a series of lectures on elasticity, undated but certainly delivered after 1897, Minkowski remarked that analogies between many different mechanical problems surely indicated a 'triumph of mathematics'. Such mechanical analogies were 'of the greatest interest' because they led to a deeper understanding of forces in motion, on the nature of which 'we are still doubtful'. It would be left to see whether mechanical construction might be able to account completely for the action of all phenomena, especially the conundrum regarding the induction of electric current. Boltzmann's mechanical constructions had opened the possibility of a purely mechanical explanation of electrical processes, and Minkowski added that he would treat the question further in his lectures.[34] Most important for Minkowski were not the physical assumptions but 'the development of movements occurring in nature'.[35] An extensive exposition of the mathematical methods of analytical mechanics really would not delay considering physical concepts (such as space, time, and force), he continued. It was essential for understanding how to approach the fundamental questions facing physics.

In 1902, Felix Klein convinced Friedrich Althoff, the Prussian administrator in charge of universities, to create a third chair in mathematics at Göttingen for Minkowski. The environment was charged with pure and applied mathematics and physics. In his lectures of the period, he continually emphasised that pure mathematics could contribute significantly to a scientific understanding of the physical universe. He introduced a course on function theory during the winter semester of 1902/03 by observing how remarkable it was that pure mathematics and mathematical physics often formulated the same mathematical problem by two different paths. He added that the process of physical observation could be made easier 'if, by free reflection, one only followed his imagination to spin more extensively the thread of existing mathematical fabric'.[36] According to Minkowski, pure mathematics and physical observation often arrived at the same result. During the summer of 1904 he opened a lecture course on the theory of differential equations by pointing to this unusual confluence.

Mathematics has the task of developing the tools necessary to grasp the logical coherence of external appearances. Its basic concepts, the axioms of physical quantities and of geometry, have arisen from experience. Mathematics constantly derives the most beautiful problems in applications from the natural sciences. And through a peculiar, pre-established harmony, it has been shown that, by trying logically to elaborate the existing edifice of mathematics, one is directed on exactly the same path as by having responded to questions arising from the facts of physics and astronomy.[37]

According to Minkowski, the structure of mathematics was established by judicious selection of axioms through the aid of 'experience', a term that apparently included both physical 'facts' and intuitive synthesis.

Deriving the basic equations

How did the four *Dozenten*—each a master of mathematical reasoning and each committed to bringing about a mathematical synthesis of electro-dynamical theory—present the electron theory during the summer of 1905?

Herglotz and Minkowski were responsible, in the first session, for deriving the basic equations (and their general integrals) for the laws of conservation of energy and impulse. They undoubtedly followed Lorentz's expository summary of 1903. As original texts, in addition to Lorentz's 1895 *Versuch* and Poincaré's textbook, the seminarists appealed to an article of Poincaré's in the 1900 Lorentz *Festschrift* of the Haarlem *Archives néerlandaises*.[38]

In his article, Poincaré showed how Newton's third law had no equivalent in Lorentz's theory, at least when only matter was considered. After calculating the ponderomotive force on all electricity inside a given volume, Poincaré introduced a principle of relative motion along with Lorentz's notion of local time. Poincaré concluded that all field theories taking account of Newton's principle of action and equal reaction would be unsatisfactory unless the fundamental ideas of electrodynamics were profoundly modified in unspecified ways. Poincaré's final call would have served to introduce the seminar to the electromagnetic view of nature, where all mechanics was to have been derived from electromagnetic theory.[39]

In the same Lorentz *Festschrift*, Wiechert had published his derivation of the retarded electromagnetic potentials. In his article, Wiechert also expressed doubts about the adequacy of modern interpretations of electro-dynamics: 'Matter and ether are for us pictures', he wrote, 'which we see from our human standpoint in nature.' It remained to be seen if these pictures corresponded to reality.[40] The differential equation for the scalar potential drew the attention of the seminarists in their second session. In the first physics paper considered, the seminar examined Wiechert's 1900 expression for the retarded potentials due to a point charge, a physical situation equivalent to the potential at great distances from a charge source of finite dimensions.[41] With an explanation of Zeeman spectra in mind, Wiechert applied his calculation for the potential to the case of an electron executing damped linear vibration.

As professor in charge of this session, Hilbert was interested in establishing the mathematical heritage behind Wiechert's solution, a heritage that Wiechert had sketched in his paper. Hilbert marked for special study the form that Eugenio Beltrami had given to Green's theorem.[42] He also indicated the work of the former Göttingen *Privatdozent* Heinrich Burkhardt on related matters, perhaps meaning to consider Burkhardt and W Franz Meyer's article on potential theory in the encyclopaedia of mathematical sciences.[43] In focusing on the solution to the potential equation Hilbert would have been able to recover much of nineteenth-century mathematical physics—from the work of Joseph Liouville, Augustin Louis Cauchy, and William Thomson in the 1830s and 1840s, to Charles Emile Picard's and Arnold Sommerfeld's studies in the 1890s. The second-order, homogeneous, partial differential equation in four dimensions was a central tool in all areas of dynamical theory. It was the formalism chosen by Lorentz to represent Maxwell's equations.

Turning to the most substantial elaboration of Wiechert's retarded potentials, the seminar considered Schwarzschild's recent treatment of the force exerted by a moving point charge, or electron, on another point charge.[44] In his elegant and simple derivation, Schwarzschild obtained components of the electrical force along the line of connection between two electrons, in the direction of the velocity of the perturbing electron, and in the direction of the acceleration of the perturbing electron. He also obtained magnetic and mechanical forces resulting from the interaction between the exciting electron at the moment of the emission of the force wave and the excited electron when it met the wave.

Schwarzschild recovered electrostatics, when both the perturbing electron and the perturbed electron had identical velocities. For this case, of course, the mechanical force had a scalar potential. When the acceleration of the excited electron was zero, Schwarzschild found that within a correction factor the force could be expressed as the sum of the Coulomb force and Hermann Grassmann's formula for the elementary force law of electrodynamics.[45] At great distances from the perturbing electron, Schwarzschild recovered well known results for the electric and magnetic fields of a moving charge.

Instead of elaborating potential theory for special physical cases, in its third week the seminar followed Lorentz by considering how electrodynamics could be formulated with a variational principle. At this time radical thinkers joined Heinrich Hertz in objecting to non-mechanically defined quantities, in particular the elusive 'action'. Among more traditionally minded physicists at the turn of the century, however, the principle of least action was seen as the *dénouement* of classical dynamics. Great value was placed in providing electrodynamics with the same formal elegance that governed the dynamics of material particles. Expositions chosen by the seminarists to illustrate the action approach were the three that Lorentz had considered in 1903: Lorentz's Lagrangian formulation of the electromagnetic field in 1892; Poincaré's reconsideration of Lorentz's paper in 1901, and Schwarzschild's formulation in 1903 of the principle of least action for the electron theory.

Tetu Hirosige has provided a thorough analysis of Lorentz's paper.[46] It is well to emphasise here, along with Hirosige, that Lorentz sought, like Hertz, to provide for electrodynamic theory the same form that had been used with such success in dynamical theory. To this end Lorentz used a kinetic-energy-like quantity for the electromagnetic field to arrive at a Lagrangian equation of motion. (Three years later, in his *Versuch* of 1895, Lorentz completely abandoned attempts to cast electrodynamics in a form like that of particle dynamics.) Poincaré's published lecture notes restated Lorentz's procedure. His treatment was equally clear and elegant.

Minkowski took charge of organising the third week of the seminar, and one of the two student reporters was Max Born, in four years destined to become Minkowski's last assistant. At the close of this session Minkowski supervised presentations of a final model of formal elegance, Karl Schwarzschild's brief formulation of the principle of least action.[47] Schwarzschild began with the electrodynamics of Lorentz and Wiechert. As a Lagrangian function he chose the difference between the scalar potential and the inner product of the vector potential and the velocity of the moving electron, $L = \phi - v_x\Gamma_x - v_y\Gamma_y - v_z\Gamma_z$ where ϕ was the scalar potential, v_i the electron velocity components, and Γ_i Wiechert's vector potential components. It was different from the choice made by Lorentz in 1892, and it is the formulation taught to students of physics today. Schwarzschild then defined the components of electromagnetic force as $F_x = -dL/dx + (d/dt)(\partial L/\partial v_x)$, and so on. With this convention, which recovered Lorentz's electromagnetic force, Schwarzschild proposed for electrodynamics the following law: In a given electric field an electrical quantity moves so that the variation of the integral $\int dt\,(-T + \Sigma\,eL)$ was a minimum between fixed times and beginning and end points. In this variational equation e was the sum of all electrical charges, and T the kinetic energy of ponderable (that is, material) masses bound up in the electricity. Schwarzschild denoted his Lagrangian L as electrokinetic potential, a quantity that corresponded precisely to Rudolf Clausius' electrodynamic potential.[48] He extended his action principle to consider the electromagnetic field and variations in electrical charge density.

Physical examples were not considered in the text of Schwarzschild and in the corresponding passages of Lorentz and Poincaré undoubtedly analysed by Minkowski. Week four of the seminar was devoted entirely to considering how electrodynamics could account for optics in moving systems. Wiechert, as much a talented experimentalist as a theoretician, was in charge. According to the seminar outline, his mandate included the 'influence of the earth's movement, local time, aberration', and other optical effects. Among his texts on the syllabus were the Adams prize essays of Gilbert T Walker and Joseph Larmor on aberration and other problems. Walker's essay was a coherent summary of Lorentz's electrodynamics and his interpretation of optical experiments: facilitating reading of the essay were Walker's decisions to follow the Heaviside notation used by Ludwig Föppl in his 1893 text on Maxwell's electromagnetic theory and to adopt Hertz's system of electrical units.[49] Larmor's text was a long ramble through Maxwellian electrodynamics. In his book, Larmor developed a novel theory of ether and matter, and he actually proposed what would later become known as the Lorentz transformation together with the physical property of time dilatation.[50] This part of Larmor's book was not noted by Lorentz in his encyclopaedia article. It is doubtful, in any case, if the Göttingen seminarists would have been struck by the passage, for Larmor's idiosyncratic exposition and poor command of written English would have sorely tried the logical and linguistic skills of German readers.

The Adams essays aside, three texts provided the backbone of the session: chapter 8 of Paul Drude's 1900 book on optics,[51] once more Poincaré's lectures on electricity and optics, and Lorentz's *Versuch* of 1895. Poincaré summarised Lorentz's work. Drude did the same, providing a more comprehensive view of the optical experiments that Lorentz had explained by his hypothesis of the stationary ether and local time. Lorentz's *Versuch*, in conjunction with his encyclopaedia article, would have provided the principal intellectual fare for this session of the seminar. The *Dozenten* evidently saw no need directly to appraise the experimental literature.

Studying Abraham's electron dynamics

The second half of the seminar focused on elaborations of the electron theory by Göttingen physicists and mathematicians. An entire week was spent on Abraham's long 1903 study of the principles of electron dynamics, a work reviewed in Lorentz's encyclopaedia article.[52] It was not an unreasonable decision on the part of the seminar to study this paper. By 1905 Abraham had demonstrated remarkable capabilities in synthesising and extending the electron theory, as formulated by Lorentz, Wien, Wiechert, and others. Abraham was a student of Max Planck's.[53] He appropriated from his professor a keen sense of the value of experiments in constructing physical theories. Like Planck, Abraham used the vector calculus to study radiative phenomena. Also like Planck, Abraham approached complicated mathematics with caution. Abraham's mathematics served physical reasoning, but he remained respectful of its power. At the beginning of his paper Abraham emphasised that 'the mathematical formulation of all the relationships developed here obtains not only greater elegance but also closer bonds to physical phenomena if the vector calculus is used.'[54] He had evidently taken pains to clarify the geometrical meaning of vectors in his exposition recently published in the encyclopaedia of mathematical sciences, and in his research article of 1903 he provided the reader with a brief lexicon—the kind used in literature reviews—before he began the detailed analysis. His approach to the electron theory, like his opinionated evaluation of his colleagues' work, was not favoured by the seminarists of 1905.[55] Although they could by no means ignore Abraham's work, it is understandable why the *Dozenten* leading the seminar would not have sought his participation.

Abraham opened his paper by emphasising that, in the theories elaborated by Wiechert and Lorentz, electron dynamics was the main concern. Electron dynamics raised a fundamental question. Could the motion of the electron, and hence its inertial mass, be determined solely by its electromagnetic field, or did the electron contain material mass in addition to mass of electromagnetic origin? The question seemed important because William Sutherland and Paul Drude had recently come out in favour of the electromagnetic view of electronic mass.[56] Abraham noted that Lorentz had recently published a formulation in which one found that the mass of the electron was not a scalar quantity, but rather had components in directions longitudinal and transverse to the motion of the electron. Abraham agreed that this result was a reasonable development. To disarm potential critics, Abraham referred at the beginning of his article to the experiments of his friend and colleague Walter Kaufmann, who had been studying electrons since 1900. Kaufmann's experiments of 1902 showed that Abraham's formulation of transverse electromagnetic mass (not Lorentz's given later in the paper) was correct.[57] Because his own careful derivation assumed only the electrodynamic view of nature, Abraham believed that Kaufmann's experimental verification provided convincing evidence that electron mass had a purely electromagnetic nature.

Abraham worked from three fundamental systems of equations. The first was a kinematic equation that limited the freedom of motion of the electron. It stated simply that the total velocity of the electron could be expressed as the sum of the translational velocity and the component of angular velocity in the direction of motion. In the second system were the electromagnetic field equations, as expressed by Lorentz, together with the scalar and vector potential equations of Theodor Des Coudres and Wiechert. The dynamical equation comprised the third system: the variation of external work plus the variation of internal work equalled the variation of the total work of the electron system. Abraham explained how these systems related to the electromagnetic view of nature. If electrical charge were assumed to be distributed uniformly throughout the volume of the electron, then the kinematic equations were those of a rigid body. He observed immediately that such an assumption could well seem arbitrary. The objection could be raised that such a volume-density distribution would necessarily deform the electron. If one supposed that, in an electron at rest, the electrical and elastic forces counterbalanced each

The Einsteins' family home in Pavia as it looks today. ©
Barbara Reeves.

The cantonal school at Aarau, 1896. T Müller-Wolfer, *Die Aargauische Kantonsschule in den vergangenen 150 Jahren* (Aarau: H R Sauerländer 1952).

Arc lamp manufactured by J Einstein & Co around 1890. Deutsches Patentamt, Munich.

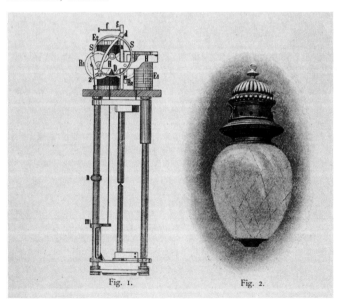

Fig. 1.   Fig. 2.

Main exhibition hall at the Frankfurt electrotechnical fair, 1891. *Offizieller Bericht über die Internationale Ausstellung in Frankfurt am Main 1891* **1:** *Allgemeiner Bericht* (Frankfurt 1893).

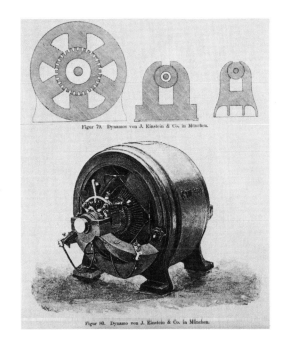

Various dynamos available from J Einstein & Co, around 1891. *Offizieller Bericht über die Internationale Ausstellung in Frankfurt am Main 1891* **1:** *Allgemeiner Bericht* (Frankfurt 1893).

Site of Einstein, Garrone & Co (on the right) in Pavia, as it looks today. ©
Barbara Reeves.

Buchau am Federsee, around 1860. Johann Evangelist Schöttle, *Geschichte von
Stadt und Stift Buchau* (Waldsee 1884).

Buchau synagogue (with tower), around 1925. Walter Staudacher, *Führer durch Buchau und das Federseeried* (Buchau [1925]).

Main synagogue in Munich, 1887. Munich, Israelitische Kultusgemeinde, *Festgabe: 50 Jahre Hauptsynagoge München 1887–1937* (Munich 1937).

Max Planck in 1895. Department of Terrestrial Magnetism, Carnegie Institution of Washington.

Göttingen mathematicians at ease around 1905; Hermann Minkowski with moustache and David Hilbert reclining, with cane. Niels Bohr Library, American Institute of Physics, New York.

Cartoon illustrating the tenth anniversary meeting of the Göttingen Association for Applied Mathematics and Physics. A line of university professors, each bearing a large book and a small one, meets a line of industrialists carrying a large and a small purse. The small objects are exchanged, after which professors and industrialists continue on side by side. The transaction is overseen by Felix Klein, cast as the Sun; the Moon is probably Henry Theodore Böttinger, the leading industrialist behind the Association. Also present is the spirit of Friedrich Althoff, the Prussian educational authority who encouraged the Association. Niels Bohr Library, American Institute of Physics, New York.

Einstein in his Princeton study. © Lotte Jacobi.

other and produced a spherical electron, then the force of the electromagnetic field had to disrupt the original balance and deform a moving
electron. In his defence, Abraham noted that, first of all, Kaufmann's
experiments did not confirm such a possibility. In addition, adherents to
the electromagnetic view of nature held the deformable electron as in
principle an unreasonable construction, for if the electron changed shape,
the work done against the electromagnetic force would give rise to a non-
electromagnetic potential energy.

To clarify his method Abraham appealed to the approach of Heinrich
Hertz. Abraham noted that, in Hertz's *Principles of Mechanics*, the latter
allowed only those kinematic connections whose existence depended on
the generation or the destruction of kinetic energy. Hertz based all energy
on the kinetic energy of moving masses and reduced all forces to kinematic
connections. To deal with the paradox that nature provided only an
approximation to the hypothesis of rigid interactions, Abraham cited
Hertz: ' "In the search for the real, rigid connections, our mechanics will
perhaps have to descend to the world of atoms." '[58] Abraham proposed
in his treatise to go even deeper, to the submolecular level of electrons.
Hertz had demonstrated to Abraham's satisfaction that it was permissible
to speak of rigid connections before forces were introduced. Following
Hertz, in his own electron dynamics Abraham avoided speaking about the
forces that acted to deform the electron. He addressed only 'external
forces' producing a velocity or angular velocity and 'internal forces' originating from the field of the electron to maintain equilibrium. In Abraham's view forces were only ancillary concepts defined by kinematic and
electromagnetic considerations. The same was true for the words *work*,
energy, and *quantity of motion*. By carefully choosing his words, Abraham
sought to develop an analogy between 'electromagnetic mechanics' and
'familiar mechanics'.[59]

Upon formulating his equations, Abraham developed the idea of electromagnetic quantity of motion and electromagnetic energy. Following
Poincaré's electrodynamics, Abraham expressed the field inside an electron in terms of impulse and angular impulse, which paved the way for a
simple calculation of electromagnetic mass and electromagnetic moment
of inertia. Having defined a notion of mass, Abraham restricted his view
to the most important class of electron movements, that of 'distinguished
motions'. From the field equations for an electron in a rigid coordinate
system, Abraham defined 'distinguished motions' as those where the field
was at rest when expressed in a coordinate system fixed to an electron.
For 'distinguished motions', the internal forces could be formulated as the
gradient of a scalar 'convection potential'. 'Distinguished motions'
included uniform translation and uniform rotation.[60] For these movements, Abraham formulated electron dynamics in terms of d'Alembert's
Principle. The resulting equation of motion was much more difficult to

treat mathematically than was ordinary mechanics because the linear and angular impulse in it were complicated functions of velocity and angular velocity; impulse depended on the previous history of the quantity of motion as determined by integrating the field equations.

At the centre of his paper, Abraham treated pure translation by a Lagrangian function that was the difference between magnetic and electrical energy. He recovered the results of William Blair Morton and George Frederic Charles Searle, emphasising that for pure translation Newton's first two laws held true when a quantity 'electromagnetic mass' was defined. The latter analogue to familiar mass was not a scalar, but rather a tensor, whose components became longitudinal and transverse mass.

It is instructive to follow Abraham's reasoning in defining the notion of electromagnetic mass.[61] He began by observing that for an electrical current flowing in a stationary wire, the current strength remained constant and determined the magnetic field. As soon as the current changed intensity, the field no longer reflected the momentary current strength; it lagged behind the current. For fast vibrations of the frequency of a Hertzian oscillator, such a relationship could be calculated from the electromagnetic waves propagating in the field. In the theory of alternating currents, however, one calculated the magnetic field from the strength of the current as if the current were stationary. This procedure was familiar as the theory of quasistationary currents.[62] Two different methods, then, were used to calculate the quantities in one physical situation. One could either begin with the electromagnetic waves and calculate the alternating current required to generate them, or one could begin with a current and calculate the electromagnetic field. Abraham drew a parallel between the second method and the electron theory. He observed that the quasistationary convection current of alternating-current theory was analogous to uniform electron motion. With quasistationary currents, those where the change of velocity was so slow that impulse could be calculated from any velocity as in the case of stationary motion, were associated quasistationary motions. In particular, self-induction in the theory of current conductors could be reflected in the quantity called electromagnetic mass.

Armed with his notion of electromagnetic mass, Abraham calculated the ratio of force divided by acceleration for longitudinal and transverse directions with respect to the motion of the electron. He found that his expression for the mass of an electron assumed the form of an asymmetric tensor. In calculating the radiation of electrons executing quasistationary motion, Abraham assumed that the electron radius was small compared with the points at which the field was calculated, that the electron velocity was slow compared with that of light, and that the direction of motion of the electron would not be changed over short periods of time by application of an external force. That is, Abraham required the radius to be small compared with the distance over which the field changed significantly. He emphasised that the principle of least action held for quasistationary, translationary movement. For Abraham it was of 'epistemological' as well as of 'economical' importance that electron dynamics could be expressed in Lagrangian form.[63] Abraham finally described the motion of a rotating electron. To provide a point of comparison with his own theory of the rigid, spherical electron, he calculated the translation of a charged ellipsoid. Among his conclusions he recovered the results of Woldemar Voigt for the precession of an electron in a magnetic field.

Rotating and accelerating electrons: Schwarzschild and Hertz

Having considered Abraham's theory of quasistationary translatory motion, the seminar moved to study quasistationary rotational motion. On the agenda was Hilbert's review of the third instalment of Schwarzschild's electron-theory paper. Schwarzschild worked to extend Abraham's study.[64] He wrote that Abraham's theory of the massless electron had been verified by the astonishing experiments of Kaufmann. Yet, he added, Kaufmann's experiments did not take into account the possibility that the electron could rotate. It would be absurd to believe that with the colossal electron velocities at the cathode, Schwarzschild went on, the electron could not also manifest a great rotational velocity. At the same time, such rotation evidently did not have much influence on the visible motion of the electron. Could the Lorentz–Wiechert electrodynamics account for these facts?

In two simple cases considered by Abraham, those of rotation without translation and rotation in the direction of translation, the influence of the rotations was small. But when the rotational axis was across the direction of translation, Abraham showed that only an external force could keep the electron on a straight path. Schwarzschild speculated that it seemed almost as if translatory energy went into making the electron rotate; certain knowledge had to be obtained about whether this was so. On such information depended the notion that an electron had no 'real', that is to say traditional, mass.

Schwarzschild wanted to show that Abraham's results, as well as the motion of an electron for arbitrary translation and rotation, could be obtained directly from a variational formulation. For his calculations he assumed quasistationary motion, that with small accelerations. He demonstrated that the rotation of an electron could not exceed an angular velocity that would have the surface of the electron rotating with a moderate fraction of the speed of light. Schwarzschild emphasised that his paper was understandably occupied with 'formal' matters, since it proceeded from a variational principle.[65] For quasistationary motion, the variational principle reduced to a minimal principle very close to that of Hamilton's. Drawing inspiration from the mechanics of Leo Königsberger, Schwarzschild related the acceleration of Abraham's 'distinguished motions' to kinetic potential.[66] In this way he was able to arrive at close analogies with ordinary mechanics.

The astrophysicist Schwarzschild was careful to proceed with the greatest possible generality. Following a path different from Abraham's physical reasoning, Schwarzschild sought from the beginning to arrive at formal elegance. His expression for the electrodynamic potentials was extremely complicated, even though he neglected lower orders of magnitude as permitted by his assumption of quasistationary motion. When finally he was able to compare his results with those of Abraham, agreement came only in the highest orders. He identified the conditions for force-free motion of the electron. These were only those cases when the axis of rotation was coincident with or perpendicular to the direction of motion of the electron.

Monstrous problems were raised by this conclusion. Classical degrees of freedom were now insufficient for evaluating the electron Lagrangian; non-classical constraints had to be applied to obtain the motion of a rigid, electromagnetic body.[67] Schwarzschild did not pause to examine this paradox closely. He continued with a description of free electron motion. The midpoint of a freely rotating electron not subject to an external force described a cylindrical helix, and the electron precessed around the direction of the helical axis provided that the helical axis, rotational axis, and direction of the midpoint velocity all fell in the same plane. He calculated the dimensions of the cylinder. If the translational velocity of the electron were between one-tenth and 97% of the velocity of light (the observed lower and upper limits for cathode rays) and if the rotational velocity were of the order of the speed of light, then the helical radius would be of the order of the electron radius. Only when the rotational velocity was much larger than the translational velocity would the radius of the helix be of sensible dimensions. Schwarzschild concluded with a peace offering: in the case of a non-rotating electron he recovered Abraham's formulae for longitudinal and transverse mass, the latter value having been verified by Kaufmann's experiments. He concluded that there was no contradiction between the behaviour of a massless electron following Lorentz–Wiechert electrodynamics and the results of experience. It was a result that Abraham had anticipated in his paper.

Together with Schwarzschild's mathematical *tour de force*, Hilbert considered the dissertation of Paul Hertz, officially his student but whose work in practice was directed by *Privatdozent* Max Abraham, whom Hertz thanked profusely at the end of the *vita* published with the dissertation.[68] Hertz attempted to provide a general theory of non-stationary electron motion. At the beginning of his study he explained why the question was important. Originally, J J Thomson had hypothesised that electrons were emitted from cathodes suddenly, as if they were inelastic spheres bouncing off a rigid wall. Hertz pointed to the unreasonableness of such a hypothesis if the cathode was considered a grille of molecules separated by spaces much larger than the dimensions of an electron. What was the energy radiated, then, by an arbitrarily accelerated electron?

Max Abraham had calculated the limiting case of radiation from an infinitesimally small acceleration, but Hertz sought the radiation from extremely large accelerations as well. Hertz emphasised that experimental investigations had not yet arrived at firm results concerning questions about the electron velocity and its changes. Hermann Haga and Cornelis Harm Wind's experiments on Röntgen rays, taken with Sommerfeld's theoretical calculations, supported the hypothesis of gradual changes. Concerning the variety of Röntgen radiation called gamma rays, the hypothesis of sudden acceleration was more probable than in the case of beta rays (Hertz assumed that gamma rays were electrons).

In the first half of his dissertation, Hertz calculated the field at an infinitely long time after an electron was disturbed. In this way he derived the energy and quantities of motion. He made use of the retarded potentials, calculating the formulae for an excited, spherical electron with uniform volume charge, for the same electron with uniform surface charge, and for an arbitrarily shaped, arbitrarily charged electron. He then returned to derive these results in a second way, beginning with accelerated motion and then passing to the case of velocity instabilities. He arrived at the energy and quantity of motion by integrating the field strength. In the second half, Hertz applied energetic methods to find the energy, impulse, and force of a disturbed electron at a finite time after a disturbance. Different from the case in ordinary mechanics, he found along with Schwarzschild that a finite—not an infinite—force was required for an instability in velocity. The forces important for giving to an electron the velocity of a slow cathode ray greatly exceeded all experimentally obtained field strengths, but Hertz allowed that they could still perhaps be produced inside radium atoms.

Hertz affirmed with Abraham that stationary motion of an electron at the velocity of light was impossible. It was not impossible, however, for an electron to attain such a velocity. In fact, a finite force could accelerate an electron suddenly to the velocity of light and keep it there. Hertz would not speculate whether such a process was realised in nature. He did note that Friedrich Paschen had indicated that at least part of what had been designated gamma rays were conventional charges, and these could attain the velocity of light.[69]

To calculate the potential due to a change in velocity, Hertz considered in detail how the process was seen in different coordinate systems. Impelling him to this approach were difficulties with integrating his equations.

(He was not concerned with the consequences of transforming from one system to another, that is, with covariance, invariance, and like notions.) To help his calculation along Hertz substituted for a suddenly accelerated electron a system of three imaginary electrons.[70] One of these travelled along the actual electron's path with its initial velocity. A second electron, of the opposite charge, was made to materialise at the moment of acceleration and travelled along the path of the actual electron with the electron's initial velocity. The third electron, charged the same as the first, materialised at the time of acceleration and followed the path of the actual electron with its final velocity. Taken together, Hertz argued, the three imaginary electrons exactly duplicated the motion of the actual electron. From his fictional construction, Hertz derived the values for the electromagnetic field given by Lorentz in his article on electrodynamics which had been published in the encyclopaedia of mathematical sciences. Hertz then calculated the radiation of an accelerated, spherical electron, recovering Schwarzschild's results for the field strength. He concluded his first part by rederiving all formulae for radiation from an energetic point of view.

In the second part of his dissertation Hertz calculated the radiation from a spherical, quasistationary electron at a finite time after it was disturbed. Hertz noted that if one postulated that the rigid electron had no material mass, then the electron had to generate internal forces to compensate for all external forces. This was Abraham's point, but Hertz was not sure if such an argument always held. Presumably, he suspected that the electron could deform under external forces. Hertz sought the force required to produce a definite electronic motion. To calculate the force, Hertz needed the electromagnetic field. He obtained it after making use of many diagrams, all of which were physical pictures of the electron and electromagnetic waves. At the end of his dissertation, Hertz considered the possibility of motion with the velocity of light, concluding with the result, astonishing to us today in view of our understanding of special relativity, that to accelerate an electron suddenly to the velocity of light and to keep it there required only a finite force.[71]

Sommerfeld: the outsider as insider

Those whose special contributions to the electron theory were considered by the seminarists resided, with the exception of Arnold Sommerfeld, at Göttingen. Weeks seven and eight were devoted to the outsider's work. Sommerfeld was at the time of the seminar professor of mechanics at the Aachen Institute of Technology.[72] He had obtained a doctorate in 1891 for a dissertation in mathematical physics under the Königsberg mathematician Ferdinand Lindemann. Sommerfeld recalled of his student days that electrodynamics had then been at a major turning point. It was still presented to us in the old manner—in addition to Coulomb and Biot-Savart, Ampère's law of the mutual action of two elements of current and its competitors, the laws of Grassmann, Gauss, Riemann, and Clausius, and as a culmination the law of Wilhelm Weber, all of which were based on action at a distance. The total picture of electrodynamics thus presented to us was awkward, incoherent, and by no means self-contained. Teachers and students made a great effort to familiarize themselves with Heinrich Hertz's experiments step by step as they became known and to explain them with the aid of the difficult original presentation in Maxwell's *Treatise*.

Hertz's results came as a revelation to Sommerfeld: 'It was as though scales fell from my eyes when I read Hertz's great papers . . .' Sommerfeld studied Hertz's work while attending lectures given by Königsberg *Privatdozenten* Hilbert and Wiechert. He became a close collaborator of Wiechert's.

In 1893 Sommerfeld went to Göttingen as an assistant in mineralogy, and rapidly became the *famulus*, or first assistant, of Felix Klein. It was a turning point in his life. He fell under the spell of Klein's new programme to make pure mathematics indispensable for physicists. Klein quickly accepted Sommerfeld as his protégé and sponsored his *Habilitationsschrift* in 1895. The *Privatdozent* Sommerfeld taught at Göttingen for five semesters. During this time he began to collaborate with Klein on their major mechanics textbook, the *Theory of Tops*. Sommerfeld was Klein's favoured disciple when in 1897 he received a call to teach mathematics at the Clausthal Mining Academy. In 1900 he became professor of mechanics at Aachen. Due in part to his studies on electron dynamics he became in 1907 professor of theoretical physics at the University of Munich.

While at Aachen Sommerfeld wrote furiously on the electron theory in what must have seemed a desperate attempt to keep up with the Göttingen theorists. During the latter half of 1903 Sommerfeld was preparing for press Lorentz's contributions to the *Encyklopädie* volume on mechanics, the editing of which had been confided to him by his mentor Felix Klein. In July, Lorentz sent to Sommerfeld for this volume a long article on Maxwell's theory; in December came Lorentz's brilliant synthesis of work in the electron theory, the treatment that became a bible for the Göttingen seminar. Throughout 1903 Sommerfeld was in correspondence with Schwarzschild, who in July had finished the final instalment of his three-part paper on electrodynamics. Herglotz, the brilliant mathematical star, had just begun to turn his attention to the electron theory, and as Klein's post-doctoral student he had the opportunity for direct contact with Göttingen *Dozenten*. Sommerfeld had some reason to feel that in a short time Herglotz could capture a university chair in mechanics or in the new rage, applied mathematics, while he would be eclipsed at the Aachen Institute of Technology.

Sommerfeld was clearly agitated when late in January 1904

Schwarzschild mailed him the proofs of Herglotz's first electron-theory paper, scheduled to appear in the *Nachrichten* of the Göttingen Scientific Society.[73] Sommerfeld sent a postcard to Schwarzschild, emphasising how Herglotz's work was 'fundamentally different' from his own, and he would provisionally not be influenced by it. Sommerfeld claimed to have a 'magic formula' that would provide the field for rectilinear electron motion. Herglotz's paper had provided a solution for small vibrations of a rotating electron, but at the moment Sommerfeld confessed to knowing nothing about vibrating processes. His own electron was a sphere with a variable radius. Schwarzschild could soon expect that something of Sommerfeld's work, the Aachen exile emphasised, would cross the desk of the *Nachrichten* editor.[74]

When his first electron-theory paper was accepted early in March 1904, Sommerfeld still found himself struggling to clarify his ideas. According to a postcard that Sommerfeld sent to Schwarzschild three weeks after Sommerfeld's paper was read before the Society, Lorentz had gone through Sommerfeld's study and queried his formulation of the vector potential.[75] Sommerfeld answered laconically and guardedly to questions posed by Schwarzschild. Apparently Schwarzschild felt that Sommerfeld should have cited Schwarzschild's 1903 electron-theory papers. Sommerfeld claimed not to have seen them. In responding to Schwarzschild, Sommerfeld was being deliberately perverse, for Schwarzschild's electron-theory papers were extensively discussed in Lorentz's second encyclopaedia article, by then in Sommerfeld's hands for more than two months. 'If you could send me the proofs of your note,' Sommerfeld replied testily to Schwarzschild, 'perhaps I can cite it.'[76] The citation never appeared.

Reflecting his professed lack of familiarity with the latest publications of his colleagues, Sommerfeld began his first electron-theory paper by recalling that theorists had until then only considered uniform, straight-line motion and stationary or quasistationary motion.[77] For accelerated motion the advanced and retarded potentials of Liénard and Wiechert were known, but these formulations did not provide answers to dynamical questions concerning the field within and outside an electron. In the first instalment of his study Sommerfeld provided a simple expression for the entire field of the electron, a formula motivated by a long mathematical digression. Much of the paper concerned not so much useful results themselves as how Sommerfeld was led to certain general formulae.

Sommerfeld formulated the differential equation of the scalar potential by following Lorentz's exposition in his encyclopaedia article on Maxwell's theory. The Aachen theorist immediately used Fourier integrals to deal with a variable distribution of charge density. Complicated expressions resulted, which Sommerfeld reduced to the potential inside and outside a spherical electron. Near the end of the paper, Sommerfeld obtained his formulae by a more elegant although equally unmotivated procedure.

He thanked his Aachen colleague, professor of mathematics Hans von Mangoldt, for having shown him how to derive his formulae from Lorentz's theory, where the electron changed shape with velocity. Undertaking such a calculation did not interest Sommerfeld, although he sketched how it could be carried out by introducing the simplifying hypotheses of constant surface and volume charge distribution. Sommerfeld was, nevertheless, concerned with recovering from his formulae the Liénard–Wiechert potentials, those present at a great distance from an accelerating electron.

Having established the field for a moving electron, Sommerfeld devoted a second communication to providing a general dynamical description of things.[78] He followed Lorentz's theory in representing the mechanical force per unit charge resulting from the electromagnetic field:

$$f = - \operatorname{grad} \left(\phi - \frac{1}{c}(vA) \right) - \frac{1}{c}\frac{\partial A}{\partial t} + \frac{1}{c}\left[[wr]\operatorname{rot} A\right].$$

Here *grad* was the gradient operator and *rot* the 'curl' operator, v the electron velocity, w the angular velocity with radius r, ϕ and A the scalar and vector potentials, c the speed of light, (wr) the scalar product and $[wr]$ the vector product of w and r. The formula resulted immediately from Maxwell's equations. Sommerfeld identified the term $(1/c)(vA)$ as Schwarzschild's electrokinetic potential. For the resulting force on an electron Sommerfeld arrived at a 'functional equation', or, as Hilbert had called it, an 'integral equation'. To convert the integral equation to a differential equation would be a difficult task, but Sommerfeld sought to lead the reader through the derivation.

He observed that electron mechanics allowed much greater latitude in terms of physical movement than did conventional mechanics. Electron mechanics required knowledge not only of place and velocity, but also of the previous motion of the electron. Sommerfeld emphasised that the moving electron interacted with its own field. He underlined that in the electron theory 'Galilean inertial motion' (the very notion used by Philipp Frank in 1909 in connection with special relativity) was not the only possible force-free motion.[79] In a paper of 1903 Herglotz had demonstrated the possibility of force-free rotation about the centre of an electron. Sommerfeld recovered this result, as well as Abraham's description of the quasistationary movement of an electron by calculating the Poynting energy flux following Poincaré's impulse method.

Electrons moving faster than light

Sommerfeld was interested in obtaining the greatest possible mathematical generality. He had no commitment to the electromagnetic view of nature, and he could thus consider electrons moving faster than the speed of light. Although in 1905 Einstein showed that an electron travelling with the velocity of light would have infinite kinetic energy, such motion was a possibility discussed widely, if intermittently, by many of Sommerfeld's physicist contemporaries. In particular, in 1900 Theodor Des Coudres, who had been a fellow *Privatdozent* with Sommerfeld at Göttingen and then received an appointment as associate professor of physics, reconsidered Oliver Heaviside's arguments concerning the possible character of faster-than-light motion.[80]

Sommerfeld noted that if a spherical electron travelled faster than light, then the field produced by the charge in the electron's nose would interact with the charge of the entire electron, but the field produced by the charge in the electron's heel would always follow in the electron's wake. A general calculation was necessary for Sommerfeld to establish his principal physical result: velocity faster than light was possible for charge distributed in the volume of the electron, but to accelerate surface charge faster than the speed of light would require application of an infinitely great force. From this result Sommerfeld concluded that for velocities greater than light the existence of surface charge came into question, 'just as we have given up the point-electrons supposed at the beginning of electron theory or as we have abandoned the hypothesis of point-atoms formerly constraining molecular physics'.[81]

When Sommerfeld considered electron motion both slower and faster than the velocity of light, he appealed to a space–time diagram. Sommerfeld was surely motivated to employ such a technique by the great interest among engineers at the time in graphical solutions and techniques, an interest to which Sommerfeld, as professor of mechanics at Aachen, would have been attuned and as a collaborator of Felix Klein's one that he would have found entirely congenial. Sommerfeld's graph was one in a family of similar representations going back at least to those of Des Coudres in 1900. It was not, however, infused with physical meaning. The abscissa of the diagram was length, measured as c multiplied by τ, the time of flight; the ordinate of the diagram was a constant of integration. The diagram indicated a flourish along the way to Sommerfeld's conclusion. He calculated the finite force necessary to sustain an electron having a constant charge density in uniform, rectilinear motion exceeding the velocity of light.

Of great importance for Sommerfeld was calculating quasistationary, rectilinear motion, where accelerations were small with respect to velocity. A velocity v and small acceleration p at time t were arranged in a power series to give a velocity $v_{t-\tau}$ at an earlier time $t-\tau$: $v_{t-\tau} = v - pt + \ldots$ Sommerfeld then calculated the integral $T = \int_{t-\tau}^{t} v_u \, du$, whose first and second time derivatives yielded velocity and acceleration. Substituting these quantities into his formula for the force resisting an accelerating, surface-charged electron travelling slower than light provided Sommerfeld with an expression identical to that which Lorentz called electromagnetic mass and that which Abraham called special, longitudinal electromagnetic mass. Sommerfeld found the same quantity—multiplied by a factor of 6/5—for the electromagnetic mass of a volume charge travelling slower than light. It was a result derived by both Abraham and Schwarzschild.

For the case of a volume charge executing quasistationary motion at a speed greater than that of light, Sommerfeld arrived at unusual results. Deceleration at velocities greater than light required a greater applied force than did acceleration, a result recently rederived for the hypothetical faster-than-light particles called tachyons.[82] It required force to bring an electron from infinite velocity to that of light. Sommerfeld divided the maintaining force into a part corresponding to overcoming the dissipative effects of radiation and a part for overcoming the inertia of the electron. Defining an apparent electron mass as force divided by acceleration, Sommerfeld observed, would result in a negative mass for particles moving faster than light.

To clarify the concept of electromagnetic mass, Sommerfeld calculated uniform, accelerated motion of a surface charge moving slower than the speed of light. He concluded, along with Paul Hertz, that it was possible to accelerate an electron to the speed of light by supplying a finite force. Then he addressed uniform circular motion, calculating electromagnetic centrifugal mass and electromagnetic transverse mass for surface and volume charges. These were identical with the values obtained by Abraham. Sommerfeld concluded that circular motion of an electron was possible without a constraining force in the radial direction, a conclusion previously reported by Herglotz.

The Aachen theorist was not blind to the implication of this calculation for understanding spectral lines. Using his expert knowledge of rotating, rigid bodies, he showed that Abraham's value of the electromagnetic moment of inertia, obtained for infinitely small rotations, was valid as well for large rotations. Sommerfeld ended the second part of his electron-theory study by considering the conditions of force-free motion. He proposed a periodic function as a solution to the problem of electron motion, and he calculated the allowable period and *wavelengths* of electron vibrations. The wavelengths turned out to be 'extraordinarily small', of the order of the electron diameter. He defined the 'spectrum' of the rotating electron as the totality of possible vibration numbers. It was an infinite series. Sommerfeld was quick to point out that his vibrations could not account for optical spectra. In his case, for an electron rotating about a fixed axis, and hence with one degree of freedom, infinitely many vibrations were possible.

The result was not anticipated in the classical theory of dispersion, where the number of degrees of freedom determined vibrations. Following this line of reasoning Sommerfeld concluded what British researchers had thought for some time, that electron mechanics could not be considered independently of the ether, a substance held to contain infinitely many electromagnetic degrees of freedom. He showed how the motion of an electron induced an elastic opposing force in the ether. Such a demonstration was important for making the electron theory seem less of a *deus ex machina* in explaining dielectric phenomena, dispersion, and the Zeeman effect.[83] Different from the free rotation of a spherical surface charge, the free rotation of a volume charge was damped. Evaluating a functional equation, Sommerfeld showed that Herglotz's result for small rotational vibrations was rigorously valid for large amplitude vibrations as well.

Sommerfeld's unwieldy Fourier expansion stimulated Gustav Herglotz to seek a simplification.[84] Sommerfeld also recognised that his calculation was cumbersome and inelegant, and he sought to simplify it. In a paper presented for him before the Amsterdam Academy of Sciences by Lorentz, one studied in week eight of the Göttingen seminar, Sommerfeld noted that the method in his first two *Nachrichten* papers had the advantage of working with a simple integral over space and time. Unlike Lorentz, who integrated first over time, Sommerfeld would consider the charge problem first. In carrying out his calculation Sommerfeld did not use Lorentz's hypothesis that the shape of an electron changed with increasing velocity, following the form of a Heaviside ellipsoid. He felt that when the electron velocity exceeded the speed of light such a hypothesis would, by extension, require an electron to assume the shape of a hyperboloid. Motion faster than light was not unphysical in his view; hyperboloid-shaped electrons were.[85]

To elaborate on faster-than-light phenomena, Sommerfeld described the 'shadow' of electron motion by considering those points in space along the path of the electron from which issued electromagnetic radiation that affected motion of the electron at a later time τ. Around every point on the path of the electron through space could be constructed a sphere of radius $c\tau$; the envelope of these spheres defined the shadow of motion. The greater v exceeded c, the smaller would be the shadow of motion. To calculate the scalar potential for motion faster than light, Sommerfeld specified three regions outside the electron. In the shadow of the electron, the equipotential surfaces were hyperboloids of revolution around the direction of motion (region 1); beyond a small border enclosing the shadow (region 2) the potential dropped to zero (region 3).

Sommerfeld led the reader to think that the notion of the shadow of motion was his own innovation; it was not, having clearly been indicated in 1900 by Des Coudres in his contribution to the well known Lorentz

Festschrift in the Haarlem *Archives néerlandaises*.[86] In his textbook on optics, Paul Drude had even referred to a picture of the surface of light-filled space for a moving, radiating system.[87] Sommerfeld's novelty lay in having obtained exact solutions for the scalar potential in and around the shadow, solutions similar to those provided more than thirty years later by Igor E Tamm and Ilya M Frank in studying Čerenkov radiation, which results from particles moving with velocities exceeding the phase velocity of light in material media. Sommerfeld's shadow of motion was analogous to the space inside Čerenkov's electromagnetic shock waves.[88] By his method Sommerfeld recovered the result that motion below the speed of light gave rise to equipotential surfaces that were ellipsoids of revolution around the direction of motion. He reiterated his stunning conclusion concerning stationary movement greater than the velocity of light: a finite force was required to maintain an electron of uniform volume density at an instantaneous infinite velocity. Accelerating surface charge faster than the speed of light, however, was impossible, because the self-field would become infinite.

In a final, major paper early in 1905, one also studied by the Göttingen seminar, Sommerfeld forged ahead with his study of the electron, clarifying motion greater than the speed of light by modifying his electron-motion graphs.[89] Distance came to be measured on the abscissa and time of flight multiplied by the speed of light remained the ordinate. As before, he associated portions of the paths with complicated integral calculations. The modified diagram was the direct predecessor of Hermann Minkowski's space–time diagram. Because Minkowski calculated with a rationalised system where the speed of light was assigned a value of unity, Sommerfeld's diagram would have easily suggested to Minkowski that Poincaré's convention of multiplying time by $\sqrt{-1}$ could be represented as a fourth spatial coordinate.[90]

The concluding paper in Sommerfeld's electron-theory series raised a number of unsettling points. Sommerfeld found that the integral equation for force-free motion greater than the velocity of light had no solution, and he was compelled to obtain results by a graphical procedure. It was a source of worry: 'This might well be the only known example where a reasonably-stated physical problem permits no solution.' Sommerfeld accordingly considered the possibility that motion faster than light was impossible: 'We must understand as impossible the process behind this nonexistence of a solution.'[91] Another problem concerned a physical picture of motion faster than light. Theoretically such motion could be achieved by application of finite forces. If the forces were suddenly removed, then the electron had certainly to fall to a velocity below that of light. Suddenly freeing the electron from constraining forces contradicted, however, Maxwell's equations, for the constraining forces arose from an electric field and they could not suddenly be removed because the field travelled with the velocity of light.

Sommerfeld recanted his earlier views. He also indicated how motion faster than light was not allowed by an energetic approach. A moving charge continuously radiated. In motion faster than the speed of light, however, part of the radiated energy was lost, again because electromagnetic energy could only travel with the speed of light. Such a loss had to be covered by the expenditure of work. As a result, motion faster than light could never be force-free. While on the subject of physical implausibilities, Sommerfeld continued Hertz's earlier remarks by observing that gamma rays could not be the hypothesised faster-than-light electrons, a view that he had previously entertained. Energetic considerations apart, he showed how electrons moving faster than light would be deflected by a magnetic field to an extent comparable with electrons moving slightly slower than the velocity of light. Gamma rays were not so deflected. Sommerfeld was encouraged to persist in considering the possibility of faster-than-light motion because his general techniques recovered the results of Hertz for motion slower than light. All arguments based on conventional physics, however, spoke against such motion.

A final, critical problem concerned the meaning of negative electromagnetic longitudinal mass for electron velocities greater than that of light. For given electron velocities, Sommerfeld plotted graphs of the function relating the applied, external force necessary for any accelerated motion greater than light (as the ordinate) and the resulting acceleration (as the abscissa). Following Abraham's clear physical reasoning but not mentioning it, Sommerfeld observed that the value of the slope of such a function would correspond to a classical notion of mass. When, for a given velocity exceeding that of light, the electron acceleration was zero, then the electron momentarily experienced stationary motion. At this point in its trajectory the value for the slope of one of Sommerfeld's 'velocity curves' would correspond to the electromagnetic, longitudinal mass of an electron undergoing stationary motion with such a velocity. The value of such a mass was always negative.

Ever a resilient theoretician, Sommerfeld noted, in a paragraph added in proof, that Wiechert had shown that one could not speak of electromagnetic mass for velocities greater than light, agreeing with Sommerfeld's negative-mass quantity.[92] Wiechert calculated, however, that the external force of the self-field was independent of electron velocity and acceleration. Such a conclusion only superficially contradicted Sommerfeld's point of view. He observed that Wiechert allowed the shape of his electron to depend on velocity; in this way, Wiechert's electromagnetic resistance was independent of velocity. Different from Wiechert, Sommerfeld had assumed throughout a spherical electron and so required electromagnetic mass to depend on velocity.

Working in the shadow of mathematics

To conclude the seminar Herglotz directed a session devoted to the theory of dispersion and the Zeeman effect. His sources were the textbooks by Drude and Poincaré, neither of which provided treatments approaching in level the sophisticated analyses offered by Sommerfeld and Schwarzschild. It is hard to see what Herglotz, a *Dozent* without training in experimental physics, was expected to contribute if not a new mathematical elaboration of these critical phenomena.

In concluding by discussing experiments of current interest, the seminar achieved a certain structural elegance. It passed from the basic equations of electron theory to, at last, the critical phenomena that the theory would have to explain. In his first paper on special relativity—then surely past the stage of corrected proofs—Einstein also concluded by considering how his theory could account for experiments. Einstein chose, however, the classical and well-known optical phenomena of the Doppler shift and stellar aberration, phenomena unencumbered (as were dispersion and Zeeman splitting) by particular assumptions about the structure of the matter. Einstein was surely the man to make bold hypotheses in this field, but unlike the Göttingen *Dozenten* he sought above all to address the most essential properties of nature. One can only guess what happened when on 31 July 1905 Herglotz and his student reporter walked to the blackboard.

It is not the place here to consider the subsequent and major contributions to electron theory made by the seminarists of 1905. One may ask, nevertheless, why the Göttingen *Dozenten* did not arrive at Einstein's special theory of relativity. They enjoyed unhindered access to published work and personal resources. Group theory was part of the atmosphere at Göttingen. Felix Klein had been the author of the 1872 Erlangen programme for unifying geometries by seeking to characterise their differential, invariant properties, and Woldemar Voigt had spent much of his career studying the transformational properties of crystals. None in the seminar, however, directly arrived at the Lorentz transformations.

By 1904 the electromagnetic view of nature had been shown to contain serious inconsistencies, yet none at Göttingen was able to formulate, much less to resolve, the fundamental contradictions between electromagnetic theory and classical mechanics. Had Des Coudres, Schwarzschild, or especially Abraham participated in the seminar its syllabus might have included or even centred on Lorentz's 1904 elaboration of electron theory, and in this way Minkowski might have been led to formulate, two years earlier, his notion of space–time, a notion that owed little to Einstein's special theory of relativity. Had Kaufmann, Riecke, or Voigt participated in the seminar more attention might have been paid to experimental measurements of electron dynamics. Even with these changes one wonders if special relativity could have emerged at Göttingen.

The vision of the seminarists was a mathematical one. Powerful machinery from pure mathematics and technical mechanics was introduced to extend the electron theory, a field of study that was barely five years old. The *Dozenten* sought to subdue nature, as it were, by the use of pure mathematics. They were not much interested in calculating with experimentally observable phenomena. They avoided studying electrons in metal conductors or at very low or high temperatures, and they did not spend much time elaborating the role of electrons in atomic spectra, a field of experimental physics then attracting the interest of scores of young physicists in their doctoral dissertations. Earlier, in 1902, Walther Ritz had written a dissertation under Voigt where he stated his famous law for spectral series.[93] The seminar took no notice of it. For the seminar *Dozenten* it did not matter that accelerating an electron to velocities greater than that of light and even to infinite velocities made little physical sense. They pursued the problem because of its intrinsic, abstract interest. When the four *Dozenten* responded to Einstein's special relativity after 1906 they did so from the perspective of their experiences in the 1905 seminar. None ever recognised subsequently how fundamentally Einstein's work differed from Lorentz's electron theory.

In seeking reasons why Einstein was more successful than the Göttingen *Dozenten* at resolving the impasse in electron theory it might be thought that Einstein did not have before him the wealth, perhaps the *embarras de choix*, that confronted researchers at Göttingen. They had access to numerous published exercises written from their own mathematical point of view, while Einstein was in matters of electrodynamics an autodidact. We may ask, nevertheless, about possible intersections between the reading lists of the 1905 seminar and the young Einstein.

In the period before 1905 Einstein's position at the Berne patent office required that he know and continue to improve his familiarity with Maxwellian electromagnetic theory.[94] In January 1903, Einstein wrote to his good friend Michele Angelo Besso with a remark that he would soon devote himself to *Elektronentheorie*, the theory of electrons.[95] He referred not to electromagnetism or electrodynamics, but to a word that had only been used in German since around 1902. For the source of the term 'theory of electrons' might Einstein have had in mind the 1902 *Göttinger Nachrichten* text of Max Abraham, where the term was given one of its first summary expositions?[96] We do know that Einstein favoured above all Lorentz's electron theory, and the Dutch theoretician was the single living authority cited in Einstein's first paper on relativity.

When in the spring of 1905 Einstein was looking for the *accepted* exposition of electron theory—and he referred to it in these words in his paper—nothing would have seemed more natural than for him to scan the first part of Sommerfeld's mechanics volume in the encyclopaedia of mathematical sciences, published in June 1904. In it Lorentz presented an introductory article on Maxwell's theory and his long review of electron theory. Einstein did not have ready access to many of the recent original papers of Lorentz. It would be strange, however, if in Berne, a university town and capital of Switzerland, there had not been then some library—of the university, *Gymnasium*, city, canton, or confederation—which subscribed to Felix Klein's well-publicised encyclopaedia. If more certain information were available concerning Einstein's study habits, one might be tempted to claim about the physical paradox described by him in the introduction to the first article on special relativity that it derived from a reading of the opening pages of Lorentz's article on Maxwell's theory. Knowing the extent of Einstein's familiarity with Lorentz's two encyclopaedia articles might resolve the long historical debate concerning whether or not Einstein in 1905 was familiar with the Michelson–Morley experiments.

Notwithstanding Einstein's possible acquaintance with these review articles, the second, electrodynamical part of his paper on special relativity was quite different from the electron-theory exposition chosen by the Göttingen *Dozenten*. Most striking is the absence in Einstein's work of any mention of electromagnetic potential or action principles, concepts lying at the very core of the expositions studied by the 1905 seminar. Because as a last-year student at the Zurich Polytechnikum Einstein had studied potential theory from the lecture notes taken by his friend Marcel Grossmann, we must assume that his decision not to consider at least this subject was a deliberate one.[97] In contrast with the Göttingen mathematicians, Einstein held the field equations and their properties, throughout his life, as the most fundamental parts of physical theory. It was immensely important for Einstein when, late in the 1930s, he was able to show that the equations of motion of a particle were contained in the field equations of general relativity.[98] The utility of other quantities and formulations depended on first understanding the field equations, in electromagnetism as well as in gravitation. By directing their attention toward the consequences of various symbolic elaborations of nature's laws, the Göttingen *Dozenten* thought that they would be able to set electrodynamic theory in order. They brought as much confusion to it as rectification.

Notes and references

1 Tetu Hirosige, 'Electrodynamics before the Theory of Relativity', *Japanese Studies in the History of Science* no 5 (1966) 1–49; Hirosige, 'The Ether Problem, the Mechanistic Worldview, and the Origins of the Theory of Relativity', *Historical Studies in the Physical Sciences* **7** (1976) 3–82, esp pp 41

ff; Stanley Goldberg, 'Henri Poincaré and Einstein's Theory of Relativity', *American Journal of Physics* **36** (1967) 934–44; Goldberg, 'The Lorentz Theory of Electrons and Einstein's Theory of Relativity', *Am. J. Phys.* **37** (1969) 982–94; Goldberg, 'Poincaré's Silence and Einstein's Theory of Relativity', *British Journal for the History of Science* **5** (1970) 73–84; Goldberg, 'Max Planck's Philosophy of Nature and His Elaboration of the Special Theory of Relativity', *Hist. Stud. Phys. Sci.* **7** (1976) 125–60; Russell McCormmach, 'Einstein, Lorentz, and the Electron Theory', *Hist. Stud. Phys. Sci.* **2** (1970) 41–87; McCormmach, 'H A Lorentz and the Electromagnetic View of Nature', *Isis* **61** (1970) 459–97. On related issues the reader is referred to McCormmach's lucid studies: 'Lorentz, Hendrik Antoon', *Dictionary of Scientific Biography* **8** (New York 1973) 487–500, and his 'Editor's Foreword', *Hist. Stud. Phys. Sci.* **7** (1976) xi–xxxv.

2 This literature is too large to be summarised here. References are provided in Hirosige's 'Ether Problem' (ref 1) 4–5. For a technical introduction to electron theory and its relationship to Einstein's special theory of relativity *circa* 1905, Ludwik Silberstein's text (*The Theory of Relativity* [London 1914], esp pp 21–122) has remained the best English-language treatment.

3 'Grundgleichungen der Elektronentheorie', Nachlass David Hilbert 570/9, Niedersächsische Staats- und Universitätsbibliothek, Göttingen. Texts mentioned in this document have been verified against K Hiemenz, *Katalog des mathematischen Lesezimmers der Universität Göttingen* (Leipzig 1907).

4 *Amtliches Verzeichnis des Personals und der Studierenden der Georg-August Universität zu Göttingen. Ostern bis Michaelis 1905.* A copy of this printed document is available in the Universitätsarchiv. Listed in it are: Blasius, Born, Houstoun, Kohlschütter, Laue, Swift, Tietze, Syula Lechnitzky (from Iglo, Hungary), Friedrich Schwietring (from Hanover), and Wenceslaus Werner (from Warsaw). No mention is made of students Belkenet [?], Jaumann [?], and Joukowski [?]. Other students may have attended the seminar, as well. The *Matrikeleintragung* of Jakob Johann Laub, at the Universitätsarchiv in Göttingen, indicates that Laub registered for it.

5 'Seminar. Sommer 1905. Elektrotechnisches Seminar. Mi. 3. V. 05'. Nachlass Felix Klein, XIX-K, Niedersächsische Staats- und Universitätsbibliothek, Göttingen.

6 H A Lorentz, *Versuch einer Theorie der elektrischen und optischen Erscheinungen in bewegten Körpern* (Leiden 1895). This book is analysed intensively by Tetu Hirosige in 'Origins of Lorentz' Theory of Electrons and the Concept of the Electromagnetic Field', *Hist. Stud. Phys. Sci.* **1** (1969) 151–209.

7 H Poincaré, *Electricité et optique: La Lumière et les théories électrodynamiques. Leçons professées à la Sorbonne en 1888, 1890 et 1899* ed J Blondin and E Néculcéa (Paris 1901).

8 H A Lorentz, 'Weiterbildung der Maxwellschen Theorie. Elektronentheorie', published as article 14 (pp 145–280) in volume 5, part 2 (ed Arnold Sommerfeld) of the *Encyklopädie der mathematischen Wissenschaften mit Einschluss ihrer Anwendungen*, under the general direction of Felix Klein. The first number of part 2, including this article of Lorentz's, was published on 16 June 1904. Lorentz's article is discussed briefly in Hirosige's 'Ether Problem' (ref 1) 43–4.

9 H A Lorentz (ref 8) p 221. Planck, 'Ueber das Gesetz der Energieverteilung im Normalspektrum', *Annalender Physik* **4** (1901) 553–64; 'Ueber die Elementarquanta der Materie und der Elektrizität', *Ann. Phys.* **4** (1901) 564–7.

10 H Poincaré, 'Sur la Dynamique de l'électron', *Rendiconti del Circolo Matematico di Palermo* **21** (1906) 129–75. The article is considered in A I Miller's 'A Study of Henri Poincaré's "Sur la Dynamique de l'Electron" ', *Archive for History of Exact Sciences* **10** (1973) 207–328.

11 H A Lorentz, 'Electromagnetic Phenomena in a System Moving with any Velocity Less than that of Light', Amsterdam, Koninklijke Akademie van Wetenschappen, *Proceedings of the Section of Sciences* **6** (1904) 809. See McCormmach's 'H A Lorentz' (ref 1), Hirosige's 'Ether Problem' (ref 1), 44–7, and K F Schaffner's 'The Lorentz Electron Theory of Relativity', *Am. J. Phys.* **37** (1969) 498–513.

12 F Klein, *Vorträge über den mathematischen Unterricht an den höheren Schulen* I ed Rudolf Schimmack (Leipzig 1907) pp 159–73.

13 Ambronn and Klein did not agree on how to conduct astronomical research at Göttingen. Ambronn to Hermann Wagner, 15 April 1910. Nachlass Hermann Wagner 14, Niedersächsische Staats- und Universitätsbibliothek, Göttingen.

14 B Gutenberg, 'Emil Wiechert', *Meteorologische Zeitschrift* **45** (1928) 183–5. Gutenberg's information is in some cases different from that given by Keith E Bullen in *Dict. Sci. Biog.* **14** (1976) 327–8.

15 P Volkmann, 'Hat die Physik Atome? Erkenntnistheoretische Studien über die Grundlage der Physik', *Schriften der physikalisch–ökonomischen Gesellschaft zu Königsberg in Preussen, Sitzungsberichte* **35** (1894) 13–22, pp 14, 18.

16 E Wiechert, 'Die Bedeutung des Weltaethers', *ibid* 4–11; 'Die Theorie der Elektrodynamik und die Röntgen'sche Entdeckung', *ibid, Abhandlungen* **37** (1896) 1–49; 'Ueber das Wesen der Elektrizität', *ibid, Sitzungsberichte* **38** (1897) 3–12.

17 Karl Schwarzschild to his parents, 26 January 1901. Schwarzschild papers, reel 16, Niels Bohr Library, American Institute of Physics, New York.

18 Heinrich Tietze, 'Gustav Herglotz', *Jahrbuch der Bayerischen Akademie der Wissenschaften* (Munich 1953) pp 188–94.

19 Herglotz to Schwarzschild, 5 April 1903 and 15 April 1903. Nachlass Karl Schwarzschild 5:XV, Niedersächsische Staats- und Universitätsbibliothek, Göttingen.

20 As indicated by Felix Klein in his *Gesammelte Mathematische Abhandlungen* **3** (Berlin 1923), appendix.

21 Ernst Hellinger, 'Mechanik. Vorlesung von Prof Dr Hilbert im W–S, 1905/06', Nachlass Gustav Herglotz C-6, Niedersächsische Staats- und Universitätsbibliothek, Göttingen.

22 Max Born, *Physics in My Generation* (New York 1969) p 101. In his long autobiography (*Mein Leben* [Munich 1975]) Born does not elaborate on the seminar.

23 H Minkowski, 'Ueber die Bewegung eines festen Körpers in einer Flüssigkeit', Berlin, Königliche preussische Akademie der Wissenschaften, *Sitzungsberichte* **40** (1888) 1095–1110. Reprinted in *Gesammelte Abhandlungen von Hermann Minkowski* **2** ed David Hilbert (Berlin 1911) 283–97.

24 H Minkowski to D Hilbert, 19 June 1889, in *Hermann Minkowski: Briefe an David Hilbert* ed L Rüdenberg and H Zassenhaus (Berlin 1973) p 36.
25 Voigt, 'Ueber das Doppler'sche Prinzip', Göttingen, Königliche Gesellschaft der Wissenschaften, Mathematisch–physikalische Klasse, *Nachrichten* [hereafter *Göttinger Nachr.*] (1887) pp 41–51.
26 H Minkowski to D Hilbert, 22 December 1890, *Briefe* (ref 24) pp 39–40.
27 R McCormmach, 'Hertz, Heinrich', *Dict. Sci. Biog.* **6** (1972) 340–50.
28 H Minkowski to D Hilbert, 31 January 1897, *Briefe* (ref 24) p 94.
29 Klein's approach is treated in chapter 7.
30 H Minkowski to D Hilbert, 11 February 1899, *Briefe* (ref 24) p 113.
31 F Klein and A Sommerfeld, *Ueber die Theorie des Kreisels* (4 vols, Leipzig 1897–1912). See also Klein's *Mathematical Theory of the Top: Lectures delivered on the occasion of the sesquicentennial celebration of Princeton University* (New York 1897).
32 H Minkowski to D Hilbert, 6 December 1898, *Briefe* (ref 24) p 111.
33 H Minkowski to D Hilbert, 11 February 1899, *ibid* p 113.
34 'Kapitel XI: Einleitung in die Elastizitätstheorie', n.d. Minkowski papers, box VIII, folder 3, Niels Bohr Library, American Institute of Physics, New York.
35 Remarks on a lecture course in analytical mechanics, 1902. Minkowski papers, box X, folder 14, *ibid*.
36 Manuscript, probably a lecture on complex analysis, dated Wintersemester 1902/03. Box IX, folder 9, *ibid*.
37 'Differentialrechnung, S. S. 1904', box IX, folder 6, *ibid*.
38 H Poincaré, 'La Théorie de Lorentz et le principe de la réaction', *Archives néerlandaises* **5** (1900) 252–78.
39 R McCormmach, 'H A Lorentz' (ref 1).
40 E Wiechert, 'Elektrodynamische Elementargesetze', *Archives néerlandaises* **5** (1900) 549–73.
41 *Ibid*.
42 E Beltrami, 'Sull'espressione data da Kirchhoff al principio di Huygens', Rome, Reale Accademia dei Lincei, Classe di scienze fisiche, matematiche e naturali, *Rendiconti* **4** part 2 (1895) 29–31.
43 H Burkhardt and W F Meyer, 'Potentialtheorie (Theorie der Laplace–Poissonschen Differentialgleichung)', published as article 7b (pp 464–503) in vol **2**, part 1, first half (ed H Burkhardt, W Wirtinger, and R Fricke) in *Encyklopädie* (ref 8). The fourth number of this publication, including Burkhardt and Meyer's article, nominally appeared on 31 July 1900.
44 K Schwarzschild, 'Zur Elektrodynamik: II. Die elementare elektrodynamische Kraft', *Göttinger Nachr.* (1903) pp 132–41.
45 Grassmann's treatment is given in R Reiff and A Sommerfeld's 'Standpunkt der Fernwirkung: Die Elementargesetze', pp 3–62 of Sommerfeld's volume *Mechanik* (ref 8).
46 T Hirosige (ref 6).
47 K Schwarzschild, 'Zur Elektrodynamik: I. Zwei Formen des Prinzips der kleinsten Action in der Elektronentheorie', *Göttinger Nachr.* (1903) pp 126–31.
48 Clausius' potential is treated in Reiff and Sommerfeld (ref 45) pp 55–62.
49 G T Walker, *Aberration and Some Other Problems Connected with the Electromagnetic Field* (Cambridge 1900).

50 J Larmor, *Aether and Matter* (Cambridge 1900) pp 167–75. Compare B G Doran's 'Origins and Consolidation of Field Theory in Nineteenth Century Britain: From the Mechanical to the Electromagnetic View of Nature', *Hist. Stud. Phys. Sci.* **6** (1975) 133–260, esp pp 243–5, 254–7.

51 P Drude, *Lehrbuch der Optik* (Leipzig 1900).

52 M Abraham, 'Prinzipien der Dynamik des Elektrons', *Ann. Phys.* **10** (1903) 105–79. Stanley Goldberg, 'The Abraham Theory of the Electrons: The Symbiosis of Experiment and Theory', *Arch. Hist. Exact Sci.* **7** (1970) 7–25.

53 According to *J C Poggendorff's biographisch–literarisches Handwörterbuch* **6** ed H Stobbe (Berlin 1936), and S Goldberg's 'Abraham, Max', *Dict. Sci. Biog.* **1** (1970) 23–5.

54 M Abraham (ref 52) p 111.

55 S Goldberg (ref 53).

56 M Abraham (ref 52) p 105.

57 *Ibid* p 107.

58 *Ibid* p 109.

59 *Ibid* p 109.

60 *Ibid* p 111.

61 *Ibid* pp 148–9.

62 M Abraham, 'Elektromagnetische Wellen', pp 483–538 in Sommerfeld's *Mechanik* (ref 8).

63 M Abraham (ref 52) p 168.

64 K Schwarzschild, 'Zur Elektrodynamik: III. Ueber die Bewegung des Elektrons', *Göttinger Nachr.* (1903) pp 245–78.

65 *Ibid* p 246.

66 Probably Leo Königsberger's *Die Prinzipien der Mechanik* (Leipzig 1901).

67 K Schwarzschild (ref 64) p 273.

68 P Hertz, *Untersuchungen über unstetige Bewegungen eines Elektrons* (dissertation, University of Göttingen 1904).

69 *Ibid* p 4.

70 *Ibid* p 29.

71 *Ibid* pp 77–8.

72 The following quotations are taken from: Paul Forman and Armin Hermann's 'Sommerfeld, Arnold', *Dict. Sci. Biog.* **12** (1975) 525–32; Thomas S Kuhn *et al*, *Sources for History of Quantum Physics* (Philadelphia 1967) [*Am. Phil. Soc. Mem.* **68**] p 138.

73 G Herglotz, 'Zur Elektronentheorie', *Göttinger Nachr.* (1903) pp 357–82.

74 A Sommerfeld to K Schwarzschild, 30 January 1904. Schwarzschild papers, reel 21, section 1, Niels Bohr Library, American Institute of Physics, New York.

75 A Sommerfeld to K Schwarzschild, 31 March 1904. *Ibid.*

76 *Ibid.*

77 A Sommerfeld, 'Zur Elektronentheorie: I. Allgemeine Untersuchung des Feldes eines beliebig bewegten Elektrons', *Göttinger Nachr.* (1904) pp 99–130.

78 A Sommerfeld, 'Zur Elektronentheorie: II. Grundlagen für eine allgemeine Dynamik des Elektrons', *Göttinger Nachr.* (1904) pp 363–439.

79 *Ibid* p 367. P Frank, 'Das Relativitätsprinzip der Mechanik und die Glei-

chungen für die elektromagnetischen Vorgänge in bewegten Körpern', *Ann. Phys.* **27** (1909) 897–902 on p 897.

80 T Des Coudres, 'Zur Theorie des Kraftfeldes elektrischer Ladungen, die sich mit Ueberlichtgeschwindigkeit bewegen', *Archives néerlandaises* **5** (1900) 652–64.

81 A Sommerfeld (ref 78) p 371.

82 Olexa M P Bilaniuk, V K Deshpande, and E C G Sudarshan, ' "Meta" Relativity', *Am. J. Phys.* **30** (1962) 718–23; Bilaniuk and Sudarshan, 'Particles Beyond the Light Barrier', *Physics Today* **22** no 5 (May 1969) 43–51 and the subsequent discussion 'More About Tachyons', *Physics Today* **22** no 12 (December 1969) 47–52. Bilaniuk *et al* acknowledge Sommerfeld's work.

83 A Sommerfeld (ref 78) p 432.

84 G Herglotz, 'Ueber die Berechnung retardierter Potentiale', *Göttinger Nachr.* (1904) pp 549–56.

85 A Sommerfeld, 'Simplified Deduction of the Field and the Forces of an Electron, moving in any given way', Amsterdam, K. Akad. Wet. *Proc. Sect. Sci.* **7** part 1 (1904) 346–67.

86 T Des Coudres (ref 80).

87 P Drude (ref 51) p 433.

88 J V Jelley, *Čerenkov Radiation* (London 1958); J D Jackson, *Classical Electrodynamics* (New York 1962) pp 494–9. In accepting the 1958 Nobel Prize for providing the theory of Čerenkov radiation, Tamm noted that when he and Frank first discussed their theory with Alexander Joffe during the 1930s, Joffe alerted them to Sommerfeld's work of 1904. Nobel Foundation, *Nobel Lectures . . . Physics, 1942–1962* (Amsterdam 1964) p 473.

89 A Sommerfeld, 'Zur Elektronentheorie: III. Ueber Lichtgeschwindigkeits- und Ueberlichtgeschwindigkeits-Elektronen', *Göttinger Nachr.* (1905) pp 201–35.

90 This point is elaborated in chapter 4.

91 A Sommerfeld (ref 89) p 202.

92 E Wiechert, 'Bemerkungen zur Bewegung der Elektronen bei Ueberlichtgeschwindigkeiten', *Göttinger Nachr.* (1905) pp 75–82.

93 R Fueter, 'Dr Walter Ritz', *Verhandlungen der Schweizerischen Naturforschenden Gesellschaft, 92. Jahresversammlung: Nekrologe und Biographien* (1909) pp 96–104, p 99; Paul Forman, 'Ritz, Walter', *Dict. Sci. Biog.* **11** (1970) 475–81.

94 Max Flückiger, *Albert Einstein in Bern* (Berne 1974) pp 53–70.

95 A Einstein to M Besso, January 1903. *Albert Einstein–Michele Besso, Correspondance, 1903–1955* ed Pierre Speziali (Paris 1972) pp 3–6.

96 M Abraham, 'Dynamik des Elektrons', *Göttinger Nachr.* (1902) pp 20–41.

97 The notebooks are kept in the Wissenschaftshistorischen Sammlung, Bibliothek der ETH, Zurich.

98 Leopold Infeld, *Why I Left Canada: Reflections on Science and Politics*, transl Helen Infeld, ed Lewis Pyenson (Montreal 1978) pp 6–7.

6   Relativity in late Wilhelmian Germany: the appeal to a pre-established harmony between mathematics and physics

Introduction

Most students of intellectual life in Wilhelmian Germany have at one time or other attempted to gauge the magnitude of their task by reading in Traugott Konstantin Oesterreich's massive bibliography and synopsis of philosophical currents. More than any other source, his text provides a measure of the bewildering profusion of competing philosophical systems that appeared around 1900.[1] There one sees theories of myriad shades and complexions, bright patches of colour that fade into each other's periphery. Never before, the impression arises, had there been such a large and apparently anarchic outpouring of concern about philosophical truth and how to achieve it. In flogging his own work, every obscure professor or social malcontent seemed eager to gather in his train, Friedrich Paulsen noted in 1907, a gaggle of disciples.[2] Fame and fortune rewarded those, like Wilhelm Ostwald, Ernst Haeckel, and Rudolf von Eucken, who gave the public what they wanted.

From our privileged vantage point we see the superficiality of philosophical texts published at that time. Leaving aside major developments in mathematical logic, one is especially struck by the extent to which philosophers failed to arrive at formulations commensurate with achievements in other fields. Creative thinkers early in the twentieth century would have agreed: philosophy only lightly scarred the enduring accomplishments of the period.

If one finds little echo of the special world systems of a Windelband, a Tönnies, or a Weber in literary fiction or scientific theories, there are nevertheless themes in Wilhelmian Germany which transcend the boundaries separating various creative endeavours. Fundamental questioning arose in nearly all scholarly and scientific circles. Accepted canons and principles sustained heavy criticism from new visions of reality and humanity's place in it. The force generating this intellectual maelstrom was a hunger for wholeness, a 'kindling fever' or emotional craving to bring the separate elements of reality into a coherent synthesis. Success would require, many intellectuals believed, a revolution in thought. From the 1890s onward, the various words for revolution—*Umwalzung, Umgestaltung, Revolution*—regularly appeared in scientific and literary writings. 'People were standing on all sides to fight against the old way of life', Robert Musil observed in 1930 about the prewar years. At a time when protests against the autocratic German state involved substantial personal risk, intellectuals mounted paper barricades to defend one or another revolutionary idea. The residue of this revolutionary thought underlies twentieth-century scholarship and especially science.[3]

Weak links between exhilaration in physical science and tedium in philosophy would have cautioned writers in the interwar period who sought the philosophical heritage of scientific discourse. Because in recent times it claims no necessary connection with natural knowledge or science, philosophy usually finds a place in scientific activity as just one of many sources for the prejudice or fantasy that inspires or constrains a working scientist. As might be expected, even though individual philosophers were rarely celebrated by physicists or chemists in their scientific treatises, philosophical predilections suffused what can be called the German scientific community at the beginning of the twentieth century. In this chapter I consider one such predilection, that relating to a revival of the notion of pre-established harmony.

We owe the idea of pre-established harmony, of course, to Leibniz. It was his solution to the problem of the interaction between mind and body—between the eternal and perfect objects studied by metaphysics on the one hand and the world of experience studied by physics on the other hand. In his view, there could be no causal interaction, intercourse, or commerce between these two domains, which were complementary aspects of the universe, just as there could be no causal connection between any two things in the physical world. Rather, all change had to be pre-ordained by God, who was to have endowed both the constituent objects of the metaphysical realm and the things of the physical realm with identical plans for future action and development. Notwithstanding his metaphysical commitments, Leibniz welcomed such mechanical or mathematical explanations as, for example, were provided in the laws of motion.

Hidē Ishiguro has emphasised about this point: 'To say that every change in an object can be explained from its nature and natural laws of the world is not to say that things behave as if they were not connected to

other things. Everything is like a mirror which reflects the whole universe.'
Exploring the lawfulness of the physical world required, in Leibniz's view,
an appeal to mechanics and mathematics. Ishiguro quotes Leibniz: 'Nature
must be explained mechanically and mathematically, provided one bears
in mind that the principles of the laws of mechanics themselves do not
derive from mere mathematical extension, but from metaphysical reasons.'
Inversely, since the abstract forms of certain mathematical relations
belonged to the metaphysical realm, they could reasonably be expected
to correspond to relationships among things in the physical realm.
Adhering to a Leibniz-like understanding of the idea of pre-established
harmony, especially after the foundation of the discipline of pure mathematics in the nineteenth century, would impel one to use mathematical
forms and symmetries as a guide to discovering nature's laws.[4]

Pre-established harmony is only one of many notions that might have
served to motivate or justify a desire to impose mathematical order on
physical phenomena. In the following pages I indicate how the notion
figured prominently in the writings of many interpreters of Einstein's
theories of relativity. The mathematicians, physicists, and philosophers
whom I consider were for the most part uneasy about viewing special
relativity as a theory concerned with measurement. The theory became
acceptable to them when, upon being recast in mathematical language, it
was de-relativised. Many writers appealed to the idea of pre-established
harmony in their attempt to interpret relativity as a theory of absolute,
four-dimensional space–time, a theory that could admit the concept of an
electromagnetic ether. On the eve of the advent of the Weimar republic,
relativity was understood to concern abstract, unphysical, absolute
space—all that its creator Albert Einstein had originally laboured to dispel.

My aim in this chapter is to isolate an intellectual phenomenon that
informed the reception of physical theories. In proposing that for many
researchers pure mathematics came to dictate the form of physical reality,
I do not mean to deny the importance of other epistemological inclinations
and proclivities manifest in the late Wilhelmian period. Many physicists
steadfastly believed that mathematics remained rooted in physical reality.
At the same time, I deliberately ignore how the notion of pre-established
harmony received support from objective successes in applying mathematics to physical problems. It lies far from my intention here to argue
that philosophical ideas in themselves precipitated a new way of understanding the relationship between mathematics and physics; although I
touch on why the notion of pre-established harmony would have received
a favourable reception in Germany, elaboration of themes in social history
are reserved for another place in the present book. Whether the pattern
revealed here finds reflections in other countries is a subject for future
investigations.[5]

A classical vision

Physicists throughout German-speaking Europe at the end of the nineteenth century believed that mathematics had only incidental value in constructing physical theories. The views of the talented experimentalist and theoretician Paul Drude are typical in this regard. When he was called to an associate professorship of physics at the University of Leipzig in 1894, Drude delivered an inaugural lecture on the role of theory in his discipline. He followed the approach of Gustav Kirchhoff in believing that the task of modern theoretical physics lay in 'describing natural phenomena completely and in the simplest way'. One did not seek to know the essence of reality, only the 'representation of the world of phenomena'. To describe nature required that physics invoke 'mathematical language'. Drude recognised that mathematics in itself was insufficient for revealing or elaborating physical laws. There was 'real danger in the application of mathematics, or, as I could better say, of rigid formalism.' The body of his address indicated how physicists had constructed, with the help of mathematics, pictures of the physical world. Such descriptions were by no means less certain than ordinary sense perception: the essence of a stone held in one's hand was known as well, or as poorly, as the essence of electricity. Truth, for Drude, could be known only subjectively as the sum of human perception of 'intelligible facts'.[6]

It is not surprising that Drude's views emerged at the same time that pure mathematics reached its zenith as a learned discipline, one with dozens of university chairs and one processing hundreds of students destined for posts in the secondary schools. Pure mathematics tended to evacuate from physics the talents of those mathematically adept physicists who, as lesser copies of Carl Friedrich Gauss, might otherwise have ranged from number theory to electrical instrumentation. Pure mathematicians believed that intercourse with the abstract, pure essence of mathematics unencumbered by physical reality was essential preparation for solving concrete problems in the dirty, real world. Educators in the civil services of the various German states found such an outlook congenial, with the result that as German industrial technology came to set a model for the world, producing technical competence remained less important than educating noble sentiments.

Paul Drude's views on mathematics were shared by theoretical physicists of the time—Max Planck, Ernst Mach, and Ludwig Boltzmann—regardless of their other epistemological inclinations. We find them present, too, in the last lectures of the influential Hermann von Helmholtz, which were edited in 1903 by Arthur König and Carl Runge. Helmholtz began by emphasising the pernicious influence on natural science of the German *Naturphilosophen*. Men long knew that in mathematics,

Helmholtz continued, one was able by the force of pure thought to find general laws. Pure thought, speculation, was also useful in formulating scientific laws. One could treat abstract things and grammatical expressions as realities and one could regard results of untested experience as necessities of thought. Helmholtz noted how this circumstance brought philosophy into ill repute. Although mathematical knowledge in itself did not reveal physical truths, the great physicist believed that mathematics played a 'vital role' for anyone who dedicated himself to physics. 'The greatest depths of mathematical analysis' would have to be plumbed to achieve a clear and distinct view of the basic laws of nature. Mathematics provided a logical structure—it was no more than that—for expressing in words the laws of physics.[7]

If there were a classical physicist who might have subscribed to the notion that beautiful mathematical formalism directly corresponded to physical reality, then it would have been Heinrich Hertz. He was a transitional figure. A master like Drude of both experiment and theory, Hertz had verified the existence of electromagnetic waves and had renovated James Clerk Maxwell's theory of electricity and magnetism. He attributed no deep meaning to the form that he gave to what we now call 'Maxwell's equations' for the electromagnetic field. Rather, he agreed to accept the equations as a phenomenological description of a reality that had still to be discovered. Hertz's last project—seen through the press by his assistant Philipp Lenard—was an attempt to formulate mechanics by eliminating the apparently obscure notion of force. In place of force Hertz hypothesised physical masses in support of which no evidence could be marshalled.[8]

We see how he began to move away from Drude's understanding of mathematics when, in the introduction to his *Principles of Mechanics*, Hertz underlined how physical understanding arose. He believed that the mind formed images of the external world. Deductions from these images paralleled, in a convincing discussion, consequences in nature of the things that were pictured. Although Hertz did not use the words 'pre-established harmony' to describe how conceptions cohered with the external world, his description of theories might well have had such a notion at its base. Later in the introduction, when he wrote that 'the physical content is quite independent of the mathematical form', he could only have meant to emphasise the harmony that existed between physical reality and mathematics. In this, Hertz's last work, there is a reluctance to acknowledge the paralysing beauty and seductiveness of the abstract form that mechanics took when phrased in terms of the principle of least action. Hertz, the codifier of Maxwell's equations for electromagnetism, vigorously resisted granting that abstract equations implied the actual existence of an electromagnetic field.[9]

Pre-established harmony reconsidered

How was it, then, that from Hertz's intimation of pre-established harmony there came, within twenty years, an effusion of sentiment in favour of the notion? The answer to such a question involves a conjuncture of several developments. Educational reform successfully challenged the pre-eminence of pure mathematicians in universities and secondary schools, and it forced them to provide evidence for the relevance of their field of study to other, more prosaic concerns. Beginning in 1900, secondary schools came to include a great deal more advanced mathematics in their curricula, and this material was taught by men trained for the most part in pure mathematics—men who reluctantly emphasised how pure thought could make sense of physical phenomena. Increasing numbers of students entered university, fired with a conviction that advanced mathematics could unify and codify disparate branches of physics. Attuned to the process of school reform, university lecturers sought to provide concrete evidence for the power of pure mathematics, and many increasingly turned their attention towards physical problems. In such a climate, an appeal to pre-established harmony would have found many sympathetic readers.[10]

The echoes of harmony, as from the music of the spheres, resonated throughout nineteenth-century German culture. The word 'harmony' was widely employed in the service of general, cultural manifestos: it was ideologically neutral, it could be invoked to support monistic or pluralistic philosophies, and it bore the unmistakable cachet of classical antiquity. With the rise of materialistic and industrial civilisation late in the century came much anguish over the decline of the 'neogrecian, harmonious ideal of humanities', as the historian Georg Steinhausen lamented in 1913.[11] In an obvious attempt to appropriate the neohumanist educational ideal of spiritual harmony that had dominated Germany for so long, science educators like Johann Norrenberg wrote about how secondary schools had to place formal understanding (*Können*) in harmony with material knowledge (*Wissen*). 'The end and aim of natural-science instruction can only be found in a symbiotic union of material and formal tasks.'[12] Because it was so central to German thinking around 1900, desire for harmony in thought and life would have sustained interest in the notion of a pre-established harmony between mathematics and the world of experience, at least once the notion had been clearly articulated.

The notion came to centre stage during a revival of interest in Leibniz's philosophy. As the founding genius behind the Berlin Academy of Sciences, of course, the great polymath received panegyric or eulogy at least once a year.[13] His work also captured the attention of dedicated editors like mathematician Carl Immanuel Gerhardt.[14] These and other references were more in the nature of scholarly exercises than confessions of belief, for in the shadow of Immanuel Kant's critical idealism and its successor programmes, few commentators could have been expected to take pre-Kantian philosophy seriously. In part as a consequence of the tide that threw everything open to question, the situation changed at the beginning of the twentieth century. The British philosopher Bertrand Russell and the French mathematician Louis Couturat both elaborated on Leibniz's philosophy in major treatises.[15] Party to this international interest was the young German neoidealist Ernst Cassirer, whose first full-length book, published in 1902, considered the scientific foundations of Leibniz's writings.[16]

In his book, Cassirer emphasised how Leibniz understood a pre-established harmony to exist between mathematics and the real world. Mathematics was in Leibniz's view the essential moderator between ideal, logical principles and the reality of nature: 'Mathematics provides the general, mental methods of determining [reality].' Cassirer underlined how Leibniz believed in 'distinct, mathematical sensuality, which is not thought of as opposed to the principles of pure understanding'. Reality, then, followed from pure reason through the application of mathematics. Cassirer paraphrased Leibniz: the real object was 'only a paradigm of the general [form] and has for itself alone no independent meaning'. For Leibniz 'time and space indicate possibilities beyond the supposition of existences.' Time and space were not in themselves real, but were determinations of relations between realities. Cassirer understood the great rationalist to believe that 'measurement is not inferred from sensual, material bodies, but from pure, dynamical laws' that were themselves 'only a fulfilment of what is represented in mathematics'.[17]

Ernst Cassirer elaborated his thoughts in a long essay of 1910 on the notions of substance and function.[18] There he directly addressed 'the natural genealogy' of physics in mathematical concepts. For the neoidealist, 'physical concepts only carry forward the process that is begun in the mathematical concepts.' Mathematical concepts were for Cassirer pure relations, upon which rested 'the unity and continuous connections of the members of a manifold'. Mathematics gave rise to the 'intellectual connection and "harmony" of reality'. Following Leibniz, Cassirer believed that theoretical concepts in natural sciences were far from being 'merely purified and idealised word-meanings'. Mathematics elaborated the full truth of physical theory. Expressed somewhat obliquely: 'Mathematics is no "logical unique", but . . . it progressively provides the "special" natural sciences with its own characteristic form of concept. The form of mathematical "deduction" is already contained in the form of physical "induction".'

Bringing his thoughts to bear on a concrete example, Cassirer elaborated how he understood the way in which electricity and light were the same sort of phenomenon. The agreement was based not merely on perception, but also on the form of mathematical equations. More than similarity, the identity in form was a logical invariant, as in pure mathematics. ' "Analogy", which at first seems concerned with the sensuous particular, goes over more and more into mathematical "harmony".' In discussing frames of reference, Cassirer appealed to Leibniz's notion of paradigm: 'That any system of bodies is at rest (for example, the system of the fixed stars) does not signify a fact that can be directly established by perception or measurement, but means that a *paradigm* is found here in the world of bodies for certain principles of pure mechanics, in which they can be, as it were, visibly demonstrated and represented.' Paradigms, which originated in observation of nature, moved in the realm of pure thought. In Cassirer's view, experiments served as a heuristic beginning for a subsequent, more general understanding:

> Though experiment is necessary to analyze an originally undifferentiated perceptual whole into its particular constitutive elements, on the other hand, to mathematical theory belongs the determination of the form by which these elements are combined into a unity of law. The system of 'possible' relational syntheses already developed in mathematics affords the fundamental schema for the connections which thought seeks in the material of the real.[19]

Views on pre-established harmony similar to those in Cassirer's long-winded exposition appeared from a number of physicists and mathematicians during the first decade of the twentieth century. Before the Third International Mathematics Congress, held at Heidelberg in 1904, mathematician Felix Klein emphasised how applied mathematics was distinct from the 'citadel of citadels', or 'formal mathematics (in the Leibnizian sense)'. He understood the latter as 'any treatment of mathematical questions looking away from the possibility of any concrete meaning for its quantities or symbols and asking only about the external laws by which the quantities and symbols may be combined'. Klein believed that pure mathematics had a referent in the physical world. In his view, mathematics could obviously be applied to aid physical understanding.[20] Klein's colleague, the experimental physicist Eduard Riecke, emphasised in 1905 how in physics, as in all sciences, one distinguished between what nature did and what men thought about nature. It was always remarkable to Riecke that 'between the world of phenomena and the world of our thought an inner harmony exists which allows us to construct models that, at least within certain boundaries, provide a correct picture of the world'.[21]

Thoughts expressed by Riecke and Cassirer resonate with those of Hermann Minkowski, the mathematician who used Einstein's special theory of relativity to elaborate during the years 1907–9 a theory of absolute, four-dimensional space–time. He understood little of Einstein's work, and his main objective lay in imposing mathematical order on recalcitrant physical laws. We have seen in preceding chapters how, in his lectures after around 1900, he continually emphasised that pure mathematics could contribute significantly to a scientific understanding of the physical universe. He explicitly invoked pre-established harmony in a course of 1904 on differential equations. Minkowski, who played a critical role in reinterpreting and disseminating Einstein's special relativity, was guided in his endeavour by a neoleibnizian vision.[22]

Pre-established harmony and Minkowskian relativity

The response to Minkowski's elaboration of Einstein's ideas came quickly. One early commentator was Wilhelm Wien, professor of physics at the University of Würzburg and winner of a Nobel Prize in 1911 for his work on radiation. Wien was a master of both experiment and theory, following in the tradition of Paul Drude. In fact, Wien succeeded Drude as coeditor of the *Annalen der Physik*, the most prestigious physics periodical in the world, upon Drude's suicide in 1906.

Wilhelm Wien began his first popular exposition of relativity in 1909 by referring to purely mathematical investigations of non-Euclidean geometries.[23] In contrast to this basically speculative tradition, he noted, a tradition stretching from Gauss to David Hilbert, experimental physics had broken the path to a new view of space and time. It had done so by induction and had enjoyed no direct contact with the mathematicians pursuing various geometries. Although he paid homage to pure mathematics, Wien was clear to identify Einstein's physical contribution. Wien noted how the Dutch theoretician Hendrik Antoon Lorentz had proposed a theory that contained 'mathematically everything that we now identify as relativity theory', but how Lorentz's work was dominated by a belief in the stationary, electromagnetic ether—a concept that Einstein had dispatched. Wien even claimed himself to have proposed the famous space–time transformations, but he insisted that neither he nor Lorentz had interpreted the transformations from the point of view of relativity theory.

In view of all these statements, then, one is especially interested in the different tone that Wien used for a summation. 'It cannot be denied that this altered grasp of space and time has something intensely convincing about it', he wrote. 'The whole system of entirely internal consistency calls to mind the conviction that the facts would have to accommodate themselves to it [that is, to the system itself].'[24] The thick prose was the work of *Privatdozent* A Sommer, who took notes during Wien's talk and then reconstructed the discourse. We nevertheless see how, despite his obligatory references to experimental evidence, Wien felt himself drawn to Minkowski's theory by its inner beauty and consistency.

Wien had followed special relativity with great interest ever since

Einstein's publication of 1905. He alerted a student of his, Jakob Johann Laub, to the new theory. During his doctoral defence late in 1906, Laub appealed to Einstein's work, and later, while Wien's post-doctoral assistant, he came to collaborate closely with Einstein. In 1910 Laub summarised his views in a long article reviewing the experimental foundation of the theory. He realised that no *experimentum crucis* could establish the limits within which special relativity was a valid theory. Before Einstein's theory could be accepted, physicists would have to refine and reflect upon the material that had been accumulating since 1905. Laub concluded his review by asserting, much as his mentor Wien had done, the unity and mathematical elegance of Einstein's work: 'Although it is true that only an experiment can decide if a physical theory is correct, it must still be emphasised that mathematics and its applications are related by an inner harmony.'[25]

What came reluctantly to physicists Laub and Wien proved a triumph for mathematician Felix Klein. During the academic year 1909/10, Klein conducted an advanced seminar at the University of Göttingen on the psychological foundations of mathematics in an attempt to sharpen his understanding of the field for which he had become a public spokesman. In discussing mathematics and language, Klein gave special notice to the notion of pre-established harmony.[26] When in 1911 he offered his thoughts on the geometrical roots of Einstein's theory of relativity, Klein paraphrased Minkowski's approach to the matter. Physicists had neither the time nor the inclination, Klein wrote, 'to see if any conceptual laws [*begriffliche Ansätze*] which they need are to be found already constructed in the store-room of pure mathematics'. Physicists sadly proceeded by reinventing the mathematics that they required. 'All that is mathematically sound', Klein emphasised, 'sooner or later goes beyond its narrow field and finds more far-reaching meaning.'[27]

The extent to which Minkowski's formulation became a favoured illustration for the notion of pre-established harmony is revealed in the work of a pair of professors from Prussian Silesia. For the theme of his rectoral address at the University of Breslau in 1911, mathematician Adolf Kneser considered the extent to which the notion of pre-established harmony accounted for the relation between mathematics and the real world.[28] After remarking on how various great men of science had used mathematics—he considered Galileo, Joseph Fourier, Carl Jacobi, and Charles Hermite—Kneser addressed the theory of relativity. It was a theory where 'hand-graspable realities are replaced by mathematical constructions'. In Minkowski's four-dimensional, covariant representation of relativity, 'the physicist perceived, from his innermost requirements, a mathematical tool which long lay ready.' Kneser made relativity act as a sentient creature: 'The new physics of the principle of relativity is eager to work with any mathematical tool, to construct with it, and always to turn to new fashions.' He emphasised how Minkowski characterised the situation as 'a pre-established harmony between pure mathematics and applied physics'. For the Breslau mathematician anything palpable in nature could be formulated mathematically. New mathematics, indeed, held the key to knowledge: 'Progress in science is unthinkable without always obtaining for new mathematical tools a scientific existence.'[29]

Adolf Kneser's elaboration came to have wider circulation through a long essay published by his Breslau philosopher colleague Richard Hönigswald.[30] The philosopher considered and rejected in turn three possible resolutions of the problem of harmony between mathematics and reality: that the harmony could be attributed to psychological factors, that the harmony and hence mathematics was really grounded in experience, or that the harmony was rooted in mathematics itself. Rejecting dualistic solutions, Hönigswald remained convinced that the trace of sensory experience existed in the structure of pure mathematics. Following Kneser, he elaborated how Fourier saw the study of all nature as a source of mathematical discovery and how for Hermite the harmony was an aesthetic, metaphysical identity between two different worlds. Hönigswald then considered the harmony problem in the relativity theory of Lorentz and Einstein. For a hero, the philosopher also followed Kneser in choosing Hermann Minkowski. To Hönigswald, harmony was revealed in the way that Minkowski's theory incorporated the results of the Michelson–Morley experiment (which had failed to detect motion of the Earth relative to an electromagnetic ether) in a theory of space and time.

Relativity theory was not 'based on nor does it "constitute" scientific experience', he wrote. 'It *belongs* to scientific experience.' Relativity 'embodies the thoughts of pre-established harmony between mathematics and nature in its epistemologically original construction.' A Leibnizian solution was the only one possible for Hönigswald, for he held that 'mathematics establishes knowledge of nature because it itself is knowledge'. Yet Hönigswald stopped short of asserting the next step—that mathematics of itself, since it embodied reality, apodeictically anticipated natural laws. One could only become accustomed, Hönigswald cited Kneser, to expect that mathematics would make sense out of empirically derived data: ' "Not with certainty beforehand" can the "remarkable consequences" of mathematics in the command of nature "be calculated"; but "as the fruit of a tree in bloom" should they "be anticipated".'[31]

Philosophical niceties

By appealing to the metaphor of a living tree, Kneser and Hönigswald hit on just the way of expressing the notion of pre-established harmony for readers who might not have been inclined to accept neoidealist ideas. The metaphor carried with it the connotation of preordained teleology, the biological 'clock' that had so impressed Hegel about Leibniz's philosophy.[32] Use of the tree in this way, of course, had for a long time been widespread in many fields of study which required schematic diagrams, *Stammtafeln*, with trunk and branches. Among European commentators of all sorts one finds the tree metaphor invoked to serve polemical ends. An obscure and apparently pseudonymous Parisian science reformer intoned in 1848 how 'science is a tree, whose large branches are agriculture, industry, and medicine; whose roots are study, experience, and observation of nature; whose fruits will always be the richness, glory, and happiness of the people who cultivate it and make it flower.'[33] When, some years later, the distinguished British professor James Clerk Maxwell cast about for a metaphor to describe the indeterminate character of human creativity, he noted how the mind 'is rather like a tree, shooting out branches which adapt themselves to the new aspects of the sky towards which they climb, and roots which contort themselves among the strange strata of the earth into which they delve.'[34]

By around 1900 the tree metaphor had come in Central Europe to resolve any number of antinomies relating to mathematics. In 1895 Felix Klein used it to merge free-spirited intuition with solidly anchored formal development. For Klein, mathematical science was a tree, 'its roots below constantly penetrating deeper into the earth, and the bent shade of its boughs freely unfolding above'. The life of the tree of mathematics depended on healthy interaction between the branches of intuition and the roots of logical principles. To understand mathematics was to understand how it had penetrated to its depths and ascended to its heights.[35] Arnold Sommerfeld, professor of mechanics at the Aachen Institute of Technology and a former student of Klein's, referred in 1904 to the 'green tree of life' of advancing knowledge when he wanted to indicate how progress in technology was bound up with that in mathematics.[36] In the hands of a young *Privatdozent* of mathematics, Hermann Weyl, a brilliant star in Klein's Göttingen constellation, the arboreal boughs connoted mathematical abstraction and formal exposition while the tree roots represented the real world of intuition and practical ends:

> Mathematics, the proud tree with its wide crown freely unfolding in the ether, actually sucks with a thousand roots its force from the soil of intuition and imagination. It would therefore be fatal, if one cut it with the shears of petty utilitarianism, or if one wanted to dig it up from the soil whence it springs.[37]

Weyl wrote the preceding lines in 1910. His fanciful rhetoric presaged important accomplishments. The same could not be said about other philosophically minded writers who came to address the notion of pre-established harmony in their doctoral dissertations.

In 1912 Heinrich Block, a student at the University of Bonn, defended his thesis on the epistemological role of the ether in the development of electromagnetism.[38] His dissertation adviser was officially Heinrich Kayser, the professor of experimental physics whose principal interest lay in spectroscopy, although it is clear from Block's acknowledgments that his main inspiration came from Alfred Heinrich Bucherer, an experimental physicist at Bonn who was then notorious in Germany for spreading extravagant claims about having verified the variation of electron mass with electron velocity. Near the end of his text, Block came to consider special relativity. He wrote about how Einstein, 'unconcerned with any physical pictures', treated moving physical systems as 'a purely mathematical question dealing with the transformations of independent variables that leave any equation invariant'.

Block was obscure about other sources as well as about Einstein. He cited Minkowski's space-and-time lecture—actually delivered at the meeting in 1908 of the German Association of Scientists and Physicians held at Cologne—as having been aired at Göttingen in 1910. In a misleading identification, Block noted how the Einstein–Minkowski principle of relativity was 'completely free' from the ether. With mathematical elegance, Block wrote, Minkowski had brought to the theory of relativity 'a unity and harmony' that had previously graced few theories.[39] Then total confusion dominated his text. Without citing Einstein's work, Block mentioned predictions about light deflection in the vicinity of massive celestial bodies, and he referred to the necessity for distinguishing between gravitational and electromagnetic mass. He concluded that even if the principle of relativity were generally true, it did not contradict the static ether advanced by Lorentz.

As Block's dissertation will have suggested, the message about pre-established harmony could be transmitted less than faithfully. One reads with alarm how a fellow student at Bonn picked up the tattered thread that Block left. The younger man was Heinrich Debus, technically a student of philosopher Oswald Külpe's but, like Block, actually advised by Bucherer.[40] Debus made liberal use of his predecessors' glosses on modern physics. Inspired by Minkowski, Debus argued in his dissertation in 1913 that the principle of relativity was 'not the direct fruit of mathematical deductions but an outcome of experimental–physical research'. The true form of the principle, however, came from the insight of pure thought: 'Because of its already elaborated methodology, to mathematics has come the satisfaction of granting this principle a genuine form free from "internal" contradiction.' Debus emphasised how mathematics had 'in fact expanded physical reality'. Although his dissertation was unusually opaque and suffered from tedious literary style, it seems as if Debus sought to transcend a mere phenomenological approach to Einstein's relativity. He believed that the principle of relativity could never be verified experimentally, and he argued that a 'realising principle' was to be found in Einstein's hypothesis of the constancy of the speed of light.[41] He paid passing mention to general relativity, but one wonders if he understood any of it.

The confusion endemic to physics and philosophy at Bonn found a sympathetic reading elsewhere. We have the case of Eva Koehler, who, after spending two years studying at Bonn where she heard Bucherer but not Külpe lecture, moved on to Göttingen. There she defended a dissertation on the ideas of absolute and relative motion under the joint direction of the philosopher Georg Elias Müller and the brilliant mathematician David Hilbert.[42] Einstein's name was entirely absent from Koehler's thin text. In her view, the principle of relativity originated in electrodynamics, and Hermann Minkowski had broadened it to bring into coherence 'the various fields of physics'.[43] For the young philosopher, as for David Hilbert, Minkowski had indicated the promised land where pure mathematics found a place in the real world.

At the beginning of the twentieth century, Germany was inundated with philosophical systems, and although it proved remarkably accommodating, the notion of pre-established harmony could not have been expected to join with the dreams of all writers. In a treatise of 1905 on epistemology in the work of contemporary scientific thinkers, Hans Kleinpeter vigorously argued that no amount of mathematics could replace physical investigation or intuition.[44] The Königsberg phenomenologist and physicist Paul Volkmann believed that 'mathematics fails in the realm of reality'.[45] Neokantian Paul Natorp objected to Minkowski's interpretation of Lorentz and Einstein, wherein space and time became 'pure abstractions of merely mathematical but not physical' content. Because he inclined to believe in immanent reality, the philosopher could not accept Minkowski's use of a 'pre-established harmony' between mathematical and empirical nature.[46]

Discussing the question of absolute space, philosopher Aloys Müller expressed his view that 'the essence of the world is not mathematics', but rather a subjective appreciation of what he called the 'physical world picture'.[47] For this reason, Müller interpreted Einstein's special theory of relativity as merely a heuristic, mathematical elaboration of Lorentz's electron theory. In 1913 Max B Weinstein, an outsider theoretical physicist no less competent at mathematical manipulation than many who held university chairs, considered Minkowski's use of complex numbers to express the real world as 'one of the greatest revolutions in our accepted views'. Yet he worried about the 'almost wrong-headed and fanatical generalisations' of relativity which were coming from all quarters. For Weinstein, a differential equation was a creation of the human mind, one that did not necessarily correspond to reality. It always remained to infuse physical constraints into mathematical formalism. To do otherwise resulted in 'only mystical symbolism'.[48] In denying something one gives reason to its existence; Leibniz stalked Weinstein, as he did Müller, Natorp, and Volkmann.

Elaborations of the doctrine of pre-established harmony gave rise to fearsome predictions. In his 1908 popular lectures on the philosophy of science, a professor at the state physical laboratory in Hamburg, Johannes Classen, examined the relationship between mathematics and physics.[49] 'Hypotheses in physics', he wrote, 'go back to the supposition of the applicability of definite, mathematically defined concepts; physical laws are the mathematical consequences of these.' Classen held mathematics to be so important that he identified Helmholtz, Hertz, and Lord Kelvin as 'famous mathematicians'.

Classen believed, along with Max Planck and Planck's former student Hans Witte, that one had to seek to provide a satisfactory mechanical explanation for electromagnetic processes.[50] He concluded that a 'unified exposition of the now divided parts of physics can only be achieved by a mathematician, who is capable of seeing the core through the [present] difficulties'. Philosophical approaches, such as those of Haeckel, Ostwald, and Mach, would be of no use to the mathematician in the new synthesis. 'He must seek his own way. For this reason, the next advance in this field will be expected only from the mathematician, not the philosopher.' Classen's solution was the classical, Leibnizian one: 'We imprint on the natural laws that we seek from within the external form of our mathematical formulae.' He continued: 'If modern physics will share in the formation of our "world view" [*Weltansicht*] we must assume that "this world" also passes into the realm of mathematical formulae; nature must be conceived as conforming to the form of mathematical thought [*die Natur muss der Form des mathematischen Denkens entsprechend vorgestellt werden*].' Yet because arguing in favour of pre-established harmony was like invoking biblical scriptures, one could never anticipate the specific revelations conjured forth by a scientist schoolman. In his lectures, Classen completely rejected the idea that four-dimensional mathematical space could have any application in physics. He based this judgment on the belief that 'a special step is required to go from purely mathematical laws to physical knowledge.'[51] One assumes that, by late 1908, after Minkowski had published his thoughts on space–time, Classen came to realise the error of his ways.

The triumph of pre-established harmony

Except for a peccadillo regarding four-dimensional space, the elements of Classen's exposition appeared in the treatments of colleagues over the next six years. With pre-established harmony in mind, commentators quickly came to assert, as Classen did, the primacy of pure mathematics for resolving problems in physical theory. In 1912, Gustav von Sensel, a Viennese *Oberlehrer* who managed to keep abreast of the latest developments in physics, provided an exposition of Einstein's relativity for an Austrian periodical. He could have expected his readers to be sympathetic to natural sciences, and to know at least the rudiments of the calculus. To such readers, Sensel conveyed the thought that, in his principle of relativity, Einstein had simply arrived at a formal resolution of outstanding problems in theoretical physics. 'Above all,' Sensel began, 'and this is of the utmost importance, one must note that it [relativity theory] rests on a *"purely mathematical"* speculation, so that to appreciate it, understanding its mathematical foundations is absolutely important.'[52]

When pure mathematician David Hilbert began to elaborate in print his programme for infusing physics with mathematical rigour, Julius Sommer responded with enthusiasm. Referring to his correspondent's attempt at providing a framework for radiation theory, mathematician Sommer wrote to Hilbert: 'The world will be grateful to you for your exemplary treatment of problems in theoretical physics.' Perhaps with Johannes Classen's strictures in mind, Sommer indicated that he had always been unhappy about the claim that theoretical physics required a 'special talent'; Hilbert's work showed, in Sommer's mind, that any mathematician could jump right in to address physical questions. To Hilbert, Sommer confided: 'I find your radiation theory as I found your geometry; instead of uncertainty, only clarity and certainty.'[53] Little did it seem to matter to Sommer that Hilbert's theory actually resolved little in the world of physics *circa* 1914.

A convinced follower of Edmund Husserl's philosophy of phenomenology, Hilbert's talented protégé Hermann Weyl attempted to deliver in 1918 a unified theory of electromagnetism and gravitation. Pre-established harmony was the engine that drove his grandiose project forward. Weyl emphasised how pure mathematics and reality formed an 'inseparable, theoretical whole'. He continued: 'We cannot merely test a single law detached from this theoretical fabric . . . We must never lose sight of this totality when we enquire whether these sciences interpret rationally the reality which proclaims itself in all subjective experiences of consciousness, and which itself transcends consciousness: that is, truth forms a *system*.' Weyl's goal was to reveal 'a few of the fundamental chords from that harmony of the spheres of which Pythagoras and Kepler once dreamed.'[54] Though his approach to physics differed greatly from Hilbert's and Weyl's and though he believed in 'physical' explanations, Einstein spoke for many others when in 1918 he invoked Leibniz to express why nature had to conform to abstract thought: 'Nobody who has really gone deeply into the matter will deny that in practice the world of phenomena uniquely determines the theoretical system, in spite of the fact that there is no logical bridge between phenomena and their theoretical principles; this is what Leibniz described so happily as a "pre-established harmony".'[55]

At the time that revolution brought an end to the German Empire, many contributors to theoretical physics sought to explicate a pre-established harmony between mathematics and physical reality. When in the 1920s abstract mathematics in the form of particle statistics and Hilbert spaces found a place in quantum physics, scarcely anyone questioned that much of the formalism should have given rise to notions—fictional waves, virtual radiation, and mysterious 'constraints' on particle motion—with absolutely no physical meaning. Mathematics, indeed, began to dictate the nature of physical reality. No one less than Einstein came in his later years to accept the immense power of pure mathematics in this regard:

> I am convinced that we can discover by means of purely mathematical constructions the concepts and the laws connecting them with each other, which furnish the key to the understanding of natural phenomena. Experience may suggest the appropriate mathematical concepts, but they most certainly cannot be deduced from it. Experience remains, of course, the sole criterion of the physical utility of a mathematical construction. But the creative principle resides in mathematics. In a certain sense, therefore, I hold it true that pure thought can grasp reality, as the ancients dreamed.[56]

This confession marks one of the most astonishing contrasts between Einstein's thought as a young man and as a mature researcher.

Like drops of rain on an alpine meadow, ideas can descend over a cultural setting, disperse, and then find their way into rivulets. In late Wilhelmian Germany, philosophical thoughts rained down on intellectual life. They adhered to the contours of the environment—changing the shade of one or another feature, dampening the ground, and contributing a continual babble, as of water streaming down a hillside. The notion of pre-established harmony interacted with the climate of physical thought in much this way. During the period following the breakdown of classical mechanics, this notion was called to support growing sentiment that favoured symbolic forms over what had been traditionally called 'physical content'. Writing in 1927, in the wake of the achievement of quantum mechanics, Ernst Cassirer noted:

> Physics has definitely left the realm of representation and of representability in general for a more abstract realm. The schematism of images has given way to the symbolism of principles. Of course the empirical source of modern physical theory has not been affected in the least by this insight. But physics no longer deals directly with the existent as the materially real; it deals with its structure, its formal context.[57]

In Cassirer's judgment is found the 'wicked intellect' that Robert Musil thought had come by 1930 to dominate civilisation. 'Mathematics has entered like a daemon into all aspects of our life', the great novelist wrote.[58]

With three generations' hindsight we understand that merely to state the circumstance of pre-established harmony is no more than to displace a deeper lying antinomy. We may draw consolation from Hegel when, in commenting on Leibniz's philosophy, he noted how it 'appears like a string of arbitrary assertions, which follow one on another like a metaphysical romance'. The machine that guided Leibniz's world—the thing that pre-ordained the clocks in each of its monads—was God. For Hegel, God in Leibniz was the 'waste channel into which all contradictions flow'.[59] Although it is not the place here to evaluate the extent to which Hegel's critique of Leibniz is persuasive, one may affirm that the inchoate notion of pre-established harmony underlay a great deal of physical thought early in the twentieth century.

Notes and references

1 T K Oesterreich, *Friedrich Ueberwegs Grundriss der Geschichte der Philosophie vom Beginn des neunzehnten Jahrhunderts bis auf die Gegenwart* (Berlin 1916).
2 Friedrich Paulsen, 'Die Zukunftsaufgaben der Philosophie', in Wilhelm Dilthey *et al*'s *Systematische Philosophie* (Berlin 1907) pp 389–421, on pp 420–1. The book is part 1, section 6 of Paul Hinneberg's *Kultur der Gegenwart*. Paulsen's indictment is one of the most savage to appear from the pen of a university professor during the Wilhelmian period.
3 'Kindling fever' and the second quotation from Robert Musil's *The Man Without Qualities* volume 1, part 1, transl E Wilkins and E Kaiser (New York 1965) p 59. Suggestive in this regard is the standard work by Fritz Ringer, *The Decline of the German Mandarins* (Cambridge, Mass 1969), which makes no mention of natural sciences. The propensity for revolutionary solutions to their problems among Wilhelmian physicists has been suggested by Russell McCormmach in 'H A Lorentz and the Electromagnetic View of Nature', *Isis* **61** (1970) 459–97, and is elaborated in Lewis Pyenson's 'La Place des sciences exactes en Allemagne à l'époque de Guillaume II', *Europa: A Journal of Interdisciplinary Studies* **4** no 2 (1981) 187–217, esp pp 199–200.
4 Hidē Ishiguro, *Leibniz's Philosophy of Logic and Language* (Ithaca 1972) pp 111–12. See also Dieter Turck's *Die Metaphysik der Natur bei Leibniz* (dissertation, University of Bonn 1967) pp 211–21; Rüdiger Böhle's *Der Begriff des Individuums bei Leibniz* (Meisenheim am Glan 1978) pp 237–50; Nicholas Rescher's *Leibniz: An Introduction to His Philosophy* (Totowa, NJ 1979) pp 65–6.
5 These remarks have been prompted by the penetrating comments of V P Vizgin, who has argued in favour of the fruitful interchange between mathematics and physics: Vizgin, ' "Die schönste Leistung der allgemeinen Relativitätstheorie": The Genesis of the Tensor-Geometrical Conception of Gravitation', in *Nature Mathematized* ed W R Shea (Dordrecht 1983) pp 298–317. Vizgin has published a major study of relativity physics in the early decades of the twentieth century: V P Vizgin, *Relyativistskaya Teoriya Tyagoteniya (Istori i Formirovanie. 1900–1915.)* (Moscow 1981).

6 Paul Drude, *Die Theorie in der Physik: Antrittsvorlesung gehalten am 5. Dezember 1894 an der Universität Leipzig* (Leipzig 1895), quotations on pp 3–4, 14–15.

7 Arthur König and Carl Runge, eds, *Einleitung zu den Vorlesungen über theoretische Physik von H von Helmholtz* (Leipzig 1903), quotations on pp 4, 25.

8 Russell McCormmach, 'Hertz, Heinrich', *Dictionary of Scientific Biography* **6** (New York 1972) 340–50.

9 Heinrich Hertz, *Principles of Mechanics* transl D E Jones and J T Walley (London 1899), quotation on p 29.

10 The point is considered at length in Lewis Pyenson's *Neohumanism and the Persistence of Pure Mathematics in Wilhelmian Germany* (Philadelphia 1983) [*Am. Phil. Soc. Mem.* **150**], and is addressed in the following chapter.

11 Georg Steinhausen, *Geschichte der deutschen Kultur* **2** (Leipzig 1913) 489–90.

12 Johann Norrenberg, 'Der Unterricht in den Naturwissenschaften', in *Die Reform des höheren Schulwesens in Preussen* ed Wilhelm Lexis (Halle 1902) pp 265–304, quotation on p 288.

13 For example, the annual addresses by the Academy president and mathematician Ernst Eduard Kummer, reprinted in *Ernst Eduard Kummer: Collected Papers* **2** ed André Weil (Berlin 1975).

14 G W Leibniz, *Mathematische Schriften* 7 vols ed Carl Immanuel Gerhardt (Berlin 1849–75); *Die philosophischen Schriften von Gottfried Wilhelm Leibniz* 7 vols (Berlin 1875–90).

15 Bertrand Russell, *A Critical Exposition of the Philosophy of Leibniz* (Cambridge 1902); Louis Couturat, *La Logique de Leibniz* (Paris 1901).

16 Ernst Cassirer, *Leibniz' System in seinen wissenschaftlichen Grundlagen* (Marburg 1902).

17 *Ibid* quotations on pp 123, 268, 245, 257, 263, 261, 297, in sequence.

18 Ernst Cassirer, *Substance and Function, and Einstein's Theory of Relativity* transl W C Swabey and M C Swabey (1923, New York 1953).

19 *Ibid* quotations on pp 166, 230, 252, 183, 257. In 1903 Bertrand Russell severely criticised the Kantian orientation of Cassirer's earlier book: 'Recent Work on the Philosophy of Leibniz', reprinted in *Leibniz: A Collection of Critical Essays* ed Harry G Frankfurt (Notre Dame, Ind 1976) pp 365–400. The criticism holds here, too.

20 Felix Klein, 'Ueber die Aufgabe der angewandten Mathematik, besonders über die pädagogische Seite', in *Verhandlungen des dritten internationalen Mathematiker-Kongress in Heidelberg vom 8. bis 13. August 1904* ed A Krazer (Leipzig 1905) pp 396–7.

21 Eduard Riecke, in Göttingen Vereinigung zur Förderung der angewandten Physik und Mathematik, *Die Physikalische Institute der Universität Göttingen: Festschrift im Anschlusse an die Einweihung der Neubauten am 9. Dezember 1905* (Leipzig 1906) p 32.

22 Minkowski's view of the relationship between mathematics and physics is elaborated in chapters 4 and 5.

23 Wilhelm Wien, 'Ueber die Wandlung des Raum- und Zeitbegriffs in der Physik', Würzburg, Physikalisch–medizinische Gesellschaft, *Verhandlungen* **40** (1909) 20–39.

24 *Ibid* quotations on pp 29–31.

25 Laub's work is considered at length in chapter 9.

26 Göttingen. Niedersächsische Staats- und Universitätsbibliothek. Nachlass Felix Klein. XXI.A. 'Material zum psychologischen Seminar (Winter 1909–10).'

27 Felix Klein, 'Ueber die geometrischen Grundlagen der Lorentzgruppe', *Physikalische Zeitschrift* **12** (1911) 17–27, on pp 20–2.

28 Adolf Kneser, *Mathematik und Natur: Rede zum Antritt des Rektorats der Breslauer Universität in der Aula Leopoldina am 15. Oktober 1911* (Breslau 1913).

29 *Ibid* quotations on pp 16, 15, 16.

30 Richard Hönigswald, *Zum Streit über die Grundlagen der Mathematik* (Heidelberg 1912).

31 *Ibid* quotations on pp 100, 106, 64.

32 *Hegel's Lectures on the History of Philosophy* transl E S Haldane and F H Simson **3** (1896, London 1968) 342.

33 Nerée Boubée, ed, *Reform agricole* no 5 (November 1848) p 17.

34 James Clerk Maxwell, 'Address to the Mathematical and Physical Sections of the British Association (1870)', in Maxwell, *Scientific Papers* **2** ed W D Niven (Cambridge 1890) 215–29, quotation on pp 226–7.

35 F Klein, 'Ueber Arithmetisierung der Mathematik', Göttingen. Königl. Gesellschaft der Wissenschaften, *Nachrichten: Geschäftliche Mitteilungen aus dem Jahre 1895* (1895) pp 82–91, quotation on p 91.

36 Arnold Sommerfeld, 'Die naturwissenschaftliche Ergebnisse und die Ziele der modernen technischen Mechanik', *Phys. Z.* **4** (1903–4) 773–82, quotation on p 773.

37 Hermann Weyl, 'Ueber die Definitionen der mathematischen Grundbegriffe', *Mathematisch-Naturwissenschaftliche Blätter* **7** (1910) 93–5, 109–13, reprinted in *Hermann Weyl: Gesammelte Abhandlungen* **1** ed K Chandrasekharan (Berlin 1968), quotation on p 304.

38 Heinrich Block, *Die erkenntnistheoretische Rolle des Aethers in der Entwickelung des Elektromagnetismus* (dissertation, University of Bonn 1912).

39 *Ibid* quotations on pp 81, 84, 87, 85, 94, 96. Biographical information comes from Block's *Lebenslauf*, published in the dissertation.

40 Heinrich Debus, *Die philosophische Grundlagen des Relativitätsprinzips der Elektrodynamik* (dissertation, University of Bonn 1913).

41 *Ibid* quotations on pp 5, 53, 54. Biographical information comes from Debus's *Lebenslauf*.

42 Eva Koehler, *Absolute und relative Bewegung* (dissertation, University of Göttingen 1913), acknowledgments and *Lebenslauf*.

43 *Ibid* pp 22–3.

44 Hans Kleinpeter, *Die Erkenntnistheorie der Naturforschung der Gegenwart* (Leipzig 1905) p 117.

45 Paul Volkmann, *Erkenntnistheoretische Grundzüge der Naturwissenschaften und ihre Beziehungen zum Geistesleben der Gegenwart* (Leipzig 1910) p xi.

46 Paul Natorp, *Die logische Grundlagen der exakten Wissenschaften* (Leipzig 1910) pp 396, 401.

47 Aloys Müller, *Das Problem des absoluten Raumes und seine Beziehung zum allgemeinen Raumproblem* (Brunswick 1911) pp 108, 118.

48 Max B Weinstein, *Die Physik der bewegten Materie und die Relativitätstheorie* (Leipzig 1913) pp 307, 309.

49 Johannes Classen, *Vorlesungen über moderne Naturphilosophen* (Hamburg 1908).

50 Hans Witte, *Ueber den gegenwärtigen Stand der Frage nach einer mechanischen Erklärung der elektrischen Erscheinungen* (dissertation, University of Berlin 1905).

51 J Classen (ref 49), quotations on pp 136, 146, 156, 160, 172, 163.

52 Gustav von Sensel, 'Das Relativitätsprinzip', *Zeitschrift für das Realschulwesen* **37** (1912) 398–409. Sensel's summary of recent developments appeared the next year: *Elektrizität und Optik behandelt vom Standpunkte der Elektronentheorie* (Vienna 1913). Though Austrian, Sensel was typical of many secondary-school teachers in Germany.

53 J Sommer to D Hilbert, 31 December 1914. Nachlass David Hilbert, Niedersächsische Staats- und Universitätsbibliothek, Göttingen.

54 Hermann Weyl, *Space–Time–Matter* transl Henry L Brose (New York 1952) pp 67, 312.

55 Albert Einstein, 'Principles of Scientific Research', in *The World as I See It* transl Alan Harris (London 1935) pp 123–7, citation on p 126. This passage omits a number of lines from the text that Einstein read in 1918 on the occasion of Max Planck's sixtieth birthday; the change is one of style rather than substance. E Warburg, M von Laue, A Sommerfeld, A Einstein, M Planck, *Zu Max Plancks sechzigstem Geburtstag* (Karlsruhe 1918) on p 31. I owe this observation to Donald Howard.

56 A Einstein, 'The Method of Theoretical Physics', in *ibid* pp 131–9, quotation on p 136.

57 E Cassirer, *The Philosophy of Symbolic Forms* **3**: *The Phenomenology of Knowledge* transl Ralph Mannheim (New Haven 1957) p 467.

58 R Musil (ref 3) p 40.

59 *Hegel's Lectures* (ref 32) pp 330, 348.

7 Mathematics, education, and the Göttingen approach to physical reality, 1890–1914

Is science elitist? To understand the development of scientific ideas, is it sufficient to focus on the key thinkers who conceived them? To describe the reception of scientific ideas, is it enough to study small circles of scientific power brokers who transmitted them to selected men of learning? Can the historian who studies scientific change limit himself to the words and deeds of people at the top, to their motives and passions, and to their traces left in letters, diaries, and in countless reports sent along the corridors of power?

Historians of science studying the transformation in physical ideas between 1890 and 1914 have answered these questions in the affirmative. They have elaborated critical scientific texts; they have attended to the lives and creative psychology of distinguished scientists; they have tabulated the productivity of university laboratories; they have considered the motives and activities of patrons of physical knowledge. Illuminating as many of these studies have been for the accomplishments of great physicists, for the most part historians of science have not addressed how it was that new ideas came to be accepted by broad layers of physical scientists.

What happened in physics at the beginning of the twentieth century is now seen—and it was then identified—as a revolution in scientific thought. For the historian, of course, the word *revolution* brings to mind the work of scholars who, in studying political revolutions, have long looked beyond the immediate activity of revolutionary captains. These scholars have focused on the interactions between revolutionary crowds, ideologues, and movement leaders. They have considered millenarians and parliamentarians in seventeenth-century England, *sans-culottes* and deputies during the French Revolution, and irregulars at the street barricade and intellectuals of the revolutionary vanguard in nineteenth- and twentieth-century situations. Scientific revolutions are obviously different from political ones, but it remains that few historians of science have elaborated how pressures 'from below' have interacted with the interests, prejudices, and unconscious actions of men at the top.

Such an interaction is the subject of the present chapter. It focuses on the relationship between two groups labouring to dispatch established patterns of scientific activity: the first is constituted by mathematics schoolteachers at the turn of the century who played, in some sense, the role of revolutionary *sans-culottes*; in the second group are university professors at the vanguard of exact sciences. I examine how the aims of the schoolteachers' spontaneous and primitive organisations were taken over by pure mathematicians in the universities. I consider how a revolution from below was diverted—co-opted, to use the currently fashionable term—by an established elite. One result was confusion over the theories of relativity.

The climate of education

It is well to recall that during the period 1870–1918 the states constituting the German Empire retained control of educational policy, despite the widespread imitation of the Prussian model. Throughout Germany the pattern of secondary education changed dramatically at the turn of the century, as indicated in chapter 1.[1] Before 1900 graduates of the classical *Gymnasien* retained many official privileges not extended to graduates of the semi-classical *Realgymnasien* and the non-classical *Oberrealschulen*, these latter two categories of school being called *Realanstalten*.[2] By a move with far-reaching implications, in 1901 the Prussian authorities granted the *Realanstalten* virtual parity with the *Gymnasien*. The other German states soon followed suit, so that the closing years of the Wilhelmian period saw a steady erosion of the demographical superiority of *Gymnasien* over their sister institutions. During the decade between 1899 and 1909, when the population of Prussia increased by 15% to 34 243 000, the secondary-school population increased by 41%. Attendance at Prussian *Gymnasien* increased by 14% to 106 794, at the *Realgymnasien* by 104% to 46 080, and at the *Oberrealschulen* by 61% to 68 085. By 1909 the Prussian *Gymnasien* hosted only 48% of secondary-school pupils, down from 59% in 1899.[3]

Historians have documented how *Realen*—instruction in modern languages, worldly technologies, and natural sciences—came to occupy a position in secondary education equal, at least in principle, to that of *Idealen*—instruction in classical languages and higher moral values not of direct use in practical affairs. In referring to this major change in education, I do not mean to ignore social determinants behind it—the demand for highly skilled technicians on the part of science-based industries and the clerical requirements of commercial firms and government offices. Like their colleagues in England and the United States, German engineers and modern-language teachers sought to achieve parity between their accreditation and more traditional certification in secondary and higher education. To study the struggle ·for academic parity is in itself not especially illuminating. Many in the middle class continued to value the *Gymnasien* more highly than·the *Realanstalten*, even after students without training in Greek and Latin were permitted to receive doctorates in philosophy and law and when, in 1899, the *Technischen Hochschulen*, or institutes of technology, obtained permission to confer a doctorate of engineering. Just as non-classical education remained for most cultured Germans a source of *Halbbildung*, or incomplete education, so in contrast to the philosophy doctorate, or PhD, the engineering doctorate was deemed an inferior diploma, one opening few doors in either academia or industry. Into the twentieth century it was by no means aberrant for the 1905 Nobel laureate in chemistry Adolf von Baeyer, someone intimate with the needs of German industry, to regard his student, the 1915 Nobel laureate in chemistry, Richard Willstätter, as culturally inferior because the latter had come through a *Realgymnasium*. Willstätter noted in turn: 'Many of my pupils lacked Latin, and to them I was a humanist.'[4]

Engineers urged that practical subjects be given more time in the schools and institutions of higher learning, while at the same time recoiling from what they considered abstract or theoretical science. When in the mid 1890s the mathematician Felix Klein established a physical–technical institute at the University of Göttingen, leading engineers feared that Klein's version of engineering would serve the ends of theory rather than solve practical problems. An engineering professor at the Berlin Institute of Technology, Alois Riedler, condemned Göttingen as the home of enemies of technical education: 'The Göttingen initiative proves that theoreticians for whom technical education is quite foreign do not understand our life's interest.'[5] When the editorial board of the *Zeitschrift* of the Association of German Engineers wrote to Klein about an altercation that he had had with Riedler, they emphasised that they sought an equal partnership between theoreticians and technologists, not Klein's elitist programme. They rejected Klein's desire that theoreticians should 'learn our skills and understand our results to be able better to accomplish what we [the engineers] authorise . . .'[6] The mathematician Gerhard Kowalewski remembered of this period that engineers sought to debase 'higher' mathematics for their needs. In practice the consequences of such an approach to science were alarming. Kowalewski pointed to the case of a man who was not certified to teach as *Privatdozent* at the Dresden Institute of Technology because he had used determinants in his *Habilitationsschrift*, or qualifying thesis.[7]

German engineers wanted especially to break the university monopoly on training schoolteachers. This posed something of a problem for university mathematicians eager to find common ground with technologists. Klein's nephew Robert Fricke, a pure mathematician teaching at the Brunswick Institute of Technology, identified the dilemma of his disciplinary colleagues. In a letter to his uncle, Fricke wrote that he did not doubt for a moment 'that the philologists would scream bloody murder if the institutes of technology were to educate future schoolteachers . . . We mathematicians stand without prejudices in the middle between technologists and philologists', Fricke concluded.[8] It is understandable why mathematicians like Fricke and Klein sought not to alienate their colleagues in philology. Philologists controlled the German *Gymnasien*, and, despite the new franchise granted to graduates of *Realanstalten*, by 1911 around two-thirds of university students still received the *Abitur*, or secondary-school leaving certificate, from a *Gymnasium*.[9]

Given the parameters of nineteenth-century German culture it is not at all surprising that *Gymnasien* continued to be favoured by the great majority of pupils destined for the universities, while the *Realanstalten* swelled with pupils headed for careers in *Realen*, that is, in industry and commerce. There remains, nonetheless, one striking departure from this expected pattern. It is a development central to the story that follows. Simply, after 1900 future physicists came through the *Realanstalten* in dramatically increasing numbers. Among those receiving a PhD in physics at a German university around 1900, 79% had previously received the *Abitur* from a *Gymnasium*. This percentage is about the same as that among students destined to take doctorates in what might be called the 'humanities'. The figure is much higher than that for other scientific disciplines, notably organic chemistry, or for other disciplinary aggregates such as the social sciences. Only 40% of those obtaining a PhD in physics in 1913, however, had come through the *Gymnasien*. In considering this decline—one more extreme than that for other academic disciplines—it must be emphasised that, from the point of view of social background, the typical young physicist in Germany at the end of the nineteenth century was virtually indistinguishable from the young classical scholar, but he differed considerably from the young organic chemist.[10] By 1913 physicists still emerged from the same, higher strata of society (tables 4 and 5). The change in schooling may quite possibly turn around the enlightened educational attitudes of the parents of future physicists, those who belonged in large numbers to the middle and higher professional classes. More than the parents of university students destined to receive doctorates in other fields, parents of physicists may have believed, just after the turn of the century, that secondary-school preparation in *Realen* constituted a socially acceptable alternative to the *Gymnasien*.

Interesting as it might be to speculate about the motives of physicists' parents in coming to support *Realen*, the topic will not be pursued here.

Table 4 Percentage of Dr phil (PhD) recipients having been educated at classical *Gymnasien*, in several disciplines and disciplinary aggregates.

	1899		1913	
	%	N	%	N
Physics	79	85	40	107
Organic chemistry	57	149	34	191
Other physical sciences	59	155	38	268
Humanities	71	65	66	973
Social sciences	73	96	42	278

The sample consisted of dissertations *published* (not awarded) in the given year which were received by the University of Pennsylvania and The Johns Hopkins University through dissertation-exchange *ententes* with individual German universities. Under the column 1899, for physics and the other physical sciences (excluding organic chemistry), the figures derive from dissertations published in the years 1896–1902. Disciplinary allegiance was determined from the name of the dissertation adviser given in the dissertation and the title of the chair of the adviser given in *Minerva*. Statistics on secondary education for the column 1899 were drawn from dissertation *Lebensläufe*, for the column 1913 from the annual *Jahres-Verzeichnis* of all German dissertations published by the Royal Library in Berlin.[10]

In this chapter, I explore some of the effects of a major transformation in secondary-school training on the physics discipline. The following pages ask about the education of physicists in the *Gymnasien* around 1900 and elaborate how their migration to *Realanstalten* by 1910 might have produced new sensibilities in young physicists. I consider the secondary-school experience that a physicist underwent, from curricula to teachers. I am concerned, as well, with responses among university physicists and mathematicians to the new educational requirements and certifying procedures. Because the most important curriculum changes were those in mathematics, before turning to educational issues it is first necessary to recall the vision brought by late nineteenth-century physicists to mathematics.

The world picture of classical physics

In the period before around 1900 physicists sought to formulate a physical world picture—a simple and elegant synthesis of all the laws of the physical world, a synthesis that could be expressed in words.[11] The search for a physical world picture in which mathematics played a secondary role was endemic among Wilhelmian physicists; even when they fundamentally disagreed about epistemological issues they were unanimous about how

Table 5 Class structure of Dr phil (PhD) recipients, in percentages for the given year and discipline or disciplinary aggregate.

	Physics	Mathematics and astronomy	Earth sciences	Nonorganic chemistry	Organic chemistry	Humanities	Social sciences
1899	$N = 56$	$N = 19$	$N = 24$	$N = 77$	$N = 99$	$N = 64$	$N = 20$
Middle and upper professional classes	52	53	42	29	25	50	40
Business community	36	39	46	61	66	44	35
Agriculture: Landowning and landworking	7	16	8	9	4	3	25
Rentier	2	0	4	1	4	3	0
1913	$N = 68$	$N = 8$	$N = 48$	$N = 42$	$N = 99$	$N = 441$	$N = 111$
Middle and upper professional classes	53	50	48	40	33	50	34
Business community	40	50	38	45	57	38	37
Agriculture: Landowning and landworking	4	0	10	14	7	2	19
Rentier	3	0	4	0	3	2	3

Under the heading 1899, for physics, mathematics and astronomy, earth sciences, and nonorganic chemistry, the figures derive from dissertations published in the years 1896–1902. All information about fathers' occupations comes from dissertation *Lebensläufe*, and follows a schema used by Fritz Ringer (same source as table 4).

mathematics was to be used. For Max Planck, professor of theoretical physics at Berlin and by 1900 a leader in the physics discipline, a physical world picture was built up from many laws, each one of which served to define concepts precisely. In 1892 Planck explained his understanding of physical laws to his pupil Ludwik Silberstein:

> Many of our most important laws of physics state not so much relationships among known concepts as the definition of one of these concepts if the rest of them are known. Better said, this is the perfecting of the definition. An entirely perfect definition does not exist because any measurement has a . margin of error.[12]

Planck's approach to the mathematisation of nature is revealed in an exchange of 1897 with Heinrich Weber, professor of mathematics at Strasbourg. Weber, a pure mathematician famous for his definitive two-volume treatise on algebra, ventured to provide a mathematically exact description of ion movement in electrolytic solutions.[13] For a solution of two electrolytes having one ion in common, Weber extended the theory of experimental physicist Friedrich Kohlrausch to arrive at a first-order inhomogeneous, partial differential equation. After defining boundary conditions by assuming a thin boundary layer initially separating the two electrolytes Weber used a method discovered by the pure mathematician Lazarus Fuchs to integrate his equations. Writing to Weber about the article Planck observed that Weber's exact solution for ion movement depended on assuming, from the first instant of time, a constant gradient between the two electrolytes. Weber's calculation was indeed consistent with his working hypotheses, Planck continued, but the physicist was 'for the most part interested' in precisely the case excluded by Weber, where two homogeneous solutions were 'sharply divided from each other in the beginning'.[14]

Planck pointed to his own, earlier calculation of the potential for a weak solution of two bipolar electrolytes. Like Weber, Planck had to integrate a partial differential equation; unlike Weber, Planck was extremely sensitive to the physical simplifications made to facilitate integration, and in his calculation he did not make use of novel mathematical techniques.[15] His own results were consistent with experiment, Planck noted to Weber, but 'the mathematical treatment is not yet completely rigorous since I introduce the condition that the transition from one to another solution is limited to a very thin but finite boundary layer and that outside this boundary layer the solutions are completely homogeneous'. Planck was quick to emphasise, of course, that 'the latter is surely not completely accurate when the boundary layer has a finite thickness.' Obtaining a rigorous solution to this problem would be 'of the highest interest'.

Weber was clearly touched by Planck's attention and, in a letter that is not available, sought to answer the critique. In his subsequent reply to

Weber, Planck explained away the instabilities associated with the outset of the propagation of an ordinary plane wave; he 'categorically omitted the instabilities, only taking account of them when a special conviction shows that they will not change anything in the situation.'[16] Planck used mathematics as a physicist would, without worrying about questions of completeness or consistency. Weber's special case was interesting for Planck even though it did not take account of physical instabilities. Planck argued, nevertheless, against attempting to provide mathematically exact solutions to physical problems by advancing overly simple hypotheses about physical reality.

Planck's vision of the role of mathematics in physics was shared by Ernst Mach, an Austrian physicist well known in Germany as a vigorous supporter of *Realen*. Indeed, as co-founder in 1887 with schoolteachers Bernhard Schwalbe and Friedrich Poske of the reform-minded journal *Zeitschrift für physikalischen und chemischen Unterricht*, Mach left no doubt about his educational sympathies. For many Germans who were unaware of epistemological debates conducted among university intellectuals, Mach appeared as a champion of modernism and practical knowledge, a man who challenged the old educational order and the abstract philosophies used to justify it. According to the schoolteacher historian Heinrich Lange, the science textbook by Mach and Johann Odstrčil, *Grundrisse der Naturlehre*, provided a logical–historical introduction to physics where concepts emerged naturally from phenomena. Mach opposed the encyclopaedic orientation of other texts that presented physics as a subject valuable for formal, intellectual training. He and Odstrčil sought 'the most naive, simple, and classical observations and thoughts from which great scientists have built physics'.[17] In Mach's simplifying approach to problems then current in epistemology lay a call to action. His method of presenting elementary physics survives to this day. Mach's approach to epistemology differed a great deal from that of Planck,[18] but like Planck, Mach expressed reservations about how contemporary mathematicians were going about their work. Writing to the famous mathematician David Hilbert in 1897, mathematician Eduard Study cited a recent letter of Mach's. Study reported that Mach 'complains about the style of mathematicians. He wants to follow the progress of mathematics but finds it impossible to do so because of the way that it is presented.'[19] Mathematics was, for Mach, nothing more than a tool for obtaining an economical description of natural laws.

For a final example of the incidental place of mathematics in the world picture of classical physics, one may cite Ludwig Boltzmann's inaugural address upon his accepting the chair of physics at the University of Munich in 1890. Boltzmann was a widely known theoretical physicist who had pioneered statistical mechanics. In his address he described how a picture of the external world constructed by physical theory should be the 'guiding star' of human reason. 'It is a peculiar drive of the human spirit to make itself such a picture and increasingly adapt it to the external world . . . The immediate elaboration and constant perfection of this picture is then the chief task of theory.' For Boltzmann, theory was 'purely an inner mental picture of the outer, physical world'. Mathematical formulae could never form the basis for any physical theory. The real theoretician used formulae as sparingly as possible, trying to express his ideas in words. Boltzmann allowed that as a picture of the physical world was elaborated, intricate formulae might have to be employed to represent part of the picture. Mathematics remained an 'inessential, if most serviceable' way of describing physical reality. The mathematician, Boltzmann averred, was 'constantly occupied with his formulae and blinded by their abstract perfection, often mistakenly assuming that the inner relations that he had found reflected processes in the real world'.[20] It is important to emphasise that Boltzmann's reservations about using mathematics to guide physical reasoning in no way constituted an attack on the enterprise of pure mathematics. He respected pure mathematicians. Shortly before his death in 1906 he stated in a response to a questionnaire sent to him by the Geneva mathematician Henri Fehr: 'Although in practice I am concerned principally with theoretical physics, I feel attracted in the highest degree to pure mathematics, and I count the hours when I studied the theory of numbers among the most beautiful in my life.'[21]

The neohumanist imperative

As will have become apparent after considering the thoughts of Planck, Mach, and Boltzmann, late nineteenth-century physics excluded the investigations of pure mathematics. This peculiar field of learning was, as Felix Klein's student Conrad H Müller noted in 1904, a creation of the nineteenth century: until the 1800s 'the unhappy separation of *Mathesis pura* and *applicata* had not yet been ordained'. Eighteenth-century German Enlightenment writers held practical, useful knowledge in high esteem, and mathematicians of this period, for example the Göttingen professor Abraham G Kästner, wrote about many applied problems and urged students to acquire practical experience with measuring apparatuses.[22]

Two developments brought about a new direction for late eighteenth-century mathematics in Germany. First, following the French model of *physique expérimentale*, physics separated from mathematics to form an independent field of study, one not requiring mathematical sophistication from its practitioners. Second, the Lagrangian approach to analytical mechanics was modified by the Göttingen mathematician Carl Friedrich Hindenburg, among others. In adopting the algebraic manipulations related to Lagrangian mechanics, Hindenburg expressly rejected the *phys-*

ique mathématique of Paris, a field that invested diverse physical phenomena with explanations involving analytical mechanics. Hindenburg saw the birth of a new era in mathematics, one in which mathematics could become more than a tool in the hands of practical-minded thinkers. To this end he established the earliest German periodical devoted exclusively to mathematics.[23] Whether or not Conrad Müller is correct in identifying Hindenburg as an ancestor of pure mathematicians, it is certain that by the middle of the nineteenth century the new discipline was well established in Germany. Pure mathematics emerged as a field that no longer made any reference to events in the physical world.

In one of the most striking features of late nineteenth-century education, pure mathematicians came to control mathematics instruction in the schools. In the nineteenth-century *Gymnasien*, mathematics was presented as an abstract and formal system, one taught more for its intrinsic pedagogical value than for its physical or technological applications; as for physics, after mid-century it was barely mentioned at all. A pupil in a late nineteenth-century *Gymnasium* would have obtained the impression that mathematics was of only peripheral value for understanding phenomena in the physical world. It was in every sense a 'pure' field of learning.

The general intellectual environment of a late nineteenth-century *Gymnasium* would have been more than hospitable to pure mathematics. Conrad Müller emphasised how closely pure mathematics was related to the spiritual ethos of neohumanism, the intellectual movement that guided the reform of German educational institutions early in the century.[24] Because the greatest part of the secondary education of any intellectual or scientist *circa* 1900 would have been based on the neohumanist ideal, it is important to underline that this ideal was characterised by an intense, scholarly search for the proportions and qualities of human existence which are suggested in ancient Greek texts. In principle, the single, all-consuming goal of neohumanism was to elaborate the perfect, absolute, and true image of humanity in Greek literature and culture and to use the resulting interpretation of classical Greece as a standard for judging German society. 'The noble simplicity and calm greatness' of Greek texts became a passion for Johannes Winckelmann. Hellenic civilisation was a secular religion for Johann Gottfried von Herder. In the view of Christian Heyne, who together with Johann Gesner taught over three hundred students in the neohumanist seminar at Göttingen late in the eighteenth century, neohumanism encouraged, in its disciplinary vehicle classical philology, a search for the ideal form of humanity by reflection on the true. 'The essence of the discipline to be sought', Heyne wrote, 'appears not in the language, but in the intimate personal touch with the good and the great.'[25]

Historians have long noted how the secondary schools and universities were redesigned by neohumanist scholars at the beginning of the nineteenth century. During the first half of the century the classical *Gymnasien* rose to a position of unprecedented importance, and the *Reifeprüfung*, or *Abitur*, was made the sole qualification for attending Prussian universities. During this time the *Gymnasium* teacher, or *Oberlehrer*, joined a secure, mandarin profession. The state requirements for admission to the teaching profession, or *Oberlehrerstand*, were made considerably more rigorous than the university requirements for a PhD. By 1820 advancement in the teaching profession was inextricably linked to a candidate's publications. 'Publish or perish' governed teachers in secondary schools of Prussia to an extent comparable with the case among university faculty. Indeed, for over a century the great majority of students in advanced philology and science seminars at the universities were not future university professors or engineers but future schoolteachers; they were the life blood of German learning.

Representing the new discipline of neohumanist scholarship, the *Oberlehrer* zealously pursued his task by carrying out original scholarship and by attempting to mould the spirit of his charges into a harmonious whole along the lines of classical truth and beauty. The new humanist ideology, together with the scholarly status given to the *Oberlehrer*, bestowed intrinsic value on secondary education. With tenacity that seems remarkable only when viewing in retrospect the rise of Germany as an empire and an industrial state, the classical *Gymnasien*, with their overwhelming emphasis on neohumanist literature, retained a virtual monopoly on providing students for university faculties and most professions until the very end of the century. The system persisted despite one evident flaw: upon leaving the *Gymnasium* at the age of eighteen, most students had to begin acquiring the basic elements of their future profession. The system also persisted despite the erosion of neohumanist scholarship and despite increasing numbers of concessions granted to the *Realanstalten*, privileges that were previously reserved for the *Gymnasien*.[26]

Pure mathematics and the schools

An affinity between pure mathematics and the ideology deemed appropriate for the *Gymnasium* eventually facilitated the creation of university mathematics seminars for training mathematics *Oberlehrer*. The innovation of the seminar in mathematics and the mathematical sciences followed the model of Friedrich August Wolf's neohumanist seminar at Halle.[27] In 1825 the University of Bonn created a seminar for training natural-science teachers as well as promoting scientific research, a seminar that may have been organised at the urging of the professor of mathematics Wilhelm Adolf Diesterweg. One of the seminar's instructors was the physicist and mathematician Julius Plücker, later the adviser of young Felix

Klein. The course of study lasted three years, and it included instruction
in all the biological and physical sciences. Upon certification, members
of the seminar were destined for assignments in the ancestors of
the *Oberrealschulen*—municipal schools known as the *höheren
Bürgerschulen*—as well as in the *Gymnasien*. The Berlin ministry was so
pleased with the seminar that in 1831 it encouraged students throughout
Prussia to attend. With the model of the Bonn seminar in mind, the
ministry agreed to finance similar ventures at Halle and, of great consequence for the discipline of physics, at Königsberg.[28]

The Königsberg seminar followed in the neohumanist tradition. Wolf's
student August Boeckh had brought the philological seminar in 1812 to
the new University of Berlin where Carl Jacobi studied. It was Jacobi
who chaired with Franz Neumann the mathematical–physical seminar at
Königsberg in the mid 1830s.[29] Jacobi and Neumann initiated their seminar
in part to fill a void in training *Gymnasium* teachers. Over the previous
generation Königsberg had hosted Johann Friedrich Herbart's pedagogical
seminar, an experiment founded in 1810 which gave candidates practical
experience in teaching children. A central element in Herbart's curriculum
was mathematics, including differential and integral calculus, astronomy,
and statics. When in 1833 Herbart left for a chair at Göttingen, his
seminar was discontinued.[30] Divided into a section for pure and applied
mathematics and a section for mathematical physics, the new Königsberg
seminar of Jacobi, Neumann, and Wilhelm Bessel marks the advent of
the modern physics discipline. The Königsberg tradition spread to many
other institutions of higher learning over the next generation, notably
Halle through Ludwig Adolph Soncke, Heidelberg through Gustav Kirchhoff, and Giessen through Friedrich Alfred Clebsch.

Most noteworthy of all the mathematics teaching seminars was that run
by Karl Schellbach at Berlin, a seminar through which passed the physicists
Emil Jochmann, Adolf Paalzow, Carl Neumann, and Friedrich Poske,
and the mathematicians Lazarus Fuchs, Leo Königsberger, Hermann
Amandus Schwarz, Georg Cantor, Eugen Netto, and Arthur Schoenflies.[31]
Finally funded in 1851, the 'institute for educating teachers of mathematics
and physics' was Schellbach's personal domain. He was a towering figure
belonging to the first generation of scientists educated under the new
Gymnasium regulations put into effect during the period 1810–20. Upon
receiving a PhD from Jena in 1834 and at the recommendation of mathematician Peter Gustav Lejeune Dirichlet, Schellbach took a post at the
Friedrich-Gymnasium auf dem Werder in Berlin. In 1840 he moved to the
Friedrich-Wilhelms Gymnasium, teaching at the War Academy as well
along with his brilliant colleagues Dirichlet, Martin Ohm, and Ernst
Eduard Kummer.

The mathematics seminar held at the University of Berlin stemmed
from an initiative taken by Schellbach in 1859 to improve the teaching of

secondary-school mathematics and physics. Unlike many of his *Gymnasium* colleagues, Schellbach retained a great interest in technology. In 1873 he summoned Hermann von Helmholtz, Emil DuBois-Reymond, Wilhelm Förster, Paalzow, and his son-in-law, the Berlin school commissioner Heinrich Bertram, to discuss a state institution for research in exact sciences and precision mechanics. Schellbach took the idea to the Kaiser. His initiative resulted in the Imperial Institute of Physics and Technology. Mathematician colleagues resented Schellbach's influence and never accepted him as an equal. In spite of his numerous publications he was never elected to the Berlin Academy of Sciences. In their headlong rush to establish credentials before members of the teaching profession, university reformers of the 1890s, most notably Felix Klein, only belatedly credited Schellbach with a key role in having popularised the so-called heuristic method of instruction.[32]

Schellbach clarified his sympathies when in 1844 he urged educational authorities to create a mathematics institute at Berlin. His was only one in a series of unsuccessful attempts to create at Berlin a German analogue to the Paris *École polytechnique*, by then well into its long decline.[33] The earlier plans were formulated by the mathematical editor Ludwig Crelle and his colleagues in the Berlin Academy and University, all of whom were eager to advance their careers by setting up a system of cross-appointments among Berlin institutions along the Parisian model. They knew that a call to provide teachers could persuade the personages responsible to allocate funding, even though their own interest lay in doing pure science. Different from the earlier proposals, Schellbach's plan seems to have been motivated by a genuine interest in producing science teachers.

Mathematics constituted the second part of philology, Schellbach wrote in his proposal of 1844.[34] Just as philology was the science of knowing the already known, mathematics was the science of knowing the unknown. It never asked if there could be no answer, and this feature distinguished it from all other branches of learning. As the science of intellectual creation, mathematics represented the most manly of all sciences, and one of the most congenial of arts. For centuries, Schellbach continued, mathematics had been along with ancient languages a second focal point for instruction. It was indispensable for certain knowledge: 'The disciplines of physics where mathematics does not yet rule are dark and unsure.'[35] Astronomy as well as the most elaborated theories of physics—optics, acoustics, magnetism—were no more than parts of applied mathematics. In Schellbach's view, most educators of the period felt that mathematics could not really be taught and that mathematically suited minds only required external shocks to allow mathematics to penetrate inside. He saw no reason, however, why such a judgment was any more true for mathematics than for other branches of learning, such as languages, law, medicine, or philosophy.

Sensitive to the contemporary employment market, creators of the mathematics and physics seminars emphasised production of secondary-school teachers. Training students to teach mathematics by educating them for research was precisely the concept adopted with success in philology seminars.[36] In the Prussian teacher-certifying regulations of 1866, mathematics candidates were for the first time explicitly required to demonstrate the ability to carry out research. Preparing teachers by inculcating them with the research ethic contained an underlying ambivalence. Teaching candidates were trained in a continually changing, encyclopaedic synthesis of advanced mathematics and mathematical physics, and certification procedures guaranteed the existence of numerous mathematics chairs in higher education. School curricula hardly required such advanced teacher training, however. Over the nineteenth century, *Gymnasien* progressively eliminated advanced mathematics from their courses; by the early 1890s even the *Realanstalten* were offering less advanced material in mathematics than they had at the middle of the century. After around 1860 practitioners in secondary and tertiary educational institutions enjoyed a reciprocal master–apprentice interchange, one based on the decline of the Königsberg synthesis and the rise of pure mathematics. Prospective mathematics *Oberlehrer* might be expected on their examinations to answer questions about complicated physical problems, but the questions would be posed in a mathematical way by mathematicians.

The new spirit of mid-nineteenth-century mathematics is reflected in the career of Hermann Grassmann, pioneer of differential geometry.[37] The son of a mathematics and physics teacher at the Stettin *Gymnasium*, in 1827 the eighteen-year-old Grassmann went to Berlin with the aim of pursuing theology. There he fell under the spell of Boeckh's philology and soon studied little else. He qualified for the teaching certification with a major field in classical philology and a minor field in mathematics. He returned to Stettin as a teacher. Soon he left for a brief and unhappy period as mathematician Jakob Steiner's successor at the Berlin *Gewerbeschule*, an ancestor of the Berlin Institute of Technology. Grassmann then went home to Stettin as a teacher of mathematics, physics, chemistry, German, and religion.

In 1839, the same year that he passed the second qualifying examination in theology, the thirty-year-old Grassmann applied for teaching certification in mathematics as a major field. For his written question he was assigned a mathematical essay on the theory of ebb and flow. Grassmann worked through a portion of Laplace's *Mécanique céleste*, submitting a brilliant and voluminous paper, a doctoral thesis by any standard. In his paper Grassmann decried 'spiritless, formal development' and mere mechanical explanation, preferring instead geometrical modes of expression.[38] His examiner from the Joachimstal *Gymnasium* in Berlin barely looked through the paper and gave Grassmann a mediocre grade.[39] The candidate was bitten by mathematics, however, and in 1844 he produced his *Ausdehnungslehre*. It remained unnoticed.

Detoured by the Revolution of 1848, during which time Grassmann and his brother ran a counter-revolutionary weekly, he conceived a great passion to continue philology. Accordingly, he mastered Franz Bopp's work and a good many Indo-European languages. In the 1862 edition of his mathematical opus, Grassmann entered a plea for recognition: 'Truth is eternal and divine. No phase in the development of truth, however small be the field that it embraces, can pass by unnoticed. It remains, even if still ruined in the dust, clothed in the raiment that weak men have given it.'[40] He asked the Prussian authorities to be called to a university chair of mathematics, but the call never came. Grassmann died at his post in Stettin, a model philologist–mathematician *Oberlehrer*.

Shortly after mid-century the discipline of pure mathematics was sustained by the presence of *Oberlehrer* candidates. At Berlin the former *Oberlehrer* Kummer and Weierstrass established a seminar devoted to pure mathematics. It was the only way, the two mathematicians argued, of creating a 'school'. In their view, training promising talent for the discipline of pure mathematics had to receive priority over training *Oberlehrer*, a position contested by the Berlin authorities. As it turned out, the Berlin seminar did precisely what its originators had hoped: it consolidated the formalist approach to mathematics of Kummer and Weierstrass, dragging along as ballast future teachers of mathematics in the *Gymnasien*.[41] In the decade of the 1860s research in pure mathematics came to be the most important task of mathematics seminars at northern German universities, those created in 1866 at Bonn by Plücker and Rudolf Lipschitz, in 1870 at Breslau by Heinrich Schröter, and in 1872 at Greifswald by Fuchs. The seminars survived by training mathematics teachers.

By the early 1880s, over 160 candidates per year took the Prussian teaching certification with a major field in mathematics and natural sciences. Candidates prepared for examinations whose guidelines were set in 1866 by the pure mathematician Schröter.[42] A seminar designed to educate future teachers of mathematics which emphasised physical problems, like that created in 1866 at Halle by the astronomer Eduard Heis, was an anomaly; the programme in pure and applied mathematics advocated by Oskar Schlömilch, the neokantian minister for *Realanstalten* in Saxony, was seen as unusual. A measure of the new orientation to pure mathematics which was expected of teaching candidates is seen in the constitution of the commissions selected to certify *Oberlehrer* in mathematics and physics. By 1870 a substantial number of the Prussian examiners were pure mathematicians with university chairs: Friedrich Richelot at Königsberg, Fuchs at Greifswald, Schröter at Breslau, Eduard Heine at Halle, Lipschitz at Bonn, Georg Weyer at Kiel, Friedrich Ludwig

Stegmann at Marburg, and Clebsch at Göttingen. Only four mathematicians on the commission were sympathetic to applied studies: Schellbach at Berlin, Ernst Schering at Göttingen, Wilhelm Hittorf at Münster, and Heis at Münster.[43] The situation was less extreme in southern Germany, at Freiburg, Würzburg, Heidelberg, and Tübingen, where mathematics seminars retained an emphasis on physical problems. In part for this reason during the last two decades of the nineteenth century reform agitation was most intense in the north, and from the north came a new synthesis for all Germany.[44]

The regime of pure mathematics consolidated its gains over the first two decades of the new German empire. Mathematics positions at the institutes of technology were filled by graduates of the new seminars in pure mathematics, who condescended to teach engineers while waiting for a university call. Physicists, in particular, increasingly had to forge their own mathematical instruments from material cast by pure mathematicians with other purposes in mind.

The chasm between school and university mathematics widened. *Oberlehrer* were trained as pure mathematicians and set to convey no more than symbolic systems to their charges, who came to appreciate little of either the utility or the abstract essence of mathematics. As a result of the orientation of mathematics *Oberlehrer* who often taught science courses in the *Gymnasien*, pupils came to hold natural sciences in contempt. The chemist Alfred Miethe recalled of his *Gymnasium* years in the 1870s at Potsdam that most pupils looked on an inclination toward natural sciences as 'the expression of a perverse temperament'.[45] Most pupils in the Rhineland *Gymnasien* during the 1860s were bored with their mathematics lessons.[46] Friedrich Paulsen remembered his mathematics *Oberlehrer* at Altona in the mid 1860s as 'the sorriest figure among all the teachers' whom he had ever known. In his autobiography Paulsen could 'hardly bear to recall that expression of complete hopelessness in his eyes', for the poor man had absolutely no control over his class.[47]

To receive the *Abitur*, however, one had to answer a mathematics question. We need not wonder about the resourcefulness of pupils at German *Gymnasien* who were faced with mathematical difficulties: they cheated to succeed. Elaborate networks were set up, like the one that the future, distinguished Göttingen mathematician Carl Runge joined in Bremen during the mid 1870s, to smuggle unqualified candidates through the *Abitur* examination.[48] Pure mathematics, pursued by scores of brilliant university lecturers, was a rising star in German academia. Eclipsed were the tens of thousands of *Gymnasium* pupils who suffered under the tutelage of the near-greats, mathematics *Oberlehrer* who issued in a continuing stream from the universities. The situation was at best unstable, at worst self-destructive. It formed the background for a pedagogical revolution from below.

The end of neohumanism

The preparation that classical neohumanism provided for classical physics ended with the sweeping reform of mathematics and physics education accompanying new teaching regulations instituted around 1900. The reform was carried through by scores of *Oberlehrer*, some of whom sacrificed brilliant careers in research or administration to agitate for parity in the curriculum between natural sciences and classical languages. Their names are unfamiliar to historians of science, but their initiative brought about perhaps the most far-reaching reform of mathematics and physics education over the past century and a half. They organised into loose federations like the Association for the Advancement of Mathematical and Scientific Instruction, founded in 1890 following the initiative of the maverick *Oberlehrer* and reform-minded editor Immanuel Carl Volkmar Hoffmann; by 1897 this association, known as the Förderverein, was publishing a widely read journal and claimed over five hundred members, most of whom were mathematics and science schoolteachers.[49] In 1910, after a long struggle, calculus was being taught in around half of the *Realanstalten* of Prussia, and most secondary-school pupils were exposed to increasingly sophisticated mathematics, especially to the notion of functions and preliminary intuitions of calculus.[50]

The reform of mathematics instruction in late Wilhelmian Germany exerted a profound effect on members of the physics discipline. By the eve of the First World War most neophyte physicists had no longer been subjected to neohumanist-inspired instruction during their formative years in secondary school. To produce teachers capable of presenting the new material, universities began to offer new courses emphasising how mathematics could be used to solve physical and technical problems. In the education of a young physicist around 1910 advanced mathematics and modern languages had come to replace Greek and Latin. The effect of such a change in patterns of physics and mathematics education cannot be characterised in a simple way. The opinion of mathematician Heinrich Emil Timerding in 1926 is worth recalling here. He observed that instruction and research in both philology and exact sciences were the fruit of neohumanism. 'Both sides of our cultural reality sprang from one source', Timerding emphasised. He continued: 'One must not confuse humanism with the study of ancient languages, but one must see it as the education of a higher humanity.'[51]

What Timerding and others such as the British defender of classical studies Richard W Livingstone could only remark on,[52] we may begin to understand. It is certain that the *Gymnasien* provided encouragement for the ideology of pure mathematics. At the same time, evidence from German secondary education suggests that, far from turning students away from classical physics, neohumanism would have served as a genial and efficient introduction to the importance that classical physicists attached to physical world pictures.

Neohumanism presented a synthesis of human beauty, civilised morality, and philosophical truth that was based on pictures of classical, Hellenic culture. Despite its declining influence in academic circles during the nineteenth century, the ideal of neohumanism remained self-contained, rational, and, once its essence is distilled from a surrounding sea of murky scholarship, fundamentally simple and easy to express in ordinary speech. The ideal ethical and aesthetic picture of humanity revealed in Greek texts manifests striking resemblance to the requirements that Planck and others imposed on the physical world picture. Just as classical scholarship was a necessary tool for clarifying the neohumanist vision, so mathematics in the view of Planck, Mach, and Boltzmann was a tool for elaborating a physical world picture.[53] The very word 'classical', used around 1890 by Boltzmann and Mach to describe traditional physics,[54] would immediately have been associated in the minds of readers with the classical philology retailed by neohumanist educators who controlled *Gymnasien* and who dominated educational ministries in the German states.

The association between these two classical pictures of the world gains in importance when it is recalled that the term 'classical physics' was identified as a doctrine in the closing years of the nineteenth century—that is, when what we today call classical mechanics had been recognised as insufficient but before convincing substitutions had been proposed. When neohumanist instruction lost its hold over future physicists, young members of this discipline would have been inclined to look favourably on the new approach to mathematics. A young physicist on the eve of the First World War would have been predisposed to accept an instrumentalist interpretation of physical laws, one where abstract mathematics joined with *ad hoc* physical hypotheses to produce complicated theoretical syntheses. So pervasive was the new instrumentalist approach (to provide it with a name) that a young physicist late in Wilhelmian Germany would have had difficulty in understanding the commitment of classical physicists to what they called a 'physical world picture'.

Why exactly did mathematical instrumentalism become established as an approach to characterising physical reality early in twentieth-century Germany? Mathematical logicians, laboratory scientists and prosecuting attorneys have schooled us to seek single causes for natural and human events. Yet in his essay *Apologie pour l'histoire* Marc Bloch suggests that the activity of large numbers of historical actors may be governed by a conjuncture of circumstances. In Bloch's view, several independent lines of activity may suddenly add up together, after the manner of the mathematical theory of wave motion, to produce a new attitude or response to historical events. Bloch's suggestion seems appropriate for considering

the question at hand. It has been maintained that classical neohumanism
lent support to the classical physical world picture and that the decline of
the influence of classical neohumanism on physicists accompanied a decline
of interest in the classical world picture. To develop the point completely,
one would have to indicate how the vision of education replacing neohumanism was conducive to the new view of mathematical instrumentalism.
Technical detail is indispensable for convincing arguments in the social
history of science. Much understanding can be achieved, nevertheless,
without direct appeal to mathematical equations and laboratory
procedures. This latter spirit governs the remainder of the present chapter,
where educational practice and mathematics instruction are considered by
focusing on the changing status of the *Oberlehrerstand* as well as on the
educational activity of Felix Klein.

The new schoolteacher

The image and professional status of the *Oberlehrerstand* changed with
the destruction of the monopoly of the neohumanists on providing students
for institutions of higher education. As with Heinrich Mann's Professor
Unrat and the professors of the unhappy pupil Törless in Robert Musil's
fictional military academy, an *Oberlehrer* became characterised as a weak,
ignorant partisan participant in current affairs, a martinet whose actions
were governed by unrefined passions over which he had little control and
many regrets. The picture of the *Oberlehrer* as a scholar declined with the
ossification of classical studies and the loss of interest in related disciplines.
Increasingly cut off from his university counterpart, the secondary-school
Oberlehrer became a prophet and a seer. He was supposed to disseminate
all forms of culture leading to an appreciation of the universe and the
place of humanity in it; he was no longer charged with advancing the
frontiers of knowledge, or even with encouraging original research among
his pupils. Historical synthesis in the service of instilling a practical appreciation for national goals and orthodox morality replaced elaboration of the
tangible picture of Greek culture and wisdom.[55]

According to the educator Rudolf Lehmann, the early nineteenth-
century ideal of the *Oberlehrer* as a *Lehrbeamter*, or scholar–humanist
teacher, was replaced at the end of the century with the image of an
Erziehungsbeamter, an instructor who synthesised and disseminated the
specialised learning pursued in the universities. The *Oberlehrer* needed to
develop, above all, the facility to enliven all dry intellectual
activity—learned or otherwise—for a new generation. The American
historian of education William Setchel Learned emphasised that the late
Wilhelmian *Oberlehrer* responded to 'not only the university investigator,
but every writer, actor, and preacher who has a message'.[56]

In 1906, at their second national gathering, *Oberlehrer* expressly rejected the dual role into which they had evolved. No longer were they scholars, they affirmed; they could only maintain an appreciation for scientific research and keep abreast of new advances. Affirming the new role of *Oberlehrer*, the modernist educator Karl Fricke asserted that their task was not to pursue specialised research but to make the results of scholarship known and available for the advancement of culture. In the period before the First World War, the individual *Oberlehrer* avoided confining himself to one subject or one year. He was encouraged to follow a class through school, teaching several subjects along the way. Pedagogy supplanted classical scholarship, even in *Gymnasium* circles. The educator August Baumeister openly welcomed the slur directed against contemporary *Oberlehrer* that they were no more than 'method mongers', because competence in teaching, not in literary activity, had become the proper measure of accomplishment in the secondary schools.

Unlike faculty in universities or institutes of technology, the late Wilhelmian *Oberlehrer* showed unmistakable signs of advancing sclerosis. With the advent of the obligatory pedagogical seminar and the years of probationary teaching, careers in secondary schools diverged from those in the universities. The PhD became a superfluous, if highly coveted, ornament for *Oberlehrer*, whose educational path was longer and more demanding than that of lawyers, doctors, theologians, and even university teachers. During the last third of the nineteenth century *Oberlehrer* gradually accumulated benefits rivalling those of university faculty. The new professional, non-scholarly status of the pedagogue was consecrated in 1906, when Prussian *Oberlehrer* finally obtained parity in salary and privileges with *Richter*, or lower-court judges.[57]

The new secondary-school *Oberlehrer* of late Wilhelmian Germany rejected the neohumanists' emphasis on the importance of a picture of the world, and, as well, he rejected the neohumanist ideal of original research and scholarship. He was a modern taxonomist, who sought to enumerate and classify the elements of a chaotic world. He was a jurist, who weighed the moral temper of the Wilhelmian Age. He was a nationalist, who sought to edify young Germans and not young Greeks, one who sought to breathe relevance into the impersonal and abstract formulae of modern Germany. The new ideology of education, especially as disseminated by younger *Oberlehrer* in the early years of the twentieth century, prepared young physicists to receive with sympathy the approach of mathematical instrumentalism, where physical properties were ascribed to mathematical formulae.

The new educational ideology was especially pronounced in the *Real-anstalten* where the future physicist would have been exposed to elementary physics and above all mathematics at the expense of Greek and Latin. In the *Realanstalten* of late Wilhelmian Germany, future physicists would have increasingly had instructors who themselves were not formed in the neohumanist mould. And it was above all in the *Realanstalten* that physicists were educated on the eve of the First World War.

The Göttingen offensive

The central spokesman driving both *Oberlehrer* and students to the new instrumentalist point of view was Felix Klein. A student of Julius Plücker's and the author in 1872 of a programme for unifying geometry, Klein by the mid 1880s directed the interest of his university colleagues to educational matters.[58] Coming to fill in 1886 the junior of two full professorships of mathematics at Göttingen, Klein worked to extend his influence in pedagogy. Under his inspiration the new statutes of the mathematical–physical seminar specified that the seminar, whose principal aim remained training secondary-school teachers, would treat questions of applied mathematics in its mathematical section and theoretical physics in its physical section.[59] When Hermann Amandus Schwarz left for Strasbourg in 1892, Klein assumed the prerogatives of senior mathematician. He took control of Schwarz's seminar's lending library, integrating it into his own non-circulating, mathematical reading-room collection. Klein stocked his reading room with books, reprints, and lecture notes in all fields of mathematical sciences.[60]

Klein's pedagogical manoeuvres supported his vision that ideal reasoning could bring about a new unification of thought in both pure and applied mathematics. 'To idealise a physical or technical problem is to make it mathematically tractable', he noted in his 1897 lectures on theoretical mechanics.[61] In a public talk of 1904 he emphasised that the struggle of theoreticians allied with technologists might be described as:

> *progressive* but in no way radical, as *calculating with given relationships in a practical way* but in no way *utilitarian*. The various parts of learning evolving equally along with each other and together with each other should unite into a comprehensive whole. If you want a precise name for what I have in mind, I can suggest the word *universalism*.[62]

Under Klein's aegis and following his vision of mathematical sciences, Göttingen became by 1905 the most influential centre of mathematics in the world.

Beginning in 1894 Klein sought support for his views among reformist *Oberlehrer*. His nephew at the Brunswick Institute of Technology, Robert Fricke, attended the 1894 Förderverein meeting at Wiesbaden. There Fricke heard the Erlangen professor of physics Eilhard Wiedemann speak on physics instruction in the schools and in higher education.[63] Fricke wrote to Klein enthusiastically about the organisation: 'I find the strivings of the *Verein* worth a great deal of attention, as much by my technical colleagues as by me.'[64] Members of the organisation reacted unsympathetically to pure mathematics, which they regarded as impeding instruction in useful sciences. Fricke provided Klein with the example of the director of the Brunswick *Oberrealschule*, Wilhelm Krumme, a man by no means opposed to the views of reformist *Oberlehrer* but someone who also held obscure ideas about higher mathematics. Krumme had studied the publications of his former teacher Julius Plücker, but he spoke of Plücker's geometry 'as something that he had never understood and that in any case belonged to the most profound creations of human intellect'. Fricke concluded that the task of *Oberlehrer* 'to communicate fresh contact with higher developments in mathematics is, as things lie, probably quite difficult to realise'.[65]

The next meeting of the Förderverein was to take place at the Göttingen *Gymnasium* in June 1895, and Klein realised that it would present him with a golden opportunity for placing 'the relationship between school and university in the foreground'.[66] He first managed to have himself designated organising chairman and carefully chose a planning committee. For the three-day meeting he arranged an excursion to the nearby Hanover Institute of Technology.[67] On the morning of the first full day of the meeting Klein lectured the Göttingen assembly in strident tones on the value of the short course that he had inaugurated for mathematics and science teachers, modelled after those of Bernhard Schwalbe at Berlin and the lectures sponsored by the Frankfurt Physical Society.[68] In an obvious appeal to reformist *Oberlehrer*, Klein emphasised the inventiveness and adaptability of the mathematical sciences at the University of Göttingen. He spoke at length about the Göttingen ideal of presenting mathematics as an undivided whole, 'rather than offering lectures in only a few areas'. Göttingen had a unified plan of studies for mathematicians and physicists, Klein observed, one that was optional and flexible so that it really did not interfere with sacred *Lernfreiheit*, the traditional freedom of German students to hear any lectures that they pleased in any order that they liked. Making possible an encyclopaedic breadth of instruction at Göttingen were seventeen instructors in mathematics, physics, and astronomy, including eight in pure mathematics. Guiding the approach to mathematics of the faculty was Klein's belief in a balance between intuitive and axiomatic formulations of the field.

Despite rhetoric such as that offered to the Förderverein, by the late 1890s Klein devoted his organisational efforts to urging that physical and technical problems be solved by extensive appeal to pure mathematics. In this way he hoped to adapt the pure mathematics discipline to changing social requirements. With new teaching regulations giving a place to applied mathematics and with engineers demanding practical instruction in mathematical methods, pure mathematicians feared that their discipline would wither and die. Opposing the suggestion of a respected engineer that all university mathematicians should have a practical speciality and teach it, mathematician Eduard Study argued that pure mathematics could not be carried on by part-time practitioners: 'Because of its extent and multiform nature, pure mathematics requires a whole man.' If the engineer's suggestion came to pass, Study emphasised, 'the flowering of pure mathematics which we now enjoy in Germany is finished.'[69] Klein's programme at Göttingen had the effect of accommodating criticisms like those offered by Study. At the same time that he introduced technical education at Göttingen, Klein greatly expanded instruction in pure mathematics. He also insisted that new faculty in physical sciences at Göttingen thoroughly master advanced mathematics. Klein's efforts reserved for pure mathematics a secure place in the cosmology of exact sciences at Göttingen. Pure mathematicians were charged with the task of impregnating physical sciences with abstract harmony.

One should emphasise here that such a charge was not coherent with the views of the early neohumanists. According to their programme, classical philology was pursued for its own sake and for the mental training that resulted from intercourse with the great and noble intellects of antiquity. Applications of the neohumanist world view to current or practical affairs were excluded. It was against this otherworldliness of neohumanism that Wilhelm II spoke out during the 1890 school conference in Berlin. Wilhelm wanted to instil in schoolchildren a national feeling and Christian morality. He himself had experienced neohumanism as a pupil at the *Gymnasium* in Cassel, and he found it repellent. Klein's argument was a unique effort at attempting to accommodate old patterns of thought within a changing social framework. Philology professors might have made the argument that their discipline was useful in educating good Germans who would gladly serve the Emperor. The evidence is that few so argued.

What drove Klein to dedicate the last thirty years of his life to achieving an imperialist vision of mathematical universalism? The historian, to be sure, cannot discard biographical evidence. Felix Klein's dissertation adviser Plücker was a physicist turned mathematician, and Klein's early approach to mathematics received little encouragement from his mathematician colleagues. Klein, like many other German professors, suffered periodic mental breakdowns from overwork. By 1890 his original work in mathematics had come to an end, and following a pattern usual for exhausted scientists and scholars he sought to make a name for himself as an innovative educator. These circumstances, however, in no way establish whether his universalist striving was a noble and selfless undertaking or a cynical attempt to manipulate his contemporaries.

Doubtless the truth is a mixture of the two extremes, and it is not the place here to attempt to arrive at more certain knowledge concerning Klein's motivation. How Klein's universalism was perceived by his contemporaries is nevertheless of great interest. Klein's official and recent biographers have seen in his Göttingen programme a genuine desire to marry mathematics with exact sciences and technology, but some among his colleagues were less sanguine. In 1910 Leopold Ambronn, associate professor of astronomy at Göttingen, summarised the view of others in a long letter to his colleague, the Göttingen geographer–geologist Hermann Wagner. Ambronn had been an observational astronomer at Göttingen since 1892, and he hoped for a full professorship. He confided to Wagner that the mathematics 'monopoly' at Göttingen was not conducive to practical astronomy. 'Klein and the men around him here are finally not working astronomers. They have let themselves be led—not to speak about personal matters—to entirely different hypotheses and fundamentals.'[70] For his part Klein was not happy with Ambronn's practical, observational work; Ambronn remained associate professor until 1920.

In his excellent study of Klein's interaction with the technologists and engineers, Karl-Heinz Manegold has emphasised how Klein brought instruction in technology to Göttingen. To serve his ends Klein created the Göttingen Association for the Advancement of Applied Physics and Mathematics, a league of industrialists and university professors. Motivating the Göttingen Association was the deep impression left on Klein in 1893 by his extended visit to the United States, where he saw how industrialists supported higher learning. To attract private purses to Göttingen Klein had to provide assurance that men of pure learning could, if properly funded, produce knowledge of use to captains of industry.

In the period before 1914 Klein was moderately successful in obtaining industrial capital, although his elaborate promises of pactical gain failed to materialise. One of his colleagues saw why this was so. Hans Lorenz, associate professor of mechanical engineering at Göttingen, issued a public challenge to his mathematician colleague. In 1903 he wrote in the *Jahresbericht* of the German Mathematicians' Association about Klein's attempt in the mid 1890s to create at Göttingen a 'general staff' for industry, leaving the institutes of technology to furnish the 'front officers'. The new programme could hardly conceal the 'abstract direction' given to preparing school teachers. As a result, Lorenz noted, the teaching corps was underdeveloped in mathematics: it was unprepared to provide instruction in applied subjects. The mistaken approach was nowhere more evident than in the Göttingen mathematics seminar, where technical mechanics was treated in a few sessions 'by lectures from the participants, without systematic preparation in a technical laboratory'.[71]

According to a letter from the editor of the *Jahresberichte* to David Hilbert, Klein was 'quite badly hurt' by Lorenz's exposition. The editor, Jena mathematics professor August Gutzmer, saw no personal motive in Lorenz's argument, although he admitted: 'The offensive against the "mathematical seminar" could well have been omitted. It could have been warned in general terms against excessive theorising and undervaluing work in the laboratory, that I concede.' Gutzmer continued with an observation, the truth of which is apparent to any modern editor: 'As editor I would have gladly dropped the point, but in the final instance the editor cannot control his contributors.'[72] Even Gutzmer, otherwise one of Klein's strongest supporters, questioned the abstract Göttingen approach to technology.

Klein soon countered Lorenz's criticism by offering a few interdisciplinary seminars in technological areas, seminars that, like the one on electro-technology which Klein co-directed in 1905, required laboratory exercises of the students.[73] To judge from the Göttingen courses listed in the *Physikalische Zeitschrift* between 1899 and 1914, however, laboratory exercises in technology occupied only a small part among the advanced seminars. Resentment over the elitist approach to technology at Göttingen appeared in journalistic accounts. Klein supported the introduction of calculus into the schools, but his nephew Robert Fricke reported in 1902: 'In the daily press appears: "Klein and Hilbert actively agitate to delay introducing instr. in differential and integral equns. into the schools." ' Fricke anticipated the worst: 'If it comes to this, we are finished in higher education.'[74]

Fricke had little reason to fear for the projects of his uncle, as criticism directed against Klein hardly impaired his influence over the institutions of exact sciences. Requiring a supporter of Klein's stature, *Oberlehrer* active in the reform struggle tolerated and even elaborated his rhetoric. By 1900 the darling of thousands of mathematics and science teachers, Klein spoke at the school conference in Berlin that led directly to the elevation of the *Realanstalten*. Using his friendship with Friedrich Althoff, the Prussian authority in charge of higher education, Klein placed his favourites in university and polytechnic vacancies throughout Prussia.

Typical of Klein's great influence is the story of mathematics at Aachen. Writing to Hilbert from the Aachen Institute of Technology, the former Göttingen instructor Otto Blumenthal detailed how higher mathematics Göttingen-style was transmitted to engineering students. Blumenthal reported in 1905 that his first advanced course on complex analysis was a disaster: only one man showed up for it. Blumenthal sought consolation from Klein's former assistant Arnold Sommerfeld, professor of mechanics at Aachen. Sommerfeld took the matter philosophically. He offered 'that it was always this way'. Blumenthal increased the practical content of his course and soon had an audience of six.[75] Despite Blumenthal's lukewarm reception, by the eve of the First World War Aachen was a satellite of Göttingen. Blumenthal confided to Hilbert that because Wilhelm Kutta had decided to decline Aachen for a post at Stuttgart, the Aachen faculty 'were for once in the beautiful position of having to call a mathematician of the applied direction'. Blumenthal never doubted that Göttingen could come up with a winning candidate. Göttingen instructor of applied mechanics Theodor von Kármán would make an excellent choice 'under the condition', Blumenthal emphasised, 'that he also understands pure mathematics.'[76] Kármán received and accepted the call. At Aachen he pioneered heavier-than-air flight.

Relativity misunderstood

The Göttingen atmosphere created by Klein and sustained by dozens of his hand-picked professors, instructors, and assistants encouraged the belief, to introduce the frequently reported remark by David Hilbert, that physics was too important to be left to physicists. The Göttingen approach to physical reality was overwhelmingly mathematical. With their superior formalisms Göttingen mathematicians set out to capture the laws of nature which had eluded physical scientists.

In one of the most influential demonstrations of the Göttingen outlook, Hermann Minkowski reformulated Albert Einstein's special theory of relativity, embedding it in a theory of absolute, four-dimensional space–time. In previous chapters we have seen that Minkowski's theory differed greatly from Einstein's. To cite only one difference, Minkowski invoked the electromagnetic ether, while Einstein argued that such a concept had no place in physics.[77]

For the Göttingen mathematicians and mathematically inclined physicists, Minkowski's judgment carried authority. His approach was taken up after his death in 1909 by David Hilbert. When asking a state official in 1913 for 5000 marks to finance guest professorships, Hilbert provided a concise summary of the Göttingen approach to physical reality. He began his plea for funds by explaining 'why at the moment mathematical fundamentals are bringing about a transformation in the basic concepts of physics'. Hilbert had in mind Einstein's theory of relativity, as elaborated by Minkowski. 'The tendency of Einstein's thought was a radical one', Hilbert stated, paraphrasing Minkowski, the mathematician who had 'provided the definitive mathematical expression to Einstein's thought'. Hilbert continued: 'Einstein's idea has become the *boldest and most powerful scientific* idea since David Hume's critique of the concept of causality.' Hilbert then mentioned the role of experiment in the genesis of relativity, thoroughly confusing the contributions of Walter Kaufmann, Max Abraham, and Albert Michelson. It did not matter, for Hilbert introduced these names only because all had been associated for a time with his university. Much more important in Hilbert's mind was to underline that the new theory had originated in *pure* thought:

Never has the most liberated scientific imagination dared to shake old views on space and time in a way analogous to Michelson's experiment and this result. The consequences of Einstein's thought, the so-called 'relativity principle', have revolutionised mathematical and physical science: in place of the old Lagrangian mechanics stands a completely new structure whose surest building blocks, Maxwell's electrodynamics, have now become the new four-dimensional 'world-mechanics'.

Hilbert considered the theory of relativity to emphasise

> how close mathematics and physics have grown and how these two sciences depend on each other. While previously mathematics occasionally considered isolated problems from physics and then only treated them in the abstract, mathematical sense, and while physics mostly asked from mathematics only technical rules for calculations or formal methods of calculation, both sciences have coalesced into a single scientific field.

The conclusion for Hilbert was obvious: more pure mathematics was needed in physics. 'It follows that the mathematician must penetrate far deeper than before into the innermost essence of physical science and the physicist should no longer remain merely a mathematical layman.' The new synthesis could not be obtained, however, merely from reading scientific papers. Mathematicians could easily learn physics, Hilbert implied; it would be more difficult for physicists to assimilate mathematics:

> In his written exposition the physicist easily jumps over important logical steps obvious to him in view of intuitive, contemporary experiments, while the mathematician often retains the key to understanding physical processes. Yet the physicist finds it for the most part impossible to follow the abstract content of a modern mathematical paper, even when the subject is close to him.[78]

Hilbert's scheme was to invite distinguished physicists to Göttingen to give short lecture series. Göttingen mathematicians, apprised of physical theory, would then be able to offer solutions to outstanding problems.

How the Göttingen spirit moved classical physicists is revealed in Gustav Mie's response to Minkowski's theory. Mie was a mineralogy student who in 1891 decided to take a doctorate under the Heidelberg mathematician Leo Königsberger. In 1897 he became instructor at the Karlsruhe Institute of Technology. By this time he was busy exploring the field concept of electrodynamics and within several years came to study the new electromagnetic view of nature. The electromagnetic ether ran as a 'red thread' through Mie's 1910 textbook on electrodynamics, noted one reviewer.[79] Because Mie addressed the physical constitution of the ether and indicated how molecules, atoms, and electrons were singularities in this peculiar substance, the philosophically minded professor at the Hamburg state physical laboratory, Johannes Classen, identified Mie as a leading exponent of the 'old school'.[80] In Classen's view, Einstein's special theory of relativity had successfully shown that the hypothesis of an ether was no longer required in physics.

In 1912, having been full professor of physics at Greifswald for seven years, Mie published an electromagnetic theory of matter which was heavily inspired by Minkowski's four-dimensional space–time. Like many others before him, Mie considered electrical charge as a singularity in the ether. He concluded by producing a physically unsatisfying nonlinear field theory, one that found few adherents among even formalist physicists.[81] Mie was quite pleased with himself for having decided to study relativity. To the astronomer Karl Schwarzschild, Mie wrote in 1912 that his theory of matter was 'in complete agreement with the relativity principle and reproduces all known facts about gravitation'. Oblivious to various attempts at measuring the variation of electron mass with velocity and perhaps even unaware of the astronomical tests for general relativity which Einstein had recently proposed, Mie regretted that in his own approach all relativistic effects were 'so small that they can't be tested experimentally'. Mie continued that in his theory 'the gravitational "constant" depends on temperature . . . but the changes are at best always of the order 10^{-11} and so not observable'. He felt that relativity theory was 'so wonderfully beautiful and Minkowski's method . . . so elegant and rich that they have raised theoretical physics to a new height'.[82]

Mie's theory of matter was based on Minkowski's space–time formalism and like Minkowski's work was essentially untestable. It provided inspiration for David Hilbert when, as the culmination of several years' intense interest in physical problems, Hilbert applied his talents to study Einstein's general relativity. Hilbert paid close attention to Einstein's Göttingen lectures on gravitation during the summer of 1915 and (with the full benefit of Einstein's many published versions of general relativity and perhaps even with some knowledge of Einstein's earlier, unpublished attempts to formulate a covariant field theory) he decided that the field equations had to be expressed in covariant form.[83] Following Minkowski and Mie, Hilbert derived the field equations by applying the principle of least action to an unspecified, general function after first having postulated two unphysical axioms. The function was the scalar curvature along with matter terms.[84]

Hilbert's result, an unphysical formulation of the covariant field equations, came as a revelation to Mie. Writing to his Göttingen colleague in 1916 Mie exclaimed:

I have read your work on the foundations of physics with growing wonderment and enrapture. Although I must naturally take much trouble in doing so, still I am excited by what I have already understood. It is to me as if I had been feeling in the dark; the theory that you have given is certainly in the right direction. But I lack the mathematical force to replace these obscure feelings with clear concepts, and I didn't hope to venture that such a powerful step as you have taken could be made.

Mie remained unconvinced, however, that general relativity was self-consistent. Recalling a discussion in 1913 with Einstein,[85] Mie observed that in general relativity there was no way to prove rectilinear motion or establish absolute coordinates. 'No physicist will let himself be convinced' about the impossibility of absolute motion so long as plane and curved waves were permitted in the theory.[86] The new mathematics troubled Mie deeply. He wrote to Hilbert in 1917:

> I have been raised as a calculating physicist, and I characteristically think of any problem as if I had numerically to calculate my way through it. This would seem to me not entirely the same as how the modern mathematician operates. Numerically to calculate is always to calculate with finite decimals.[87]

Mie raised the issue of a physicist's use of mathematics because he feared that Hilbert and Einstein would misunderstand his criticism of general relativity. In 1912 he did not hesitate to follow the method of the new mathematician–physicists, insofar as he could understand it; by 1917, left behind by the mathematics, Mie reverted to his earlier sensibilities as a classical physicist.

From the beginning Einstein did not think much of Mie's theory of matter. In 1913 he wrote to his astronomer friend Erwin Finlay Freundlich that Mie's theory was 'fantastic and has, according to my opinion, a vanishingly small inside chance' of being right.[88] He thought that Hilbert's treatment was similarly flawed. It 'doesn't please me', Einstein wrote to physicist Paul Ehrenfest. 'It is unduly specialised concerning "matter", unduly complicated, not honest ($\equiv$ Gaussian) in construction. (Pretention of being a superman by concealing his methods.)'[89] In Hilbert's theory, according to Einstein, physics was obscured by a variational method operating on an abstract 'world-function'. Einstein elaborated to mathematician Hermann Weyl how unconvincing it was that in Hilbert's theory 'firm considerations stemming from the relativity postulate are linked to such unfounded hypotheses about matter, [hypotheses] concerning the structure of electrons'. Einstein did not in principle oppose Hilbert's mathematical treatment; he simply insisted that a physical argument had to be retained: 'I am prepared to admit that the search for the suitable hypothesis, or the Hamiltonian function for the construction of electrons, comprises one of the most immediate tasks of the theory. But "axiomatic method" can be of little help in this.'[90] Einstein had already spent several years working to connect special relativity with the electron theory, and he regarded with suspicion Hilbert's grandiose formulation.[91]

To his disappointment, Einstein in 1917 had to circumvent formal difficulties in his cosmological research by proceeding in an empirical fashion. He felt forced to introduce a 'cosmological constant' to make his field equations coherent with a static universe of constant curvature.[92]

Einstein's cosmology was received with great interest by none other than Felix Klein. In 1890 Klein had considered the geometry of the universe in relation to the law of gravitation,[93] and in 1917 he reconsidered the thorny question once more from the point of view of Hilbert's formulation of general relativity. Klein's approach was not pleasing to Einstein. He wrote to Klein in 1917: 'It still seems to me that you very much over-rate the value of purely formal points of view. These are quite precious if there is an already-discovered truth finally to be formulated, but they almost always fail as a heuristic aid.'[94]

Klein and Einstein corresponded intensely throughout 1918, but Einstein remained unconvinced about Klein's formal approach to cosmology. Remarking on one of Klein's models for the universe, Einstein was polite but firm: 'From the physical standpoint I believe that I can advance the opinion that this mathematically elegant, since four-dimensional uniform interpretation of the universe, does not correspond to reality.'[95] Einstein resisted the cavalier Göttingen approach to physics, an approach where, by starting with aesthetically pleasing constructions in pure mathematics, one could expect to achieve a deeper understanding of physical reality.

The Göttingen approach to mathematical physics provided impetus for the twentieth-century attitude towards physical reality, but it was only one manifestation of the new instrumentalist point of view. It has been suggested here that the new view resulted after pressure from below, from legions of reformist *Oberlehrer*, was guided through official channels by Felix Klein and his university colleagues. In understanding this process of change, obscure *Oberlehrer* and their wards are as important as *Geheimrat* Klein and his retainers.

What precedes has focused on why younger physicists around 1913 would have found the classical, physical world picture old-fashioned and even incomprehensible, and why they would have been favourably predisposed to the overtures of mathematical instrumentalism extended by the pure mathematicians of Klein's circle at Göttingen. The explanation deals with proximate motivations for changing patterns in the ideas of large numbers of historical actors. The argument indicates how the historian of science might begin to understand, from another perspective, one dimension of the peculiar revolution in physical thought that took place in Germany on the eve of the First World War, a revolution that fixed the attitude of twentieth-century physicists towards mathematics.

Returning to the metaphor drawn from the French Revolution, in the story presented here the university mathematician Felix Klein chaired a revolutionary Convention that channelled the activity of schoolteacher *sans-culottes*. A new ideology of mathematical instrumentalism was disseminated by both the elite revolutionary vanguard and the mass of radicalised scientists-of-the-line. The prevalence of the new ideology illuminates the reception of relativity in Germany. What I have described will not explain the turns in Albert Einstein's path to the covariant field equations of general relativity, even though such a traditionally phrased question may be informed by the analysis outlined above. My analysis is intended to suggest how one may approach the social history of scientific ideas by starting with the little figures in history of science, the men and women who accepted, rejected, ignored, or misunderstood work that has come to be seen as central for modern science.

Notes and references

1 The amount of material on the school reforms of 1890–1900 is staggering. Standard chronology is found in the histories of Friedrich Paulsen, a reformer openly hostile to mathematics and natural sciences. A recent reconsideration of the standard account is James Charles Albisetti's *Kaiser, Classicists, and Moderns: Secondary School Reform in Imperial Germany* (dissertation, Yale University 1976), a study that specifically avoids discussing mathematics and natural science. Standard accounts emphasising mathematics and science instruction include: Felix Klein, *Vorträge über den mathematischen Unterricht an den höheren Schulen. I: Von der Organisation des mathematischen Unterrichts*, recorded by R Schimmack (Leipzig 1907); Herbert Göllnitz, *Beiträge zur Geschichte des physikalisch–chemischen Unterrichts an den höheren Schulen Deutschlands seit der Mitte des 19. Jahrhunderts* (Leipzig 1920); Paul Bode, *Die Reform des mathematischen und naturwissenschaftlichen Unterrichts an den höheren Schulen in der Gegenwart* (dissertation, University of Leipzig 1911). Recent studies include: Jürgen Sievert, *Zur Geschichte des Physikunterrichts* (dissertation, University of Bonn 1967); Heide Inhetveen, *Die Reform des gymnasialen Mathematikunterrichts zwischen 1890 und 1914* (Bad Heilbrunn 1976).
2 Friedrich Paulsen provides a discussion of the tripartite nature of German secondary education, as it developed during the nineteenth century, in *German Education: Past and Present* transl T Lorenz (London 1908).
3 A Tilmann, 'Die Entwicklung des höheren Schulwesens in Preussen im letzten Jahrzehnt', *Monatschrift für höhere Schulen* 9 (1910) 289–303.
4 R Willstätter, *From My Life*, ed A Stoll, transl L S Hornig (New York 1965) pp 89–90.
5 A Riedler, in remarks following an article of Klein's, *Zeitschrift des Vereines deutscher Ingenieure* 40 (1896) 990.
6 Vorstand des Vereines deutscher Ingenieure to Klein, 26 June 1896. Nachlass Felix Klein VI-C, Niedersächsische Staats- und Universitätsbibliothek, Göttingen (henceforth: NSUB Gött.).
7 G Kowalewski, cited in Armin Hermann's 'Sommerfeld und die Technik', *Technikgeschichte* 34 (1967) 313.
8 R Fricke to F Klein, 5 May 1896. Nachlass Felix Klein IX, NSUB Gött.

9 A Tilmann, 'Die Entwicklung' (ref 3); Richard H Samuel and R Hinton Thomas, *Education and Society in Modern Germany* (London 1949) pp 45–56.

10 Lewis Pyenson and Douglas Skopp, 'Educating Physicists in Germany *circa* 1900', *Social Studies of Science* **7** (1977) 329–66.

11 Russell McCormmach has identified the importance of world pictures for classical physicists in his 'Editor's Foreword', *Historical Studies in the Physical Sciences* **6** (1975) xi–xiv.

12 M Planck to L Silberstein, 30 December 1892. Manuscripts Collection, Rush Rhees Library, University of Rochester, New York.

13 H Weber, 'Ueber die Differentialgleichungen der elektrolytischen Verschiebungen', Berlin, Akademie der Wissenschaften, Mathematisch–physikalische Klasse, *Sitzungsberichte* (1897) 936–46.

14 M Planck to H Weber, 28 November 1897. 8° Cod. Ms. philos. 205, NSUB Gött.

15 M Planck, 'Ueber die Potentialdifferenz zwischen zwei verdünnten Lösungen binärer Elektrolyte', *Annalen der Physik* **40** (1890) 561–76.

16 M Planck to H Weber, 19 December 1898. 8° Cod. Ms. philos. 205, NSUB Gött.

17 H Lange, 'Geschichte der Methodik des physikalischen und chemischen Unterrichtes in der Volksschule', in *Geschichte des deutschen Unterrichts in der Volksschule. II: Geschichte der Methodik des Unterrichtes in den Realen* ed Carl Kehr (Gotha 1888) p 204.

18 In the first decade of the twentieth century an epistemological debate erupted between Planck and Mach. An indication of the dimensions of the exchange is given in Lewis S Feuer's *Einstein and the Generations of Science* (New York 1974) pp 342–4. That both Planck and Mach used compatible vocabulary would seem to lend support to my analysis.

19 E Study to D Hilbert, 7 January 1897. Nachlass David Hilbert 396, NSUB Gött.

20 L Boltzmann, 'On the Significance of Theories', in L Boltzmann's *Theoretical Physics and Philosophical Problems, Selected Writings* ed B McGuiness, transl P Foulkes (Dordrecht 1964) pp 33–4.

21 L Boltzmann, cited in Henri Fehr's 'Enquête sur la méthode de travail des mathématiciens: Résultats, III', *L'Enseignement mathématique* **8** (1906) 45.

22 C H Müller, 'Studien zur Geschichte der Mathematik insbesondere des mathematischen Unterrichts an der Universität Göttingen im 18. Jahrhundert', *Abhandlungen zur Geschichte der mathematischen Wissenschaften* **17** (1904) 59, 73, and 99.

23 *Ibid* p 128; Wilhelm Lorey, *Das Studium der Mathematik an den deutschen Universitäten seit Anfang des 19. Jahrhunderts* (Leipzig 1916) p 28.

24 C H Müller, 'Studien' (ref 22) p 127. See Lewis Pyenson's *Neohumanism and the Persistence of Pure Mathematics in Wilhelmian Germany* (Philadelphia 1983) [*Am. Phil. Soc. Mem.* **150**] pp 20–3.

25 Quotations in William Setchel Learned's *The Oberlehrer: A Study of the Social and Professional Evolution of the German Schoolmaster* (Cambridge, Mass 1914) pp 32, 44.

26 Walter Jens, 'The Classical Tradition in Germany—Grandeur and Decay', in *Upheaval and Continuity: A Century of German History* ed E J Feuchtwanger

(London 1973) pp 67–82. Among many other sources see the excellent history by Franz Pahl, *Geschichte des naturwissenschaftlichen und mathematischen Unterrichts* (Leipzig 1913) pp 169ff.

27 W Lorey, *Staatsprüfung und praktische Ausbildung der Mathematiker an den höheren Schulen in Preussen und einigen Norddeutschen Staaten* (Leipzig 1911) p 103; Johannes Norrenberg, 'Der Unterricht in den Naturwissenschaften', in *Die Reform des höheren Schulwesens in Preussen* ed Wilhelm Lexis (Halle 1902) p 273; W Lorey, *Studium* (ref 23) p 63.

28 J Sievert, *Geschichte* (ref 1) pp 47–50.

29 W Lorey, *Staatsprüfung* (ref 27) p 105.

30 *Ibid* pp 102–3.

31 Felix Müller, *Karl Schellbach, Rückblick auf sein wissenschaftliches Leben* (Leipzig 1905) p 24.

32 *Ibid* p 16; K Schellbach, *Erinnerungen an den Kronprinz Friedrich Wilhelm von Preussen* (Breslau 1890) pp 21–2; F Klein, *Vorträge* (ref 1) p 91; Francisque Marotte, *L'Enseignement des sciences mathématiques et physiques dans l'enseignement secondaire des garçons en Allemagne* (Paris 1905) p 26.

33 W Lorey, *Studium* (ref 23) pp 40–51.

34 K Schellbach, 'Plan zur Gründung eines mathematischen Institutes zu Berlin', in F Müller's *Karl Schellbach* (ref 31) pp 41–56.

35 *Ibid* p 41.

36 W Lorey, *Studium* (ref 23) p 103. The connection between *Gymnasium* education and higher mathematics has been suggested in the remarks of Marguerite Gerstell: 'Prussian Education and Mathematics', *American Mathematical Monthly* **82** (1975) 240–5.

37 Friedrich Engel, 'Hermann Grassmann', *Jahresberichte der deutschen Mathematiker-Vereinigung* **18** (1909) 344–456; **19** (1910) 1–13.

38 *Ibid* **18** p 350.

39 *Ibid* **19** p 4.

40 *Ibid* **18** p 354.

41 W Lorey, *Studium* (ref 23) pp 120–3.

42 *Ibid* p 99.

43 W Lorey, *Staatsprüfung* (ref 27) p 77.

44 Gerhard Hessenberg, 'Willkürliche Schöpfungen des Verstandes?' *Jahresberichte der deutschen Mathematiker-Vereinigung* **17** (1908) 158; W Lorey, *Studium* (ref 23) pp 104–5.

45 A Miethe, in Alfred Graf's *Schülerjahre, Erlebnisse und Urteile namhäfter Zeitgenossen* (Berlin 1912) p 166.

46 F Klein, 'Hundert Jahre mathematischen Unterrichts an den höheren Schulen Preussens', *Jahresberichte der deutschen Mathematiker-Vereinigung* **13** (1904) 350.

47 F Paulsen, *An Autobiography* transl T Lorenz (New York 1938) p 148.

48 Iris Runge, *Carl Runge und sein wissenschaftliches Werk* (Göttingen 1949) p 16. [Göttingen, Akademie der Wissenschaften, Mathematisch–physikalische Klasse, *Abhandlungen*, no 23.]

49 W Lorey, *Der Deutsche Verein zur Förderung des mathematischen und naturwissenschaftlichen Unterrichts. E.D., 1891–1938: Ein Rückblick zugleich auch*

auf die mathematische und naturwissenschaftliche Erziehung und Bildung in den letzten fünfzig Jahren (Frankfurt 1938) pp 8–18.

50 Rudolf Schimmack, *Die Entwicklung der mathematischen Unterrichts-Reform in Deutschland* (Leipzig 1911) pp 74–6; Walter Lietzmann, *Die Organisation des mathematischen Unterrichts an den höheren Knabenschulen in Preussen* (Leipzig 1910) pp 199–200.

51 H E Timerding, 'Forschung und Unterricht', in *Geschichte der Physik: Vorlesungstechnik* ed Karl Scheel in *Handbuch der Physik* 1 ed H Geiger and K Scheel (Berlin 1926) 199.

52 R W Livingstone, *A Defence of Classical Education* (London 1916) pp 2–3. Livingstone's defence was attacked by H G Wells in 'The Case against the Classical Languages', in *Natural Science and the Classical System in Education* ed Edwin Ray Lankester (London 1918) pp 183–95.

53 R McCormmach, 'Editor's Foreword', *Hist. Stud. Phys. Sci.* 7 (1976) xi–xxxv; S Goldberg, 'Max Planck's Philosophy of Nature and his Elaboration of the Special Theory of Relativity', *ibid* 125–60.

54 L Boltzmann, 'On the Significance of Theories', in *Theoretical Physics* (ref 20) pp 33–40; 'On the Development of the Methods of Theoretical Physics in Recent Times', in *ibid* pp 77–100.

55 W S Learned, *The Oberlehrer* (ref 25) pp 82–98; James E Russell, *German Higher Schools: The History, Organization and Methods of Secondary Education in Germany* (New York 1899) pp 356–73; Jacob William Albert Young, *The Teaching of Mathematics in the Higher Schools of Prussia* (London 1900) pp 13–18.

56 Quotations given in W S Learned's *The Oberlehrer* (ref 25) pp 75–80.

57 *Ibid* pp 85–7.

58 Klein's manoeuvres are discussed *passim* in Klein's *Vorträge* (ref 1), Schimmack's *Die Entwicklung* (ref 50), Lietzmann's *Die Organisation* (ref 50), and Paul Staeckel's *Die mathematische Ausbildung der Architekten, Chemiker und Ingenieure an den deutschen technischen Hochschulen* (Leipzig 1915). Klein's institutional activity promoting technical education at Göttingen is ably treated in Karl-Heinz Manegold's *Universität, Technische Hochschule und Industrie: Ein Beitrag zur Emanzipation der Technik im 19. Jahrhundert unter besonderer Berücksichtigung Felix Kleins* (Berlin 1970).

59 'Statuten des mathematisch–physikalischen Seminars zu Göttingen, November 1886'. Universitätsarchiv 4 V K/20, Göttingen.

60 F Klein, 'Mathematisch–physikalisches Seminar', typescript dated 1914. Nachlass Felix Klein II-E, NSUB Gött.

61 F Klein, 'Theoretische Mechanik I. Vorlesungen im WS 1897/98'. Nachlass Gustav Herglotz C-7. *Ibid.*

62 F Klein, *Ueber die Aufgaben und die Zukunft der Philosophischen Fakultät, Rede zur Feier des Geburtstages . . . des Kaisers . . . 29 Januar 1904* (Göttingen 1904) p 7.

63 W Lorey, *Deutsche Verein* (ref 49) p 19.

64 R Fricke to F Klein, 4 May 1894. Nachlass Felix Klein, IX, NSUB Gött.

65 R Fricke to F Klein, 9 May 1894. *Ibid.*

66 F Klein to Ludwig, draft, 21 May 1894. Nachlass Felix Klein VI-A. *Ibid.*

67 See Klein's notes on organising the meeting, October 1894, in Nachlass Felix Klein VI-B. *Ibid*.

68 F Klein, 'Ueber den mathematischen Unterricht an der Göttinger Universität', *Unterrichtsblatt für Mathematik und Naturwissenschaften* **1** (1895) 20–4. The *Unterrichtsblatt* was the official journal of the Förderverein. The Berlin and Frankfurt lectures are mentioned in Lorey's *Deutsche Verein* (ref 49) p 19.

69 E Study, 'Einige Bemerkungen zu der neuen preussischen Prüfungsordnung', *Jahresberichte der deutschen Mathematiker-Vereinigung* **7** (1899) 136.

70 L Ambronn to H Wagner, 15 April 1910. Nachlass Hermann Wagner 14, NSUB Gött.

71 H Lorenz, 'Der Unterricht in angewandten Mathematik und Physik an den deutschen Universitäten', *Jahresberichte der deutschen Mathematiker-Vereinigung* **12** (1903) 567–9.

72 A Gutzmer to D Hilbert, 27 December 1903. Nachlass David Hilbert 123, NSUB Gött.

73 'Sommer 1905. Elektrotechnisches Seminar. Mi 3.V.05'. Nachlass Felix Klein XIX-K. *Ibid*.

74 R Fricke to F Klein, 29 April 1902. Nachlass Felix Klein IX. *Ibid*.

75 O Blumenthal to D Hilbert, 3 November 1905. Nachlass David Hilbert 30. *Ibid*.

76 O Blumenthal to D Hilbert, 4 January 1912. *Ibid*.

77 See chapter 4.

78 D Hilbert to H A Krüss of the Berlin Kultusministerium, untitled typescript, 1913. Nachlass David Hilbert 494, NSUB Gött.

79 H Hörnig, reviewing Mie's *Lehrbuch der Elektrizität und des Magnetismus: Eine Experimentalphysik des Weltäthers für Physiker, Chemiker, Elektrotechniker* (Stuttgart 1910) in *Physikalische Zeitschrift* **10** (1909) 855.

80 J Classen, 'Ueber das Relativitätsprinzip in der modernen Physik', *Zeitschrift für den physikalischen und chemischen Unterricht* **23** (1910) 257.

81 G Mie, 'Grundlage einer Theorie der Materie', *Ann. Phys.* **37** (1912) 511–34, **39** (1913) 1–40, **40** (1913) 1–66. Mie's earlier work is mentioned in Max Jammer's *Concepts of Mass* (New York 1964) pp 174–5. Mie's later theory of matter is analysed in the classic work of Wolfgang Pauli, *Theory of Relativity*, transl H Brose (New York 1958) p 192, and more recently in Marie-Antoinette Tonnelat's *Principles of Electromagnetic Theory and Relativity* (Dordrecht 1966) p 269.

82 G Mie to K Schwarzschild, 27 October 1912. Schwarzschild papers, reel 7, sec. 4, Niels Bohr Library, American Institute of Physics, New York.

83 Eugene Guth has argued that Hilbert arrived at the covariant field equations after a thorough study of Einstein's previous work in general relativity. E Guth, 'Contribution to the History of Einstein's Geometry as a Branch of Physics', in *Relativity* ed Moshe Carmeli *et al* (New York 1970), pp 161–207, esp 183–4. Jagdish Mehra has contested Guth's remarks. Mehra believes that Hilbert 'discovered the field equations simultaneously with and independently of Einstein'. J Mehra, *Einstein, Hilbert, and the Theory of Gravitation* (Dordrecht 1974) pp 74, 81.

I suspect that Hilbert wrote his paper with a full knowledge of all of Einstein's work printed by November 1915, the time that he and Einstein published their final results. In the period before 1915 Einstein considered covariant field equations, but he discarded the idea and did not publish his thoughts. Covariance would have been a simple, formal requirement for Hilbert to impose on the field equations, especially so given his deep reverence for Minkowski's formulation of special relativity.

When Einstein visited Göttingen during the summer of 1915, Hilbert was greatly impressed. Hilbert wrote: 'During the summer we had here as guests the following: Sommerfeld, Born, Einstein. Especially the lectures of the last on gravitational theory were an event.' Hilbert to Schwarzschild, 17 July 1915. Schwarzschild papers, reel 5, sec. 3, Niels Bohr Library, American Institute of Physics, New York.

Hilbert would have had four months to familiarise himself with Einstein's work before he published his paper. The *dénouement* of Einstein's and Hilbert's efforts has been studied in some detail by John Earman and Clark Glymour in 'Einstein and Hilbert: Two Months in the History of General Relativity', *Archive for History of Exact Sciences* **19** (1978) 291–308.

84 D Hilbert, 'Die Grundlagen der Physik, I', Göttingen, Akademie der Wissenschaften, Mathematisch–physikalische Klasse, *Nachrichten* (1915) 407.

85 At a special session during the 1913 meeting of the German Association of Scientists and Physicians, Einstein responded to the comments and criticisms of Mie and others concerning his gravitational theory. *Phys. Z.* **14** (1913) 1262–6.

86 G Mie to D Hilbert, 13 February 1916. Nachlass David Hilbert 254, NSUB Gött.

87 G Mie to D Hilbert, 26 December 1917. *Ibid.*

88 A Einstein to E F Freundlich, 1913. Photocopy in the Einstein Archives, Princeton University Library.

89 A Einstein to P Ehrenfest, 24 May 1916. Einstein–Ehrenfest Correspondence, Archive for History of Quantum Physics, American Philosophical Society, Philadelphia.

90 A Einstein to H Weyl, 23 November 1916. Photocopy in the Einstein Archives, Princeton University Library.

91 R McCormmach, 'Einstein, Lorentz, and the Electron Theory', *Hist. Stud. Phys. Sci.* **2** (1970) 41–87.

92 A Einstein, 'Kosmologische Betrachtungen zur allgemeinen Relativitätstheorie', Berlin, Akademie der Wissenschaften, Mathematisch–physikalische Klasse, *Sitzungsberichte* (1917) 142–52, translated in: A Einstein *et al*, *The Principle of Relativity* (New York 1923).

93 F Klein, 'Zur Nicht-Euklidischen Geometrie', *Mathematische Annalen* **37** (1890) 557–8. See John D North's *The Measure of the Universe* (Oxford 1965) p 108.

94 A Einstein to F Klein, 15 December 1917. Photocopy in the Einstein Archives, Princeton University Library.

95 A Einstein to F Klein, 2 June 1918. *Ibid.*

8 Physical sense in relativity: Max Planck edits the Annalen der Physik, 1906–1918

Introduction

The centre of gravity for a scientific discipline lies in its periodical press. Disciplinary journals control the quality and direction of research, define acceptable limits to scientific debates, provide a measure for individual achievement, and confer status on trusted advisers. In the case of the strongest journals in a discipline, the editorial hand is firm and the editor's vision, conservative. For these reasons, over the past six or seven generations scientists have often felt called to create new journals that could respond to the needs of one or another emerging speciality. Journals devoted to physical chemistry, colloidal chemistry, applied mathematics, number theory, astrophysics, and even general relativity have in this way come into being.

Since disciplines keep a close rein on publishing, it comes as no surprise that some revolutionary scientific ideas appear in print beyond the reach of disciplinary approbation or censure. Forums for authors with major restructurings to propose have included general scientific journals, the proceedings of learned corporations, popular magazines, and privately printed monographs. At various points in their careers these were the favoured publishing outlets for Charles Darwin, Oliver Heaviside, Sigmund Freud, Alfred Wegener, and Enrico Fermi. The historian of science is especially interested, then, in situations when an established, disciplinary journal accommodates a theory that fundamentally reorients scientific discourse. In such cases journal editors shape how the innovation is received. A sensitive editor can ensure that an otherwise unsettling theory is quickly absorbed into the fabric of existing knowledge.[1]

In this chapter I consider how during the years 1906–18 the editor of the most prestigious physics journal in the world evaluated incoming manuscripts treating Albert Einstein's theories of relativity. The journal was the *Annalen der Physik*, the principal publishing outlet for Einstein's own early scientific work. The editor was Max Planck, professor at the University of Berlin and Germany's most distinguished theoretical physicist. In writing to his coeditor Wilhelm Wien, Planck expressed opinions about the work of a large number of his contemporaries who sought to contribute to Einstein's formulations. Planck emerges from this correspondence as a cautious, conservative physicist vitally interested in extending the 'revolutionary' theories of relativity.[2]

Planck sought to have the theories of relativity accepted because they resolved long-standing problems in classical physics. The principle of relativity, Planck noted in 1910, 'removes from the previously existing physical world picture the nonessential components brought in only by the circumstance of human perception and habits, and so it purges physics of anthropomorphic impurities originating in the individual nature of the physicist'.[3] By winnowing manuscripts submitted to the *Annalen* and by encouraging work that seemed promising, Planck hoped to soften the 'hard struggles' that he knew the theories would have to face.[4]

Because this story turns on the character of one scientific journal, I begin the present chapter by tracing the development of the *Annalen der Physik* from its foundation in the eighteenth century to the beginning of the twentieth. After considering the circumstances surrounding Planck's and Wien's editorial charge, I elaborate on Planck's vision of theoretical physics, especially the theories of relativity, as this vision is revealed in his editorial judgments. A central feature of Planck's approach to relativity involved mistrust of mathematical formalism. As we have seen in the preceding chapter, he believed that the laws of physics transcended the language, mathematics, in which they were expressed. For Planck in the period around 1910, the formal elegance of a physical proposition mattered less than the extent to which it could be used to treat related problems. 'The measure of the worth of a new physical hypothesis', he wrote, 'lies not in its vivid expression but in its ability to perform well.' In his view performance was related to experimental verification: 'All physical questions are decided not by aesthetic points of view but by experiments.'[5]

The *Annalen*

Beginning with the end of the nineteenth century, the *Annalen der Physik* has traced its ancestry to the efforts of Friedrich Albrecht Carl Gren, a late-eighteenth-century professor of physics and chemistry at the University of Halle. Like many of his physical scientist contemporaries, Gren rose through the early stages of a pharmacy career and received a medical doctorate before turning all his interests to physical sciences. Inspired by the chemical journal of his teacher Lorenz von Crell, in 1790 the thirty-year-old Professor Gren brought into being the *Journal der Physik*, a periodical publication for 'mathematical and chemical branches of natural science'. Within four years the journal began a new series, the *Neues Journal der Physik*, again under Gren's watchful eye. Gren used both journals as vehicles to promote his views in favour of the phlogiston theory of chemical combustion.[6]

Upon Gren's death in 1798 his editorial responsibilities fell to Ludwig Wilhelm Gilbert. Like Gren, young Gilbert had lost his father. Gilbert's mother sent him to study at the progressive Philanthropin, a school in Dessau where the influential pedagogue Johann Bernhard Basedow lectured. Gilbert went on to hear physical sciences at the University of Halle and came under the spell of Gren, nine years his senior. *Dozent* and *ausserordentlicher* professor in 1795, Gilbert took over direction of Gren's *Journal* upon his mentor's death. Scientific editing for polymath Gilbert was by no means a single-minded life's focus. During his early years as editor he wrote a three-volume travel guide for Germany. That he was eager to begin editing three years before he received Gren's chair suggests that he received either direct compensation or scholarly renown for his labours. He called his journal the *Annalen der Physik*.[7] During Gilbert's stewardship, the *Annalen* appeared irregularly and published eclectically.

Gilbert's successor was the distinguished bibliographer Johann Christian Poggendorff. Like Gren apprenticed to an apothecary and like both Gren and Gilbert having as a youth lost his father, young Poggendorff arrived in Berlin to study chemistry. He soon made a mark as a talented electrical experimentalist. Having thought of running a scientific journal, upon Gilbert's death in 1824 the twenty-six-year-old Poggendorff presented himself to the publisher, the firm of Johannes Ambrosius Barth, as the next man in charge. His candidacy accepted and his services presumably rewarded by the press, Poggendorff changed the journal's title to the *Annalen der Physik und Chemie*. Only six years after assuming his charge did Poggendorff receive a professorial title from Prussia. After a decade of editing, Poggendorff was awarded an honorary PhD and came to be employed as an associate professor of physics at the University of Berlin. With Poggendorff's genius for organisation, the journal issued 160 volumes in fifty-two years, most of the articles conforming to the editor's empiricist inclinations.[8]

By the time that Poggendorff died in 1877, the physical sciences in Germany had been transformed, and the role of a scientific editor had come to require a new kind of talent, support, and organisation. Poggendorff's successor, Gustav Heinrich Wiedemann, belonged to the first generation of physicists, in the modern sense of the word. The son of a

Berlin merchant who died when Wiedemann was a boy, the future physicist passed through *Gymnasium* in Berlin. Introduced to physical science
by an uncle, Wiedemann then went on to receive in 1847 a doctorate in
physics at the University of Berlin. His physics education came in the
private laboratory of his experimentalist and empiricist professor, Gustav
Magnus, who discouraged his students from pursuing mathematical
physics. As a result, Wiedemann studied the works of Siméon-Denis
Poisson on his own. *Privatdozent* at Berlin in 1850, he married a daughter
of the chemist Eilhard Mitscherlich's the next year. After twenty years of
professorial appointments in physics at Basle, Brunswick, and Karlsruhe,
in 1871 he obtained at the University of Leipzig the first German chair in
physical chemistry. When Poggendorff died in 1877, the publisher of the
Annalen approached Wiedemann to become editor.[9]

Under Wiedemann's direction the journal emerged as the favoured
forum for original physics publications in a country that was soon to
lead the world in this discipline. The transformation occurred because
Wiedemann encouraged original contributions and increased the number
of theoretical papers. At the same time, the change related to a new
administrative arrangement. With Wiedemann's ascension the Berlin
Physical Society undertook to contribute to the costs of publication, and
it delegated Germany's most distinguished physicist, Hermann von
Helmholtz, as its factotum in the editorial office. Beginning in 1877 the
title page of the *Annalen* specified this organisation, Helmholtz's name
appearing in type smaller than that used for the editor, Wiedemann.
Helmholtz's death in 1893 resulted in the aging Wiedemann's asking his
own physicist son Eilhard to become coeditor. Finding a replacement for
the overseer Helmholtz took several years. The new representative of the
Berlin Physical Society (from 1898 the *German* Physical Society) appeared
on the title page in 1895. He was Max Planck, recently appointed professor
of theoretical physics at the University of Berlin.

Gustav Wiedemann died in 1899. The coeditor son, an otherwise undistinguished physicist at the University of Erlangen, did not feel up to the
task of carrying on in the absence of his father and mentor. By this time
it should have been evident to German physicists that the *Annalen* had
grown beyond the point where one physicist could edit it. Such a realisation did not surface in either Berlin or Leipzig; the press and no doubt
the Physical Society sought out the most promising, established young
physicist to continue Wiedemann's work, still under Planck's watchful eye.
Perhaps to prevent regional jealousies from emerging, the journal fell into
the hands of Paul Drude, recently appointed professor of theoretical
physics at the University of Leipzig. In an attempt to distribute responsibility for the journal over a broader segment of the German physical
community, Drude had behind him a *Kuratorium*, or council, of five
professors of physics: experimentalists Friedrich Kohlrausch, Georg

Quincke, Emil Warburg, and Wilhelm Conrad Röntgen, and theoretician Planck. The title of the journal changed to emphasise its status as an organ of physicists: it became, once more, simply the *Annalen der Physik*.

Drude was a natural choice as editor. Son of a physician, in 1887 he received a doctorate for a dissertation on theoretical crystallography directed by physicist Woldemar Voigt at the University of Göttingen.[10] Drude worked as Voigt's assistant until 1894, when he was called to become associate professor of physics at the University of Leipzig. In 1900 he went as successor to renovate and direct the moribund physics institute at the University of Giessen. His institute there was a small one, attracting fewer doctoral students in physics than nearly any other German university, and his budget was commensurate with the institute's low popularity. The position carried few administrative responsibilities.[11]

By the time that he went to Giessen, Drude had accumulated a remarkably long and varied list of publications. He was at his finest when he interpreted and extended Maxwell's electrodynamics, as elaborated by Heinrich Hertz. Drude belonged to a tradition exemplary in the work of Helmholtz and Hertz, where theoreticians were also expected to be at home with experiment. The marriage of theory and experiment in Drude's published work was more harmonious than that found in the research of any of his distinguished young contemporaries, including Philipp Lenard, Wilhelm Wien, and Emil Wiechert. Having by around 1900 published scores of papers, monographs and textbooks, Drude was viewed as the heritor of Helmholtz's and Hertz's mantle. It was entirely natural that he should have been called to direct the journal that had published most of his work. To edit a voluminous and prestigious review, direct a small institute, and continue to produce first-rate research was a difficult task, even for someone with Drude's talents. All physicists in Germany looked to Drude's rising star.

When in 1905 Emil Warburg resigned from the University of Berlin to become the third president of the Imperial Institute of Physics and Technology, his position, the most prized chair of physics in Germany, went to Drude. Over the preceding ten years Warburg had set a breathtaking record as institute director. He issued about eight doctoral dissertations a year, more than any other German professor of physics. His students published more than students at any other physics institute, some 220 publications between 1895 and 1905. By the middle 1920s around one-third of his students from this period held professorships.[12] Going from physics at Giessen to physics at Berlin would have implied great changes in one's style of research, teaching, and administration, even without the additional burden of editing the *Annalen*. Drude did not make the transition. His personal research and writing slowed. He was overwhelmed.

Drude called out in anguish to his friend Wilhelm Wien at Würzburg, asking that Wien change places with him. A country boy who liked living in an uncongested city, Wien blanched at the thought of directing the Berlin institute, for it, constructed on piles driven into the banks of the Spree and with a high tension electrical cable running underneath, was entirely unsuited for delicate physical measurements. Finding no honourable way out, and not communicating his desperation to colleagues at Berlin, Drude committed suicide. It was only one year after he had arrived in the imperial city. The shock rippled through the world of physics. Weeks after Drude shot himself, Max Levin, a post-doctoral student at Göttingen, wrote about the event to Ernest Rutherford, professor at McGill University in Montreal. He understated that Drude 'was somewhat overworked, but a satisfactory explanation has not been found'.[13]

Planck and Wien take charge

It was in these circumstances, then, that Max Planck stepped forward to become editor of the *Annalen*. To share editorial responsibilities he asked Wilhelm Wien, then professor of physics at the University of Würzburg in the South German state of Bavaria. As was the case with Drude, Wien's appointment provided visible evidence that the Berlin Physical Society sought to represent all German physicists, those in and beyond Prussia. Wien is best known today for work in synthesising experimental research which led to the quantum theory of radiation, but his activity spanned all of physics. He was an early and vocal partisan of the electromagnetic view of nature and an elaborator of the electron theory. Like Planck, Wien became an immediate supporter of Einstein's special theory of relativity. Different from Planck, in the 1920s Wien appeared in the company of the anti-Semitic, anti-relativity physicists Johannes Stark and Philipp Lenard.[14]

In a letter to Wien written in 1906, Planck proposed how the new *Annalen* would be managed. The Berlin theoretical physicist wanted both his and Wien's name to appear side by side on the journal's title page, as was the case for the *Zeitschrift für physikalische Chemie*, edited by Wilhelm Ostwald and Jacobus Henricus van 't Hoff. Wien would handle the day-to-day matters associated with the journal, although when a manuscript was to be rejected or revised, Planck had to be consulted. Beginning his association with the most prestigious physics journal in the world, Wien asked Planck about the proportion of manuscripts that had been rejected by Drude's editorial hand. Planck could not supply precise figures, but he estimated that only 5% to 10% of submissions had been returned to authors.[15] With hindsight this remarkable statistic helps to explain the appearance in the *Annalen* of a consistent quantity of dull, unoriginal, and insignificant articles. Although under Planck's and Wien's direction the rejection rate seems to have risen (an educated guess would place it at around 15% or 20% in 1914), no clearer indication than this can be provided of the extent to which physics publication in Wilhelmian Germany was available to almost any determined and flexible author.

Planck closed his letter with the hope that Wien would soon receive word from Friedrich Althoff, the powerful civil servant who supervised professorial appointments at all institutions of higher learning in Prussia.[16] As he clarified two days later, Planck had in mind that Wien come to Berlin as Drude's successor. Wien, who did receive but declined the call, worried about the enormous responsibilities entailed by such a position, in conjunction with editing the *Annalen*. Planck assured Wien that Drude had had the possibility of diminishing his work load, but that he had made no move to do so.[17] Though we lack the letters that Wien wrote to Planck, it is clear that the younger man at Würzburg consistently deferred to his senior colleague. To the extent that he wanted to be involved with it, Planck controlled the *Annalen*.

The public Planck projects an image of a distant, superior sage. Even in the few instances when he reflected on his life, as in his scientific autobiography, personal remarks were with rare exceptions bypassed. In corresponding with his coeditor Wien, recipient of the 1911 Nobel Prize in physics (Planck would receive it only seven years later), Planck allowed a bit of his private side to show. Planck enjoyed writing letters. As his own research slowed because of advancing age and administrative commitments, his scientific correspondence swelled, and he found the circumstance 'enormously stimulating and invigorating'.[18] Business documents, Planck's letters to his near-peer telegraphed succinct judgments about manuscripts by authors knocking on the door of the *Annalen*. To Wien, Planck expressed himself in a way that he could never allow in a publication. 'Completely without value . . . nothing new . . . contradictions' are evaluations that issue from Planck's pen. One is struck by how these comments on the substance of manuscripts are distinguished in Planck's letters from his evaluation of personality and character. Planck divorced the business of physics in the *Annalen* from personal questions, insofar as he was able. Even to his coeditor of some twenty years, Wilhelm Wien, Planck never entirely warmed up. The two always addressed each other as 'Sie'.

From this brief description of Planck's temperament it follows that he would have gone to great lengths to keep caustic polemics from appearing in his journal. A controversy in the *Annalen* was not a pleasant affair. A regular contributor, Einstein, wrote in 1910 to his young colleague, Paul Hertz, that he wanted to speak with Hertz about the latter's recent publication (probably on the mechanical foundation of thermodynamics) rather than address a reply for publication. 'A quarrel in the *Annalen*', Einstein wrote to Hertz, 'is not a laughing matter.'[19] We can see the extent to which Planck strove to avoid controversy on a personal level from Planck's advice to Wien, in 1906, that the *Annalen* reject a manuscript of Carl

Wilhelm Max Koppe's on the concept of relative motion and the Foucault pendulum. The manuscript represented an attempt by Koppe, a fifty-three-year-old professor at the Andreas Realgymnasium in Berlin and a long-time contributor to the proceedings of the Berlin mathematical society and to the *Zeitschrift für den physikalischen und chemischen Unterricht*, to join a debate in the pages of the *Physikalische Zeitschrift* over an article on the same subject by Polish physicist Alfred Denizot.[20] In Planck's view, Koppe's article would be 'superfluous' for *Annalen*. At the same time, Planck feared that, if published, it could give rise to a fearsome controversy. Denizot had previously had a manuscript rejected by the *Annalen*, and Planck no doubt felt that Denizot would have reason to claim persecution at the hands of the journal.[21] When apprised of Planck's feeling that his manuscript contributed nothing new, Koppe replied that he really wanted to have the paper appear in the *Annalen*. Planck wrote to Wien that a way out would be to accept Koppe's paper on the condition that he rewrite it to exclude mention of Denizot's work.[22] Koppe dropped the matter and sent a version of his article to the *Physikalische Zeitschrift*, where it appeared immediately.[23]

The odyssey of a manuscript submitted in 1906 on the principle of relativity and electromagnetism, written by Alfred Heinrich Bucherer, indicates how Planck and Wien processed articles through their journal. Bucherer was an unusual German physicist who, after having studied at several universities in the United States, returned at an advanced age to take a doctorate at the University of Berlin. In a series of short communications and in an elementary textbook, Bucherer sought around 1905 to contribute to the exciting and mathematically elaborate discussion on the electron theory. He worked apparently oblivious of recent, sophisticated publications by Karl Schwarzschild, Paul Hertz, and Arnold Sommerfeld.[24] Planck carefully scrutinised Bucherer's submission. It was a mess. The coeditor of the *Annalen* found that according to Bucherer's interpretation of the principle of relativity, a moving current of air would impart its velocity to a light wave, a result in contradiction with Fizeau's classic experiment. Even worse, Bucherer did not seem aware that Maxwell's equations held for any uniformly moving system. Because Bucherer was a *Privatdozent* and had worked on Kaufmann's experiments, Planck was in favour of leniency. He urged a revision rather than outright rejection. Generosity was especially indicated, Planck noted to Wien, because Drude had previously rejected a paper of Bucherer's on thermoelectric fluids.[25]

Bucherer, however, refused to make changes in his paper, and he asked for a collective opinion by the curators of the *Annalen*.[26] The matter passed to Planck and Wien's 'overseers'. They opted to support the editors, and wrote to Bucherer about their decision. Bucherer replied that he would not entertain a compromise, as Planck had advocated. Planck hoped, with this response, that the matter would die, and that Bucherer would not in the future come to the *Annalen*.[27] Bucherer's thoughts went no farther than a preliminary paper published previously in the *Physikalische Zeitschrift*.[28] A number of years later Bucherer claimed to have verified the Lorentz theory of electrons by measurements of Becquerel rays, to the uninformed delight of mathematician Hermann Minkowski and the unbridled scepticism of experimentalist Alfred Bestelmeyer.[29]

Historian Stanley Goldberg has shown how elaboration and verification of special relativity remained foremost in Planck's mind during the years before 1910.[30] Planck emerged as one of the very first physicists to extend Einstein's work, and between 1905 and 1914 he was the principal or supplementary adviser for more than a dozen doctoral dissertations that were based at least in part on Einstein's special theory of relativity.[31] When Einstein's paper appeared in print, Planck had already expressed interest in the limits of the mechanical explanation of electrical phenomena, for in 1905 he was principal adviser of a dissertation by Hans Witte on precisely this subject.[32] In the wake of Einstein's work, Planck encouraged his student Kurd von Mosengeil to pursue a theoretical investigation of relativistic thermodynamics. In 1906 Planck saw Mosengeil's dissertation through the press and revised the text for the *Annalen* after the premature death of his student.[33]

Planck by no means limited himself to theoretical studies. One of his charges was Erich Hupka, officially working under the direction of experimentalist Heinrich Rubens. From the acknowledgment in his dissertation it is clear that theoretician Max Planck provided much guidance for Hupka's attempts in 1908 and 1909 to measure the change in electron mass with electron velocity. Other experimentalists had attempted to obtain such precise measurements, but none of the results were unambiguous. Hupka wanted to provide a definitive decision between the predictions of Max Abraham's theory of the rigid electron and the predictions of the Lorentz–Einstein theory (which Hupka called, along with many others of the day, not 'Relativitätstheorie' but 'Relativtheorie'—'relative theory' instead of 'relativity theory'). Hupka worked with cathode rays, then established to consist of electrons moving at velocities approaching that of light. Negatively charged cathode rays were deflected by a magnetic field, the amount of deflection depending only on the apparent electron mass. The young physicist could establish the kinetic energy of electrons emitted from a cathode in a vacuum tube, and he could calculate, for a given magnetic field strength, deflections of the cathode rays according to Max Abraham's theory and the relativity theory. His observed deflections fitted the latter.[34]

When he published his dissertation in monograph form and as an article in the prestigious *Annalen der Physik*, Hupka found himself at the centre of a sharp controversy with Wilhelm Heil, who had just finished a dissertation under Planck's direction which critically examined Walter Kaufmann's measurements of the change in electron mass with electron velocity for beta rays.[35] Taking into account the reliability of the data, Heil concluded that experimental evidence did not provide a conclusive decision among the three competing electron theories: those of Bucherer, Abraham, and the 'Relativtheorie'. Planck had the two doctoral candidates working in ignorance of each other. According to a letter that Planck wrote to Wilhelm Wien, at the time that Heil finished, the young researcher did not know about Hupka's work.[36] Heil wrote a sharp critique of Hupka's dissertation and sent it to Planck for publication in the *Annalen*. Planck naturally felt that Heil's subject was 'very important', but he urged Heil to moderate his language. Planck informed Hupka about the impending publication. He worked with both researchers to eliminate personal remarks from their position papers.[37] Their public discussion resolved little.

The gatekeepers

Planck's attitude towards mathematics, especially how he distinguished mathematical formalism from physical reasoning, is clearly revealed in his editorial correspondence with Wien. The Berlin theoretician, of course, was the very model of a physicist *brahmin*. A university professor like his father, Planck grew up in an atmosphere redolent with the responsibilities and prerogatives of professorial station. His interests turned almost exclusively towards abstract learning, many steps removed from direct contact with the world of practical activity. Planck's research reflects in physics the widespread desideratum of nineteenth-century German, neoclassically-inspired learning, where one was expected to elaborate on the world in 'general' terms. As we have seen previously, in Planck's time, culture was supposed to be *allgemein*, general, rather than *fachlich* or *realistisch*, specialised or practical. Generality, furthermore, implied a primary emphasis on linguistic skills, in philology and in natural sciences.[38]

Though a master of mathematical methods, Planck passionately sought to express the fundamental laws of the universe in words. From the fundamental laws, he believed, could be constructed what he and others called a world picture of physical reality. It would be as a vast landscape, not unlike those projected by nineteenth-century, German, neoclassical artists, wherein all parts of physics stood in harmony with each other. When words failed him and he held only mathematical formulae—as seems to have been the case in 1900 upon his first formulation of the quantum theory of radiation—he was unable to draw unambiguous conclusions.[39] Planck had little patience with mathematically pretentious glosses on the principle of relativity. Into such a category fell about half of the relativity manuscripts that passed across his desk. His thoughts on several submissions are especially illuminating in this regard.

In 1908 Emil Kohl, associate professor of physics at the University of Vienna, submitted a two-part manuscript that developed a new theory of electrodynamics and provided a critique of the Michelson experiment. Kohl assumed that electricity was a continuous fluid distributed throughout space. He came to the same results obtained by Lorentz, Planck noted, but only after having made special hypotheses about the ether. Planck urged Wien to ask Kohl to limit his observations to the Michelson experiment. The outcome was as requested.[40]

In rejecting a later manuscript of Kohl's that set out a theory of electrons, Planck emphasised that among all Kohl's many equations he had not found 'a single one in which a new relationship between measurable quantities is provided'.[41] (Kohl is the physicist who in 1911 was edged out by Einstein for a chair at the German university in Prague.[42]) In a similar class was a manuscript of Anton Weber's on special relativity. In Planck's view it did not have 'enough physical results to be accepted by the *Annalen*'. It would make only 'ballast' for the journal.[43] Weber, a professor of physics and mathematics at the Royal Bavarian Lyzeum in Dillingen, was only able to make his thoughts public in a note published in the *Physikalische Zeitschrift*.[44]

Planck considered as 'entirely worthless' two long manuscripts submitted in 1911 by Emil Arnold Budde on the Klinkerfues and Michelson experiments to detect motion relative to the ether. Sixty-nine-year-old Budde directed the Charlottenburg factory of the firm Siemens & Halske; he had published extensively in the *Annalen* and had in 1888 directed the abstracting journal *Fortschritte der Physik*. Budde wrote in the style of an engineer. Planck found that Budde was completely ignorant of the literature and that his attempted critiques of the two experiments were embarrassingly bad. His work contained 'no original thought that is not already found in the scientific literature, and done better there'.[45] Both of Budde's papers, rejected by Planck, appeared in the *Physikalische Zeitschrift*. In his paper on the Michelson experiment, Budde criticised Max von Laue's textbook of 1911 on the special theory of relativity. Laue replied to Budde's accusations with devastating effect.[46]

On a manuscript of F Grünbaum's which was ultimately rejected, Planck commented in 1911 that it was 'correct, but it includes nothing really new and its physical interest is only very indirect'. The paper duplicated a lecture that applied mathematician Hans von Mangoldt had published in the *Zeitschrift* of the German Engineers' Association and reprinted in the *Physikalische Zeitschrift*.[47] It was not clear to Planck if or how Grünbaum used Mangoldt's work, and whether he supplied anything more than mathematical formulae to Mangoldt's physical content. Grünbaum's article appeared shortly thereafter in the *Physikalische Zeitschrift*.[48]

To judge from its contents the bi-weekly *Physikalische Zeitschrift*, controlled by Göttingen physicists and in this period edited variously by Emil Bose, Friedrich Krüger, Hans Busch, Max Born, and Hermann Theodor Simon, was often desperately short for copy. Publishing both notes and long-winded analyses, the journal became a dumping ground for work rejected by Planck and Wien. Even so, some manuscripts declined by the *Annalen* did not find their way into the more catholic journal, presumably because the treatments were obviously derivative or out of fashion. One such case was a long manuscript elaborating Vilhelm Bjerknes's hydrodynamical analogue for electromagnetism, submitted in 1912 by a certain H Rudolph. In 1910 Rudolph had published a small book purporting to unite the principle of relativity, Planck's quantum of radiation, and gravitation in a mechanical picture of the world.[49] Planck would not have Rudolph's elaboration of this theory. Bjerknes's mechanical theory had appeared in the *Annalen*, along with a rejoinder by Hans Witte, but 'direct and definitive rejection' was Planck's advice for Rudolph's manuscript, a text that failed to distinguish between force and pressure and one that remained confused about the physical meaning of differential quotients.[50]

The preceding papers were written by unimportant authors whose work was far from original. Not all submissions were so easily weighed. In 1910 Planck reluctantly assented to a manuscript by Waldemar Sergius von Ignatowsky on the notion of a relativistic rigid body. Ignatowsky in fact met with Planck and told Planck that Wien was not happy with his manuscript. Planck commented on Ignatowsky's confusion over Einstein's notion of signal velocity, but in the end decided to accept Ignatowsky's paper.[51] He had to handle Ignatowsky with care, because Ignatowsky and Eugen Jahnke—both aging *Dozenten* at Berlin-area institutes of technology—had proposed to create a journal specialising in theoretical physics, a competitor for many articles that would otherwise be sent to the *Annalen*. Planck approached the project, which did not bear fruit, with circumspection. To Wien he confided that it might be 'quite a good idea' to take some theoretical work out of the *Annalen*, but he dreaded the consequent emergence of 'a sharp division between theoretical and experimental research'. He believed that theory had always to be grounded in experimental reality.[52]

It appears from Planck's correspondence with Wien that the most perplexing submissions on relativity were those invoking complicated mathematical machinery to elaborate formal, working hypotheses. Planck especially believed that the *Annalen* had to adopt a clear policy with respect to submissions dealing with the principle of relativity. Manuscripts that focused on the formulation of definitions—as was the case in the recent spate of literature on the relativistic rigid body—had to be referred to mathematical journals or to the more accommodating *Physikalische Zeitschrift*.[53]

Planck urged that a 1913 manuscript by the twenty-three-year-old Polish physicist Felix Joachim Wiśniewski be declined. 'The author defines every last thing in a formal way and assumes that, behind it all, these definitions have a physical meaning. But nothing new comes from it.' Wiśniewski's gravitational theory might have had some strong points, but in Planck's view there were 'too few solid, deciding factors for a completely informed gravitational theory'. At this time Planck believed that even Einstein's theory was not necessarily in the right direction, and it would have to be tested during the upcoming solar eclipse of 1914.[54] In two previous papers published in the *Annalen*, Wiśniewski had begun to elaborate a new gravitational theory, but Planck decided that the journal did not have to continue to support Wiśniewski's tedious and pedestrian mathematical speculations.[55] A second communication on the quantum theory, submitted by Wiśniewski in 1914, also received definitive rejection by Planck.[56]

For Planck, mathematical exposition had to be clear as well as relevant to physical concerns. In 1913 he accepted one short paper from Jun Ishiwara,[57] a Japanese theoretical physicist who had studied extensively in Europe, but later that year Planck convinced Wien to reject another of Ishiwara's papers on electrodynamics. The second treatment contained serious mathematical infelicities, such as defining one quantity without further comment as a 'Quasisinnevektor'. In the expositions, as in other publications of Ishiwara's, the author was not always clear and the text would have to be rewritten completely. Planck did not want to hurt Ishiwara's feelings. He suggested to Wien that in rejecting the manuscript one could say that it was not publishable in the present form. In any event, Ishiwara had already published the result in a Japanese journal. In all probability Ishiwara sent the rejected manuscript to the *Physikalische Zeitschrift*, where it appeared in 1914.[58]

The above extracts tend to present Planck as a stern gatekeeper. In reality he encouraged work that he thought promising, even if it did not issue from the pens of his students. He followed Walther Ritz's emission theory of radiation with great interest, even though he did not believe in it.[59] In 1908 Planck advised Wien to accept a paper that the young Viennese physicist Philipp Frank had submitted, where Frank showed how the Lorentz transformation could reduce to a Galilean transformation and applied the principle of relativity to Hertz's equations for moving bodies. Planck was in favour of the paper even though the distinction between Einsteinian and Hertzian relativity as elaborated by Frank remained unclear to him.[60] He felt that his journal was fortunate to have Breslau *Oberlehrer* Ferencz Jüttner's 'quite interesting' research on kinetic molecular theory and relativity. Planck urged Wien not to cut the manuscript of one of Jüttner's papers.[61] He proposed that a text on gravity by Finnish physicist Gunnar Nordström be accepted even though it did not offer 'fundamental' insights. Nordström was a talented man who had previously not appeared in the *Annalen*, and Planck wanted to encourage Nordström's work. He was especially glad that in Nordström's paper the foreigner retained the constancy of the velocity of light, a principle that Einstein and Abraham had recently dropped. The *Annalen* had to be hospitable, in Planck's view, to promising first communications.[62]

After the covariant field equations of general relativity emerged late in 1915, Planck found the *Annalen* besieged by authors wanting to contribute to the topic. In March 1916 Einstein sent the *Annalen* a long article setting out the definitive form of general relativity,[63] but many others who knocked at Planck's door with texts elaborating the theory were far removed from centres of power and prestige in the discipline. Einstein gave the wide-ranging engineering professor at Berlin Hans Reissner 'many explanations and criticisms', and so helped him to complete a paper on the self-gravitation of an electrical field.[64] The young Viennese theoretician Friedrich Kottler elaborated in 1916 the principle of equivalence in a short paper printed without much editorial deliberation.[65] Both Reissner and Kottler had previously published on relativity and gravitation.

Planck also argued in 1916 that two manuscripts by the Norwegian physicist Thorstein Gunnar Wereide be accepted, even though as a foreigner and, according to Planck, an 'autodidact', Wereide proceeded in an unorthodox manner and wrote with many spelling mistakes. Wereide had published, the previous year, a monograph in English which summarised many of his ideas.[66] One of the papers that Wereide sent Planck, on energy exchange between ether and matter, borrowed from Niels Bohr's atomic theory. Planck urged that it be published because in such a new field standards were different from those in older fields. The manuscript had been rejected by the *Physikalische Zeitschrift*, Planck noted, and that journal's poor judgment was a boon for the *Annalen*.[67]

Among the many manuscripts sent to the journal which elaborated general relativity came one from the Königsberg *Oberlehrer* Ernst Reichenbächer, according to Planck a 'basically cultured theoretician', who attacked the general problem of the connection between electricity and gravitation. Reichenbächer limited his study to a two-dimensional field, which he then expanded to the four-dimensional world of Hermann Minkowski. Planck was sympathetic to Reichenbächer's approach, but he was not overly sanguine about its future. 'The value of such a theory', Planck felt, lay in 'what it finally delivers'. The payoff, in Planck's view, lay in 'simplicity and intuitiveness [*Einfachheit u. Anschaulichkeit*] and above all [in] whether it has such characteristic consequences that can be tested by experiment'. Reichenbächer's theory failed on both counts. Planck found especially perplexing a law of Reichenbächer's where the radius of curvature of a negative electron was enormously larger than the electron radius. In general Planck felt that the theory was not terribly new if one was familiar with the theory of conformal mappings in two planes. In Planck's view the manuscript was not yet ready for publication. The first, mathematical part had to be clarified; the second, physical part had to deal with the theories of Gustav Mie, David Hilbert, and Einstein.[68] Reichenbächer's manuscript went back to him. Three months later a revision arrived on Planck's desk. Planck was uncertain to which of Einstein's papers Reichenbächer appealed. He urged that Reichenbächer speak with Einstein and so resolve their differences. The meeting was amicable.[69] Reichenbächer's paper appeared in 1917 as the first attempt at a unified field theory in the wake of Einstein's covariant field equations.

Near the end of the war, the problem of mathematical expositions came to weigh heavily on Planck's shoulders. When in 1917 Hermann Weyl sent his first attempt at a unified field theory to the *Annalen*, Planck wrote to Wien that Weyl stood at the very 'height of research of his time'. Although he observed that Weyl did not cite all the literature and mentioned nothing about experimental verification of the theory, Planck noted with approval that Weyl based his work firmly on Einstein's 'general gravitational theory'. Studies like Weyl's were, in Planck's view, of clear value, but a larger problem remained. Weyl's paper depended heavily on mathematical machinery from non-Euclidean geometry, and Planck would have preferred to see more weight attached to physical reasoning and discussion. He did not want to decide in general the extent to which studies like Weyl's belonged in the *Annalen*, although he offered that possibly 'non-Euclidean geometry as such, separated from physical tasks, will be treated better in mathematical journals, as has been the case until now'.[70]

Planck the editor

Scientific editing calls many kinds of people. In pursuing riches some pander to public tastes. Others seek a special outlet for a particular kind of wisdom or a learned corporation. All scientific editors purport to instruct; their enterprise is an educational one. So it is with Max Planck, an exemplary teacher. In addition to producing a number of doctoral dissertations on the theories of relativity, he corresponded with Wien about the submissions of as many as a score of additional authors writing on relativity. The *Annalen der Physik* was controlled by robust and young researchers at the height of their abilities. No different from other people, physicists mature in their positions, but this circumstance is no reason to burden editors with the image of exhausted thinkers. The editors of the *Annalen der Physik* continued educational and scientific activity at the same time that they processed the work of their colleagues. The most valuable commodity at their disposal, time, went to imposing their prejudices on the visible and permanent residue of their discipline—learned publications.

Although Planck was wary in approaching mathematical formalism, he remained in awe of talented mathematician colleagues. He wrote to Wien in 1912 that Hilbert's radiation theory was quite interesting from the point of view of formalism and general applicability, but that it brought no new physical understanding. 'For all that,' Planck offered, 'it is to be welcomed when the mathematicians begin to be interested in physical problems.'[71] Planck was not alone in his opinion about the role of mathematics in physics. His coeditor colleague Wilhelm Wien approached mathematics in a similar way. Wien wrote to David Hilbert in 1910 about his sadness at the death of mathematician Hermann Minkowski, whose last papers on relativity theory, 'in which he went entirely into physical points', were of great interest.[72]

Like Wien, Albert Einstein would have been sensitive to Planck's strictures. Tensor analysis came to him as a method of last resort. 'You have absolutely no idea', Einstein wrote to physicist Paul Hertz in 1916, 'what I went through as a mathematical ignoramus until I arrived in this harbour.'[73] The widely travelled Paul Ehrenfest, later Einstein's close friend, shared this view of mathematics. Ehrenfest wrote to Paul Hertz around 1906 about how he had taught himself higher mathematics, and so his education had many holes: 'Often quite elementary mathematical methods are essentially unknown to me.' In another letter to Hertz from this period, Ehrenfest emphasised that a surprising majority of the talented physicists and mathematicians whom he had met considered 'mathematics a "veritable devil"—naturally a man-eating one'. Ehrenfest added: 'I calculate with this fleeting intimation instinctively, and I have the conviction that you must have quite often [experienced] the same sentiment.'[74]

The attitude of these physicists toward the role of mathematics in formulating physical laws stands in sharp contrast to that of younger theoretical physicists in the period after the First World War. 'Physical sense' was for the younger men increasingly seen to be of less importance than the requirement that a theory be clothed in elegant mathematics. Writing to Wolfgang Pauli about Pauli's long essay on the theories of relativity, the septuagenarian mathematician Felix Klein reported the belief of his mathematician colleague David Hilbert, 'that one could explain the essence of nature by mere mathematical reflection'.[75] Hilbert's attitude came to permeate physics in the 1920s. Unfamiliar mathematical expressions replaced classical physical notions, and theorists like Werner Heisenberg, Wolfgang Pauli, and Paul Adrian Maurice Dirac imputed new physical meaning to sophisticated mathematical expressions. Niels Bohr convinced physicists to accept a new, indeterminist epistemology that could accommodate the success of formal methods in quantum mechanics. Those sharing an older vision, however, hesitated to accept the new point of view and, with a few exceptions, refrained from contributing to the structure of the new world picture.

In view of his persistent belief in many features of the late nineteenth-century 'physical world picture', Planck appears as a sympathetic figure striding across two epochs. He consistently pointed the way to the new physics of relativity and quanta; in this regard his pedagogical and epistolary activities were as valuable as his original scientific communications. At the same time he resisted abandoning beliefs about physical reasoning and the use of mathematical tools which he had acquired when in the nineteenth century he wrestled with the foundations of thermodynamics. Especially in his role as editor of the *Annalen der Physik*, Planck acted as Moses for twentieth-century physicists. He guided and disciplined his colleagues through nearly twenty years of bewildering revelations, but he never touched the soil of the promised land.

Notes and references

1 On the role of editors in scientific publishing see Susan Sheets-Pyenson, *Low Scientific Culture in London and Paris, 1820–1875* (dissertation, University of Pennsylvania 1976), University Microfilms International no 77-10, 216, and her subsequent studies: 'War and Peace in Natural History Publishing: The *Naturalist's Library*, 1833–1843', *Isis* **72** (1981) 50–72; 'From the North to Red Lion Court: The Creation and Early Years of the *Annals of Natural History*', *Archives of Natural History* **10** (1981) 221–49; 'Darwin's Data: His Reading of Natural History Journals, 1837–1842', *Journal of the History of Biology* **14** (1981) 231–48; 'A Measure of Success: The Publication of Natural History Journals in Early Victorian Britain', *Publishing History* **9** (1981) 21–36.

2 Max Planck, 'Die Stellung der neueren Physik zur mechanischen Natur-anschauung', *Physikalische Zeitschrift* **11** (1910) 922–32, on p 928. Stanley Goldberg's lucid treatment of Planck's views is never far from discussion here. Goldberg, 'Max Planck's Philosophy of Nature and His Elaboration of the Special Theory of Relativity', *Historical Studies in the Physical Sciences* **7** (1976) 125–60.

3 M Planck, 'Stellung' (ref 2) p 931.

4 *Ibid* p 930.

5 *Ibid* pp 929, 931.

6 Karl Hufbauer, 'Gren, Friedrich Albrecht Carl', *Dictionary of Scientific Biography* **5** (New York 1972) 531–3; Hufbauer, *The Formation of the German Chemical Community, 1720–1795* (Berkeley 1982) pp 120–37.

7 Ludwig Choulant, 'Versuch über Ludwig Wilhelm Gilbert's Leben und Wirken', *Ann. Phys. Chem.* **76** (1826) 453–71.

8 W Baretin, 'Johann Christian Poggendorff', *Ann. Phys. Chem.* **160** (1877) v–xxiv; Friedrich Klemm, 'Poggendorff, Johann Christian', *Dict. Sci. Biog.* **11** (1975) 49–51.

9 Hans-Günther Körber, 'Wiedemann, Gustav Heinrich', *Dict. Sci. Biog.* **14** (1976) 529–31.

10 S Goldberg, 'Drude, Paul Karl Ludwig', *Dict. Sci. Biog.* **4** (1971) 189–93.

11 Information on doctoral students from Lewis Pyenson and Douglas Skopp, 'Educating Physicists in Germany *circa* 1900', *Social Studies of Science* **7** (1977) 329–66, on p 350; information on budgets from Paul Forman, John L Heilbron, and Spencer Weart, *Physics circa 1900: Personnel, Funding, and Productivity of the Academic Establishments* (Princeton 1975) [*Hist. Stud. Phys. Sci.* **5**] p 61.

12 Hans Ramser, 'Warburg, Emil Gabriel', *Dict. Sci. Biog.* **14** (1976) 170–2; Pyenson and Skopp, 'Educating' (ref 11), p 355.

13 Wilhelm Wien, *Aus dem Leben und Wirken eines Physikers* (Leipzig 1930) pp 24–6. In the notes to his remarkable novel, *Night Thoughts of a Classical Physicist* (Cambridge, Mass 1982) p 200, Russell McCormmach emphasises that 'Drude never asked for help, and so Planck and others concluded he didn't need or wish it.' Max Levin to Ernest Rutherford, 25 July 1906. Rutherford Correspondence. Rare Book Department, McGill University, Montreal.

14 Hans Kangro, 'Wien, Wilhelm Carl Werner Otto Fritz Franz', *Dict. Sci. Biog.* **14** (1976) 337–42.

15 M Planck to W Wien, 28 July 1906. Handschriftenabteilung, Staatsbibliothek Preussischer Kulturbesitz, Berlin, Federal Republic of Germany [henceforth SPK Berlin].

16 *Ibid.*

17 M Planck to W Wien, 30 July 1906. SPK Berlin. See Wien's *Leben* (ref 13) pp 24–6. This letter of Planck's is noted in McCormmach's *Night Thoughts* (ref 13) p 200.

18 M Planck, *Scientific Autobiography and Other Papers*, transl Frank Gaynor (New York 1949) pp 49–50.

19 A Einstein to Paul Hertz, postcard dated 15 August 1910. Collection of Rudolf H Hertz, Roslyn Heights, New York, and available on microfilm in the Einstein Archives, Princeton.

20 Alfred Denizot, 'Zur Theorie der relativen Bewegung und des Foucaultschen Pendelversuches', *Phys. Z.* **6** (1905) 342–5; L Tesar, 'Die Theorie der relativen Bewegung und ihrer Anwendung auf Bewegungen auf der Erdoberfläche', *ibid* 556–9; Denizot's reply, *ibid* 559 and 677–9; P Rudzki, 'Theorie der relativen Bewegung', *ibid* 679–80.

21 M Planck to W Wien, 28 July 1906. SPK Berlin.

22 M Planck to W Wien, 12 October 1906. SPK Berlin.

23 Max Koppe, 'Zum Foucaultschen Pendel', *Phys. Z.* **7** (1906) 604–8, 665–6.

24 Alfred H Bucherer, 'Das Feld eines rotierenden Elektrons', *Phys. Z.* **6** (1905) 225–7; 'Die Rotation eines Elektrons mit Volumladung', *ibid*, 269–70; 'Das deformierte Elektron und die Theorie des Elektromagnetismus', *ibid*, 833–4; *Mathematische Einführung in die Elektronentheorie* (Leipzig 1904). Bucherer's work is considered in Goldberg's 'Planck's' (ref 2) 129–32.

25 M Planck to W Wien, 29 November 1906. SPK Berlin.

26 M Planck to W Wien, 21 December 1906. SPK Berlin.

27 M Planck to W Wien, 26 January 1907. SPK Berlin.

28 A H Bucherer, 'Ein Versuch, den Elektromagnetismus auf Grund der Relativbewegung darzustellen', *Phys. Z.* **7** (1906) 533–57.

29 A H Bucherer, 'Messungen an Becquerelstrahlen. Die experimentelle Bestätigung der Lorentz–Einsteinschen Theorie', *Phys. Z.* **9** (1908) 755–62, including the debate following Bucherer's presentation at the 1908 meeting of the Naturforscher in Cologne.

30 S Goldberg, 'Planck's' (ref 2).

31 Between 1906 and 1914 Planck was principal director for the following dissertations which in whole or part related to relativity and the electron theory: Hans Witte, *Ueber den gegenwärtigen Stand der Frage nach einer mechanischen Erklärung der elektrischen Erscheinungen: Abschn. 1: Begriff, Grundlagen, Einleitung* (1905); Kurd von Mosengeil, *Theorie der stationären Strahlung in einem gleichförmig bewegten Hohlraum* (1906); Walther Meissner, *Zur Theorie des Strahlungsdruckes* (1907); Wilhelm Heil, *Zur Theorie der Kaufmannschen Versuche über die elektromagnetische Ablenkung der β-Strahlen* (1909); August Gehrts, *Reflexion und Sekundärstrahlung lichtelektrisch ausgelöster Kathodenstrahlen* (1911); Hans Schneider, *Die Energie der glühenden CaO entweichenden Elektronen* (1911); Hermann Bönke, *Zur mathematischen Theorie der Polarlicht-Erscheinungen* (1912); Erich Henschke, *Ueber eine Form des Prinzips der kleinsten Wirkung in der Elektrodynamik des Relativitätsprinzips* (1912); Ernst Lamla, *Ueber die Hydrodynamik des Relativitätsprinzips* (1912); Walter Schottky, *Zur Relativtheoretischen Energetik und Dynamik. Abschnitt I und II* (1912); Karl Körner, *Ueber die Ritzsche Theorie des Zeemaneffektes* (1913); Erich Kretschmann, *Eine Theorie der Schwerkraft im Rahmen der ursprünglichen Einsteinschen Relativitätstheorie* (1914).

   Information assembled from the *Jahres-Verzeichnis der an den deutschen Universitäten erschienenen Schriften*, 1906–14. Beginning in 1904/05 this annual publication provided the names of dissertation advisers.

32 H Witte, *Erklärung* (ref 31).

33 S Goldberg, 'Planck's' (ref 2) 133–7.

34 E Hupka, *Die träge Masse bewegter Elektronen* (dissertation, University of Berlin 1909).

35 W Heil, *Kaufmannschen Versuche* (ref 31).

36 M Planck to W Wien, 30 November 1909. SPK Berlin.

37 M Planck to W Wien, 6 July 1910. SPK Berlin. E Hupka, 'Beitrag zur Kenntnis der trägen Masse bewegter Elektronen', *Ann. Phys.* **31** (1910) 169–204; Wilhelm Heil, 'Diskussion der Versuche über die träge Masse bewegter Elektronen', *ibid* 519–46.

38 L Pyenson, *Neohumanism and the Persistence of Pure Mathematics in Wilhelmian Germany* (Philadelphia 1983) [*Am. Phil. Soc. Mem.* **150**] pp 9, 29–30.

39 Thomas S Kuhn, *Black-Body Theory and the Quantum Discontinuity, 1894–1914* (Oxford 1978). In general, Kuhn's book does not address the issues raised here.

40 M Planck to W Wien, 26 November 1908. SPK Berlin. Emil Kohl, 'Ueber den Michelsonschen Versuch', *Ann. Phys.* **28** (1909) 259–307.

41 M Planck to W Wien, 30 November 1909. SPK Berlin.

42 József Illy, 'Albert Einstein in Prague', *Isis* **70** (1979) 76–84.

43 M Planck to W Wien, 7 November 1910. SPK Berlin.

44 Anton Weber, 'Konvektions- und Röntgenstrom in der Relativitätstheorie', *Phys. Z.* **11** (1910) 134.

45 M Planck to W Wien, 30 May 1911. SPK Berlin.

46 Emil Budde, 'Das Dopplersche Prinzip für bewegte Spiegel und ein Versuch von Klinkerfues', *Phys. Z.* **12** (1911) 725–9; 'Zur Theorie des Michelsonschen Versuches', *ibid* 979–91, including discussion of Budde's paper at the 1911 Naturforscherversammlung in Karlsruhe.

47 Hans von Mangoldt, 'Längen- und Zeitmessung in der Relativitätstheorie', *Phys. Z.* **11** (1910) 937–44.

48 M Planck to W Wien, 9 February 1911. SPK Berlin. F Grünbaum, 'Ueber einige ideelle Versuche zum Relativitätsprinzip', *Phys. Z.* **12** (1911) 500–509.

49 H Rudolph, *Die mechanische Erklärung der Naturerscheinungen, insbesondere der Relativbewegung, des Planck'schen Wirkungselements und der Gravitation* (Coblenz 1910).

50 M Planck to W Wien, 29 June 1912. SPK Berlin. Hans Witte, 'Besonderes und Allgemeines zur Weltätherfrage: Eine Erwiderung auf einen Artikel von Herrn V Bjerknes', *Ann. Phys.* **32** (1910) 382–410.

51 Woldemar von Ignatowsky, 'Der starre Körper und das Relativitätsprinzip', *Ann. Phys.* **33** (1910) 607–30. M Planck to W Wien, 13 July 1910. SPK Berlin.

52 M Planck to W Wien, 13 June 1910. SPK Berlin.

53 M Planck to W Wien, 9 February 1911. SPK Berlin.

54 M Planck to W Wien, 29 June 1913. SPK Berlin.

55 Felix de Wiśniewski, 'Zur Minkowskischen Mechanik', *Ann. Phys.* **40** (1913) 387–90, 668–76.

56 M Planck to W Wien, 14 June 1914. SPK Berlin.

57 M Planck to W Wien, 31 July 1913. SPK Berlin. Jun Ishiwara, 'Ueber das Prinzip der kleinsten Wirkung in der Elektrodynamik bewegter ponderabler Körper', *Ann. Phys.* **42** (1913) 986–1000.

58 M Planck to W Wien, 14 December 1913. SPK Berlin. Jun Ishiwara, 'Grundlagen einer relativistischen elektromagnetischen Gravitationstheorie', *Phys. Z.* **14** (1914) 294–8, 506–10.

59 M Planck to W Wien, 19 January 1909. SPK Berlin.

60 M Planck to W Wien, 9 October 1908. SPK Berlin. Philipp Frank, 'Das Relativitätsprinzip der Mechanik und die Gleichungen für die elektromagnetischen Vorgänge in bewegten Körper', *Ann. Phys.* **27** (1908) 897–902.

61 M Planck to W Wien, 9 February 1911. SPK Berlin. Ferencz Jüttner, 'Das Maxwell'sche Gesetz der Geschwindigkeitsverteilung in der Relativtheorie', *Ann. Phys.* **34** (1911) 856–82; 'Die Dynamik eines bewegten Gases in der Relativtheorie', *ibid* **35** (1911) 145–61.

62 M Planck to W Wien, 28 January 1913. SPK Berlin. Gunnar Nordström, 'Träge und schwere Masse in der Relativitätstheorie', *Ann. Phys.* **40** (1913) 856–78.

63 M Planck to W Wien, 6 March 1916. SPK Berlin. A Einstein, 'Die Grundlage der allgemeinen Relativitätstheorie', *Ann. Phys.* **49** (1916) 769–822.

64 Hans Reissner, 'Ueber die Eigengravitation des elektrischen Feldes nach der Einsteinschen Theorie', *Ann. Phys.* **50** (1916) 106–20. Reissner credited Einstein for assisting him.

65 Friedrich Kottler, 'Ueber Einsteins Aequivalenzhypothese und die Gravitation', *Ann. Phys.* **45** (1916) 955–72.

66 Thorstein Wereide, *Statistical Theory of Energy and Matter* (Kristiania [Oslo] 1915).

67 M Planck to W Wien, 1 March 1916. SPK Berlin. Thorstein Wereide, 'Die statistisch–mechanische Grundlage der allgemeinen Quantentheorie', *Ann. Phys.* **49** (1916) 966–75; 'Die Energieaustausch zwischen Materie und Aether', *ibid* 976–1000.

68 M Planck to W Wien, 25 August 1916. SPK Berlin.

69 M Planck to W Wien, 12 November 1916. SPK Berlin. Ernst Reichenbächer, 'Grundzüge zu einer Theorie der Elektrizität und der Gravitation', *Ann. Phys.* **52** (1917) 134–73.

70 M Planck to W Wien, 10 August 1917. SPK Berlin. Hermann Weyl, 'Zur Gravitationstheorie', *Ann. Phys.* **54** (1918) 117–45.

71 M Planck to W Wien, 4 October 1912. SPK Berlin.

72 W Wien to David Hilbert, 15 April 1910. Nachlass Hilbert, Niedersächsische Staats- und Universitätsbibliothek, Göttingen.

73 A Einstein to Paul Hertz, 22 August 1916. Collection of Rudolf H Hertz, Roslyn Heights, New York, and available on microfilm in the Einstein Archives, Princeton.

74 Paul Ehrenfest to Paul Hertz, two undated letters. Collection of Rudolf H Hertz, Roslyn Heights, New York.

75 Felix Klein to Wolfgang Pauli, 8 May 1921. Armin Hermann, Karl von Meyenn, Viktor F Weisskopf, eds, *Wolfgang Pauli. Wissenschaftlicher Briefwechsel mit Bohr, Einstein, Heisenberg u.a. Band I: 1919–1929* (New York 1979) p 31.

9 Einstein's early scientific collaboration

Introduction

With his earliest work towards the general theory of relativity Einstein joined a direction in physics that, as he saw it, was marked by a prevalent interest in field theory. He recalled in 1933 that, 'like most physicists, at this period I endeavoured to find a "field law", since, of course, the introduction of action at a distance was no longer feasible in any plausible form once the idea of simultaneity had been abolished.'[1] The many field-theoretical studies carried out during the years around 1905 were of two kinds. Some physicists were using field theory in the form of Maxwellian electrodynamics to develop descriptions of the electron as well as a complete system of physics founded on the electromagnetic world view. Others sought to formulate a field theory of gravitation which could be integrated with electromagnetic theory. Physicists who had serious objections to the programme of the electromagnetic world view tried to answer them by examining gravitation with field-theoretical formalisms.

One way to study Einstein's position in the field-oriented physics of this period is by examining his early scientific collaboration. By 1913 Einstein had written scientific articles with five other scientists and had corresponded extensively with perhaps a score more. Some of his early contacts are well known. While at Berne, Einstein discussed his ideas with the brothers Paul and Conrad Habicht, with Maurice Solovine, and with Michele Angelo Besso, all of whom were trained in physics but not associated professionally with a university. Then, between 1908 and 1910, several young, established physicists, including Max von Laue, Rudolf Ladenburg, and Arnold Sommerfeld, visited Einstein to discuss, for the most part, problems in quantum theory.[2]

215

After 1909 Einstein collaborated with Sommerfeld's student Ludwig Hopf on the quantum theory, and with Jakob Johann Laub, Walther Ritz, Erwin Finlay Freundlich, and his old friend Marcel Grossmann on the theories of relativity. Unlike Grossmann who helped Einstein with mathematical problems, Laub, Ritz and Freundlich provided him with the opportunity to discuss his physical ideas on the special theory of relativity and gravitation theory. Laub and Ritz were the first coauthors of papers with him, and, beginning in 1911, Freundlich corresponded extensively with Einstein about astronomical problems in general relativity. Einstein's relationship with these three physical scientists differed greatly from his associations with other scientists in the period before 1914. Through them he was able to keep informed of developments in the physical science community.

In the following pages I use Einstein's collaboration with Laub, Ritz, and Freundlich to illuminate his relationship to the physical science community in late Wilhelmian Germany. I examine to what extent the attitudes toward mathematics of Einstein's collaborators stemmed from the intellectual climate at the University of Göttingen, where, between 1902 and 1910, each of the three had studied for at least two years. Then I discuss their collaboration with Einstein and remark on their importance in the development of Einstein's general relativity. Finally, I discuss the reception of the special and general theories of relativity in light of the effects that the collaboration with Einstein had on Laub's and Freundlich's careers.

Physical science at Göttingen, 1895–1914

Preceding chapters have explored special features of mathematical physics at the University of Göttingen. It is well to emphasise, nevertheless, that by the first decade of the twentieth century, the university had become a leader in all fields of the exact sciences.[3] Since the institutional configuration behind this leadership bears on the stories of Laub, Ritz, and Freundlich, its dimensions will be considered at the outset.

In 1894, several Göttingen institutes accommodated physics research and instruction. The most important of these was the physical institute with one division for experimental physics under Eduard Riecke and a second division for what was variously called mathematical physics or theoretical physics under Woldemar Voigt. The less important Göttingen observatory under Ernst Schering also treated mathematical physics as well as theoretical astronomy and geodesy. The Göttingen mathematical physics seminar under Felix Klein sought to unify physical science; Klein was joined by Riecke, Voigt, Schering, the mathematician Heinrich

Weber, and Wilhelm Schur, director of the division of applied astronomy of the observatory.

Between 1895 and 1898 exact sciences underwent a transformation. An institute of physical chemistry was created for Walther Nernst, then an associate (*ausserordentlichen*) professor of mathematical physics, and a division for technical physics, that is, for applied mechanics and applied electrical studies, was added to the physical institute. The observatory was reorganised upon Schering's death in 1898. Both Schering's chair and the directorship of the observatory's theoretical division remained vacant. Instead, Martin Brendel became associate professor of applied astronomy, and Emil Wiechert was appointed to the new position of associate professor of geophysics. Although Wiechert's duties included the management of the observatory's terrestrial magnetism laboratory, for all practical purposes he directed a fourth geophysical division of the physical institute.

In 1905, Göttingen physical science underwent a last reorganisation in the Wilhelmian period. The technical physics division of the physical institute became an independent institute for applied mathematics and mechanics under the joint direction of Carl Runge, professor of applied mathematics, and Ludwig Prandtl, associate professor of applied mechanics. Hermann Theodor Simon then became director of a new division of the physical institute devoted exclusively to applied electricity. At the same time, Wiechert was elevated to the directorship of an independent institute of geophysics. Finally, the theoretical divisions of the observatory were officially united under the direction of Karl Schwarzschild.

The driving force behind these institutional changes was Felix Klein. As the titles of some of the new institutes indicate, Klein sought to promote interdisciplinary studies at Göttingen. He believed that such studies furthered industrial applications of science and that they played a critical role in the development of new scientific ideas.[4] From about 1902 he organised numerous interdisciplinary seminars in the physical sciences, and between 1895 and 1910 he succeeded in establishing nine new senior faculty positions in interdisciplinary physical sciences. Several of the seminars and faculty appointments emphasised technical physics.

Largely as a result of Klein's leadership, mathematics occupied the central position in Göttingen physical science. Klein himself preferred intuitive reasoning with models and geometrical pictures to axiomatic, logical exposition. His view of mathematics was a reaction against the trend current at the end of the nineteenth century to separate pure mathematics from applied mathematics and often to include theoretical physics in the latter. Mathematicians generally considered pure mathematics the product of pure reason obtained without any reference to experiment, a 'set of *formal implications* independent of all content'.[5] Applied mathematics was thought by most researchers to consist of applications of the relationships revealed by pure mathematics to material facts or physical processes and to depend on an intuitive grasp of physical postulates and models. Analysis, algebra, and logic were part of pure mathematics, whereas geometry and mechanics belonged to applied mathematics.[6]

The division between pure and applied mathematics did not alter the curriculum that pure mathematicians generally claimed. During the period before the First World War, pure mathematicians regularly taught mechanics and geometry to physicists. Some physicists felt that they were not receiving an adequate mathematical education. Carl Runge reported to the Fifth International Congress of Mathematicians in 1913: 'Some of my correspondents bitterly complain of the mathematical training of students of physics in consequence of the professors of pure mathematics ignoring some mathematical theorems and methods, that are of greatest importance to the physicist.' Runge felt that a closer cooperation between pure and applied mathematicians would do much to alleviate the problem:

> On the whole there seems to be no need for special mathematical courses for students of physics, nor does it seem necessary to compel them to attend more mathematical lectures. But a need seems to be strongly felt for mathematicians and physicists to draw closer together. The spirit of the mathematical teaching should be altered, so as to make it more practical and easier to apply to physical problems. At present the gap is very wide and is not tending to close up.[7]

Klein's efforts to bridge the gap between pure and applied mathematics were reflected in the work of other Göttingen mathematicians: they frequently employed rigid-body mechanics and electrodynamics when investigating other problems. David Hilbert, Wiechert, Max Abraham, and Gunnar Nordström often used the Maxwell–Lorentz electromagnetic theory in interpreting both special and general relativity, and Max Born and Gustav Herglotz for some time tried to reconcile special relativity with classical notions of rigid-body motion. Their emphasis on mechanics seems to have been related to the strong Göttingen programme in technical physics and to Runge's and Prandtl's research on engineering problems associated with hydrodynamics.

Interest in electrodynamics at Göttingen focused on the elaboration of the electromagnetic view of nature. After 1900, the electromagnetic view of nature received widest circulation through the various theories treating the dynamics of the electron.[8] Of the scientists concerned with electron theories between 1900 and 1910 more worked at Göttingen than anywhere else. Alexander Wilkins, Walter Kaufmann, Emil Bose, Schwarzschild, Abraham, and Wiechert published on the electron theory while at Göttingen; Paul Drude and Arnold Sommerfeld, who had been *Privatdozenten* at Göttingen in the 1890s, submitted papers on the subject to the Göttingen Scientific Society. Göttingen mathematicians were attracted to the electron theory by its promise for unifying all of physical theory, but, as we have seen in preceding chapters, they were sometimes not overly careful about giving what physicists would consider realistic formulations of the physical processes that they were investigating.

It should be emphasised that the Göttingen *physics* faculty was not sympathetic to Einstein's theory of relativity. None of the six physicists who responded at length to Einstein's theories were senior members of the discipline when at Göttingen. The two most sensitive physicists of the six, Abraham and Born, found the theories difficult to understand. Wiechert, the professor of geophysics, was the only other physics instructor to write on both theories; unfortunately, he never understood either. Three more members of the physics faculty, Kaufmann, Johannes Stark, and Ritz, wrote on special relativity without commenting on general relativity. Kaufmann and Stark, both *Privatdozenten* in physics, were excellent experimentalists; Kaufmann initially rejected and Stark never accepted special relativity. Ritz, also a *Privatdozent*, rejected special relativity in favour of an emission theory of light.

In view of the nearly unanimous rejection of relativity among physicists at Göttingen it is not surprising that only three Göttingen physics *graduates* wrote on special or general relativity before 1919. Of the three students of Voigt's (who himself referred to Einstein's relativity only in passing),[9] two had previously been educated in Britain: Robert Alexander Houstoun had received a master's degree from the University of Glasgow in 1902, and Alfred Arthur Robb had obtained a bachelor's degree from Cambridge in 1897. Both Houstoun and Robb studied theoretical optics under Voigt from 1902 to 1905, but their Göttingen studies apparently did not influence their work on special relativity.[10] The third student of Voigt's to write on special relativity was Walther Ritz.

Other Göttingen physics students who later wrote extensively on special and general relativity were Moritz Schlick and Max von Laue,[11] Voigt's protégés, and Paul Ehrenfest[12] and Johannes Droste. Their work, too, does not appear to have been influenced by Göttingen physicists. However, young Gunnar Nordström, who had come to study physical chemistry in 1906, was quickly converted to the mathematical physics of Minkowski.[13] Nordström's switch to mathematical physics was not unusual[14]; Laub, Ritz, and Freundlich were all drawn equally strongly to Göttingen mathematics.

Ritz arrived in Göttingen in the spring of 1901 after having studied at the Federal Institute of Technology in Zurich.[15] He was several years behind Einstein in his studies there, and there is no evidence that the two met while they were students. Unlike Einstein, Ritz followed attentively the lectures given by Minkowski and Adolf Hurwitz on mechanics and pure mathematics. In 1901, Ritz went to Hilbert in Göttingen with an enthusiastic recommendation from Minkowski.[16] Ritz was strongly attracted to physics and chose to work on a dissertation in optics under

Voigt.[17] By the time that Ritz left Göttingen in 1903, he had acquired an impressive command of many mathematical tools. He also carried away some knowledge of Wiechert's, Abraham's, and Kaufmann's work on the electron theory.

After having studied briefly at the universities of Krakow and Vienna, Laub matriculated at Göttingen in October 1902 as a mathematics student.[18] He remained until 1905. In October 1903, Hilbert noted that Laub was 'diligently' attending his lectures on differential equations.[19] At the same time, Minkowski, who had been called to Göttingen from Zurich the year before, assigned Laub the task of writing up his introductory lectures on mechanics.[20]

Freundlich studied at Göttingen from 1905 to 1910.[21] Unlike Ritz and Laub, Freundlich came to Göttingen with the familiarity of both technical science and pure mathematics which Klein sought to cultivate. After completing *Gymnasium* in Wiesbaden, Freundlich studied shipbuilding for two semesters at the Institute of Technology in Charlottenburg. He worked for a year and a half as a volunteer in a shipyard in Stettin until ill health forced him to retire. In the spring of 1905 he finally enrolled as a mathematics student at Göttingen. He was unusually talented in mathematics and shared Klein's philosophy of mathematics education.[22]

Although Ritz, Laub, and Freundlich all had come to Göttingen to prepare for careers in the physical sciences, they also received a thorough exposure to mathematics. They were not the only physicists so influenced. In 1895 Sommerfeld submitted his *Habilitationsschrift* at Göttingen under Klein and became a *Privatdozent* there. We have seen previously how the experience profoundly marked his approach to physics.[23] Through their Göttingen education, Ritz, Laub, and Freundlich also acquired an appreciation of electrodynamics: Ritz treated it in his dissertation, Laub wrote his dissertation on one facet of electron physics, and Freundlich followed Minkowski's and Born's work in electrodynamics. Their Göttingen education, however, did not provide them with experimental experience or allow them to acquire sensitivity to experimental results. These they received elsewhere: Ritz carried out experimental work as a postdoctoral assistant to Aimé Cotton in Paris and, later, as an assistant to Friedrich Paschen at Tübingen, Laub earned his doctorate working with Wilhelm Wien at Würzburg on an experimental dissertation, and Freundlich had practical experience in engineering earlier and eventually became an observational astronomer.

Laub and Einstein

Sometime late in 1905 Laub moved from Göttingen to Würzburg to study under Wilhelm Wien, director of that university's physical institute. Unlike

Göttingen scientists, Wien did not assign to mathematics a central, unifying role in physics, but reserved that for theoretical physics. Mathematical physics—as opposed to theoretical physics—was in his view only concerned with developing mathematical tools.

Wien felt that theoretical physics was ideally constituted for the task of unifying physics. Far from being the exclusively deductive science of the Kantian point of view, it incorporated inductive as well as deductive method—the two being nearly indistinguishable—and it claimed as its 'real and exclusive task' the 'establishment of functional connections',[24] that is, the establishment of laws that govern as many physical processes as possible. Specifically, Wien hoped that theoretical physics would bring unity to physics by establishing an electromagnetic foundation of mechanics. 'It is doubtless one of the most important tasks of theoretical physics', he wrote, 'to link the now completely isolated areas of mechanical and electromagnetic phenomena and to derive the differential equations of each from a common foundation.'[25]

Laub began to work on his dissertation under Wien in 1905. An extension of Wien's recent work on secondary radiation,[26] his subject was an experimental investigation of secondary cathode ray emission, a phenomenon in which a cathode ray beam of electrons was used to generate a secondary stream of cathode rays when it struck and ionised a target. Since his dissertation was connected with the problem of a theory of atomic structure,[27] Laub's work was an ideal doctoral thesis: it involved research of great current interest that could be summarised and clarified through new and more precise experiments. At his dissertation defence in November 1906, Laub defended the special theory of relativity, to the consternation of his examining committee.[28] Wien, however, was satisfied with his work, and Laub passed. Laub continued to labour on secondary cathode ray emission under Wien during the period 1907–8,[29] but he directed the major part of his work towards Einstein's special theory of relativity.

In June 1907 Laub published his first paper on special relativity, concentrating on a discussion of Fresnel's drag coefficients.[30] (Drag coefficients described how a ponderomotive body apparently imparted a small portion of its velocity to light, as observed, for example, in the 1851 experiment of H L Fizeau, which measured the velocity of light in moving columns of water. By 1895, Lorentz had explained the first-order drag coefficient from his equations of electromagnetism by using disturbances in a stationary ether.[31]) Laub derived the first-order drag coefficients without making use of the ether, although according to Laue he confused group and phase velocities.[32]

Wien encouraged Laub. In a letter to Sommerfeld of June 1908, Wien wrote: 'I have recommended that Laub apply the Lorentz transformation to dispersion theory. I did this because the theory of drag coefficients is not rigorous since it only uses the concept of dielectric constants and not that of dispersion.'[33] A year earlier, at the 1907 Dresden meeting of the Association of Scientists and Physicians, Wien had argued that the assumption of media that displayed anomalous dispersion contradicted the second postulate of the relativity theory.[34] The contradiction still puzzled him, and he asked Laub to investigate the problem from a point of view in sympathy with Einstein's ideas. In 1908 Wien believed that the special theory of relativity was part of the electron theory. By encouraging Laub, Wien acted on his view that theoretical physicists, not mathematicians, could best formulate a new foundation for the electron theory.

In early February 1908, Laub wrote to Einstein, who was then at the patent office in Berne, to inquire if it would be possible for him to spend three months with him to work on the theory of relativity. Laub assured Einstein of his great interest in the theory: he considered Einstein's work fundamental not only for electrodynamics but for all of physics.[35] Einstein's reply to Laub is lost, but it must have been favourable. Over the next three months, he and Laub collaborated on two articles dealing with the special theory of relativity.[36] These were the first papers that Einstein wrote with another person.

In his letter to Sommerfeld of June 1908, Wien indicated that the notion of force in Einstein's special theory of relativity would have to be modified by future work in dispersion theory. Without doubt, he had in mind the subject of Laub's recent collaboration with Einstein. Einstein and Laub had taken up the problem of defining force in the special theory of relativity, a critical issue around which would turn many debates over the next three years.[37] Specifically, they criticised Minkowski's 1908 paper on the basic equations for electromagnetic processes, where he first discussed in print his ideas on space–time.[38]

In his electromagnetic equations Minkowski required that the electromagnetic force of a particle in motion always be normal to the particle's path in four-dimensional space–time. Einstein and Laub pointed out that this formulation of the electromagnetic force did not allow for current flow in a wire, or, in other words, that Minkowski's force denied that a direct current flowing through a wire in a magnetic field gave rise to a polarisation current in addition to the ponderomotive force, an experimentally observable phenomenon. They argued that Minkowski took as the entire ponderomotive force only that component of the force that was normal to the particle's velocity. This conception of force was equivalent to the assumption that the rest mass of the particle remained unchanged. Einstein and Laub formulated an expression for the ponderomotive (or electromagnetic) force and then sought to demonstrate that their formulation was consistent with the laws of dynamics, in particular with Newton's third law. To show consistency with the latter was important, because

Minkowski had attempted to place all of mechanics on an axiomatic foundation without making use of this law.

The difference between Einstein and Laub's work and Minkowski's is that between a physical and a mathematical theory: Einstein and Laub examined the physical consequences of several possible formulations of electromagnetic force, not including Minkowski's four-dimensional mathematical formulation, to find a theory that integrated several physical laws and phenomena; Minkowski, on the other hand, was concerned primarily with the mathematical consequences of one particular formulation of electromagnetic force and did not investigate whether or not the formulation was consistent with other electromagnetic laws. Laub and Einstein stressed physical arguments, but their understanding of the development of physical theory was not the same as the view that physical theory grows out of or is based on experimental physics.

Their first paper on the electromagnetic force was followed by a series of treatments by Abraham, Born, Nordström, Ehrenfest, Jun Ishiwara, and Ludwik Silberstein.[39] These physicists shared their objective of clarifying the nature of force in the special theory of relativity. Einstein subsequently turned to other problems, in particular to formulating a theory of charged particles, and did not consider the problem of force within the special theory of relativity again after 1908.[40]

In the second paper,[41] written in April 1908, Einstein and Laub were concerned with explaining a puzzling effect discovered by Harold Albert Wilson: when a dielectric was rotated in the gap between the plates of a connected capacitor in the presence of a magnetic field, an equal and opposite charge collected on the plates. For convenience Einstein and Laub assumed that each particle of the dielectric, although actually in rotation, was only in linear motion. They used Minkowski's equations of motion with appropriate boundary conditions to arrive at the observed charge separation on the two capacitor plates. Einstein and Laub claimed that their calculation differed from one based on Lorentz's electron theory and that the Wilson experiment gave identical results for the two theories because the magnetic permeability was unity in each case.[42]

Einstein and Laub carried out a theoretical study that appealed to experimental physics. When Max von Laue objected to the way in which Einstein and Laub used boundary conditions in the article, for example, they responded by affirming the physical nature of their calculations.[43] In this paper, as in the previous one, Einstein and Laub sought to distinguish the special theory of relativity from the Lorentz electron theory which seemed to many physicists to be identical with it but which in fact was based on a different understanding of physics. Einstein and Laub maintained that the special theory of relativity provided different explanations for certain electromagnetic processes. They did not use experimental propositions to modify the special theory of relativity and they did not attempt to use their results to decide between the contending theories.

After collaborating with Einstein, Laub continued to work on both theoretical and experimental problems in the special theory of relativity. The initial focus of his work was dispersion theory. Late in 1908 Laub formulated an elementary theory of dispersion based on the special theory of relativity. He concentrated on the influence of molecular motion on dispersion in gases.[44] Laub's study was doubtless proposed by Wien, although Einstein was also sympathetic to the attempt to relate the special theory of relativity to molecular theory. In January 1909 Laub used his knowledge of experimental ray physics in his work on dispersion theory.[45] He noted that Wien's as yet unpublished experiments on Doppler-shifted canal-ray spectra contradicted Stark's so-called photochemical law, which stated that energy was transferred only in those collisions between canal ray particles and gas atoms which were greater than a specific threshold.[46] Arguing against Einstein, Lorentz, Sommerfeld, and Peter Debye, Laub insisted that 'all particles contained in radiation bundles share equally in the light processes.'[47] From his equations Laub was able to indicate second-order relativistic effects in dispersion theory. In November 1909 Laub summarised his work in a paper presented to the Heidelberg Academy of Sciences by Philipp Lenard.[48] He described several primary and secondary relativistic effects that, he felt, could be distinguished in canal ray phenomena, and he demonstrated that second-order relativistic effects could be distinguished in Zeeman splitting.

Laub's work in dispersion theory was not extended by other physicists. The dispersion problem touched on too many critical unresolved issues in quantum theory, statistical mechanics, the electron theory, and the special theory of relativity. Most physicists continued to use Paul Drude's classical dispersion theory until 1921 when, after working on the problem for many years, Rudolf Ladenburg approached the interaction of matter and radiation in dispersion phenomena from the point of view of quantum mechanics.[49]

In chapter 6 we saw how, by 1910, Jakob Laub had come to appeal to a neoleibnizian notion of pre-established harmony in explaining the agreement between the mathematical formulation of special relativity and its experimental verification.[50] Laub's friend Einstein was of a different mind in this regard, for he viewed mathematics as a tool to be employed only after the physical situation had been conceptualised.[51] The senior man in Switzerland, however, was by no means estranged from his collaborator because of this difference of opinion. Through Laub, Einstein had access to developments in mathematics and mathematical physics during the period around 1908. Lacking a university appointment, Laub was free to travel throughout German-speaking Europe. He cultivated connections with mathematicians and relayed information to Einstein in Berne. His services as informant were important to Einstein, for the latter's position in the patent office allowed him little opportunity to consult scientific journals or speak with people in the forefront of science.[52]

A letter from Laub to Einstein written in May 1908, soon after they had completed their joint papers, illustrates his concern to keep Einstein informed. He reported that the theoretical physicist Matthias Cantor was not convinced of either the special theory of relativity or Minkowski's space–time because he felt that they were both based on old foundations. 'Why the foundations are not correct', Laub commented, 'God knows; I don't ask him any longer, and I don't worry about it.' Laub was amazed by what Cantor liked about Minkowski's work: Cantor applauded the way space and time coordinates were treated as homogeneous quantities and was impressed 'that one can treat that as a rotation'. Laub asked Cantor about the real meaning of time as a fourth spatial coordinate, but he received no answer. Laub concluded from this: 'I believe he has let himself be impressed by non-Euclidean geometry.' Cantor and the professor of mathematics, Eduard von Weber, were planning to introduce Minkowski's work in the physics colloquium at Würzburg. Laub noted that he would add some remarks to their presentation, for he was sceptical about Minkowski's work. 'Were not your work available', he wrote to Einstein, 'we would at best have reached the same position with the Minkowski transformation equation for time (as far as the physical interpretation is concerned) as with Lorentz's "local time".'[53]

Ritz and Einstein

In May 1909 Einstein was appointed associate professor of physics at the University of Zurich. Just before he took up the new position Einstein sent off a short note to the *Physikalische Zeitschrift* which he had written with Walther Ritz. The note presented a brief clarification of the differences between Einstein's and Ritz's work on the theory of radiation.[54] At the time, Ritz was *Privatdozent* in Göttingen. Since the paper is dated from Zurich, it may have been worked out while Ritz visited Einstein in Switzerland. Einstein's collaboration with Ritz produced no further result; Ritz died four months after the paper was written.[55]

After receiving his doctorate from Voigt at Göttingen, Ritz continued his studies under Lorentz at Leiden and under Aimé Cotton at Paris. After 1903, however, his precarious health interfered with the course of his scientific work and travels. In 1908 Ritz finally became *Privatdozent* at Göttingen. There he worked intensely to create a new theory of optical spectra and a new electrodynamics, building both upon his previous work in optics under Voigt.[56] Ritz believed in relativity, but he did not want to include in his theory the result that the mass of a particle depended upon its velocity. Furthermore, Ritz thought that Einstein was preserving a form of the ether when he postulated that the velocity of light was independent of its source. In the electrodynamics of Maxwell and Lorentz, the ether had provided a mechanical explanation for the constant velocity of light. Ritz sought an 'emission' theory of light instead of a Maxwellian field theory; he assumed that the velocity of light particles depended upon the velocity of the source from which they were emitted.

Even before his move to Göttingen, Ritz had become increasingly interested in gravitational theory. This interest emerged while he worked at Tübingen during the winter of 1907–8 in close contact with several physicists who were attempting to frame a new gravitational theory within electrodynamics. The leading figure of the Tübingen group was Richard Gans, who had been a supporter of the electromagnetic view of nature in the years after 1900.[57] Gans had first discussed the problem of gravitation in 1905, when he addressed the Association of Scientists and Physicians at Meran on 'Electricity and Gravitation'.[58] His talk was largely a favourable review of Lorentz's and Wien's gravitational theories and contained few of his own ideas. Gans supported the Lorentz–Wien theory until 1912, when he realised that it implied the instability of neutral particles with respect to the energy flux of the gravitational field.[59]

Another physicist at Tübingen who was sympathetic to electrodynamical theories of gravitation was Friedrich Paschen. In 1909 he approved a doctoral dissertation by Fritz Wacker that extended the Lorentz–Wien theory.[60] Since Paschen did not write on gravitation theory himself, we must judge by Wacker's work what kind of argument Paschen found acceptable. Wacker's dissertation was an elaboration of an article that he wrote in 1906 on the relationship between electromagnetism and gravitation.[61] Wacker assumed that Abraham's expressions for the longitudinal and transverse mass of the electron also held for the longitudinal and transverse mass of the planets with respect to their motion in the ether. Wacker then used Lorentz's explanation of the gravitational law to arrive at an expression for the gravitational force on a planet due to the Sun. Assuming with Lorentz that the Sun was stationary in the ether, Wacker carried out two calculations for the anomalous precession of the perihelion of Mercury. Taking Abraham's model of the rigid electron, Wacker found 5.8 seconds of arc per century; assuming Lorentz's model of the deformable electron, Wacker calculated 7.2 seconds per century. Neither calculation came close to the observed value of around 40 seconds per century.

Immediately after leaving Tübingen, Ritz treated gravitation theory in his long 1908 paper on an electrodynamics based on a particle emission theory.[62] First, Ritz reiterated Maxwell's conclusion that the intrinsic energy of a gravitational field that was constructed in analogy with an electromagnetic field would appear to be a negative quantity. Rejecting Lorentz's 1900 gravitational theory which had been based on hypotheses concerning the relative strengths of electrostatic and repulsive forces, Ritz applied his own electromagnetic theory to gravitation. Assuming that gravitation propagated with the velocity of light and that gravitational force was of the same general form as electromagnetic force, Ritz examined the problem of planetary orbital residues. He was only able to account for a forward precession of 41 seconds of arc per century for Mercury by using a theory that also yielded values of 8 seconds per century for Venus and 3.4 seconds per century for the Earth.

Ritz admitted that the last two values were unacceptably large, although he did not interpret this discrepancy as a serious threat to the emission theory. Ritz also mentioned his ideas on gravitation in a popular 1908 review on the role of the ether in physics.[63] Finally, in April 1909, Ritz finished a long article devoted exclusively to gravitation.[64] He summarised the limitations of all existing gravitational theories and concluded that the perihelion shift of Mercury and the value of the gravitational constant 'will possibly be deduced from the laws of electrodynamics when they are known with more certainty'.[65]

In April 1909, that is, at about the same time that he published on gravitation, Ritz also wrote his short note on electrodynamics with Einstein. It may be assumed that Ritz told Einstein of his ideas on gravitation and of those of the Tübingen group. The information may have contributed to Einstein's renewed interest in the electron theory and to a temporary halt in his work on general relativity. A brief review of Einstein's early ideas on gravitation will put the implications of his contact with Ritz at this time into perspective.

Einstein based his work on gravitation on a hypothesis and on propositions that were all experimentally verifiable. In 1907 he first postulated as a basic principle the equality for all bodies of vertical acceleration during free fall in a gravitational field.[66] As a result of this principle Einstein arrived at the proposition that time in special relativity theory was influenced by gravitation according to the relation $\sigma = \tau \left[1 + (\phi/c^2)\right]$. Here τ was the value of time in the absence of a gravitational field, ϕ the potential of a uniform gravitational field and c the speed of light. The quantity σ, 'local time', was time measured in an accelerated frame of reference. Einstein concluded his paper by giving two results of the principle that he had formulated: first, the path of light in a uniform gravitational field was curved; second, spectral lines originating from a stationary body were affected by the body's gravitational field. He added that the effects were too small to be observed. When Einstein sent a copy of the article to his friend Conrad Habicht, he mentioned a third physical effect that he was trying to work into his gravitational ideas. Einstein said that he was 'busy on a relativistic theory of the gravitational law with which I hope to account for the still unexplained secular changes of the perihelion movement of Mercury', but so far he had not succeeded.[67]

The details of Ritz's influence on Einstein cannot be established, but I want to suggest that through the exchange of ideas with Ritz, Einstein realised that the electron theory, gravitation, and the principle of relativity were all integrally connected and that gravitation was best approached by first reformulating the electron theory according to the principle of relativity. Ritz and Einstein both believed in the existence of a connection between gravitation and electrodynamics. Einstein saw the key to the connection in Ritz's demonstration that no classical theory of radiation was possible.[68] In late 1909 Einstein decided that the limitations of classical radiation theory had to be investigated before a connection between electrodynamics and gravitation could be established, and to this end he plunged into the electron theory.[69]

Freundlich and Einstein

Late in December 1919 Einstein wrote to the Prussian Minister for Science, Art, and Education to thank his office for a grant of 150 000 marks to help research in general relativity. He felt that the offer was too generous during a period of economic hardship and might 'rightfully cause bitter feelings in the public'. In any event, Einstein considered the offer unnecessary, if only the German astronomical establishment would devote some of its effort to general relativity. He underlined the uncooperativeness of German astronomers by asking the government to provide a special position for the only living German astronomer who had contributed to the general theory of relativity, Erwin Finlay Freundlich.[70]

Upon receiving a doctorate in 1910, Freundlich found a position at the Berlin observatory located in the suburb of Babelsberg. (At this time the Berlin area had three major observatories: the university one under Wilhelm Förster, the non-university one at Babelsberg, and the Prussian astrophysical observatory on the so-called Telegraphenberg in Potsdam under the direction of Karl Schwarzschild.) Freundlich first came into contact with Einstein's work on gravitation at the observatory when Leo Wenzel Pollak, who was then demonstrator in the institute for cosmic physics at the German university of Prague and who was friendly with Einstein, visited the observatory in August 1911. It was Freundlich's task as the junior observer to welcome visitors. Conversation turned to Einstein's work, and Pollak told Freundlich that Einstein wanted astronomers to examine his theory. Freundlich's wife recalls that that very evening her husband wrote to Einstein and offered to collaborate with him.[71] There is no record of Einstein's reply. Rather, for some time Pollak acted as an intermediary between the two.

Soon after his visit to Berlin, Pollak wrote to Freundlich from Prague, sending him the proof sheets of Einstein's latest paper, 'On the Influence of Gravity on the Deflection of Light'. The paper contained Einstein's first published statement that the deflection of light rays near the Sun might be observed during a solar eclipse and that there should be gravitational red shift in the spectrum of the Sun.[72] At the end of the paper Einstein expressed the hope that astronomers would become interested in the questions that he had posed. Pollak commented: 'Prof. Einstein has given me strict orders to inform you that he himself very much doubts that the experiments could be done successfully with anything except the Sun . . . [I beg you] to send further reports to me, or perhaps to Prof. Einstein, about your views on an astronomical verification.' Pollak had asked Freundlich whether or not the deflection of light could be measured around other heavenly bodies such as planets or satellites.[73]

During the autumn of 1911 Einstein and Freundlich began collaboration in earnest. A regular pattern emerged in their correspondence: Einstein would ask Freundlich whether or not a particular astronomical observation were possible, and Freundlich would give an answer which included unexpected facts or judgments. After Pollak's visit, Freundlich enquired of Einstein if processes in the solar atmosphere might mask the gravitational deflection. In his first letter to Freundlich on 1 September 1911 Einstein acknowledged the problems of using the Sun to observe the effect:

> I know very well that to obtain an answer through experience is no easy matter, since refraction in the solar atmosphere might interfere. Nevertheless, one can say with certainty: if no such deflection exists, then the assumptions of the theory are not correct. One must keep in view that these assumptions, even if they seem obvious, are nonetheless rather daring. If only we had a much bigger planet than Jupiter. But nature has not made it her business to make the discovery of her laws convenient for me.[74]

The 'assumptions' to which Einstein referred concerned the principle of equivalence. In his paper Einstein had noted that the deflection for the planet Jupiter was one hundredth of the deflection for a ray of light grazing the Sun. In his letter Einstein continued to disagree with a suggestion that Freundlich had made, namely, that it might be possible to measure the light deflection using Jupiter.

Three weeks later Einstein wrote to Freundlich about the limits of observational astronomy. He asked whether or not gravitational deflection could be observed during the day using the Sun, and he wanted to know why the observed gravitational red shift of the fixed stars should be different from the gravitational red shift of the Sun. 'I do not grasp how spectral analysis [of the effect] may be useful, since the Sun emits all the types of light that the stars we might consider also emit. Or are there enough stars that have no bright lines or even no lines at all where the Sun has absorption lines? I am curious how you envision the methods.'[75] These questions formed the basis of one line of Freundlich's astronomical research during the next several years. After attempting unsuccessfully to measure deflection using photographs of previous eclipses,[76] Freundlich tried to use photographic plates taken by William Wallace Campbell at the Lick observatory to measure the daytime light deflection.[77] Campbell thought that the experiment had no chance of success, and Freundlich eventually found the plates unsuitable.[78] Freundlich then began to look into the stellar gravitational red shift, which had been known for some time through anomalies in the Doppler-shifted spectra of various stars.[79]

By 1913 Freundlich had already corresponded with Einstein for two years and yet had never spoken with him. When Einstein was elected to the Berlin Academy of Sciences in that year, Freundlich congratulated him and at the same time told Einstein of his plans to marry.[80] Einstein wrote back in August 1913 and invited Freundlich and his bride to hear him address the Swiss Society of Natural Sciences at Frauenfeld. In his letter Einstein also commented on two of Freundlich's projects.

> I, myself, am fairly firmly convinced that the light rays actually experience a curvature. I am extraordinarily interested in your plan to observe stars near the Sun by day. This should be possible if there are no suspended particles in the atmosphere with sizes of the order of the length of light waves, which very slightly deflect the light. I fear that this could wreck your plan. But you will be better informed about these conditions than I.[81]

For several months afterwards Einstein remained hopeful that a daylight photograph of light deflections was possible despite information to the contrary from the Zurich astronomer Julius Maurer; but he worried about effects in the atmospheres of the Sun and the Earth which might give a negative result.[82]

In his letter of August 1913 Einstein also remarked on Freundlich's work with double stars. Willem de Sitter had recently written a short note in which he claimed that double star data could be used to disprove Ritz's emission hypothesis.[83] Freundlich had noted that current astronomical evidence could not support de Sitter's claim.[84] Einstein emphasised the importance of the problem for his theories: 'I am also very curious about the outcome of your examination of double stars. If the velocity of light depends even to a very tiny part upon the velocity of the light source, then my whole theory of relativity, including my gravitational theory is false.'[85]

By the time of the Frauenfeld conference Freundlich began to encounter opposition to his work with Einstein. He had been attempting to organise an expedition to the Crimea to test Einstein's deflection prediction during the August 1914 solar eclipse.[86] However, Freundlich's superiors at the Berlin observatory were not sympathetic to his plans. Freundlich wrote to Einstein soon after their Frauenfeld meeting and explained that the director of the Berlin observatory, Hermann Struve, would not provide the funds for a projected expedition. Einstein replied early in December 1913: 'After receiving your last letter I immediately wrote to Planck, who has made serious efforts for the matter and has undertaken to talk the matter over with Schwarzschild. *I will not write to Struve.* If the [Berlin] Academy does not want [to give], then we will get that little bit of money from private sources.'[87] Einstein concluded that letter by saying that he would try to fund the proposal with the help of his friend Fritz Haber, and, if that failed, he would contribute to the expedition from his own pocket. The Academy granted Freundlich 2000 marks towards collecting the necessary equipment; according to Freundlich's wife, the young astronomer also contacted the chemist Emil Fischer, who 'gave him 3000 marks for the journey and supplied him with another 3000 marks from Krupp'.[88]

As the expedition approached, Einstein's support for it weakened. To Besso, Einstein wrote in March 1914: 'Now I am fully satisfied and I no longer doubt the correctness of the whole system, whether the observation of the eclipse will succeed or not. The reasonableness of the matter is too evident.'[89] All of Freundlich's plans, however, were aborted by the outbreak of the First World War. His equipment was impounded by the Russians and he was not able to make any photographic plates. After being interned briefly in Russia, he was exchanged for several Russian officers held in Germany and returned to Berlin early in September 1914.[90]

The reaction of the scientific establishment

Neither Laub nor Ritz nor Freundlich was a member of the German scientific establishment when he collaborated with Einstein, nor did any become members later. Ritz died soon after working with Einstein. The unsuccessful careers of Laub and Freundlich invite inquiry. For both, the collaboration with Einstein led to a confrontation with a university chair holder over issues in Einstein's development of the relativity theory.

Laub

In 1909 Einstein wrote to Laub, then in Würzburg, urging him to accept a post as assistant to Philipp Lenard at Heidelberg. 'Do tolerate Lenard's whims, as many as he may have. He is a great master, an original thinker!'[91] Lenard was indeed a brilliant experimentalist. He was on less secure grounds as a theoretician, but he held his theoretical work in high regard. Lenard had devoted much effort to investigating the photoelectric effect; he had demonstrated by early 1905 that the number of electrons emitted from a photoelectric metal was proportional to the energy of the incident light and that the electron velocity—and hence the kinetic energy of the emitted electron—varied inversely with the wavelengths of the incident light.

Several months later Einstein revolutionised physics by interpreting the photoelectric effect in terms of a quantum hypothesis. Lenard won a Nobel Prize in 1905 for his work in experimental physics, but he never forgave Einstein for overshadowing him with respect to the work on the photoelectric effect.[92] Furthermore, as Laub recalled many years later, Lenard was 'no great partisan of "mathematical" physics'.[93] Early in 1912, when the Heidelberg faculty had the opportunity of creating a new associate professorship of theoretical physics, Lenard objected strenuously. Friedrich Pockels described Lenard's reaction in a letter to Laub: 'He [Lenard] wanted to deny theoretical physics any right to an independent existence [saying] that he was enough of a theoretician himself, etc. For example, he wanted to refuse on principle [to accept] purely theoretical workers as doctoral candidates.'[94]

Soon after his arrival in Heidelberg Laub found himself involved in a serious dispute with Lenard. The conclusion of Laub's paper, presented by Lenard in 1909 to the Heidelberg Academy of Sciences, that relativistic effects could be observed in gaseous dispersion,[95] was difficult to verify and had been challenged by one of his colleagues.[96] Lenard was not happy with this situation. As Laub related in letters to Johannes Stark, his position required an inordinate expenditure of time.[97] Nevertheless, throughout 1910 Laub worked on a long review for Stark's *Jahrbuch*, summarising all the experimental evidence in favour of the special theory of relativity.[98] During the same time his relations with Lenard deteriorated. In June 1910 Laub complained to Stark that he was having difficulty in getting along with Lenard.[99] It was becoming increasingly apparent that Lenard would not allow Laub to become *Privatdozent*. On 25 November 1910 Laub wrote to Stark that he was looking for a position in America, most probably referring to one at the Massachusetts Institute of Technology or at the University of Illinois.[100] Laub told Stark that his references were Runge, Einstein, Wien, Pockels, and Lenard. At this point he was evidently still speaking with Lenard. However, a few weeks later, in a letter to Einstein which is now lost, Laub reported that he had broken with Lenard.

When Einstein learned of the final altercation, he was furious. 'Lenard is really a perverted fellow! Put together entirely of bile and intrigue! However, you are considerably better off than he. You can get away from him, but he must keep house with the monster until he bites the dust. I will do what I can to obtain an assistant's post for you.'[101] After Einstein wrote to his colleagues Anton Lampa and Walther Nernst on Laub's behalf, Laub found a position as associate professor of geophysics at the National University of La Plata in Argentina.[102] Einstein's young coworker arrived at his new post in April 1911; he joined a growing circle of German physicists and mathematicians south of the Tropic of Capricorn.[103]

Laub's personal beliefs estranged him further from the German-speaking physics establishment. Like Einstein during this period, Laub was a pacifist sympathetic to socialism. In 1916 Laub publicly expressed his moral and political views in the conclusion of a report on the physical institute of the National Institute for Secondary School Teachers in Buenos Aires, of which he had been director for the preceding three years. To Laub the First World War was a tragedy which exemplified all that was morally reprehensible in the world. The war threatened to destroy culture and civilisation by fomenting antagonisms between different groups. His report continued:

> The spiritual end of science consists in this: to strive towards the highest ideal of our life, the one that rises above the individual and the nation, the one that has to be sacred to everyone and can be expressed in one simple word: humanity. We confess to be convinced that science will heal our misery, eliminate the artificial hatred between different peoples, and subordinate the petty and oppressing significance of capital to the reign of the free spirit.[104]

Laub believed that science could secure the material needs of mankind both by freeing it from the bonds of capitalist economic structure and at the same time by providing a spiritual unity. Statements concerning the importance of spiritual goals in science were not unusual among German-speaking scientific academics at this time,[105] but only a few, among them Einstein, associated themselves with pacifism or alluded to socialist ideas.

Laub continued to produce studies on many experimental and theoretical subjects between 1911 and 1917. In early 1917 the institute where Laub was employed underwent a transformation as a result of political turmoil.[106] Laub moved to Spain and then to Berlin after the war. During this period, Laub's politics veered even farther left. In 1919, together with Rudolf Grossmann of the Ibero-American Institute in Hamburg, he translated a 1917 address given by Horacio Oyhanarte on the necessity of Argentine neutrality.[107] Grossmann was a highly respected scholar, who, like several others in this period, published communist political ideas under a pseudonym.[108] In 1920 Laub found permanent employment with the Argentine foreign service in Europe. He served in various posts for nineteen years, and he was a consul at Warsaw when Hitler crossed the Polish corridor in September 1939.[109]

Subsequently, Laub spent the Second World War in Argentina. Throughout these years, he retained personal ties with the scientific world, vacationing with Nernst[110] and corresponding extensively with C A Krukow on the development of high-frequency radio transmission.[111] In 1945 Laub tried to rejoin the European scientific community, although both Einstein and Laue suggested that the scientific world had changed and that he would have difficulty adjusting to it.[112] Finally, in 1953, Laub obtained the position of associate in the physical institute at Fribourg, Switzerland. In 1962 he died, unknown and without means.[113]

Freundlich

Several months after his attempt to observe the 1914 eclipse Freundlich began to consider the anomalous perihelion precession of Mercury. He first examined the attempts of Hugo von Seeliger to provide a classical explanation for the shift. In February 1915 Freundlich questioned Seeliger's hypothesis that the presence of interplanetary dust accounted for anomalous planetary residues in general.[114] Freundlich's article may have been prompted by Einstein's as yet unpublished conjecture or calculation showing that general relativity was able to account for these anomalies. Perhaps because he did not have a convincing calculation from general relativity in hand, Freundlich decided to attack Seeliger on Seeliger's own ground. In his critique Freundlich made no use of non-Newtonian gravitational theories. Rather, he attempted to demonstrate, by using the results of classical astronomy, that Seeliger's theory could not yield correct values for the residues.

In criticising Seeliger, Freundlich was challenging the doyen of German astronomy who, for the past twenty years, had been working on alternative gravitational theories and explanations of anomalies in planetary motion.[115] Seeliger's power in the German astronomical community was unquestioned. His conservatism on political and scientific matters was well known, and a direct challenge to his scientific standing could have been expected to receive little encouragement from German astronomers.[116] Furthermore, Seeliger was a veteran of many scientific debates and knew from experience how best to defend his own integrity while at the same time discrediting that of an opponent. Seeliger's reply to Freundlich came five months later. It was a credible defence of the dust hypothesis, and it made Freundlich's attack appear ridiculous.[117]

Freundlich then continued his investigation of the astronomical consequences of general relativity from another point of view. While Seeliger was drafting his reply, Freundlich reconsidered the red shift in the Fraunhofer lines of certain classes of fixed stars.[118] He examined the predictions of a red shift for massive bodies given by Einstein's general relativity theory and by Nordström's Euclidean gravitational theory,[119] and he referred to Schwarzschild's 1914 paper on an experimental measurement of the solar red shift.[120] Freundlich's primary observational data were Campbell's measurements of the stellar red shift in Class B stars.[121] Making use of his previous work on double stars, Freundlich calculated that, if Hans Ludendorff's result for the mass of spectroscopic Class B double stars were correct, then Einstein's and Nordström's theories both predicted enormous mass densities for those stars. When Freundlich's paper appeared, Seeliger decided he could use it to discredit his opponent further. In January 1916 Seeliger showed that Freundlich's relativistic formula for the determination of stellar densities was wrong.[122] Furthermore, Seeliger insisted that Campbell's and Ludendorff's measurements disproved the stellar gravitational red shift. Freundlich immediately wrote a two-line defence of his own calculations, and he resolved to await additional quantitative evidence.[123]

Freundlich's exchange with Seeliger displeased his immediate superior, Hermann Struve. Struve had descended from a long line of Russian astronomers and since 1904 had been director of the Berlin–Babelsberg observatory.[124] For a generation, Struve had calculated masses and densities of planetary moons by working with orbital residues.[125] He was incensed by Freundlich's attack on Seeliger, for he thought that Freundlich lacked astronomical evidence to support his statements. Struve was convinced that Freundlich would be technically incapable of verifying Einstein's general relativity at the upcoming solar eclipses of 1918 and 1919, as the junior astronomer proposed to do. Late in 1915 Struve had Freundlich removed from the observatory.[126]

Einstein was shaken by Struve's action. He felt that Seeliger had overreacted in his initial reply to Freundlich. In early December 1915 Einstein wrote bitterly to Sommerfeld in Munich: 'Tell your colleague Seeliger that he has a horrible temper. I enjoyed it recently in a reply in which he corrected the astronomer Freundlich.'[127] Two months later Einstein was even more concerned, for Seeliger's second rebuttal had appeared. In a letter to Sommerfeld Einstein observed:

> It should always be credited to Freundlich that he has invented the statistical method that allows fixed stars to be used to answer the question of the line shift. Even if he has made that dreadful arithmetical error . . . still the value of the whole calculation should not be forgotten for that reason. Mistakes can be corrected and are, indeed, always corrected with time. [The achievement] lies in discovering a path and making it passable.
>
> From my point of view the matter looks like this. Freundlich was the only colleague who effectively supported me up to now in my endeavours in the area of general relativity. He has devoted to the problem years of thought and work, as far as that was possible with his fatiguing and dull duties at the observatory.
>
> Freundlich has yet a second achievement. I will not speak of the refutation of Seeliger's theory of the perihelion movement of Mercury, since that work might be considered pushing at an open door. But Freundlich has shown that modern astronomical devices suffice to prove light deflection around Jupiter, something I had not thought possible . . .[128]

Einstein alluded to Freundlich's incorrect formula for the relativistic mass density, an error that Seeliger had criticised. Freundlich's reputation suffered from this error for many years. When Freundlich produced calculations of the solar light deflection in 1931, the exchange with Seeliger made his work immediately suspect. Campbell remarked in a letter to Robert J Trümpler:

> Confidentially I am also telling Dr Pritchett that Dr Freundlich was compelled to resign from the Berlin–Babelsberg Observatory about the year 1915 by its Director Hermann Struve because of Freundlich's trickery and dishonesty in scientific matters, as shown by Seeliger . . . To give you the right angle on Freundlich, I advise you to read [his] article, if you have not already done so. The whole incident was described to Dr Moore and others here a fortnight ago by Professor Georg Struve, an astronomer in Berlin University and Babelsberg Observatory, who has been making observations with the Lick telescope during the past three months. He also remarked that Freundlich has no standing whatever with German astronomers.[129]

Freundlich's subsequent attempt to find a position in German astronomy is worth considering briefly. In 1917 or 1918 Einstein arranged a meeting between Planck and Struve to discuss Freundlich's becoming *Privatdozent*. Struve told Planck in no uncertain terms what he thought of Freundlich.[130] Einstein continued to intervene on Freundlich's behalf. In 1918, after meeting with the Prussian minister in charge of science, Einstein wrote to Freundlich: 'The man is massive and not unsympathetic. He agreed with all I said, but promised nothing, so that I don't know whether my visit was of any use. But I made an impression. I warned him that S. will react with excuses to which no importance should be attached and asked him to consult with Planck.'[131] 'S.' was evidently either Struve or Seeliger. Finally, early in 1918, Einstein was able to support Freundlich through his own recently formed Kaiser Wilhelm Institute for Physical Research. By March 1919 Einstein had succeeded in placing Freundlich as an observer at the Potsdam astrophysical observatory. Largely because the Weimar authorities wanted to create a showcase for pure science at any cost, Einstein obtained for Freundlich a key position in the new Einstein Institute at Potsdam.[132]

Conclusion

Laub, Ritz and Freundlich held in common one understanding of theoretical physics. They believed that applied mathematics and experiments were important for developing the implications of theory, although theory did not grow out of either mathematics or experiment. Laub supported special relativity, Ritz the emission theory, and Freundlich general relativity against alternative possibilities, because, in their opinion, these theories expressed clearer pictures of the physical world. Each was thoroughly educated in applied mathematics at Göttingen, but none made extensive use of complicated or unusual mathematics in his work on relativity and gravitation. All were proficient in experimental and observational physics, yet none sought to base theory upon observed results. Their approach to theoretical physics was similar to that of Einstein, who, from the time of his youth, saw himself as a theoretical physicist seeking to develop a unified picture of the physical world.

The most characteristic intellectual quality of Einstein's work is a creative independence of mind. As has been suggested in several recent studies, his receptive attitude towards new ideas is also expressed in his admiration for the iconoclasm inherent in Ernst Mach's philosophy.[133] Einstein was open to stimulating ideas wherever he found them, whether the author was director of a laboratory or an old schoolmate. Einstein's independence also led him to favour an uncomplicated way of life. It has been maintained that Einstein's independence of mind and bohemian predilection placed him in a philosophical anti-establishment milieu centred in German-speaking Switzerland.[134] In view of his early scientific collaboration, we may ask whether or not his independent course can be considered part of a larger anti-establishment current. Some material seems to speak against this proposition. Einstein associated with other young theoretical physicists outside the physics establishment who sought radical approaches for unifying physics, but the group cannot be called an intellectual movement, for the radical theoretical physicists subscribed to no single programme or world view. One finds few ideological congruences in the lives and works of those, such as Laub, Freundlich, and perhaps Abraham, who would have to be included in such a current. Some establishment physicists actively sought new non-mechanical unifications of physical science that were similar in many respects to the ideas of younger physicists.

To consider whether or not Einstein and his collaborators might have been part of an anti-establishment current in Wilhelmian physics, it is important to know if their non-academic and, in the cases of Laub and Ritz, non-German background and their social and political attitudes were shared by a distinct group outside the mainstream of physics who had corresponding scientific views. Preliminary studies seem to indicate that so many German physics students of the period had a similar background, that information of this type, taken by itself, allows no conclusions. Over fifteen per cent of all doctorates awarded in the physical sciences (excluding organic chemistry but including mathematics) in Germany *circa* 1900 were earned by non-German Jews; this percentage is much higher than that for organic chemistry, the social sciences, or the humanities.[135]

The large number of non-Germans obtaining doctorates in mathematics and physics implies that, like Einstein's collaborators, a substantial fraction of young mathematicians and physicists were not members of the German academic elite. Now the precise outlines of intellectual currents in physics have to remain conjecture. We are only beginning to understand how to define and delineate the physics community in German-speaking Europe during the period before 1914. We lack detailed information concerning the way various minor currents emerged to occupy a central role within the theoretical physics discipline. We have not yet charted the evolution of interdisciplinary formations such as astrophysics, cosmic physics, physical chemistry, and geophysics, and we have not yet begun to examine networks of scientific communication.

Several excellent analyses have recently appeared which bring into view the broad outline of theoretical physics in Wilhelmian Germany.[136] The road is open for a detailed examination of scientific productivity and career patterns in theoretical physics within all of German-speaking Europe, the Low Countries, Scandinavia, and Russia which would bring us closer to a balanced understanding of the rise of contemporary physics in perhaps its most important setting.

Einstein's early scientific collaboration places his approach to physics in clearer perspective. Although many researchers in late Wilhelmian Germany were sympathetic with attempts to unify physics, only a few exceptional physicists in established positions, such as Planck and Laue, paid serious attention to Einstein's physical interpretation of the theories of relativity. If Einstein did not share the neglect that his collaborators suffered, it was only because, by 1909, the latitude and genius of his physics made it extraordinarily difficult for other physicists to damage his reputation by personal vindictiveness. His young collaborators became victims of the rejection of his thought by the Wilhelmian physical science establishment.

Notes and references

1 Albert Einstein, *Origins of the General Theory of Relativity* (Glasgow 1933) p 6.
2 See Carl Seelig's *Albert Einstein: A Documentary Biography*, transl M Savill (London 1956) pp 78, 86, 116.
3 Sources used in assembling information on the institutional evolution of Göttingen physical science include: *Die Physikalischen Institute der Universität Göttingen: Festschrift im Anschlusse an die Einweihung der Neubauten am 9. Dezember 1905* . . . (Leipzig 1905); Felix Klein and Eduard Riecke, eds, *Ueber angewandte Mathematik und Physik in ihrer Bedeutung für den Unterricht an den höheren Schulen, nebst Erläuterung der bezüglichen Göttinger Universitätseinrichtungen* (Leipzig 1900); Karl-Heinz Manegold, *Universität, Technische Hochschule und Industrie: Ein Beitrag zur Emanzipation der Technik im 19. Jahrhundert unter besonderer Berücksichtigung Felix Kleins* (Berlin 1970); Wilhelm Ebel, ed, *Catalogus Professorum Gottingensium 1734–1962* (Göttingen 1962); Karl J Truebner *et al*, eds, *Minerva: Jahrbuch der gelehrten Welt* **1** (1891–92) *et sqq.*

4 L Pyenson, *Neohumanism and the Persistence of Pure Mathematics in Wilhelmian Germany* (Philadelphia 1983) [*Am. Phil. Soc. Mem.* **150**] pp 57–67. See also chapter 7 of the present book.

5 L Couturat, *Les Principes des mathématiques* (Paris 1905) p 4. Emphasis in the original.

6 Among many other statements, see the distinction made by Marcel Grossmann between pure and applied mathematics for the International Commission on Mathematics Instruction. Grossmann, 'Der mathematische Unterricht an der Eidgenössischen Technischen Hochschule', published as bulletin 7 of the series *Der mathematische Unterricht in der Schweiz*, ed Henri Fehr (Basle and Geneva 1911) pp 29–31.

7 Carl Runge, 'The Mathematical Training of the Physicist', *Proceedings of the Fifth International Congress of Mathematicians* **2** (1913) 599.

8 Among several excellent articles concerning the electromagnetic view of nature, see Tetu Hirosige's 'Electrodynamics Before the Theory of Relativity, 1890–1905', *Japanese Studies in the History of Science* no 5 (1966) pp 1–49; Russell McCormmach's 'H A Lorentz and the Electromagnetic View of Nature', *Isis* **61** (1970) 457–97; McCormmach's 'Lorentz, Hendrik Antoon,' *Dictionary of Scientific Biography* **8** (1973) 487–500.

9 Woldemar Voigt, 'Phänomenologische und atomistische Betrachtungsweise', in Emil Warburg's volume *Physik* (Leipzig 1915) p 731, which is part of Paul Hinneberg's series *Die Kultur der Gegenwart*. See Stanley Goldberg, 'Voigt, Woldemar', *Dict. Sci. Biog.* **14** (1976) 61–3.

10 Robert A Houstoun, *A Treatise on Light* (London 1915) pp 465–6. Houstoun here neither rejected nor accepted Einstein's principle of relativity. Robb attempted to put special relativity upon an axiomatic basis by defining rigorously the relations 'before' and 'after'. See Alfred A Robb's *Optical Geometry of Motion: A New View of the Theory of Relativity* (Cambridge 1911); *A Theory of Time and Space* (Cambridge 1914). Robb came to reconsider the problem of measuring distance and time through a comment by Joseph Larmor at the British Association Meeting of 1902. Alfred A Robb, *Absolute Relations of Time and Space* (Cambridge 1921) p v. On Robb, see G Windred's 'The History of Mathematical Time', *Isis* **26** (1934) 199–202.

11 Letter to the author from R A Houstoun, 16 December 1972. A copy is located in the Niels Bohr Library of the American Institute of Physics, New York.

12 On Ehrenfest at Göttingen, see Martin J Klein's *Paul Ehrenfest: I. The Making of a Theoretical Physicist* (Amsterdam 1971).

13 When Nordström arrived in Göttingen, Nernst had just been called to Berlin, and Fritz Dolezalek was the new director of the Göttingen physical chemistry institute. In late 1906 Nordström completed a paper under Dolezalek's direction on Wilhelm Hittorf's transference number for potassium hydrate. Thereafter nearly all of his published work dealt with electrodynamics or Einstein's theories of relativity. H Tallqvist, 'Gunnar Nordström', *Finska Vetenskaps-Societeten Minnestrecknigar och Föredrag* (1924), separatum.

14 P P Ewald arrived in Göttingen about the same time to study chemistry under Otto Wallach. He quickly transferred to Hilbert's mathematics. Interview between Ewald and George Uhlenbeck and Thomas S Kuhn, 29 March 1962,

240   *Einstein's early scientific collaboration*

Archive for History of Quantum Physics, American Philosophical Society, Philadelphia.

15 The usual source for Ritz's life is Pierre Weiss's biography in *Walther Ritz Oeuvres* ed P Weiss (Paris 1911) pp vii–xxii. A remarkable study is Paul Forman's 'Ritz, Walter,' *Dict. Sci. Biog.* **11** (1975) 475–81. Forman notes that Ritz went under the spelling 'Walter', whereas according to Weiss's *Oeuvres* it has become usual to write 'Walther'.

16 Hermann Minkowski to David Hilbert, 11 March 1901, in *Hermann Minkowski: Briefe an David Hilbert* ed Lili Rüdenburg and Hans Zassenhaus (Berlin 1973) p 139.

17 W Ritz, 'Zur Theorie der Serienspektren' (ref 15) pp 1–77.

18 J Laub, *Ueber sekundäre Kathodenstrahlen* (dissertation, University of Würzburg 1907), 'Lebenslauf', and Amt für öffentliche Ordnung (Göttingen) to Lewis Pyenson, 23 January 1974.

19 *Gerd Rosen, 37. Auktion, 2. Teil. Bücher und Autographen* (Berlin 1961), item 2002.

20 Sheet 4 of a manuscript, 'Mechanik I, Göttingen, Winter-Semester 1903/04', box IX, folder 4 of the Minkowski papers. Niels Bohr Library, American Institute of Physics, New York.

21 Eric Forbes, 'Freundlich, Erwin Finlay', *Dict. Sci. Biog.* **5** (1971) 181–4; E Freundlich, *Analytische Funktionen mit beliebig vorgeschriebenen unendlichblättrigen Existenzbereiche* (dissertation, University of Göttingen 1910), 'Lebenslauf'.

22 At the time that he was finishing his dissertation Freundlich attended Klein's seminar on philosophy and pedagogy of mathematics. 'F Klein, Material zum psychologischen Seminar, Winter-Semester 1909–1910', Klein Nachlass, XXI, A. Niedersächsische Staats- und Universitätsbibliothek, Göttingen.

23 Thomas S Kuhn *et al*, *Sources for the History of Quantum Physics, an Inventory and Report* (Philadelphia 1967) [*Am. Phil. Soc. Mem.* **68**] p 139.

24 W Wien, 'Ziele und Methoden der theoretischen Physik', *Jahrbuch der Radioaktivität und Elektronik* **12** (1915) 241–59. The passage cited is on p 246.

25 W Wien, 'Ueber die Möglichkeit einer elektromagnetischen Begründung der Mechanik', *Annalen der Physik* **5** (1901) 501.

26 Wien gave Laub an inscribed copy of his paper, 'Ueber die Energie der Kathodenstrahlen im Verhältnis zur Energie der Röntgen- und Sekundärstrahlen', *Ann. Phys.* **18** (1905) 991–1007. In *Gerd Rosen, Auktion 36, 2. Teil: Bücher und Autographen* (Berlin 1961), item 4004, Laub wrote that Wien's paper was 'very important . . . in connection with Einstein's Nobel Prize work'.

27 J Laub (ref 18) p 86. A shortened version of the dissertation was published under the same title in *Ann. Phys.* **23** (1907) 285–300. The thesis was presented by August Witkowski to the Krakow Academy of Sciences and published in its *Bulletin international, Classe des sciences mathématiques et naturelles* (1907) pp 61–87.

28 C Seelig, *Einstein* (ref 2) p 72.

29 J Laub, 'Ueber die durch Röntgenstrahlen erzeugten sekundären Kathodenstrahlen', *Ann. Phys.* **26** (1908) 712–26.

30 J Laub, 'Zur Optik der bewegten Körper', *Ann. Phys.* **23** (1907) 738–44; 'Die Mitführung des Lichtes durch bewegte Körper nach dem Relativitätsprincip', *Ann. Phys.* **23** (1907) 989–90.

31 Tetu Hirosige, 'Origins of Lorentz' Theory of Electrons and the Concept of the Electromagnetic Field', *Historical Studies in the Physical Sciences* **1** (1969) 151–209 on pp 202–5.

32 M Laue to A Einstein, 4 August 1907. Deutsches Museum, Munich.

33 W Wien to A Sommerfeld, 15 June 1908. Archive for History of Quantum Physics, American Philosophical Society, Philadelphia.

34 W Wien, 'Turbulente Bewegung der Gase', listed in *Physikalische Zeitschrift* **8** (1907) 722. See the discussion between Wien and Sommerfeld in *ibid* **8** (1907) 841–2.

35 J Laub to A Einstein, 2 February 1908. Einstein Archives, Princeton.

36 A Einstein and J Laub, 'Ueber die elektromagnetischen Grundgleichungen für bewegte Körper', *Ann. Phys.* **26** (1908) 532–40; 'Bemerkungen zu unserer Arbeit', *Ann. Phys.* **28** (1909) 445–7; 'Ueber die im elektromagnetischen Felde auf ruhende Körper ausgeübten ponderomotorischen Kräfte', *Ann. Phys.* **26** (1908) 541–50.

37 A Einstein and J Laub, 'Ueber die im elektromagnetischen Felde . . .', *ibid*.

38 H Minkowski, 'Die Grundgleichungen für die elektromagnetischen Vorgänge in bewegten Körpern (1908)', in *Hermann Minkowski: Gesammelte Abhandlungen* ed David Hilbert (Leipzig 1911) **2** 352–404.

39 These papers have been treated in several secondary sources: G H F Gardner, *The Concept of a Rigid Body in Special Relativity* (dissertation, Princeton University 1953) pp 9–14; S Goldberg, *Early Responses to Einstein's Theory of Relativity, 1905–1911: A Case Study in National Differences* (dissertation, Harvard University 1968), pp 119–29; Klein, *Ehrenfest* (ref 12) p 152. See also Ludwik Silberstein's *Theory of Relativity* (London 1914) pp 283 ff.

40 Russell McCormmach, 'Einstein, Lorentz, and the Electron Theory', *Hist. Stud. Phys. Sci.* **2** (1970) 41–87, on pp 69–81.

41 A Einstein and J Laub, 'Ueber die elektromagnetischen Grundgleichungen' (ref 36).

42 Subsequently, M and H A Wilson verified Einstein and Laub's theory in their article, 'On the Electric Effect of Rotating a Magnetic Insulator in a Magnetic Field', London, Royal Society, *Proceedings* A **89** (1913) 99–106.

43 A Einstein and J Laub, 'Bemerkungen' (ref 36).

44 J Laub, 'Ueber den Einfluss der molekularen Bewegung auf die Dispersionserscheinungen in Gasen', *Ann. Phys.* **28** (1908) 131–41.

45 J Laub, 'Zur Theorie der Dispersion und Extinction des Lichtes in leuchtenden Gasen und Dämpfen', *Ann. Phys.* **29** (1909) 94–110.

46 See Armin Hermann's *The Genesis of Quantum Theory, 1899–1913*, transl C W Nash (Cambridge, Mass 1971) pp 72–7; John L Heilbron's *A History of the Problem of Atomic Structure from the Discovery of the Electron to the Beginnings of Quantum Mechanics* (dissertation, University of California, Berkeley 1964) p 178.

47 J Laub (ref 45) p 95.

48 J Laub, 'Zur Theorie der longitudinalen magneto-optischen Effekte in leucht-

enden Gasen und Dämpfen', Heidelberg, Königliche Akademie der Wissenschaften, Mathematische Klasse, *Sitzungsberichte* (1909) separatum.

49 R Ladenburg, 'On the Quantum-Theoretical Interpretation of the Number of Dispersion Electrons', transl G Field in *Sources of Quantum Mechanics* ed B L van der Waerden (New York 1968) pp 139–57. Max Jammer, *Conceptual Development of Quantum Mechanics* (New York 1966) p 181.

50 J Laub, 'Ueber die experimentellen Grundlagen des Relativitätsprinzips', *Jahrbuch Radioakt. Elektr.* **7** (1910) 405–63, on p 463.

51 See chapters 1 and 3.

52 Banesh Hoffmann, with the assistance of Helen Dukas, *Albert Einstein: Creator and Rebel* (New York 1972) pp 85–6.

53 J Laub to A Einstein, 18 May 1908. Einstein Archives, Princeton.

54 A Einstein and W Ritz, 'Zum gegenwärtigen Stand des Strahlungsproblems', *Phys. Z.* **10** (1909) 323–4.

55 See ref 15.

56 On Ritz's spectral theory, see A d'Abro's *Rise of the New Physics* (New York 1951) **2** 181–3, 190. On Ritz's emission theory, see Klein's *Ehrenfest* (ref 12) p 155.

57 Guido Beck, 'Ricardo Gans', *Conferencia pronunciada en la sesión del 10 de Julio de 1954 de la Academia Brasileira de Ciencias en Rio de Janeiro* (Rio de Janeiro 1954); Enrique Gaviola, 'Richard Gans', *Ciencia e Investigación* (Buenos Aires) **10** (1954) 381–4.

58 R Gans, 'Gravitation und Elektromagnetismus', *Phys. Z.* **6** (1905) 803–5.

59 R Gans, 'Ist die Gravitation elektromagnetischen Ursprungs?' *Festschrift Heinrich Weber* (Leipzig 1912) pp 75–94.

60 F Wacker, *Ueber Gravitation und Elektromagnetismus* (Borna-Leipzig 1909). Richard Gans claimed in 1909 that he had 'instigated' Wacker's work. Gans, 'Lebenslauf', 4 October 1909. Göttingen, Institut für Geophysik, 'Gesellschaft der Wissenschaften 1909'.

61 F Wacker, 'Ueber Gravitation und Elektromagnetismus', *Phys. Z.* **7** (1906) 300–302.

62 W Ritz, 'Recherches critiques sur l'électrodynamique générale', in *Oeuvres* (ref 15) pp 419–22. First published in *Annales de chimie et de physique* **13** (1908).

63 W Ritz, 'Du Rôle de l'éther en physique', *ibid* p 455. First published in *Scientia* **3** (1909).

64 W Ritz, 'La Gravitation', *ibid* pp 478–92. First published in *Scientia* **5** (1909).

65 *Ibid* p 491.

66 A Einstein, 'Ueber das Relativitätsprinzip und die aus demselben gezogenen Folgerungen', *Jahrbuch Radioakt. Elektr.* **4** (1907) 411–62. Section 5 of the paper was entitled 'Relativitätsprinzip und Gravitation'.

67 Letter from A Einstein to C Habicht, 24 December 1907, quoted in Seelig's *Einstein* (ref 2) p 76.

68 A Einstein, cited in Leopold Infeld and Jerzy Plebański, *Motion and Relativity* (Warsaw 1960) p 201.

69 R McCormmach, 'Electron Theory' (ref 40) p 84.

70 Letter from A Einstein to K Haenisch, 6 December 1919. S Grundmann, 'Der deutsche Imperialismus, Einstein und die Relativitätstheorie (1914–1933)', in

Relativitätstheorie und Weltanschauung: Zur philosophischen und wissen-schaftspolitischen Wirkung Albert Einsteins (Berlin 1967) pp 260–1. The letter is also reproduced in *Albert Einstein in Berlin 1913–1933, Teil I: Darstellung und Dokumente* ed Christa Kirsten and Hans-Jürgen Treder (Berlin 1979) p 176.

71 Katje Freundlich to Lewis Pyenson, 29 April 1973. A copy is located in the Einstein Archives, Princeton.

72 A Einstein, 'On the Influence of Gravitation [*sic*] on the Propagation of Light', transl W Perrett and G B Jeffrey, in *The Principle of Relativity* (London 1923) pp 99–108.

73 L W Pollak to E Freundlich, August 1911. Einstein Archives, Princeton.

74 A Einstein to E Freundlich, 1 September 1911. Einstein Archives, Princeton.

75 A Einstein to E Freundlich, 21 September 1911. Einstein Archives, Princeton.

76 A Einstein to Michele Besso, 4 February 1912. Pierre Speziali, ed, *Albert Einstein–Michele Besso Correspondance, 1903–1955* (Paris 1972) p 46. The matter is exhaustively studied by Jeffrey Crelinsten in his *Reception of Einstein's General Relativity among American Astronomers, 1910–1930* (dissertation, University of Montreal 1982) pp 71–8.

77 W W Campbell to G E Hale, 4 November 1913. Einstein had written to Hale on 14 October 1913 to request such a search, and he had previously contacted Campbell about eclipse measurements. George Ellery Hale correspondence, located on microfilm in the Niels Bohr Library of the American Institute of Physics, New York. See Hoffmann's *Einstein* (ref 52) p 112.

78 E Freundlich, 'Ueber einen Versuch, die von A Einstein vermutete Ablenkung des Lichtes in Gravitationsfeldern zu prüfen', *Astronomische Nachrichten* **193** (1913) 369–72.

79 E Freundlich, 'Ueber die Gravitationsverschiebung der Spektrallinien bei Fixsternen', *Astron. Nachr.* **202** (1915–1916) 17–24.

80 K Freundlich (ref 71).

81 A Einstein to E Freundlich, August 1913. Einstein Archives.

82 A Einstein to E Freundlich, 27 October 1913. Einstein Archives.

83 W de Sitter, 'Ein astronomischer Beweis für die Konstanz der Lichtgeschwindigkeit', *Phys. Z.* **14** (1913) 429.

84 E Freundlich, 'Zur Frage der Konstanz der Lichtgeschwindigkeit', *Phys. Z.* **14** (1913) 835–8.

85 A Einstein to E Freundlich (ref 81).

86 Freundlich first announced plans to observe the eclipse in ref 78, p 372. The article was dated January 1913.

87 A Einstein to E Freundlich, 7 December 1913. Einstein Archives.

88 C Kirsten and H-J Treder, *Einstein* (ref 70) p 166. K Freundlich (ref 71).

89 *Einstein–Besso Correspondence* (ref 76) p 53.

90 K Freundlich (ref 71).

91 A Einstein to J Laub, n.d. Einstein Archives.

92 *Nobel Lectures in Physics, 1901–1921* (Amsterdam 1967) p 137.

93 J Laub to Carl Seelig, 10 September 1959. Bibliothek der Eidgenössischen Technischen Hochschule, Zurich.

94 F Pockels to J Laub, 12 March 1912. Deutsches Museum, Munich.

95 J Laub, 'Effekte' (ref 48).

96   Most probably August Becker. F Pockels to J Laub, 5 November 1911. Deutsches Museum, Munich.

97   J Laub to J Stark, 15 March 1910. Staatsbibliothek Preussischer Kulturbesitz, Berlin.

98   J Laub, 'Grundlagen' (ref 50).

99   J Laub to J Stark, 13 June 1910. Staatsbibliothek Preussischer Kulturbesitz, Berlin.

100 J Laub to J Stark, 25 November 1910. Staatsbibliothek Preussischer Kultur-besitz, Berlin. See also Gilbert N Lewis to J Stark, 24 January 1911, Deutsches Museum, Munich, where Lewis asks Stark for his opinion of Laub, who has just applied for a job. I thank Stanley Goldberg for pointing out the Lewis letter to me. By January 1911, Laub had been offered an assistant professorship in theoretical physics at the University of Illinois, almost certainly the position briefly held by Max Abraham in 1909. Laub to Emil Bose, January 1911, Fundación Bose, Buenos Aires. Stanley Goldberg, 'Abraham, Max', *Dict. Sci. Biog.* **1** (1969) 23–5.

101 A Einstein to J Laub, 11 November 1910. Einstein Archives.

102 A Einstein to J Laub, 15 November 1910, quoted in *Gerd Rosen, 37* (ref 19) item 1978.

103 J Laub to Paul Ehrenfest, 24 April 1911. Ehrenfest Correspondence, Archive for History of Quantum Physics, American Philosophical Society, Philadelphia. The circumstances of Laub's call to La Plata and his activity in Argentina are considered at length in Lewis Pyenson's *Cultural Imperialism and Exact Sciences: German Expansion Overseas, 1900–1930* (New York: forthcoming).

104 J Laub, 'El Departamento de Física y su Enseñanza', in *El Instituto Nacional del Professorado Secundario en la primera década de sú existencia* (Buenos Aires 1916) pp 301–36, on pp 335–6.

105 Two physicists who often phrased their work in terms of spiritual goals at this time were Gustav Mie and Max Planck. G Mie, 'Naturgesetz und Geist', *Deutsche Revue* **41** (1916) 150–63. Stanley Goldberg, 'Max Planck's Philosophy of Nature and His Elaboration of the Theory of Relativity', *Hist. Stud. Phys. Sci.* **7** (1976) 125–60.

106 L Pyenson, *Cultural Imperialism* (ref 103).

107 Horacio B Oyhanarte, *Argentiniens Neutralität. Rede, 24–25. Sept. 1917,* transl J Laub and R Grossmann (Hamburg 1920) [*Auslandspolitische Schriften des Ibero-Amerikanischen Instituts* no 1]. Laub's preface is dated Charlottenburg, 20 January 1920.

108 Under the name Pierre Ramus, Grossmann wrote *Generalstreik und direkte Aktion im proletarischen Klassenkampfe* (Berlin 1910); *Jahrbuch der freien Generation: Volkskalender und Dokumente der Weltanschauung des Sozialismus-Anarchismus* (Paris 1910); *Die Neuschöpfung der Gesellschaft durch den kommunistischen Anarchismus* (Vienna-Klosterneuburg 1923).

109 The Argentine Diplomatic Service to the author, 12 March 1973. A copy is located in the Einstein Archives at Princeton.

110 W Nernst to J Laub, 25 July 1934, *Gerd Rosen, 37* (ref 19), item 2035.

111 *Gerd Rosen, 36* (ref 26), item 3968. A transcript of a manuscript by Laub, 'Die Herkunft des hochfrequenten Drahtfunks und seine Vorteile gegenüber

dem üblichen drahtlosen Rundfunk' (Fribourg, Switzerland, n.d.), is located at the Leo Baeck Institute in New York.

112 A Einstein to J Laub, 2 June 1946, 16 April 1947, 18 July 1953. M Laue to J Laub, 21 July 1947. *Gerd Rosen, 36* (ref 26), item 2366; *Gerd Rosen, 37* (ref 19), items 1979, 1980, 2021.

113 Laub died on 22 April 1962. *Registre des décès de l'arrondissement de Fribourg 37* p 235, no 193. I know of no obituaries or éloges. See Lewis Pyenson's 'Laub, Jakob Johann', *Neue deutsche Biographie* **13** (1982) *s.v.*

114 E Freundlich, 'Ueber die Erklärung der Anomalien im Planetensystem durch die Gravitationswirkung interplanetarer Massen', *Astron. Nachr.* **201** (1915) 49–55.

115 H von Seeliger, 'Ueber Zusammenstösse und Theilungen planetarischer Massen', Munich, Königliche bayerische Akademie der Wissenschaften, Mathematisch–physikalische Classe, *Abhandlungen* **17** (1891) 457–90; 'Ueber das Newtonsche Gravitationsgesetz', *Astron. Nachr.* **137** (1895) 129–36; 'Ueber das Newtonsche Gravitationsgesetz', Munich, Akademie, *Sitzungsberichte* **26** (1896) 373–400; 'Kosmische Staubmassen und das Zodiakallicht', *ibid* **31** (1901) 265–92; 'Das Zodiakallicht und die empirischen Glieder in der Bewegung der innern Planeten', *ibid* **36** (1906) 595–622; 'Die empirischen Glieder in der Theorie der Bewegungen der Planeten Merkur, Venus, Erde und Mars', *Vierteljahrsschrift der Astronomischen Gesellschaft* **41** (1906) 234 ff. See Arthur S Eddington, 'Hugo von Seeliger', London, Royal Astronomical Society, *Monthly Notices* **85** (1925) 316; Jammer (ref 49) pp 127–8; A Einstein, 'Considerations on the Universe as a Whole', in *Theories of the Universe* ed M K Munitz (New York 1957) p 276; John D North, *The Measure of the Universe* (Oxford 1956) p 48.

116 O Struve and V Zebergs, *Astronomy of the Twentieth Century* (New York 1962) pp 39–40. In 1910 Max Planck considered Seeliger, along with Rayleigh, van der Waals, and Arthur Schuster, as one of the 'old men' who would not be interested in devoting the first Solvay Congress to problems of quantum physics. M Planck to W Nernst, 11 June 1910. Quoted by Jean Pelseneer in 'Historique des instituts internationaux de physique et de chimie Solvay depuis leur fondation jusqu'à la deuxième guerre mondiale'. A copy of Pelseneer's manuscript is located in the Archive for History of Quantum Physics at the American Philosophical Society, Philadelphia.

117 H von Seeliger, 'Ueber die Anomalien in der Bewegung der innern Planeten', *Astron. Nachr.* **201** (1915) 273–83.

118 E Freundlich, 'Ueber die Gravitationsverschiebung der Spektrallinien bei Fixsternen', *Astron. Nachr.* **202** (1915) 1.

119 Nordström produced several different gravitational theories during the period 1912–15 which were expressed in terms of four-dimensional Minkowskian space–time. For reviews of Nordström's work see M Abraham's 'Neuere Gravitationstheorie', *Jahrbuch Radioakt. Elektr.* **11** (1914) 497–508; M Laue's 'Die Nordströmsche Gravitationstheorie', *ibid* **14** (1917) 263–313; A L Harvey's 'A Brief Review of Lorentz-Covariant Theories of Gravitation', *American Journal of Physics* **33** (1965) 449–60.

120 K Schwarzschild, 'Ueber die Verschiebungen der Bänder bei 3883 Å im Sonnenspektrum', Berlin, Königliche preussische Akademie der Wissen-

schaften, Mathematisch–physikalische Klasse, *Sitzungsberichte* (1914) pp 1183–1213. See Eric Forbes' 'A History of the Solar Red Shift Problem', *Annals of Science* **17** (1961) 140.

121 W W Campbell, 'On the Motions of the Brighter Class B Stars', *Lick Observatory Bulletin* **6** (1911) 101–24; 'Some Peculiarities in the Motions of the Stars', *ibid* pp 125–35.

122 H von Seeliger, 'Ueber die Gravitationswirkung auf die Spektrallinien', *Astron. Nachr.* **202** (1916) 83–6.

123 E Freundlich, 'Bemerkung zu meinem Aufsatz in A. N. 4826', *Astron. Nachr.* **202** (1916) 147–8.

124 F W Dyson, 'Karl Hermann Struve', *Mon. Not. R. astron. Soc.* **81** (1921) 270–2.

125 L Courvoisier, 'Hermann Struve', *Astron. Nachr.* **212** (1920) 33–8.

126 In the matter of Freundlich's dismissal, the evidence is circumstantial but compelling. H Struve to O Naumann, 20 December 1915, in Kirsten and Treder's *Einstein* (ref 70), pp 169–71. Compare Forbes, 'Freundlich' (ref 21), who writes that Freundlich was fired in 1913 over his publication of relativistic calculations concerning the perihelion shift of Mercury.

127 A Einstein to A Sommerfeld, 9 December 1915, in *Einstein–Sommerfeld Briefwechsel* ed Armin Hermann (Basle 1968).

128 A Einstein to A Sommerfeld, 2 February 1916, *ibid*.

129 W W Campbell to R J Trümpler, 21 October 1931. Einstein Archives.

130 A Einstein to E Freundlich, no date. Einstein Archives.

131 A Einstein to E Freundlich, no date. Einstein Archives.

132 See Grundmann's 'Imperialismus' (ref 70) pp 210–15 for the founding of the Kaiser Wilhelm Institutes and their support of Freundlich's work in general relativity, as well as for the construction of the Einstein Institute at Potsdam.

133 H Steinberg, 'Grundzüge der philosophischen Auffassungen Albert Einsteins', in *Relativitätstheorie und Weltanschauung: Zur philosophischen und wissenschaftspolitischen Wirkung Albert Einsteins* (Berlin 1967) esp pp 46–58; Gerald Holton, 'Mach, Einstein and the Search for Reality', in Holton's *Thematic Origins of Scientific Thought* (Cambridge, Mass 1973) pp 219–59.

134 Lewis S Feuer, *Einstein and the Generations of Science* (New York 1974) esp pp 26–46. See the reviews of Feuer's book by John L Heilbron, *Science* **185** (1974) 776–8, and by L Pyenson, *Isis* **66** (1975) 586–90.

135 These statistics are drawn from a study of all German PhD dissertations published in 1899. L Pyenson and D Skopp, 'Educating Physicists in Germany circa 1900', *Social Studies of Science* **7** (1977) 329–66.

136 Russell McCormmach, 'On the Growth of the Physics Discipline in the Nineteenth Century', address published as 'Editor's Foreword' in *Hist. Stud. Phys. Sci.* **3** (1971) ix–xxiv; R McCormmach, 'On Academic Scientists in Wilhelmian Germany', *Daedalus* (summer 1974) pp 147–71; R McCormmach, 'Wilhelmian Theoretical Physics and the Physical World Picture', paper presented at the first meeting of the Joint Atlantic Seminar on the History of Physics, University of Montreal, 22 March 1974; Paul Forman, John L Heilbron, Spencer L Weart, *Physics circa 1900: Personnel, Funding and Productivity of the Academic Establishments* (Princeton 1975) [*Hist. Stud. Phys. Sci.* **5**].

Index

The author

Lewis Pyenson, born and raised in southern New Jersey, was educated as a physicist and a historian of science. He is the author of *Neohumanism and the Persistence of Pure Mathematics in Wilhelmian Germany* and *Cultural Imperialism and Exact Sciences*. He serves as Associate Editor of the semi-annual *Historical Studies in the Physical Sciences* and sits as a Curator of the Osler Library for the History of Medicine at McGill University. Since receiving a PhD in 1974 from The Johns Hopkins University, he has taught in French at the University of Montreal. He is married to historian of science Susan Sheets-Pyenson and has two children.